History of the Ancient World: A Global Perspective

Gregory S. Aldrete, Ph.D.

THE
GREAT
COURSES

PUBLISHED BY:

THE GREAT COURSES
Corporate Headquarters
4840 Westfields Boulevard, Suite 500
Chantilly, Virginia 20151-2299
Phone: 1-800-832-2412
Fax: 703-378-3819
www.thegreatcourses.com

Gregory S. Aldrete, Ph.D.

Professor of Humanistic Studies and History
University of Wisconsin–Green Bay

Professor Gregory S. Aldrete is Professor of Humanistic Studies and History at the University of Wisconsin–Green Bay. He received his A.B. from Princeton University in 1988 and his Ph.D. from the University of Michigan in 1995. His scholarship spans the fields of history, archaeology, and philology.

Among the many books Professor Aldrete has written or edited are *Gestures and Acclamations in Ancient Rome* (1999), *Floods of the Tiber in Ancient Rome* (2007), *Daily Life in the Roman City: Rome, Pompeii, and Ostia* (2009), *The Greenwood Encyclopedia of Daily Life I: The Ancient World* (editor, 2004), and *Unraveling the Linothorax Mystery: Reconstructing and Testing Ancient Linen Body Armor* (with S. Bartell and A. Aldrete, in press).

Professor Aldrete has received numerous awards for both his teaching and research. In 2009, he was a recipient of the American Philological Association Award for Excellence in the Teaching of Classics at the College Level. From 1997 to 1998, he was a University of Wisconsin System Teaching Fellow, and from 2007 to 2008, he was a University of Wisconsin–Green Bay Teaching Scholar. In addition, Professor Aldrete has received three prestigious year-long research fellowships: two Humanities Fellowships from the National Endowment for the Humanities (NEH) and the Solmsen Postdoctoral Fellowship at the Institute for Research in the Humanities in Madison. He was chosen as a fellow of two NEH seminars held at the American Academy in Rome, was a participant in an NEH Institute at UCLA, and was a Visiting Scholar at the American Academy in Rome. In 2006, his university honored him with its highest awards for both teaching and research: the Founders Association Award for Excellence in Teaching and the Founders Association Award for Excellence in Scholarship.

Professor Aldrete maintains an active schedule of lectures to the general public, including speaking to retirement groups; in elementary, middle, and high schools; and on cruise ships; and he has been named one of the National Lecturers for the Archaeological Institute of America. ∎

Table of Contents

Table of Contents

Table of Contents

History of the Ancient World: A Global Perspective

Scope:

This course traces the development of civilizations around the world, from the appearance of the first cities in various places around 3500–3000 B.C. until the establishment of the first true European empire under Charlemagne and the golden ages of the Abbasid Caliphate in Baghdad and the Tang dynasty in China, all during the 9th century A.D.

The lectures are chronologically organized, but they interweave history with the examination of key aspects of culture, including art, literature, philosophy, religion, and architecture. We begin by looking at the earliest urban civilizations, which arose independently in Mesopotamia, Egypt, India, and China, with an emphasis on how each unique physical environment indelibly and dramatically shaped the civilization that developed in each location.

In Mesopotamia, we follow a sequence of cultures: the Sumerians, Akkadians, Babylonians, Hittites, Phoenicians, Assyrians, Chaldeans, Persians, and Sassanians. In India, we follow the growth of the Indus Valley, Vedic, and Aryan civilizations and the achievements of the Mauryan and Gupta dynasties. In China, we observe the successive Shang, Zhou, Qin, Han, Sui, and Tang dynasties, while in the eastern Mediterranean, the pre-Greek Minoans and Mycenaeans are described, as is the subsequent path of classical Greek civilization, including the famed cities of Athens and Sparta and the Hellenistic world created by Alexander of Macedon. In the western Mediterranean, the fortunes of the Etruscans, Carthaginians, Romans, and various barbarian nations are all outlined. Turning to North and South America, we survey the Olmec, Chavin, Moche, Teotihuacàn, and Mayan civilizations. In Africa, the establishment of kingdoms such as Meroe, Ghana, and Axum are traced, and in Oceania, we chart the explorations of the Polynesian seafarers. Even some long-lasting hunter-gatherer societies, such as the Australian Aborigines, are examined. The course comes to a close chronologically with the rise of Islam and the establishment of the Islamic Caliphates and the effect of this on Europe and the Near East.

Throughout this course, particular attention is given to key similarities and differences among the many civilizations studied, and so, in addition to traditionally organized lectures that provide an overview of the history and culture of a certain civilization, this course features a number of special lectures that explicitly and exclusively juxtapose illuminating aspects of widely disparate civilizations. For example, an entire lecture is devoted to comparing the epic poetry of Vedic India with Homer's *Iliad*. Two lectures explore the moment of intellectual questioning that occurred simultaneously in many cultures in the 6th and 5th centuries B.C. that resulted in new philosophies and religions such as Confucianism and Daoism in China, pre-Socratic philosophy in Greece, Buddhism and Jainism in India, and Zoroastrianism in Persia. A set of four interrelated lectures offers parallel biographies of five great conquerors and empire builders: Philip of Macedon and his son, Alexander the Great; Chandragupta Maurya and his grandson Asoka of India; and Shi Huangdi, the first emperor of China.

One lecture investigates the nature of history writing itself and compares the very different methods used by three fathers of the historical craft: Herodotus, Thucydides, and Sima Qian. Another set of three lectures places two of the greatest empires of all time—the Roman Empire and Han China—side-by-side to assess how they dealt with analogous problems and challenges, such as administration, leadership, incorporating newcomers, and coping with technological limitations. Two lectures take a thematic, comparative approach to explore the topics of warfare and the symbolic expression of power through art and architecture. Thus you will learn how the Mayan, Roman, and Chinese military systems each expressed aspects of their respective cultures, and how monuments as varied as the tribute frieze of Persepolis, Trajan's Column in Rome, the tomb of Shi Huangdi, and the reliefs of Cerro Sechin in Peru all embody similar themes.

This course combines a sweeping survey of all of world history, from the beginnings of civilization up until the origins of the modern world were established, with targeted in-depth analysis of key figures, moments, and inventions. Its goal is to provide a solid foundational knowledge of the ancient world and deeper insight into the present. ■

The Great Empire of the Han Dynasty
Lecture 25

China's Han dynasty was founded by a one-time peasant whose unlikely rise to power was assisted by a period of turmoil and his own talent for choosing advisors and inspiring loyalty. He combined the Legalist bureaucracy of the Qin dynasty with a kinder, gentler Confucian philosophy that made life easier for the peasants and allowed greater social mobility among the middle and upper classes. Later Han emperors were more militaristic, and the empire reached its greatest extent under Wudi. It also made great technical, artistic, and economic strides.

Empires East and West

- Around the eastern Mediterranean Sea, in India, and in China, we have traced events up to around 200 B.C. In all these areas, brief but geographically vast empires have collapsed, leaving in their wake a confused political landscape.

- At this point, in China and the western Mediterranean, a single political power would emerge that would not only unite the entire area under its control but would establish a relatively stable empire that would last for at least 400 years: the Han Empire and the Roman Empire.

- China's Han dynasty and the Roman Empire were about the same size in terms of both population and geographic extent. Even after they fell, they continued to exert considerable influence by becoming, in their respective parts of the globe, the dominant image of and model for an empire—the yardstick by which all subsequent empires would be judged.

Liu Bang—The Peasant Emperor

- After Qin Shi Huangdi's death in 210 B.C., things rapidly deteriorated. His son could not control the power struggles among his advisors, and he had to be even more oppressive than his father. The common people were fed up, the intellectuals and the upper classes stewed with resentment, and the treasury was empty.

- The country began to erupt with rebellions, some led by aristocrats and some by peasants. After several confused years, a rebel leader named Liu Bang arose from the chaos to found a new dynasty, the Han, named after a tributary of the Yangtze River.

- Liu was an extremely unlikely emperor. A peasant, as a youth he was known as lazy, uneducated, unemployed, and overly fond of wine and women. Somehow, he reformed his ways, became village headman, and finally a general in one of the armies of rebellious peasants.

- Liu was a poor general; he lost every battle he personally commanded except one. His real talents lay in knowing how to choose subordinates, delegate authority, and mediate disputes. Ultimately, this was enough.

- Liu was illiterate and had to rely heavily on scholars in his bureaucracy, and he retained a certain peasant's contempt for these effete men of abstract learning. Nevertheless, he understood their importance and brought about a sort of golden age of Chinese culture and civilization.

The Han System of Government

- Liu's stable government started with the strong, centralized state of Shi Huangdi but took on a kinder, gentler form. He attempted to combine the Confucian model of the compassionate, virtuous ruler who cared about his subjects with the efficiency and order of Legalism.

- He addressed the peasants' unhappiness by cutting down on forced labor and temporarily reducing taxes. He appeased intellectuals and upper class landowners by rescinding the Qin ban on Confucian and Zhou classics and encouraging intellectual pursuits.

- The bureaucracy was highly ordered and hierarchical but not hereditary. Those wishing to enter government service had to pass an elaborate system of examinations which were based on knowledge of Confucian classic texts.

- The rulers established a national university to teach the Confucian texts for these exams. In theory, the exam system rewarded merit; in practice, the system naturally favored sons of landowning families, who had greater wealth and time to devote themselves to study.

- The country was divided into 100 administrative regions that were subdivided into 1,500 districts. A multilayered bureaucracy of 20 levels and an estimated 130,000 individuals oversaw everything from the collection of taxes to the construction of public works.

- The Han rulers did away with the Qin restrictions on travel, books, and thought. They also continued some Qin policies, such as conscription, the use of forced labor to build canals and roads, and standardization of weights, measures, currency, and writing.

Wudi and the Late Han Dynasty

- Early Han emperors continued in the vein of benevolent Confucian rulers. But by the time the emperor Wudi came to power in 141 B.C., the balance began to shift back toward the more centralized and heavy-handed model of Qin rule.

- Wudi was known as the martial emperor because he pursued an aggressive policy of military expansion. He also favored a more powerful, centralized form of government in which a number of important industries, including iron, salt, copper, and liquor, were taken over by the state and regulated the food supply, establishing the "ever-normal granary system."

- Wudi mustered enormous armies of more than 100,000 soldiers, which were dispatched in several directions. In the south, what today is northern Vietnam was brought under Chinese control. He also conquered southern Manchuria and Korea and pushed China's western borders into central Asia.

- Wudi's greatest military challenge was to the north, where he repeatedly mounted expeditions against the nomadic steppe nomads known as the Xiongnu. There is a debate among scholars about who they were; some identify the Xiongnu with the people later known as Huns.

- The Chinese historian Sima Qian described the Xiongnu thus:

  They move about in search of water and pasture and have no walled cities or fixed dwellings, nor do they engage in any form of agriculture. ... Even the little boys start out learning to ride sheep and shoot birds and rats with a bow and arrow. ... Their only concern is self-advantage, and they know nothing of propriety or righteousness.

- Wudi mounted several expensive campaigns against the Xiongnu, but as nomads, they could not be pinned down and simply rode away if they did not feel like engaging the Han armies. Wudi eventually managed to drive the Xiongnu out of Chinese territory and built a series of fortified garrisons along the northern frontier. Such efforts were only partly successful, and barbarian incursions would be a recurrent theme throughout later Chinese history.

- The people eventually grew tired of Wudi's constant military campaigns. Instead of responding with greater repression, however, Wudi apologized, expressed regret for past mistakes, and promised to be a better ruler in future. He halted expansionism and warfare and spent the rest of his life promoting agriculture and trade.

Late Han Cultural Achievements

- One of the most significant aspects of the Han economy was the silk trade. This fabric was a Chinese monopoly much coveted not only within China but among all civilizations that were exposed to it. The result was the famous Silk Road linking China with the outside world and extending across all of Asia to Europe.

- By 100 B.C., silk was known to the Romans, who became avid consumers of it, but no direct contact seems to have been established between the governments of Rome and China. Indeed, there is evidence that some of the middlemen in this trade, such as the Parthians, deliberately kept Rome and China in ignorance of each other so that they could continue to profit from the trade.

- The economic prosperity of the Han Empire fostered both cultural and technological achievements. True paper made from wood pulp was first invented around A.D. 100. Other practical but far-reaching inventions included the horse stirrup, the spinning wheel, the horse collar for plowing, the wheelbarrow, ships with multiple masts, sternpost rudders, and magnetic compasses.

- More abstract advances included the calculation of the value of pi and the discovery of the circulation of blood, something that was not realized in Europe until William Harvey's work in the 17th century.

- In the decorative arts, the type of fine porcelain now known as china was first produced during the Han dynasty. One invention of this era that combined both science and artistry was a kind of primitive seismograph.

- One famous scholar of the period—a historian, astronomer, and mathematician—was a woman named Ban Zhao. She received an education atypical for women at that time and is best known having authored a book called *Lessons for Women*, an influential text on the proper role of women in society.

- *Lessons for Women* reflects Confucian doctrine in the sense that Ban Zhao accepted traditional gender roles, but she also said that women should be educated and respected. She believed that such harmony could best be achieved between intellectual equals.

The Fall of the Han Dynasty

- The Han dynasty is traditionally broken into two phases: the Early, or Western, Han (c. 206 B.C.–A.D. 9) and the Later, or Eastern, Han (A.D. 25–220). During the 14-year gap between them, a number of colorful figures led popular uprisings.

- Like Wudi, the Later Han rulers expended a great deal of time and resources dispatching armies to contain the ever-menacing Xiongnu and to recapture rebellious border regions. These border regions were valuable in themselves and also acted as buffer zones, protecting China from foreign invasion.

- In the final decades of the Later Han period, many of the same old problems began to rear their heads again. Oppressive taxation sparked peasant revolts, court intrigues weakened the central government, generals broke away and became local warlords, northern barbarians became more aggressive, and the economy labored under the various strains. Eventually these forces became overwhelming, and the last Han emperor abdicated the throne in A.D. 220.

Suggested Reading

Lewis, *The Early Chinese Empires*.

Twitchett and Loewe, eds., *The Cambridge History of China*, vol. 1.

Questions to Consider

1. Compare and contrast the Han approach to running China with that of the Qin. Which dynasty's method do you think was better and why?

2. What elements of Han society encouraged the cultural and intellectual achievements of the era?

The Great Empire of the Han Dynasty
Lecture 25—Transcript

We've now reached the halfway point of this course, so it might be an appropriate moment to pause and take stock of what's happening in each of the main regions that we've been following. Around the eastern end of the Mediterranean Sea, in India and in China, we've traced events up to around 200 B.C. In all these areas, brief-lived but geographically vast empires have collapsed, and have left behind confused political landscapes. Alexander the Great's huge empire has fragmented into the many kingdoms established by his generals. In China, after the death of Shi Huangdi, his planned dynasty that would last for 1,000 generations in practice turned out to survive for two, and unified China has disintegrated back into little warring kingdoms. Finally, in India, the temporary unification of the country by Chandragupta and Asoka ended with the death of the last Mauryan king in 184 B.C., and India likewise has splintered into lots of little kingdoms. Here, in India, the resulting plethora of small, constantly-warring states will become the normal situation for hundreds of years, and no conqueror and no giant empires will emerge for nearly 600 years, until finally the Gupta Empire will unite northern and central India.

In China and the Mediterranean, however, something very different will take place. Beginning around 200 B.C. in both of those regions, a single political power will emerge that not only will unite that whole region under its control, but also, and maybe even more impressively, will establish a stable empire that will last for at least four centuries. These two successful, long-lasting regimes are the Roman Empire and the Han Empire; and not only do these two empires exist at right about the same time and they endure for roughly the same length of time, but they're also approximately the same size in terms of both population and geographic extent.

Because of the many similarities and parallels between the Han and the Roman empires, they're well worth examining together. Since the Han Empire follows directly after the actions of Shi Huangdi and either perpetuates or sometimes reacts against many of his policies, I'll first give a brief overview of the Han Empire. In cultural and intellectual terms, there's a lot of continuity between the Han and the previous Chinese dynasties, and since we've already looked at those aspects of Chinese culture, in this lecture I'll really just concentrate on outlining Han political history.

Then, we'll shift our focus to a new geographic region that we haven't yet explored in this course, the Western Mediterranean, and it's from there that Roman civilization will arrive. Since Rome represents a completely new civilization from a completely new region and is also a culture that will exert a great deal of influence, we'll stick with the Romans for five lectures, following their development all the way from its earliest stages up until the high point of the Roman Empire in the 2nd century A.D.

Then, having outlined the history of these two great contemporary empires, one of the East and one of the West, I'll pause in the narrative to spend a couple lectures explicitly comparing and contrasting certain key aspects of Han and Roman civilization, and some of these aspects, I think, help to explain their success, their longevity, and their lasting fame. That's the plan for the next 10 lectures or so; let's get started.

In China, after Qin Shi Huangdi's death in 210 B.C., things rapidly went downhill. His son couldn't control the various power struggles among his advisors and ended up ruling in an even more oppressive and heavy-handed manner than his father had. The common people were completely tired of the heavy tax load, of the forced labor, and the really harsh legal system that's been imposed. The intellectuals and the upper classes, they're stewing with resentment at their treatment, and the treasury had been drained by all the giant public works projects. The country began to erupt in rebellions by different factions, some led by aristocrats who wanted to regain their former power and reestablish old-style feudalism, and some rebellions were led by peasants who were just hoping to gain some freedom.

After several confused years, one of these rebel leaders named Liu Bang rose of the chaos to found a new dynasty, the Han. (The name, by the way, came from a tributary of the Yangtze River.) Liu Bang was really an extremely unlikely candidate to become the next emperor and to establish what will turn out to be one of China's most influential dynasties. Liu Bang was a peasant who, at least when he was younger, was described as being lazy, uneducated, and unemployed. Furthermore, he had a reputation that he was a bit overly fond of wine and women. Despite that seemingly unpromising beginning, he reformed his ways, became the headman of his local village, and from there became a general in one of the armies of rebellious peasants. Even then, his skills as a general weren't very good. He lost every single battle that he personally commanded except one. But his real talent lay in knowing how to choose subordinates, how to delegate authority, and how to mediate among his various followers who didn't get along very well. It's these, what we might call, people skills that allowed him to hold together unlikely alliances and eventually he's able to command the allegiance of all these different subordinates. That was enough to elevate him to the emperorship, and to enable him to rule successfully once he got there.

Liu Bang is one of only two individuals in the whole long history of China who rose all the way from peasant to emperor. Because he was illiterate, he had to rely heavily on scholars in the bureaucracy, and he retained a certain peasant's contempt for what he saw as these overly-effete men of abstract learning. One story, for example, told about him says that sometimes he'd grab the distinctive hat that was worn by scholars and rip it off their heads and then urinate in it as a sign of his contempt for them. Nevertheless, he understood how to use those bureaucrats to his advantage, and this uneducated commoner brought about a period that, at least later, would be viewed as almost a Golden Age of Chinese culture and civilization. In later times, the Chinese would continue to call themselves "Men of Han" or "Sons of Han," because this was respected as the greatest dynasty, which established the model that all later dynasties followed.

Liu Bang's cleverness in establishing a stable form of government lay in keeping the strong, centralized state that Shi Huangdi had built, but adding to it or turning it into a somewhat kinder, gentler form. He attempted to combine the Confucian model of the compassionate, virtuous ruler who cared about his subjects with the efficiency and the order of Legalism. He addressed the unhappiness of the peasants by reducing the forced labor that was required on them and, at least for a while, reducing taxes. He got the intellectuals and the educated upper classes on his side by rescinding the Qin ban on Confucian and Zhou classics, and he actively encouraged intellectual pursuits instead of suppressing them. All of this resulted in a flowering or a renaissance of intellectual life in China.

Liu Bang found ways to harness the talents of the class of educated men and turned those towards the service of the state, and he did this by establishing a system that was both highly ordered and hierarchical but not hereditary. This was essential, because rather than offering advancement based on birth, instead this system rewarded those who had skills and energy. The actual mechanism by which you identified these people was through an elaborate system of examinations, and the exams were based on your knowledge of Confucian classic texts. Aspiring civil servants could take these exams, and if they did well on them they could rise in the bureaucracy based on their intellectual and organizational abilities. China was divided up into 100 governmental regions, and these were further subdivided into 1,500 districts. A very elaborate, multilayered bureaucracy was formed that had 20 different levels, and it's been estimated that there were 130,000 individuals working in this bureaucracy and overseeing everything from the collection of taxes to the construction of public works. The Han rulers also set up a national university that eventually would enroll 30,000 students, and they were there studying to pass those civil service exams and try to do well at them.

In theory, the exam system purely rewarded merit, and so, again, it should allow poor people to overcome their origins. In practice, the system did naturally favor sons from the wealthier landowning families, because they were the ones who had more wealth and time to devote themselves to the study that was necessary. But nevertheless, it did serve as a way to identify the most gifted and the most industrious. Whereas before, the main social division had been a rigid distinction between peasant and aristocrat, now it's a more fluid line between peasant and landowner/bureaucrat.

While the Han did away with the hated Qin restrictions on travel, books, and even thought, they did continue some Qin policies, such as conscription into the army. They also continued the use of forced labor to build especially canals and roads, and they continued the standardization of things such as weights, measures, and currency, and the Chinese script. The Han Dynasty would last about four centuries, from 202 B.C.–220 A.D., but that Han fusion of Legalism and Confucianism, mingling practicality and ethics, would become the model for all subsequent Chinese dynasties, and it really set the pattern for government that would endure for about 1,500 years in China.

Liu Bang's immediate heirs, as well as later Han emperors, continued to follow the precedent that he'd established of the benevolent Confucian ruler. But by the time we get to later Han emperors such as Wudi, who came to power in 141 B.C., that balance began to shift a little bit back towards the more centralized and heavy-handed model of Qin rule. Wudi, who ruled down until 87 B.C., was known as the Martial Emperor because he pursued a very aggressive policy of military expansion, and under him China would expand to its largest extent during the Han period. He also favored a more powerful, centralized sort of government in which a lot of different industries, including things like iron making, salt collection, copper, even liquor were taken over by the state, which would control them as monopolies. He also actively regulated the food supply. He set up something that was called "the ever-normal granary system," in which the government would buy up big quantities of grain in years that there was a good harvest, they would store it up, and then they'd sell it for subsidized, lower than market prices during years in which there were bad harvests. This was an early attempt at government regulation of prices, and it didn't wholly work; it wasn't entirely successful. But it does, I think, demonstrate a concern for preventing starvation among the empire's populace. To support his big and active military, under Wudi taxes were steadily raised.

With the resources of all China to draw upon, Wudi was able to put together huge, huge armies, sometimes more than 100,000 soldiers, and he sent these off in various directions. Towards the south, in what today is northern Vietnam, that area was brought under Chinese control this time. He also conquered southern Manchuria and Korea, and he kept pushing the borders of China to the west, out into central Asia. His biggest challenge, though, was to the north, where repeatedly he'd mount expeditions against the nomads of the steppe who lived in that region.

The main enemy among these various nomads was a confederation of tribes known as the Xiongnu. They were fierce warriors who fought always from horseback; and currently there's a big debate among scholars, some of whom identify the Xiongnu with the people later known as the Huns. It's not really sure if the Huns and the Xiongnu were exactly the same group, but whether they were or not, they were very similar in lifestyle and the sort of tactics that they used in warfare. They're true nomads, so they didn't establish any permanent cities or camps, they only had temporary settlements, and they specialized in being horse archers, and they were absolutely deadly shooting their arrows from horseback. The famous Chinese historian Sima Qian wrote a description of them, and in this description he describes them as being:

> They are people who move about in search of water and pasture and they have no walled cities or fixed dwellings, nor do they engage in any form of agriculture. ... Even the little boys start out learning to ride sheep and to shoot birds and rats with a bow and arrow. ... Their only concern is self-advantage, and they know nothing of propriety or righteousness.

Wudi mounted a number of very expensive campaigns against the Xiongnu, but since there were no cities to attack, no real territory to conquer, he couldn't pin the nomads down, and they'd simply ride away if they didn't feel like fighting the Han armies. In the words of the frustrated Han generals, they said that the Xiongnu "move about on swift horses and in their breasts beat the hearts of beasts. They shift from place to place like a flock of birds. Thus it is difficult to corner them and bring them under control."

Despite their evasiveness, Wudi did eventually manage to drive the Xiongnu out of Chinese territory, and he tried to keep them out by establishing a series of fortified outposts and little garrison towns all along the northern frontier of China. These efforts were, again, only partly successful, and there were constant incursions and raids from these barbarian groups, and these sorts of raids would be a recurrent theme all throughout Han and, indeed, into later Chinese history.

Just like under Shi Huangdi, however, the people eventually grew tired of Wudi's constant military campaigns, which ended up depleting the resources, depleting the treasury, of the Chinese empire. But then, instead of responding like Shi Huangdi with even greater repression, Wudi did something really unusual: He actually apologized and he changed his behavior and his policies. He issued an edict in which he expressed regret for his past mistakes, and in which he promised that he'd be a better ruler in the future. True to his word, he halted expansionism and warfare in favor of spending the rest of his life promoting things like agriculture and trade.

In the north, for example, instead of funding more military expeditions, Wudi built a canal connecting the Yellow River to the original Han capital of Chang'an, and by doing so he linked up two important regions and fostered economic activity within China. During the Han period, trade and commerce thrived, both as a result of government policies and due to the security, the safety, and the stability that had been brought by the state.

One of the most significant aspects of the Han economy was the silk trade. Silk is produced by little worms, and the fabric that's made from them was a Chinese monopoly that's coveted not only within China, but among all the civilizations that became exposed to it. In particular, the cultures of the Near East and the Mediterranean very, very quickly developed a taste for this luxury good once they knew of it. The result was the establishment of the famous Silk Road, which linked China with the world outside and that extended across all of Asia to Europe. The origins of the particular route probably go back quite a bit, all the way maybe to the time of the Zhou Dynasty, but it's under the Han that it became much more prominent and that regular caravans started to go back and forth. These caravans would load up with silk and begin in China; then they'd go to Central Asia, where the goods would have to be transferred from horses to these Bactrian camels. The camels were sturdy, they could carry up to 500 pounds each, and, most importantly, they could survive the very, very harsh and cold conditions that were prevalent in the Asian deserts. Then those goods would go over those deserts, they would pass through several groups of middlemen, and ultimately they'd end up on the shores of the Mediterranean Sea. By at least 100 B.C., silk was known to the Romans, and they liked it; they became avid consumers of it. But, interestingly enough, no direct contact seems to have been established between the governments of Rome and China. There's some evidence that the middlemen in the Silk Road trade, people such as the Parthians, actually deliberately tried to keep the two sides in ignorance of each other so that they could continue to profit from the trade by being the middle guys.

The production of silk is sometimes credited with bringing huge amounts of currency to China, but producing silk is a labor-intensive thing. It's been estimated that to produce 150 pounds of silk, you have to have no fewer than

750,000 silkworms, and all those worms have to be cultivated, fed, and have their cages cleaned regularly.

The economic prosperity of the Han Empire fostered both cultural and technological achievements. Especially impressive here were some of the new inventions and technologies that came out of this time. In keeping with the whole emphasis on bureaucracy and scholarship and the exams, it's during the Han era that true paper, paper made from wood pulp, was first invented, probably around (the best guess is) 100 A.D. Prior to that in China, scribes had written on little strips of bamboo or wood, which sometimes were tied together to make large sheets. But true paper was much lighter, it offered a bigger surface to write upon, and it's much more useful for recording documents, records, and things like that.

During the Han Dynasty, the forerunner of the newspaper may also have had its first appearance, or at least something that was a regularly-published government bulletin. This was known as a *tipao*, and it would contain official announcements and little bits of news. Some of the other practically-minded but still influential inventions that came out of Han China included the horse stirrup, the spinning wheel, the horse collar that made plowing more efficient, and the wheelbarrow, which allowed you to transport loads much more easily. In the realm of maritime science, this was a Golden Age for Chinese seafaring. Chinese ships were built with multiple masts, with true sternpost rudders (that's a big innovation), and magnetic compasses; so all of these things were features of Chinese ships. Chinese scholars also made more abstract advances, including calculating the value of Pi in geometry, and also discovering the circulation of blood within the human body, which was something that wasn't realized in Europe until William Harvey worked on that in the 17th century. In the decorative arts, the type of fine porcelain that today we just generically call "china" was produced in this era as well, and Han artists crafted beautiful ceramic vessels and even pots shaped like animals out of this material. One particularly neat invention of this time that combined both science and an element of artistry was a primitive seismograph for recording earthquakes, and this consisted of a big bronze vessel that had eight bronze dragons around the lip of it, and they'd react to any sort of vibration or tremor by dropping pearls from their mouths.

One famous scholar of this time who was an historian, astronomer, and mathematician was also a woman. She was named Ban Zhao, and she came from a famous family of other eminent scholars and also generals in the military. Atypical for women of the time, she received a fairly advanced education, and she's best known today for having authored a book that's called *Lessons for Women*. This became a very influential text on the proper role of women in society. In general, it pretty much reflects or embodies standard Confucian doctrine, which, as you might expect, emphasizes devotion and selfless behavior. Ban Zhao accepted the traditional gender roles and she stressed that a good wife should be modest, should obey her husband, and should do the tasks that were expected of her; so things like weaving and food preparation, which were stereotypically women's work. But, on the other hand, she also said that women should be educated and that they should be respected. She said a harmonious marriage is the ultimate goal, but while a woman should be subservient, Ban Zhao also believed that the ideal harmony could best be achieved between intellectual equals. There's a famous passage in one of her books that says:

> Humility means yielding and acting respectful, putting others first and oneself last. … Industriousness means going to bed late, getting up early, never shirking work morning or night, and completing everything that needs to be done neatly and carefully.

The Han Dynasty can be broken up into two main phases: There's the Early Han, sometimes called the Western Han, who ruled from 206 B.C.–9 A.D., and then there's the Later or Eastern Han, who ruled from about 25–220 A.D. During the 14-year gap between them, there were a whole bunch of really very colorful figures. This was a time of confusion and a number of these people led popular uprisings. One of these was a rebel female leader named Mother Lu who started out as a rich landowner and ended up as a pirate. There's another group of rebels who called themselves the Red Eyebrows, and they'd actually paint their eyebrows red; and the idea here was they're imitating demons, which supposedly had red eyelids, and this was done to intimidate their enemies.

Like Wudi, the Later Han spent a lot of time, money, and resources sending armies to try and contain the Xiongnu, who were always an ever-present threat, and to try and bring back into the realm of China various border regions—again, like Vietnam, Korea, and Manchuria—that tended to break away during times of weakness or confusion. Those border regions also served as buffer zones; they protected China from invasion from external forces. The Han stimulated trade with other states; they were an outward-looking dynasty. In the final decades of the Later Han period, many of those same old problems, though, began to rear their heads again. Too much taxation sparked peasant revolts; constant intriguing at court weakened the central government; generals started to break away and set themselves up as local warlords or kings; the northern barbarians got more aggressive and kept raiding the border regions; and all of this put a strain on the economy. Eventually all these forces together acted together and became overwhelming, and the last Han emperor abdicated the throne in 220 A.D.

Next, we'll turn to the other great empire-building culture of this same time, the Romans, and we'll trace the course of their development from its humble beginnings up to a high point at which the Roman Empire rivaled the Han Empire in size, in wealth, and in sophistication.

People of the Toga—Etruscans, Early Rome
Lecture 26

Before the Romans, the Etruscans ruled the Italian Peninsula, and many of the cultural features we think of as quintessentially Roman were actually traits the Romans adopted from them. Once they overthrew their sometimes tyrannical Etruscan overlords, Rome quickly expanded to dominate the Western Mediterranean more through dogged persistence and generosity to the conquered than military might. By 264 B.C., Rome's unique geographic and cultural position had poised the budding empire to dominate the Hellenistic world and beyond.

The Geography of Ancient Italy

- The Italian peninsula is surrounded by water on all sides except to the north. Italy has more miles of coastline than any European country except Greece.

- Two mountain chains played significant roles in the development of the Italic peoples: the tall and formidable Alps that separate the peninsula from the rest of Europe and the Apennine Mountains that run north to south almost the entire length of the peninsula like a spine.

- Because of the Apennines, all the large expanses of flat farmland are found on Italy's coasts. There are three important arable expanses: one around Rome called Latium, one in the south around the Bay of Naples called Campania, and one to the north of Latium called Etruria.

- Between Italy and Africa is the island of Sicily. Both southern Italy and Sicily had been heavily settled by Greek colonists. Compared to the rest of early Italy, these regions were rich, powerful, and culturally sophisticated.

- The city of Rome is located 15 miles inland from the sea at the first natural ford across the Tiber River; thus it occupies a key transportation node. Rome is roughly in the middle of the Italian Peninsula, and Italy is roughly in the middle of the Mediterranean Sea. Thus, Rome was in an ideal location to dominate first Italy and then the whole Mediterranean.

Early Rome and the Etruscans

- The traditional date for the founding of the city of Rome is April 21, 753 B.C. Subsequent Roman history is divided into 3 periods by form of government: the monarchy (753–509 B.C.), the republic (509–31 B.C.), and the empire (31 B.C. onward).

- Archaeological evidence tells us the site of Rome has been inhabited since at least 1000 B.C. The most famous foundation legend tells of twin brothers, Romulus and Remus, allegedly the offspring of the god of war, Mars, and raised by a friendly she-wolf.

- As adults, the twins decided to build a city on the spot where the wolf had found them, but they argued over who should be king. Romulus murdered Remus and named the new city after himself. In a sense, this legend is entirely appropriate, as much of Roman history will involve ambitious men fighting for control of Rome.

By Verity Cridland.

The Etruscans predate the Romans, and the Romans owe much to them.

- In reality, Rome was a tiny village of thatched huts, one among hundreds similar, undistinguished Italic communities. Another extensive, powerful, and sophisticated civilization dominated the northern half of the Italian peninsula: the Etruscans, based in the region of Etruria.

- Early in their history, Rome fell under Etruscan yoke; almost half of the seven legendary kings of Rome have Etruscan names. This experience deeply engrained in the Romans a distrust of any one man (such as a king) holding supreme power and made them paranoid about being controlled by foreigners.

- The Etruscans are a bit mysterious. No Etruscan histories survive to tell their story; we know them only through their enemies' writings and through archaeological evidence. Despite their resentment, the Romans copied many things from the Etruscans, including the toga, gladiatorial combat, temple architecture, and divination through the examination of animal organs.

Rome Becomes a Republic

- The seventh king of Rome was Tarquinius Superbus, meaning Tarquin the Proud, an arrogant Etruscan tyrant. In 509 B.C., one of Tarquin's relatives raped Lucretia, the wife of a Roman nobleman. She committed suicide. This outrage sparked a general rebellion against the Tarquins, and they were expelled from Rome.

- The leader of this uprising was a man named Brutus, who swore a famous oath over the woman's dead body to never let another king rule Rome. Brutus's oath established a familial tradition of opposition to kings that would have profound consequences 500 years later.

- The Romans set up a new government, the Roman Republic, in which political power was spread among a hierarchy of officials elected by an assembly of all citizens. Even the highest office in the new system, the consulship, was held by two men who each had equal power. Brutus was elected as one of the first two consuls.

- All Roman magistrates served for one-year terms. Originally, these positions could only be held by members of a hereditary aristocracy, known as the patricians. Over time, these restrictions were relaxed. Once you had held any of these posts, you automatically became a member of the Roman Senate for the rest of your life.

- Later, as the common citizen began to feel the patrician class was monopolizing and abusing power a tribune of the plebs was created to defend the rights of nonpatricians. Tribunes had the ability to veto and to propose new legislation.

Roman Ambition and Power

- The ambition of all Roman patricians was to move up the ladder of offices, known as the *cursus honorum*, or the "course of honor." Rome was an intensely competitive society. This competition for status, or *dignitas*, was crucial for much of Roman history.

- The ways one could gain *dignitas* were myriad: Being elected to an office, winning a military victory, building a public work, becoming wealthy, winning a legal case, delivering a good speech, marrying into a prestigious family, giving charity to the poor, and many more. But *dignitas* was fleeting and constantly had to be renewed. It was also a zero-sum game, meaning that if you gained some, somebody else had lost some.

- Between the founding of the Republic and roughly 250 B.C., Rome went from being one of hundreds of Italic cities to being the dominant power in all of Italy. This was a long, gradual process, during which Rome was almost constantly at war with one or more of its neighbors. Rome often had to fight the same enemy multiple times before subduing it.

- As Etruscan faded, the Romans claimed Etruria. Rome's immediate neighbors in central Italy were a group of cities called the Latin League, cosignatories to a treaty that placed them all on equal footing. To the south was another powerful federation of cities, the Samnites. The Romans fought three major wars against the Samnites and eventually subdued them.

- To facilitate the rapid movement of troops, the consuls began building the great Roman road system. The main north-south road is the Appian Way, named after the consul who constructed it. The roads also became the visible symbols of Roman domination.

- The Romans had an unusual way of treating the people they conquered. The normal procedure in the ancient world was that the defeated city would be sacked and its inhabitants would be killed or sold into slavery. Instead, the Romans granted the local aristocrats—and, on occasion, even entire cities—full Roman citizenship.

- More commonly, cities were given half-citizenship, which meant they had the private rights of citizens, such as legal protections, but not the public rights, such as voting. Other cities became Socii, or allies of Rome. The one universal obligation imposed on the conquered was to provide troops for the Roman army.

- Rome could be a generous overlord, but they could also be savage, particularly if a city revolted. Then they might raze the city and enslave or slaughter the populace.

- Rome did not enjoy any notable military superiority. They often suffered terrible defeats. But the Romans did develop a kind of dogged persistence. Romans also became accustomed to the idea that being at war was a normal condition. Between the mid-4th century and late 2nd century B.C., there were fewer than 10 years during which Rome was not at war with someone.

The Pyrrhic Victory at Tarentum

- The final set of wars Rome fought during this period was against the wealthy Greek cities of southern Italy. The most powerful of these was Tarentum. In 280 B.C., Tarentum hired a mercenary general named Pyrrhus of Epirus and his nearly 30,000 combat-hardened Greek mercenaries and 20 war elephants.

- In the subsequent battle, the Romans were wiped out, although they inflicted heavy casualties on Pyrrhus's army. The normal procedure would be an exchange of envoys, a peace treaty, and for Rome to pay a fine. But the Romans refused to negotiate raised a second army.

- In an exact repeat of the first battle, the Romans were soundly defeated but took a significant number of Pyrrhus' troops with them. After this battle, Pyrrhus famously commented, "If I win another victory like these, my army will be finished."

- Once again, the Romans summoned their reserves, mustered new armies, and sent them south. At this point, Pyrrhus simply gave up and took the remnants of his force back to Greece, having decisively won all the battles, but lost the war.

- Rome moved into southern Italy and brought all its cities under their control. By 264 B.C., Rome had conquered nearly the entire Italian peninsula, including roughly 3 million people, of whom 1 million possessed some form of citizenship. The city of Rome had swollen to around 150,000. The stage was now set for Rome to cross the seas.

Suggested Reading

Borrelli et al., *The Etruscans*.

Cornell, *The Beginnings of Rome*.

Warren, Heichelheim, and Yeo, *A History of the Roman People*.

1. What were the most significant legacies and influences of the Etruscans on the Romans (in both a positive and negative sense)?

2. Is there any equivalent to the key Roman value of *dignitas* in modern society?

People of the Toga—Etruscans, Early Rome
Lecture 26—Transcript

We now shift to a new geographic region, the western Mediterranean, and to a new culture, the Romans; or, as they called themselves, the "People of the Toga." Over the next five lectures, rather than jumping around from culture to culture, we'll stay with the Romans and we'll trace the rise of Roman civilization from its beginnings as a kind of grubby cluster of mud huts alongside the Tiber River up until the time when they're a vast and powerful empire that stretches from Britain to Mesopotamia.

As always, when embarking on a new region, though, first I need to make a couple comments about its particular geography. The Italian peninsula, with its very distinctive boot shape, stretches north-south for about 750 miles, and it's surrounded on all sides by water except up to the north. In fact, Italy has more miles of coastline than any European country except for Greece. There are two mountain chains will play significant roles in the development of the people who live in Italy. First of all, across that northern barrier, are the Alps. These are tall, formidable mountains, and effectively they form a wall that separates Italy from the rest of Europe. There are a couple passes through the Alps, but they're very difficult to traverse and so, pretty much like Egypt, Italy has very strong natural boundaries, and for a while those boundaries will insulate and protect it from foreign invasion. Second, there are the Apennine Mountains, and this is a chain that runs north/south almost the entire length of the Italian peninsula; you can think of the Apennine's as like a spine, running down Italy. Unlike the Alps, they aren't high, there are lots of places you can cross over them; but they and their surrounding foothills ensure that the center of the Italian peninsula is composed of hilly terrain, and what that means in practical terms is that all the good farmland, all the flatlands, are only found along the coasts of Italy. Below Italy, and between it and Africa, is the crucial island of Sicily. Remember, both southern Italy and Sicily had been heavily settled by Greek colonists; so that's a Greek region. Compared to the rest of Italy, to northern and central Italy, those regions were richer, more powerful, and more culturally sophisticated.

When we turn to the city of Rome, it's located about roughly 15 miles inland from the sea, and it's located at the very first natural ford across the Tiber

River; and so Rome occupies a key transportation node. The site of Rome is roughly in the middle of the Italian Peninsula, and Italy is roughly in the middle of the Mediterranean Sea. So, by an accident of geography, Rome is ideally situated in a central location to expand and dominate first Italy and then the entire Mediterranean.

The traditional date for the foundation of the city of Rome is April 21, 753 B.C. That's actually the starting point for the Roman calendar, which counts years since the foundation of the city. Subsequent Roman history is very nicely divided up into three distinct periods by the form of government: First of all, we have the Monarchy, when Rome was ruled by kings, at that goes from the foundation at 753 down to 509 B.C. Next, you have the period of the Republic, when Rome had a somewhat democratic form of government, and that goes from 509 B.C.–31 B.C. Finally, the last period of Roman history is the Empire, during which, as the name implies, Rome was ruled by emperors. That last period begins in 31 B.C. and it goes for at least 400 years. The exact date of when it ends is something that scholars debate about and is a question we'll look at later in this course.

Despite the enormous importance that the Romans attached to the foundation of their city, and all the many stories that they later told about the origins of their city, it's very hard for scholars to determine the truth of those stories. There are no contemporary surviving accounts, and the accounts that we do have are, quite honestly, propagandistic. Archaeological, physical evidence can tell us that the site of Rome was inhabited from at least around 1000 B.C.; there are some graves that go back that far. The most famous of all the foundation legends states that the city of Rome was established by twin brothers, Romulus and Remus, who were supposedly the offspring of the god of war, Mars. Through a complex series of circumstances, they were abandoned as babies, and then were supposedly rescued by a friendly she-wolf, which was actually aided by a helpful woodpecker—often the woodpecker gets left out of that story—and both of those were animals associated with the god Mars. As adults, Romulus and Remus decided to return to the spot where the wolf had found them and to found the city, but immediately they got into an argument over who should be the king of the new city. The result of that argument was that Romulus claimed the throne by murdering his brother Remus and then he named the new city after himself. This is an odd choice for a foundation story, because it features at its core a fratricide; that's the event that begins Roman history. But, in a sense, it's an entirely appropriate story because much of Roman history will indeed consist of ambitious men fighting one another to see who will control Rome.

Keep in mind that at this time, back at the beginning of Roman history, Rome was just a tiny, insignificant little village of thatched huts, and it's only one of hundreds of other such little villages scattered all throughout Italy. There was, however, already at that time an extensive, powerful, and sophisticated civilization that dominated the northern half of the Italian peninsula. These were the Etruscans, and early in their history, Rome fell under the control of the Etruscans. In fact, of the seven legendary kings of Rome, about half of them have names that are Etruscan names; so it looks like they were actually Etruscan kings imposed on Rome. So Rome went through a period when it's ruled by foreign kings, and this experience is going to leave long-lasting psychological scars on the Romans and, in particular, it deeply engrained in them a distrust of any one man—such as a king—holding supreme power in the state. It also made the Romans a little bit paranoid about being controlled by any foreigners, and we'll see those two themes pop up repeatedly throughout the rest of Roman history.

The Etruscans themselves are a little bit of a mystery people. No Etruscan histories survive to tell us their own story in their own words, and so we really only know them through the writings of their enemies and from some archaeological evidence. Two of the most important Etruscan cities were Cerveteri and Tarquinia, and you can still visit those today. At those sites, there are very few buildings, but what you do have are lots of tombs underground, and the walls of those tombs are covered with absolutely spectacular wall paintings.

Despite their resentment of Etruscan domination, the Romans ended up copying a lot of things from them, and a number of aspects of Roman civilization that at least in popular perception are thought of as being distinctively Roman in reality are actually derived from the Etruscans. I'll give you two notable examples of such borrowings: The first is the toga, which was the mark of a Roman citizen, and only a Roman citizen by law could wear the toga. The toga was actually stolen from the Etruscans; it's the traditional outfit worn by Etruscan kings. A second thing that the Romans stole or borrowed from the Etruscans was gladiator games. Those actually originated as a part of funeral rites for dead Etruscan leaders. A lot of aspects of Etruscan culture, particularly religion, found their way into Roman culture, including things such as the style of temple architecture and the practice of divination, attempting to tell the future by examining the internal organs of animal; and that's a habit that we've already seen, for example, among the ancient Mesopotamians.

As time went on, the Romans increasingly resented being ruled over by the Etruscans. The seventh king of Rome was a guy named Tarquinius Superbus, which means "Tarquin the Proud," and, as his name suggests, he wasn't a very nice person. He did things like having several Roman noblemen murdered, he ignored advice from the Senate, he surrounded himself with bodyguards, and in general he fit the model of an arrogant tyrant. In 509 B.C., one of Tarquin's relatives raped a woman named Lucretia, who's the wife of a Roman nobleman. She subsequently committed suicide; but this outrage sparked a rebellion against the Tarquins, and they were kicked out of Rome. The leader of this uprising was a man named Brutus, and he swore a very famous oath over Lucretia's dead body. The oath of Brutus goes: "By this woman's blood, and by all the gods, I will pursue and punish Tarquin and his children, and never again will I let them or any other man be king in Rome." Brutus's oath not only resulted in the end of the monarchy, but it also established a familial tradition of opposition to kings within the Brutus family that would have profound consequences 500 years down the road; and we'll see that when we get to the story of Julius Caesar.

Still smoldering with resentment of the one-man rule of the kings, the Romans now set up a new form of government, the Roman Republic, in which political power was spread at least somewhat among the citizens. The Romans established a hierarchy of offices, of government officials, and all of these were elected by the citizens. So deeply opposed were the Romans to the whole idea of one man being the leader of the state that even the highest office in the new system—the equivalent of our president—the Roman office of something called the consulship was held not by one guy each year, but by two men who had equal power. This was really a unique arrangement; and if those two consuls for the year were in accord with one another, it could be very effective, but, as you can imagine, if they disagreed with one another you had potential for terrible governmental gridlock. Brutus was elected as one of the very first consuls.

To make sure that no man remained permanently in office like a king, all Roman magistrates served one-year terms; so you're in a year, then you're out. Originally, those positions could only be held by members of a hereditary aristocracy, a group who were known as the patricians, literally "the fathers"; but, over time, that restriction would be relaxed. Once someone had held any one of those posts in the government, you automatically became a member of the Roman Senate for the rest of your life. Because the Senate was made up of the most distinguished men in Rome, the opinions of the Roman Senate, even when they weren't legally binding, tended to carry enormous weight.

There was also one more magistracy that was added a little bit later, and this got tacked on as a result of resentment that the patricians were monopolizing and sometimes abusing power. This final office was called the Tribune of the Plebs, and it's a special office charged with defending the rights of non-patricians. To accomplish this, the Tribunes had the veto power; they could veto anything that they thought was unfair. They also had the power to propose new laws.

The ambition of every Roman patrician was to move up that ladder of offices, and this was a thing known as the *cursus honorum*; literally, the "course of honor." Rome was an intensely competitive society. The Romans were constantly comparing themselves with their peers and vying with their peers for prestige. This competition for status is absolutely crucial to understanding Roman history, and the whole idea of it is best expressed by a Latin word for which there really isn't an equivalent in English. That word is *dignitas*. *Dignitas* could be translated as "status," "prestige," "notoriety," "fame," "celebrity," "reputation," or "clout," but it's really all of those things rolled up together into one. Your *dignitas* was the intangible sum of your importance. It's not just your influence, but it's a measure of how much of a big shot you were; how much people were talking about you; how much you're in the public eye. The ways by which you could gain *dignitas* were infinite: You could gain *dignitas* if you're elected to an office; if you won a military victory; if you built a new building for the city; if you were simply rich, you had a certain amount of *dignitas*; if you won a high-profile law case; if you delivered a good speech; if you married into a famous family; all of these things could give you *dignitas*. Lots and lots of different acts could gain you *dignitas*.

The problem with *dignitas* was that it's fleeting, so you're constantly losing it as well; and you always had to be renewing your *dignitas*. Think about the concept of celebrity-hood today; it's like that: The person that everybody's talking about this week, next week is forgotten unless they've done something new to put themselves back in the public eye. That's like *dignitas*. Also, *dignitas* was a zero-sum game, meaning that if you gained some, probably somebody else had to lose some. *Dignitas* was public, it's competitive, and it's the most important thing to a Roman aristocrat. It's more important to them than life itself. The quest for *dignitas* was the engine that motivated and drove much of Roman behavior and history.

That's a quick outline of some of the main institutions of the Roman Republic, and all of this didn't just spring into being overnight in 509 B.C., it took a couple centuries for this whole system to develop. But everything was pretty much in place by the end of the 4th century B.C.

Next, let's look at how Rome went from being one of hundreds of little Italic cities to being the dominant power in all of Italy. This was a long, gradual process; it lasted all the way from the foundation of the Republic down to about 250 B.C., so about two or three centuries. During this period, Rome was almost constantly at war with one or more of its neighbors; and in the end, Rome tended to emerge successful from these wars, but they're often difficult with many setbacks. Rome often had to fight the same enemy multiple times before they managed to subdue them.

If we look first up to the north, Etruscan power by this time was fading away, and so the Romans were able to encroach in upon this territory and eventually claim all of it for themselves. In central Italy, Rome's immediate neighbors were a group of cities called the Latin League; and Rome had made a treaty with the Latin League in which Rome and the League were on equal footing, and they agreed to act as allies and to help one another. Together with the League, Rome fought many battles against mountain tribes, and eventually defeated them. But once this was done, Rome then turned against its former allies in the Latin League and attacked them, and one by one conquered the cities of the Latin League. The Latin League cities were all very similar in culture and language and habits to the Romans, and so they're easily assimilated. Down to the south was another powerful federation of cities, and these were known as the Samnites. The Romans fought three major wars against the Samnites, and in these wars they suffered some very humiliating defeats; but eventually they subdued the Samnites and they took over their territory, too.

One effect of the Samnite campaigns was that in order to facilitate moving troops rapidly south, the Consuls began building for the first time the great Roman road system, which eventually is going to link up Rome with all corners of its empire. The Roman roads were really marvels of engineering; some of them are still in use today, 2,000 years later. That first main north-south road going down from Rome is called the Appian Way, and it's named after the consul, Appius, who built it. In addition to their practical purposes, these roads had an important symbolic value. Wherever the Romans went, and in this way they're almost like an animal, the Romans marked their territory, and the way they marked their territory was by building roads; and so those roads became visible symbols of Roman domination.

Throughout this whole process of unifying Italy under their control, the Romans had a very unusual way of treating the people that they conquered. The normal procedure in the ancient world when two cities went to war was that the defeated city would tend to be sacked, burnt down often, and its inhabitants would be killed or sold into slavery. But the Romans adopted a different strategy: Sometimes, rather than killing and enslaving the local inhabitants, the Romans would grant them full Roman citizenship. Sometimes they'd do this just to the aristocracy of the city; occasionally entire cities were given Roman citizenship. More commonly, the Romans would give these cities something called half-citizenship, which meant that they had the private rights of citizens, such as legal protections, but not the public rights, such as voting. A third thing the Romans would sometimes do is, after they conquered a city, they'd declare it a Sociis, and that meant an ally of Rome. But in all these cases—whether they're made full citizens, half citizens, or allies—the one universal obligation imposed by the Romans on the conquered Italic peoples was that they had to provide soldiers to the Roman army. They didn't require taxes, but they required everybody to provide men for the Roman army. Making this the main obligation of the cities they conquered gave Rome unlimited manpower to draw upon. Those men who went off and served with the Roman army also became Romanized. They'd learn Latin if they didn't know it already; they'd pick up roman customs; they'd start to see themselves as Romans. Through this process, Rome Romanized the rest of the Italians and the Latin language became the common language of the entire Italian peninsula.

Rome could be a generous overlord, this idea of sharing citizenship; but they could also be cruel, particularly if a city to which they'd given privileges then revolted against them. In these cases, they'd move in, stomp on the city, raze it to the ground, and enslave or kill the entire populace.

It's important to stress that in all of these wars Rome really didn't have any special superiority in terms of their tactics, their leadership, or their equipment; they often suffered terrible defeats. But the Romans did have a sort of dogged persistence in the way that no matter how many times they got defeated, they'd just keep coming back, and they'd never give up until they won the war, no matter how severe the setbacks. During this period, the Romans also became accustomed to the idea that being at war was a normal condition. Today, we like to think of peace as the normative state for nations and wars are exceptional interruptions; but for the Romans, it's just the opposite. For example, during about a 200 year stretch from the mid-4th century down through the 2nd century B.C., there were only 10 years approximately during which Rome wasn't at war with someone. One historian once noted that the Romans displayed an almost biological imperative to go out and inflict massive violence on somebody every year.

In later years, the Romans would tell lots of stories about heroes and courageous figures from this era, and sometimes it's hard to separate out fact from fiction. But the qualities that were displayed by these early heroes of Roman history became identified as the set of characteristics that the Romans liked to believe defined them as a people.

One example of such an early hero was a guy named Mucius. In his story, Rome was being attacked by the Etruscans, and the Etruscan king and his army had surrounded the city. In order to save Rome, Mucius volunteered to sneak into the enemy headquarters and to assassinate the Etruscan king. Mucius succeeded in infiltrating the camp, but then he killed the wrong person and he got captured. The Etruscan king decided that he'd torture Mucius with fire, and so he had a blazing urn brought into the room. But rather than being intimidated by this threat, Mucius looked him straight in the face and very boldly made a famous declaration. Mucius said: "I am a Roman citizen. My name is Gaius Mucius. I came here to kill my enemy and I am not afraid to die. … Watch me and learn how unimportant the body is to those who have dedicated themselves to a greater cause."

Mucius then thrust his right hand into the flames and he held it there, showing absolutely no emotion while the flesh literally crisped up and burnt off his bones. Upon seeing this, the king was so astonished (or maybe frightened) that immediately he just released Mucius, let him go, and he ended the war, I think wisely preferring not to fight against a nation of such fanatical opponents. To honor and commemorate this deed, the Romans gave Mucius a new surname, and this was a name that would be passed down to all of his descendants. He became Mucius Scaevola, which loosely translates as "Mucius the Lefty," because he no longer had a right hand. In this episode, Mucius displayed not only obviously bravery but ingenuity, and the stereotypical Roman determination never to give up.

The benefits of Rome's policy of incorporating captured states and the sort of unwavering determination that we just saw with Mucius can both clearly be clearly seen in the last set of wars that Rome fought in this period, and these were wars against the wealthy Greek cities in southern Italy. The most powerful of those cities was a place called Tarentum. When the inevitable war with the Romans broke out in 280 B.C., Tarentum used its wealth to go hire the best mercenaries in the world to protect itself. The Tarentines went to the mainland of Greece and they hired a mercenary general, a guy named Pyrrhus of Epirus; and Pyrrhus had delusions of being a second Alexander the Great (he wasn't that good, but he was a very good soldier). Pyrrhus arrived in Italy with an army of 30,000 professional combat-hardened Greek mercenaries and he even had 20 war elephants. He fought a battle with the Romans, and in that battle, the Romans fought hard, but compared to Pyrrhus and his professionals, they're outclassed; so the Romans were wiped out, although they did manage to inflict heavy casualties on Pyrrhus's army.

In the Hellenistic world, the normal procedure at this point would've been to exchange some envoys, sign a peace treaty, and probably Rome would pay a big fine. But the Romans did something odd here: They refused to negotiate, and instead they went back to their reserves of Italian manpower and they raised a second army, and they sent this new army down against Pyrrhus. In really an exact repeat of the first battle, the Romans fought hard, but they're soundly defeated. Once again, though, they managed to kill a good number of Pyrrhus's troops. After this battle, Pyrrhus famously commented, "One more victory like this, and I'm done for." It's from that kind of costly military triumph where you win but really in some sense lose that today we get the phrase a "pyrrhic victory."

Pyrrhus must have imagined that after crushing the Romans twice, that would be the end of the war and the Romans would finally negotiate; but instead, the Romans went back to the Italians, they summoned their reserves, they mustered a new army, and they sent it south. At this point, Pyrrhus simply gave up. He took the remnants of his force and he fled back to Greece. He won all the battles, but he lost the war. His final reaction to this whole experience was to compare fighting the Romans with fighting a hydra. Those of you familiar with Greek mythology will know that a hydra is a mythological monster that when you chop off one of its heads, two more grow in its place.

With Pyrrhus out of the way, Rome moved into southern Italy and brought all of that area under its control. By 264 B.C., Rome had conquered the entire Italian peninsula and now could draw on the resources and the manpower of all of Italy. It's been estimated that this was about three million people, of whom about one million possessed some version of citizenship, and the population of Rome itself had swollen to about 150,000.

The stage was now set for Rome to begin thinking about crossing the seas and expanding outside of Italy. The conquest of Italy had been helped by the fact that most of the other people who lived there were similar to the Romans in culture and language. But in the next lecture, we'll see what happens when Rome moves outside of Italy and encounters civilizations and people who are truly different from them. The next lecture will also include the greatest threat that the Romans ever faced, and it's a threat that nearly brought them to the brink of total destruction.

The Crucible—Punic Wars, Roman Imperialism
Lecture 27

R ome's success in conquering the Mediterranean world stemmed from the crucible of the Punic Wars and the defeat of their greatest enemy, the Carthaginian general Hannibal. In the First Punic War, Rome was forced to become a great naval powers and captured its first province, Sicily, taking its first steps toward becoming an empire. In the Second Punic War, Rome faced Carthage on the European mainland; Hannibal brought the war to the city's gates before his slow, dispiriting defeat. But Rome's spectacular external successes resulted in self-destructive internal tensions, including unequal distributions of wealth and *dignitas*.

What Was Carthage?

- During the next several centuries of the Republic, Rome took over most of the Mediterranean basin region, starting with a series of conflicts pitting Rome against the other major, young, growing powers in the western Mediterranean—the city-state of Carthage.

- The resulting Punic Wars were the closest Rome ever came to total defeat, yet they were also the stepping stone to Rome's ultimate success. In 264 B.C., the year Rome captured the last independent Italian city, marks the beginning of the First Punic War.

- Carthage and Rome shared a number of interesting similarities: Both cities were founded around the same time; both were strategically located (Carthage was almost due south of Rome, on an excellent harbor on the African coast at the Mediterranean's narrowest point); both cities were centers of a young empire; and both were ruled by aristocracies with aggressive, expansionist outlooks.

- Unlike Rome, Carthage did not incorporate its conquered territories but forced them to pay tribute. While the early Romans were primarily farmers, the Carthaginians were merchants. They possessed a huge navy; when they needed an army, they hired mercenaries. Their political structure was an odd mixture of oligarchy (primarily the wealthy merchant families) and a democracy.

The First Punic War

- When one looks at a map of the Mediterranean, it is clear that strife between the expanding rival empires of Rome and Carthage was inevitable. Geography also dictates and explains the place where this war broke out—the island of Sicily, a key transportation choke point both empires wanted to possess.

- The Romans had one serious problem: they had no navy. In fact, the Romans were generally suspicious of the sea and were terrible sailors. Nonetheless, they decided to build a fleet. Luckily, a Carthaginian ship fell into their hands, so they used it as a model.

- The goal of naval battles at the time was usually ramming the enemy's ships. This strategy favored nautical skill. Realizing that they could not match the seamanship of the Carthaginians, the Romans invented a long, movable gangplank with an iron spike on the end and used it to nail their ships to the Carthaginian ones. The Roman marines then ran across the gangplank onto the Carthaginian ship, effectively turning a naval battle into a land one.

- The Romans won several shocking victories and invaded and occupied most of Sicily. Unfortunately, the Romans never learned to be good sailors. Eventually their fleet was caught in a terrible storm that destroyed two-thirds of their ships in a single afternoon.

- With typical Roman determination, they spent the next two years building and training another fleet, which an even worse storm sent to the bottom of the sea. It took them four years to build and train yet another fleet, which they dispatched in 249 B.C. under the command of Publius Claudius Pulcher.

- The Romans were decisively defeated. The surviving ships were caught in another storm and completely wiped out. Meanwhile, Carthage finally had an excellent land commander, Hamilcar Barca, who landed in Sicily and swiftly recaptured most of the cities.

- The Romans' luck finally turned when a political faction that opposed the war took over the government at Carthage. They dismantled most of the Carthaginian fleet and refused to send Hamilcar any supplies or reinforcements. Rome rebuilt its fleet and recaptured most of Sicily. The two sides signed a peace treaty in 241 B.C.

- There were three important effects of the First Punic War: 1) Carthage had to pay a large cash indemnity to Rome. 2) Carthage had to give up all claims on Sicily. 3) Rome formally annexed Sicily, and it became the first overseas Roman province. A Roman governor was appointed, and the Sicilians had to pay taxes. The Sicilians were not granted any form of citizenship.

The Second Punic War

- Despite its defeat, Carthage was still very strong. Since their expansion northwards had been thwarted and there was only desert to the south and Egypt to the east, the next logical place for Carthage to go was Spain. Hamilcar landed there and brought many of the Spanish tribes under his control.

- Meanwhile, Rome began to expand north and west along what is today the coast of France. The Romans and Carthaginians came into conflict over the city of Saguntum, and thus the Second Punic War broke out in 219 B.C. Hamilcar's son, Hannibal was now in charge of Carthage's colonies in Spain, and as it turned out, he was one of the greatest military geniuses of all time.

- Hannibal knew the key to Roman success was their ability to draw on the manpower reserves of the Italian half-citizens and allies, so he conceived of a bold plan to separate Rome from this resource— invading Italy itself, winning a few battles, and inspiring the Italians to turn against Rome.

- To get his army from Spain to Italy, he daringly crossed the Alps—which were high, icy, and infested with murderous hill people—with an army of 40,000 men and 37 elephants. He made it through, arriving in northern Italy with 20,000 men, one elephant, and one eye left.

- The Romans promptly dispatched an army to wipe out Hannibal's small, weakened force, but Hannibal outwitted the Roman commander, and the Romans were slaughtered. The Romans raised a second army, which Hannibal drew into an

Crossing the Alps was only one remarkable feat among many for Hannibal.

ambush and wiped out. The Romans then took nearly two years to raise two complete armies, which marched out together under the command of both consuls to confront Hannibal at Cannae in 216 B.C.

- Normal strategy dictated that Hannibal put his best troops in the center. He reversed this putting his weakest troops at the center and ordering them to slowly give ground before the Roman advance. As the Roman center pressed forward, Hannibal's best troops drove off the inferior Roman flanks and swept around the Roman center. The Romans were completely encircled. Their formations broke down, and the battle turned into a massacre.

The Slow Rout of Hannibal

- The Battle of Cannae was one of the darkest moments in Roman history. It threw the Romans into a frenzy of panic and despair. Hannibal marched to the gates of Rome, but the Romans barricaded themselves in and refused to surrender. Lacking siege equipment, Hannibal was soon forced to depart.

- After the disaster of Cannae, the Romans selected a new leader, a man named Fabius, who adopted a new strategy: Do not give Hannibal the chance to kill more Romans. The Roman armies followed Hannibal everywhere he went, but whenever Hannibal turned to attack, Fabius backed off. He became known as Fabius Cunctator—Fabius the Delayer.

- In the aftermath of Cannae, as Hannibal had hoped, some Italian cities revolted against Rome, but the vast majority remained loyal. It was now that Rome's earlier policy of generosity and inclusivity bore fruit. Hannibal was reduced to roaming up and down Italy, unconquered and undefeated, for the next 12 years.

- Rome sent other armies to Spain under the talented young general Publius Cornelius Scipio. He conquered the Carthaginian territories in Spain and killed Hannibal's brother. Scipio next invaded North Africa, forcing the Carthaginian government to order Hannibal to return to defend Carthage.

- The two great commanders came together in 202 B.C. at the Battle of Zama, and Hannibal was defeated. Carthage surrendered in 201 B.C.

The Aftermath of the Punic Wars

- There were five important effects of the Second Punic War: 1) Carthage had to pay a large cash indemnity. 2) Spain and North Africa were transformed into several tax-paying Roman provinces. 3) Carthage had to give up its territory and military. 4) The Roman army was transformed from a militia into a professional army with new equipment and tactics. 5) Scipio and his family acquired enormous amounts of *dignitas*.

- Scipio acquired a new name: Scipio Africanus, or Scipio the Conqueror of Africa. In the long run, this last effect may have been one of the most important, as the rough equilibrium among aristocrats began to tilt in favor of just one man, and his family came to dominate affairs at Rome.

- Rome next it turned its attention to the kingdoms created by the breakup of Alexander's empire. The East was Greek; it was richer, more urbanized, and more culturally sophisticated. It was also something of an unknown land to the Romans.

- The Roman war machine proved too much even for Alexander's successors. One by one, they were conquered, and Rome reorganized their territories into tax-paying provinces. Scipio's family dominated these governorships as well.

- The Roman conquest of Greece and Asia Minor brought Rome into contact with Greek culture, with its rich tradition of literature, art, and philosophy. It also brought the Greeks themselves to Rome; thousands of them were enslaved and transported to Italy. Many educated Greek slaves became the tutors to Roman children.

- Rome and the Romans became rich as the result of their Eastern conquests. By 167 B.C., all taxes for Roman citizens were abolished, yet the revenue of the Roman state increased by a factor of six. Individual Romans, particularly the generals, became fabulously wealthy.

The Paradox of the Late Republic

- On the surface, Roman imperialism looked like an unqualified success. But lurking within were forces that would soon result in the collapse of the Roman Republic.

- Dreams of wealth led many poor Roman farmers to sell their farms and join the army. Some soldiers got rich, but most returned to Italy poor and homeless. Thus, an unforeseen long-term consequence of Roman imperialism was the disruption and loss of small family farms.

- Meanwhile, successful generals were returning to Italy with great wealth, but the only real investment option in the ancient world was land. Coincidentally, there were all these small family farms being sold or falling into debt and being auctioned off.

- Land without labor was useless, but Roman imperialism was producing an endless supply of cheap labor—slaves. Meanwhile, more wars produced more poor veterans, rich generals, sold-off farms, and slaves in an endless cycle.

- Roman veterans were resentful because they had done their duty but ended up poor, farmless, and ignored. Roman aristocrats were unhappy because wealth and *dignitas* from the wars were being monopolized by a few men and their families.

- The half-citizens and allies were unhappy because they wanted full Roman citizenship in return for the conquests they had made possible. The millions of foreigners who had been conquered, enslaved, and shipped off to Italy were extremely unhappy and angry for obvious reasons.

- Finally, the political system which the Romans had evolved to run a city was now laboring under the strain of administering a vast empire.

Suggested Reading

Goldsworthy, *The Fall of Carthage.*

Harris, *War and Imperialism in Republican Rome.*

Questions to Consider

1. Some scholars have characterized Rome's conquest of the Mediterranean world as the result of a deliberate policy of aggression, while others maintain that it largely resulted from a chain of accidents. Which stance do you agree with and why?

2. What do you think were the most significant factors in Rome's emergence as the dominant power in the Mediterranean over its rival states, such as Carthage and the Hellenistic kingdoms?

The Crucible—Punic Wars, Roman Imperialism
Lecture 27—Transcript

In the last lecture, we looked at the first several centuries of the Roman Republic, and that's a time when Rome had conquered the entire Italian peninsula. In this lecture, we'll examine the next couple of centuries of the Republic, during which Rome will take over most of the Mediterranean basin. This expansion begins with a series of conflicts that will pit Rome against the other major, young, growing power in the western Mediterranean, the city-state of Carthage. The resulting Punic Wars between Rome and Carthage were a true turning point in all of Roman history. They're simultaneously the closest that Rome would ever come to total defeat but they're also the stepping stone to Rome's ultimate success. They also featured Rome's greatest nemesis, the brilliant Carthaginian general, Hannibal.

The year 264 B.C. was a fateful moment for Rome, because in that year Rome captured the last remaining independent Italian city, and, in the same year, Rome got involved in their first overseas conflict: the First Punic War against Carthage. Carthage and Rome shared a number of very interesting similarities: Both cities, at least according to legend, were founded around 750 B.C.. Both cities were located in a centralized, strategic position; in Carthage's case, Carthage was on the coast of North Africa with a very good harbor right at the bottleneck where the Mediterranean Sea was the narrowest. Both cities were centers of a young empire; and both cities were ruled by aristocracies who had very aggressive, expansionist outlooks. Carthage began as a trading outpost of the Phoenician city of Tyre, but eventually the Carthaginians broke away and set up their own empire; and, at the time when they came into conflict with Rome, they'd already brought most of the local North African tribes under their command. (The term "Punic War," by the way, is derived from the fact that the Latin word for "Phoenician" is "Punic.")

Unlike Rome, Carthage didn't incorporate its conquered territories, but instead it forced them to pay tribute. Another difference is that while the early Romans were primarily farmers, the Carthaginians were mainly merchants; and so, because of this, Carthage had a very large merchant fleet and they carried on an active trade, both in staple goods and luxury items all over the Mediterranean basin. When the Carthaginians needed an army, they tended to use their wealth to hire mercenaries; but their real military strength was their navy, because to protect their trading ships, they'd developed probably the largest and most powerful and most sophisticated navy in the Mediterranean at this time. The political structure of Carthage was a very odd mixture of oligarchy and democracy, but in reality power was in the hands of a small group of wealthy merchant families.

The key to understanding all of the Punic Wars is geography. When you look at a map of the Mediterranean, it's clear that strife between the expanding rival empires of Rome and Carthage was inevitable. Geography also dictates and really explains the place where that war broke out: the island of Sicily. In 264 B.C., Sicily lay exactly between their two spheres of influence. It's a key transportation chokepoint that both empires wanted to possess, and so predictably, those conflicting interests soon sparked an incident that resulted in a mutual declaration of war.

The Romans now had a very serious problem to contend with: They'd committed themselves to a war over an island, and it's a war that's to be fought against the dominant naval power of the region. Problem was, Rome had no navy. Even worse, the Romans in general were suspicious of the sea, and they were terrible sailors. But, with the usual Roman determination, they decided to build an entire fleet to try and match that of Carthage. They really didn't have the experience or the knowledge for how to build warships, but they did have a stroke of luck when a Carthaginian warship fell into their hands, so the Romans simply used it as a model and imitated it. They trained their own rowers by lining them up on benches on land to practice.

The goal of naval battles at this time was usually for one ship to maneuver so as to ram the other and sink it. This was a strategy that favored the person who had the most nautical skill. Realizing that they could not match the seamanship of the Carthaginians, the Romans came up with a brilliant invention. They attached a long, movable gangplank with a big, iron spike at its end to the front of their ships, and in the subsequent battle they'd use this to nail their ship to the Carthaginian one. The Roman marines could then run across the gangplank onto the Carthaginian ship and effectively they found a way to turn a naval battle into a land one, which was something the Romans were very good at. With this strategy, the Romans won, initially, several shocking victories, and they invaded and occupied most of the island of Sicily.

Unfortunately, the Romans really never learned to be good sailors, and so when the signs of a storm appeared in the distance, the Roman admirals ignored it. Their fleet was caught in a terrible storm and by the time the storm had passed, only 80 out of 250 Roman ships were left. Tens of thousands of Romans drowned in one afternoon. But, with typical Roman determination, they spent the next two years building and training another fleet, which they then sent out. Unfortunately, they still hadn't learned how to read the weather, and an even worse storm caught that fleet and sent it to the bottom of the sea as well.

Even for the industrious Romans, it took four years for them to build and train yet another fleet, and they sent this one out in 249 B.C. under the command of a man named Publius Claudius Pulcher. Before the battle, Pulcher, as was customary, took the omens, and this consisted of placing sacred chickens on the deck of his ship and then scattering grain in front of them. If the chickens ate, it was considered a good omen, but if they refused to eat, it was a bad one; and the more eagerly the chickens ate the grain, the better the omen. In this case, the sacred chickens—maybe they were seasick—refused to eat at all; a terrible omen. Becoming enraged, Pulcher exclaimed, "If the chickens won't eat, then let them drink," and he threw them overboard and they drowned. As you can guess, whether due to the bad omen, the murder of the sacred chickens, or because the Carthaginians had finally learned to avoid those Roman boarding bridges, the Romans were decisively defeated. Just to make things worse, on the way home, the surviving ships were caught in another storm and wiped out. As if all of this wasn't bad enough, Carthage at this point finally came up with an excellent land general, a man named Hamilcar Barca. By the way, the name Barca means "thunderbolt," and this was a very fitting name because he immediately landed in Sicily and he swiftly recaptured most of the cities.

At this point, the Romans's luck finally turned when a new political faction who was opposed to continuing the war took over at Carthage. They dismantled most of the Carthaginian fleet, they refused to send Hamilcar any more supplies or any more reinforcements, and meanwhile Rome had been building and training yet another fleet, and so with it they're finally able to recapture most of Sicily once again. The two sides then signed a peace treaty in 241 B.C.

There were three important effects of that First Punic War: First of all, Carthage had to pay a large cash indemnity to Rome, a fine. Second, Carthage had to give up all claims on Sicily. Third, Rome formally annexed Sicily, and it became the first overseas Roman province. When Rome did this, it represented an important change in their policy. The Romans didn't immediately share citizenship with the citizens. Instead, a Roman magistrate was appointed as governor, and the main requirement imposed on the Sicilians was to pay taxes; they weren't given citizenship. From that point on, that's the way the Romans would treat conquered territories: They'd convert them into tax-paying provinces.

Despite that defeat, Carthage was still very strong; it wasn't so much that Rome had won that war, but that Carthage had given up. Another conflict between those two young, growing empires really was inevitable. Once again, if we look at a map, we can understand where the war started. Carthage had tried to expand northward into Sicily, but they'd been thwarted. If they went to the south, there's only desert, so there's nothing there. If they went to the east, they hit Egypt, a powerful country, so they couldn't go that way. The obvious logical place, just looking at a map, for Carthage to go next was to the west and to Spain. Sure enough, Hamilcar landed in Spain and ended up conquering most of the Spanish tribes and bringing them under Carthaginian control. When Hamilcar went off to Spain, he took with him his nine-year old son, Hannibal. According to legend, at least, before they left Carthage, Hamilcar made Hannibal swear everlasting hatred for Rome. Eventually, after a decade or two, Hamilcar died and his son, Hannibal, then took over his work in Spain.

Meanwhile, Rome had begun to expand northward, and they're starting to move along what is today the coast of France. The Romans, coming up from France, and the Carthaginians, coming up from Spain, ran into conflict with each other yet again. The point at which they came into conflict was a city called Saguntum, which was located on the east coast of what today is Spain; and with that event, the Second Punic War broke out in 219 B.C. This was the war that would push Rome to the brink of total defeat, because Hannibal, as it turned out, just happened to be one of the greatest military geniuses of all time. Hannibal, I think correctly, diagnosed that the key to Roman success was their ability to draw on that huge manpower reserve of Italy, to call on the half-citizens and the allies to just keep making new armies. Hannibal came up with a bold plan to separate Rome from that resource. His plan was to invade Italy itself, to win a couple battles, and then hopefully those Italian cities would revolt and turn against Rome in order to regain their independence. To get his army from Spain to Italy, Hannibal adopted another daring plan, which was to cross the Alps, those high, icy mountains that were infested with murderous hill tribes.

In 218 B.C., Hannibal set out from Spain with an army of about 40,000 men and 37 elephants. Incredibly, he made it across the Alps, although the ice, the snow, the landslides, and the nasty hill tribes took such a toll that by the time he finally arrived in Northern Italy after crossing them, he was down to only 20,000 men, one elephant, and one eye. The Romans promptly sent out an army to try and wipe out Hannibal's small and weakened force, but Hannibal was such a military genius that he figured out a way to completely outwit the Roman commander, and he slaughtered all the Romans. In expected fashion, the Romans went back, drew on their manpower, and raised a second army, and they sent that one out after Hannibal. Again, Hannibal was outnumbered, but cleverly he drew the Romans into an ambush along a lakeside that was in the fog, and once again he wiped them out.

The Romans now were beginning to get pretty worried. Here's a guy who seemed able to beat however many armies they sent after him; so this time they took two years to raise not one but two complete Roman armies that then marched out together under the command of both consuls. This final confrontation happened at a place called Cannae in 216 B.C., and the Battle of Cannae is still studied today as an absolute textbook example of brilliant strategy. When two sides lined up for battle in the ancient world, the normal procedure was that you'd put your best soldiers in the middle and you'd put the more unreliable ones at the two sides. Hannibal reversed this; he put his best troops to the left and the right. He knew that his weaker soldiers in the middle couldn't beat the Romans, so he told them, "Once the battle starts, if you need to, just give ground; just start to back up as necessary before the

Roman advance." The battle started; the Roman center pressed forward; they thought they had the victory. Meanwhile, though, Hannibal's best troops on the left and right side drove off the inferior Roman troops they faced, and then they began to sweet around the Roman center. In the end, the main body of Roman troops got completely encircled and they're attacked from all sides. Their formations broke down, and the battle turned into a massacre.

In one afternoon, Hannibal's troops hacked to death with swords the incredible sum of 65,000 Romans. This is carnage on an almost unimaginable scale. This is a battle that ranks among the bloodiest days in all of military history. Just to try to put this in perspective, consider that more Romans were probably killed in this one afternoon than Americans died in the entire 20-plus years of the Vietnam War.

The Battle of Cannae was one of the darkest moments in Roman history, and it threw the Romans into an absolute frenzy of panic and despair. In Hannibal, they'd finally met an enemy who was able to defeat any number of men that the Romans threw at him. Hannibal marched right up to the gates of Rome itself, but the Romans barricaded themselves in and refused to surrender. Hannibal, who really didn't have any siege equipment with him, was soon forced to just move on in order to keep his army fed.

After the disaster of Cannae, the Romans selected a new leader, and this was a man named Fabius. Fabius adopted a new strategy, and the core of this strategy was very, very simple: Don't give Hannibal the chance to kill any more Romans. The Romans raised new armies, and they sent them out after Hannibal, and they followed Hannibal everywhere he went. But whenever Hannibal turned to attack, Fabius simply backed off and refused to fight. As a result, he became known as Fabius Cunctator, which means "Fabius the Delayer." In the aftermath of Cannae, as Hannibal had hoped, some of those Italian cities revolted against Rome and, seeking their independence, came over to his side. But the vast majority of Italian cities remained loyal to Rome, even at this, its time of maximum weakness. It's really here, in these dark days of the Second Punic War, that Rome's earlier policy of generosity and inclusivity, of sharing citizenship to some degree, bore fruit. With most of the cities staying loyal to Rome, Hannibal's strategy failed, and poor Hannibal was reduced to roaming up and down Italy, unconquered, undefeated, but frustrated, looking for somebody to fight. That went on for the next 12 years.

The Romans may have been afraid of Hannibal—they're not going to fight him; they're not going to give him another chance to fight Romans—but they didn't have any such fear of other Carthaginian commanders; and so Rome went back to its manpower, it raised a couple more armies, and it sent those off to Spain. After some initial setbacks, the Roman command fell to a young general named Publius Cornelius Scipio and, as chance would have it, Scipio turned out to be another military genius. He conquered all the Carthaginian territories in Spain, and he even killed Hannibal's brother. Hannibal only learned of that when the Romans threw the severed head of his brother into the Carthaginian camp. Scipio next invaded North Africa itself, and by doing so he forced the Carthaginian government to recall Hannibal and told him to come back to Africa to defend Carthage. The two great commanders, Hannibal and Scipio, finally came together and fought one another in 202 B.C. at the Battle of Zama. At that battle, Scipio's generalship proved at least a match for Hannibal, or maybe his troops were simply better than Hannibal's since Hannibal's troops by now were getting pretty old. But at any rate, Hannibal was defeated. Carthage surrendered in 201 B.C. and Rome had won the Second Punic War.

There were five important effects of the Second Punic War: First of all, Carthage had to pay a large cash indemnity, a big fine. Second, Spain and North Africa were turned into taxpaying Roman provinces under the control of Roman governors. Third, the city of Carthage had to give up all of its territory and all of its military; and so Carthage now was effectively finished, this was the end of them. The last two effects, though, weren't really so much on Carthage, they're on Rome: The fourth effect was that the Roman army simply got a lot better and a lot more professional over the course of the Second Punic War. Under Scipio, it's transformed from what was in reality a militia of citizen soldiers into a professional army with soldiers who served long-term, careerists. They also adopted new equipment, they had a new sword, new tactics, and from now on the Romans really would have a distinct qualitative edge over most of the people they fought. This is really a classic example of the old cliché that what doesn't kill you makes you stronger. The Romans almost got killed in the Second Punic War, but afterwards they were a lot stronger.

The fifth and last effect of the Second Punic War was that Scipio got lots, and lots, and lots, and lots of *dignitas*. After all, he's the man who defeated Hannibal and saved Rome. As a result of this, he acquired a new name, and from now on he'd be known as Scipio Africanus, or "Scipio the Conqueror of Africa." In the long run, this final effect here may be the most important one, because for the first time, the rough equilibrium that had existed among different aristocrats competing for *dignitas*, competing for prestige began, that equilibrium was broken and it began now to tilt in favor of just one man; and Scipio, and really Scipio's family, came to dominate affairs at Rome.

Rome was now clearly the foremost power in the Western Mediterranean, so next it turned its attention to the east. The Eastern Mediterranean was the Hellenistic world; these were the various kingdoms that had been left behind or created by the breakup of the empire of Alexander the Great. Remember, the East was Greek; it tended to be richer, it tended to be more urbanized, and it tended to be more culturally sophisticated. The East was also a little bit of an unknown for the Romans. For example, after one of their early victories of a Roman general over an Eastern kingdom, the Roman Senate actually had to be given a special geography lecture so that they could understand what they had just acquired. The Roman war machine, though, proved too much, it was too efficient, and the Romans conquered even the successors of Alexander the Great. One by one, they're knocked off, and Rome reorganized their territories into taxpaying Roman provinces under a governor. Scipio's family continued to dominate. For example, Scipio's brother got one of the key commands to oversee one of these campaigns in the East, and after that, he got to change his name to Scipio Asiaticus, "Scipio, the Conqueror of Asia."

The Roman conquest of Greece and Asia Minor also had two big effects on Rome: First of all, the Romans were exposed to Greek culture with all of that rich tradition of literature, art, and philosophy that I've already talked about. When they went back to Rome, they brought this culture with them in the form of stolen artwork, they brought it in the form of stolen books or manuscripts, and they brought it in the form of the Greeks themselves, because thousands of Greeks got enslaved and transported back to Italy. Often the educated Greek slaves became tutors to Roman children, they became teachers back in Rome, so the next generation of Romans was raised knowing Greek culture and having greater cultural sophistication. A very nice example of this new generation of highly educated Romans can be seen when, in a fit of what's really Hannibal-inspired paranoia, Rome decided to obliterate the helpless city of Carthage. The general given this particular task was, of course, another member of the Scipio family, and he burnt Carthage to the ground and sold all of its inhabitants in slavery. This Scipio, though, was one of these guys from the new generation who'd been raised to appreciate Greek culture; and, according to legend, as he watched the city burn to the ground, he was moved to recite passages from Homer in flawless Greek about the burning of Troy. So the Romans now were just as brutal, but they recited Greek poetry as they burned your city down.

Secondly, as a result of the conquest of the East, Rome and the Romans became rich, really rich, for the first time. Money poured into both the public treasury of the state and the pockets of lucky Romans, especially the generals. By 167 B.C., so much money was pouring in from the East that all forms of taxation for Roman citizens could be abolished; and it's been estimated that the revenue of the Roman state increased in this period by a factor of six. Individual Romans, especially those generals and people like the Scipios, became fabulously wealthy.

I'll end this lecture with a paradox. On the surface, Roman imperialism and overseas expansion look like a complete success. Rome has gained wealth; they've gained territory, power, prestige, and culture. But lurking within this apparently happy picture were forces that would soon result in the collapse of the Roman Republic. To put it simply: The paradox was that Rome's success at external conquest resulted in deadly internal tensions.

Roman imperialism created a kind of vicious circle that ultimately ended up making every segment of Roman society unhappy and resentful. Here's how this worked: With dreams of becoming rich, many poor Roman farmers sold their farms and joined the army. But, after decades of serving, a couple of them got rich, but the vast majority returned to Italy poor and now homeless. A lot of them ended up hanging around the city of Rome, either unemployed or underemployed. The population of Rome in this period exploded, reaching the phenomenal size of about a million people by the 1st century B.C. One unforeseen long-term consequence of Roman imperialism was the disruption and the loss of small family farms.

Meanwhile, successful generals were coming back to Italy with all this wealth; but what did you do with wealth in the ancient world? You could spend some, but the only real investment you had was to buy land. What do you know, just as these aristocrats loaded with cash were looking to acquire some land, you had all these small family farms being sold or falling into debt and being auctioned off. The net effect was the Italian countryside was transformed from a whole bunch of little, private family farms to a small number of giant plantation-like estates owned by a few rich men. All that land without labor was useless, but, what do you know, coincidentally, Roman imperialism just happened to also be producing an endless supply of cheap labor in the form of slaves captured in war and sent back to Italy.

Roman imperialism created a huge cycle that fed upon itself. More wars produced more poor veterans, more generals, more sold-off farms, and more slaves. But in the end, almost everybody involved was unhappy. Quite reasonably, Roman veterans were resentful because they felt they'd done their duty for the state, but as a result they'd ended up poor, farmless, and ignored. Quite reasonably, many Roman aristocrats were unhappy because all the wealth and *dignitas* from these wars was being monopolized by just a few men and families, like the Scipios, and everybody else was being left out. Quite reasonably, the half-citizens and the allies in Italy were unhappy because they felt that by this time, they deserved to be granted full Roman citizenship—and they did—and they wanted to share in the wealth of the conquest. Last, quite reasonably, all those millions of foreigners who'd been conquered, enslaved, and shipped off to Italy were unhappy and angry.

For all its apparent success, Roman imperialism had ultimately produced a huge, boiling cauldron of resentment in which almost every segment of Roman society was unhappy and harboring a grievance. Finally, the whole political system that the Romans had evolved to run a city was now laboring under the strain of administering an empire. In the next lecture, we'll see what happens when all that resentment finally boils over and explodes.

The Death of the Roman Republic
Lecture 28

R ome's success in conquering the Mediterranean ultimately destroyed the Roman Republic. The murder of the Gracchi brothers by the Senate brought hidden social and economic tensions in the city of Rome into public view, while slave revolts and the Social War exposed problems throughout the Italian Peninsula. But the actions of two military men—Pompey the Great and Julius Caesar—did the most to destroy traditional Republican institutions while simultaneously setting the stage for the empire.

The Gracchi

- The period from 133 to 31 B.C., known as the late Roman Republic, is also one of the best-documented eras in Roman history. It features many of the most colorful and well-known Romans, including Pompey the Great and Julius Caesar.

- Two brothers, grandsons of Scipio Africanus, became worried about the tensions building in Roman society. The elder, Tiberius Gracchus, was elected tribune in 133 B.C. and he put forward a law to limit the amount of land that could be owned by any one person and to distribute excess government-owned land to poor Roman citizens.

- A number of senators became enraged at this proposal and beat Tiberius and 300 of his followers to death.

- In 123 B.C., the younger brother, Gaius Gracchus, took up where his brother left off. He was elected tribune and promptly put forward Tiberius's proposal, plus a whole slate of additional laws: that the state supply subsidized grain to the inhabitants of the city; that the Latin allies in Italy finally be granted full citizenship; and that more roads be built to help rural farmers.

- The Senate was upset again, but leery of further bad press did not kill Gaius themselves; they let it be known that if anyone else killed him, the Senate would give that person the weight of Gaius's head in gold. Soon enough, Gaius was assassinated, too.

- What was the Gracchi's motivation? Were they really altruistic and idealistic, or were they self-interested, ambitious aristocrats pretending to be the friends of the common people? The ancient sources are split on this issue, as are modern historians.

The Social War and Slave Revolts

- The first of the resentful groups in Roman society to break with Rome was the Italian allies, or Socii. They felt, with considerable justification, that they had earned the right to full Roman citizenship. In about 91 B.C., a confederation of Socii revolted.

- The resulting Social War was particularly brutal and bitter, since both sides fought using the same tactics and strategy; it was, in essence, a civil war. It lasted for three long, terrible years, but Rome finally pounded its allies into submission.

- In the peace treaty, the Romans were compelled to bestow full citizenship on all the allies. The Social War is therefore a tragic example of Roman conservatism since, although they won, the Romans had to give the allies what they had wanted in the first place. It was a completely unnecessary and wasteful conflict.

- This era also witnessed massive slave revolts, the most famous of which was led by a Thracian gladiator named Spartacus. These were all eventually suppressed, but not without considerable bloodshed and cruelty.

Pompey the Great

- Pompey, the son of a famous and wealthy general, was an extremely ambitious young man during the Social War but was too young to hold any elected office. Unable to bear missing all the *dignitas* the war offered, he used his family's money to raise a private army and joined the war against the Socii.

- After some further military adventures, he arranged his own triumph—a great and rare honor for exceptional victorious Roman generals. He then schemed to be given additional military commands and won further victories, returning to Rome and celebrating another triumph when he was still only 35 years old.

- Having never held office, Pompey was not a member of the Senate. Despite this, he let it be known he wanted to be consul. Again, he got his way. One of the duties of the consul was to preside over meetings of the Senate, and he was embarrassingly ignorant of procedure.

- Pirates infested much of the Mediterranean, so Pompey arranged for a tribune to propose a law giving him unprecedented powers to suppress the pirates. He was granted a huge sum of money, 500 ships, an army of 120,000 soldiers, and authority over all the waters and coasts of the Mediterranean. This went against both standard appointment procedure and earlier precedents of dividing up the Roman military.

- Next, Pompey again manipulated legislative loopholes to attack and kill a troublesome eastern king named Mithridates. Mithridates escaped and fled into the wilds of central Asia. Pompey's hero was Alexander the Great, and now, like Alexander, Pompey went on a rampage through the east.

- Pompey was heading for Egypt when he got a piece of bad news: Mithridates had keeled over and died of old age. His command was now over, and he had to end his conquests. But he had made both Rome and himself incredibly rich; his fortune and *dignitas* were now incalculable.

- Pompey had gained more power, wealth, and influence than any Roman before him, but in doing so, he had undermined almost every Republican institution. At this point, he might simply have taken over Rome, but he had enough respect for tradition that he disbanded his army and went into semiretirement, exercising power from behind the scenes.

Julius Caesar the General

- The political career of Pompey's protégé, Gaius Julius Caesar, got off to a fairly conventional start with a number of elected offices. With the older man's connivance, he was elected consul in 59 B.C. His other consul for the year was a man named Bibulus, but Caesar completely dominated affairs and ignored the wishes of his colleague.

- Caesar was next appointed governor of Cisalpine Gaul, a relatively small and peaceful province with only a small army. To the north was Gaul itself, which was a vast, unconquered region roughly equivalent to modern France, Belgium, and the Netherlands.

- Immediately on becoming governor, Caesar began raising a private army. Once it was ready, he launched an invasion of Gaul and spent the next nine years fighting continuously. He amassed a huge personal army of tough veteran soldiers who were completely loyal to him and revealed a true talent for war.

Julius Caesar proved himself by subduing Gaul.

- Caesar's 10 years of campaigning enslaved and killed millions of Gauls. Even the Romans thought Caesar's actions were questionable, and a bill was put before the Senate that Caesar be turned over to the Gauls as a war criminal, but Caesar was careful to always have a tribune or two under his control.

- Finally, the senate ended Caesar's governorship, ordered him to disband his armies, and told him to return to Rome. Deciding that his *dignitas* was more important than the state, he crossed the Rubicon River, and marched on Rome, becoming guilty of treason.

- Surprised, the Senate turned to the only man with the power to oppose Caesar: Pompey. The person who had arguably done the most to undermine the institutions of the Republic now found himself cast as its defender.

- What followed was a colossal civil war fought across the Mediterranean, from Spain to Greece. Pompey was overconfident and was decisively defeated at the Battle of Pharsalus. Pompey fled to Egypt, which was still an independent kingdom, but fearing Caesar's wrath, the Egyptians murdered him the moment he set foot on the beach.

Julius Caesar the Dictator

- Caesar was now the sole ruler of Rome. The problems facing him were how to reward his war veterans and how to rule Rome as something other than a king.

- Caesar settled 80,000 veterans in colonies, granting full or half-citizenship to many. He built public works at Rome and reformed the calendar, bringing it back into alignment with the seasons.

- He began his rule by having himself elected consul over and over again, but eventually this provoked resentment among Roman aristocrats. He then turned to Roman tradition and the temporary post of dictator used in times of extreme emergency. He had himself appointed dictator for life.

- The Romans' resentment was not helped by Caesar's arrogant behavior. He had the Senate decree that everyone must take an oath of allegiance to him personally. He named the month of July after himself. He had statues of himself put in temples. He had priesthoods established in his honor. He was rude to senators, not even pretending they were his peers.

- There was a general sense that Caesar was too much like a king, and in Roman history, when you had trouble with a king, you turned to a member of the Brutus family. One of Julius Caesar's closest friends was a direct descendant of the Brutus who had expelled Tarquin and founded the Republic.

- In 44 B.C., a conspiracy was formed around this Brutus, and on March 15, 44 B.C.—the Ides of March—Brutus and a group of senators stabbed Julius Caesar to death. The Romans were rid of Caesar, but the Roman Republic was locked into a pattern of civil war.

Suggested Reading

Beard and Crawford, *Rome in the Late Republic*.

Scullard, *From the Gracchi to Nero*.

Questions to Consider

1. Do you think the Roman Republic could have been saved if the Senate had enacted the reforms of the Gracchi?

2. Whose career ultimately did more to undermine the institutions of the Roman Republic: Pompey or Caesar? Which specific actions were the most harmful?

The Death of the Roman Republic
Lecture 28—Transcript

The Late Roman Republic covers an approximately 100 year period extending from 133 B.C.–31 B.C., and it's in this time that the various tensions and resentments that had been developing all throughout the Roman Republic ultimately reached a crisis point, and it will result in the dissolution of the Roman Republic.

We begin with two brothers who were actually the grandsons of Scipio Africanus, and so these are guys that came from the most elite and privileged class in Roman society. But despite that aristocratic lineage, the elder brother of these two, named Tiberius Gracchus, looked around and became worried about these tensions that were building in Roman society, and he determined to do something about it. Accordingly, in 133 B.C., he ran for and was successfully elected to the office of Tribune. Supposedly, he was inspired by the sight of going down the road and seeing all of these dispossessed Roman farmers and all these big estates being worked by foreign slaves. Taking advantage of the power of Tribunes to propose new laws, Tiberius Gracchus put forward a new piece of legislation directly to the vote of the people without first running it past the Roman Senate.

At the heart of his proposal was a suggestion for a law that would limit the amount of land that could be owned by any one person. There's also a provision for distributing excess government-owned land to poor Roman citizens. In response to this proposal, at an assembly, a number of senators and their followers became enraged and they literally broke up the benches that they were sitting on to make clubs and with those they beat to death Tiberius and 300 of his followers. This was a shocking event, but it was a vision of other things to come, because in the Late Republic, Roman politicians would begin to substitute open violence for political debate; and so this kind of political violence would become typical over the next couple decades.

That wasn't the end of this attempt at reform, though, because in 123 B.C., the younger brother, Gaius Gracchus, decided to take up where his elder brother Tiberius had left off. Gaius now ran for and was elected Tribune, and he promptly put forward the very same proposals that Tiberius had. Gaius looked around at the problems of the Republic, and he was very much aware that there were other unhappy groups in Roman society; so he now tacked on a whole slate of additional proposals. He proposed that the Roman state give subsidized grain to all the inhabitants of the city, and that's something that would help the urban poor. He also proposed that the Latin allies in Italy finally be granted full citizenship; and he proposed building more roads, which would help out rural farmers with communication.

Once again, though, the Senate was very upset by all these actions; but when they'd beaten to death Tiberius, they'd gotten what today we might refer to as bad press. This time around, they themselves didn't kill Gaius Gracchus; instead, they simply let it be known that if somebody else just happened to kill Gaius, then they would give that person the weight of Gaius's head in gold. Soon enough, an enterprising man murdered the younger Gracchus, chopped off his head, and, in order to maximize his profit, he drained out Gaius's brain and filled the cavity with lead. Supposedly this little bit of creativity earned him 17 pounds of gold. It's interesting to speculate whether or not the tragedies of the next 100 years might have been avoided if the Gracchi's proposals had been accepted; but the Roman ruling class was resistant to change and wouldn't concede anything.

One of the unanswerable questions concerning the Gracchi brothers is: What really was their motivation? Were these two guys, even though they're from the aristocracy, were they really altruistic, were they really idealistic reformers who were just trying to do what they thought was best for the health of their country? Or were they perhaps self-interested, ambitious aristocrats who'd merely come up with some clever new ways to gain power by pretending to be the friends of the common people? It's also interesting to wonder about what might've happened if the Romans had passed all of Gaius's legislation; would doing that have extended the life of the Roman Republic? There's really no way to know the answer to any of these questions, but what was now certain was that the Republic was headed for disaster.

The first of the various resentful groups in Roman society to finally get fed up and explode was the Italian allies. For hundreds of years, they fought in Rome's wars; they even stayed loyal when Hannibal invaded; so now they felt, with really a lot of justification, that they'd earned the right to be granted full Roman citizenship. The Romans, though, refused to give it to them; so finally, in 91 B.C., a confederation of Italian allies revolted against Rome. The resulting conflict was called the Social War; that's because it comes from the Latin word *socii*, meaning "the allies." The Social War was a particularly brutal and bitter war. Both sides were fighting with the same tactics; both used the same strategy; and really what it was, was a civil war. It lasted for three long, destructive, terrible years; but ultimately, Rome was able to pound its allies into submission.

But, in the terms of the peace treaty that ended the Social War, the Romans were compelled to give full citizenship to all the Italian allies. The Social War is really a tragic example of Roman conservatism, of their resistance to change, because even though the Romans won the war, in the end they simply had to give the allies what they wanted in the first place, so it's completely unnecessary. It's a waste, and it's a war that really should've been avoided.

This same era also saw a number of huge slave revolts; so the slaves got fed up, too. The most famous of these slave revolts was led by a Thracian gladiator named Spartacus. All of those slave revolts were also eventually suppressed, but not without a lot of bloodshed and cruelty. Again, the most obvious example was Spartacus and 6,000 of his followers ended up being crucified all along the Appian Way.

The Roman Republic was really now tottering along under all of these strains, and the next half-century, the last half-century of the Republic, was a complex time loaded with all sorts of dramatic events, political machinations, and a lot of famous people. I think the best way to tell the story this time is to focus on the biographies of just two pivotal figures who lived throughout those decades, and in telling their stories I'll also tell most of the history of the era.

The older of these two guys was a man named Pompey. Pompey was the son of a famous and wealthy general, and really the key to understanding Pompey is that he's extremely ambitious. When the Social War and some subsequent infighting among various Roman factions broke out, Pompey was too young to hold any elected office. But he just couldn't stand the thought that he was missing out on a golden opportunity to gain *dignitas*, so he used his family's money to raise a private army of three legions, mostly recruited from his father's veterans, and at the head of this personal force he marched off to join the fighting. Pompey, it turned out, had some military talent; and in the resulting wars he proved so bloodthirsty that he earned an interesting nickname: Carnifex Adulescens, which literally means "the Young Butcher."

After some additional military adventures, he came back to Rome and he wanted to celebrate a triumph. A triumph was a big parade awarded as a rare honor awarded to exceptional victorious Roman generals. Remember, at this point, Pompey was still only in his 20s; but he's someone in his 20s with a private army, so he got his way. Pompey wanted his triumph to be bigger and better than anyone else's, so initially he planned to ride into Rome in a chariot that was drawn by four elephants. Unfortunately, he encountered a practical problem when those four elephants proved to be too big to fit inside the city gates. This little incident perfectly symbolizes the fact that just as Pompey's elephants were too big to fit through the gates of Rome, so, too, Pompey's ambitions were going to prove to be too big to fit within the Republican framework of Rome's constitution.

Pompey then schemed to get some additional military commands, and he won some further victories. Eventually he returned to Rome and he celebrating another triumph, and at this point he's still only 35 years old. But he'd never yet been elected to a formal office in the Roman state, and so Pompey wasn't even a member of the Roman Senate. Despite that, though, he now let it be known that he wanted to be Consul of Rome, even though there's a minimum age requirement for that top position of consul that he's nowhere near. But, again, who can tell Pompey no? He got his way. Pompey had created an entire political career that circumvented the normal route to the consulship. But by this point, he's so powerful that you just can't ignore him. One of the duties of the consul was to preside over meetings of the senate, but since Pompey had never been a senator, he knew nothing about how to run meetings of the Senate. To remedy this, some of the senior senators actually quickly had to write up a little pamphlet called "How to Run Meetings of the Senate" and give it to Pompey.

Next on Pompey's agenda was another military command so that he could gain even more glory, even more *dignitas*. One of the big problems at this time was piracy. Pirates infested almost the entire Mediterranean Sea; they're plundering Roman merchant ships seemingly at will. Pompey now manipulated affairs so that a Tribune, who's really being bribed by Pompey, proposed a law that would give Pompey unprecedented military power to suppress the pirates. With Pompey's backing, this law passed; so Pompey's given a huge sum of money, he's given a fleet of 500 ships, and an army of 120,000 soldiers, and if that's not enough, he's given authority over all the waters and coasts of the Mediterranean Sea. This whole thing went completely against standard procedure for these sorts of appointments. Earlier, the Roman precedent had been to divide up the Roman military among many different commanders so that no one person commanded too many troops; but Pompey now basically got it all. In what really was a brilliant campaign that only lasted only 40 days, Pompey wiped out all the pirates.

For his next amazing feat, Pompey again manipulated some legislative loopholes in order to be given an army, and under the specific terms of his appointment, he's given that army to command until a particularly troublesome Eastern king named Mithridates was dead; so Pompey had the army until Mithridates was dead. Pompey marched out, he very quickly defeated Mithridates, but the king escaped and Mithridates ran off into the wild somewhere in Central Asia; he just disappeared, he's hiding out in a cave someplace. Mithridates was no longer a threat, and his country had been captured and turned into a province; but instead of pursuing Mithridates, Pompey now took advantage of the terms of his command, which was "You have an army until Mithridates is dead," an Pompey now took his army and invaded and captured the entire eastern coastline of the Mediterranean. If you think who else went conquering in the East, it was Alexander the Great; and Pompey here, his hero was Alexander, so now, like Alexander, Pompey was going on a rampage through the East. He's exactly imitating Alexander, and he started to head for Egypt, which was where Alexander went. But right before he got there, he got a piece of bad news, and the bad news was way up to the north, somewhere in the mountains, Mithridates had finally keeled over and died of old age. Remember the terms of his appointment? "You have the army until Mithridates is dead?" This now meant that Pompey's command over that army was over, so he had to stop his conquests.

By this point, though, Pompey's expedition had made both Rome and himself unbelievably rich. As a result of Pompey's little rampage through the East, the tax income of the Roman state tripled, and Pompey's personal fortune and his *dignitas* were now incalculable. Since Alexander had founded cities that he named Alexandria, Pompey now founded at least 11 cities that he called (you can guess) Pompeiopolis.

Pompey had gained more power, wealth, and influence than any Roman before him, but in doing this, he'd repeatedly broken the rules. He'd risen to power working outside the system and he'd really undermined those old Republican institutions; and this set precedents that you couldn't undo. But, at this point when he reached the pinnacle of his power and he might have just taken over Rome, he still had enough respect for tradition that he disbanded his army, he returned to Rome, and he just went into a kind of semiretirement where he's controlling things, but he's exercising power behind the scenes.

We'll now leave Pompey for a bit and turn to one of his younger contemporaries, a man named Gaius Julius Caesar. Caesar's very first public act already hints that he's going to prove to be, if possible, even more ambitious than Pompey. As a young man, Caesar had to give a funeral oration at the burial of an aunt, but instead of just praising the old woman, Caesar got up and took the opportunity to remind the crowd that he claimed to be descended from a god. That's a fairly egotistical statement for a young man who hadn't done anything yet.

Unlike Pompey, Caesar's political career started off fairly conventionally. He held a number of elected offices, he held them in the right order, and at he held them at the right ages. But like Pompey, Caesar also had an Alexander complex; and one day when he's serving in the army in Spain, he supposedly burst into tears. When his aides said, "What's wrong?" he said that he'd been thinking that, at that same age, Alexander had already conquered the world.

Caesar began as a protégé of Pompey, and with some help from the older man he got elected to the consulship in 59 B.C. The other consul for that year—remember, there are always two—was a man named Bibulus, but Caesar totally dominated things and he basically ignored whatever Bibulus wanted. Eventually Bibulus felt so left out that he just retired to his house and left Caesar in charge of the Roman state.

This complete dominance of Caesar over Bibulus resulted in a popular joke at the time. Normally, legislation would be signed with the names of the two consuls for that year, but people said that in the year 59, bills weren't signed with the usual words "in the consulship of Caesar and Bibulus" but instead were signed with the phrase "in the consulship of Julius and Caesar."

Caesar then faced a bit of a crisis, because he knew that the moment he stepped down from office, his enemies would prosecute him in the law courts for illegal actions. Because a Roman official couldn't be prosecuted while in office, if he could immediately go to another office, he'd be safe, at least for a while. Caesar therefore arranged to be appointed governor of a little province called Cisalpine Gaul. This was a small, pretty peaceful province with only a small army. But it's immediately south of Gaul, and Gaul was a huge unconquered region that's roughly equivalent to modern France, Belgium, and the Netherlands as well, and Gaul was inhabited by lots and lots of warlike tribes. Caesar saw this as opportunity, and immediately upon becoming governor, he started to raise a private army, just like Pompey had done. Once that army was ready, he launched his own personal invasion of Gaul. Caesar would ultimately spend nine years fighting continuously in Gaul. He'll raise many more legions to support these campaigns; he'll build up a huge personal army of tough veteran soldiers who were totally loyal to him because that's who they got their rewards from, not the Roman state. Caesar also turned out to be a military genius in his own right. He shared the hardship of his men, and he had a very keen tactical sense.

Caesar's actions in Gaul were blatant imperialism. He'd conquer one tribe, and then he'd say, "In order to make sure that this newly conquered territory is safe, I really have no choice but to attack all the neighbors"; and when those were beaten, it would just create more hostile neighbors; and so on. Caesar's 10 years of campaigning in Gaul killed or enslaved millions of Gauls. Even the Romans thought Caesar's actions were a little bit questionable. At one point a bill got proposed in the Senate that Caesar should be turned over to the Gauls as a war criminal for his unwarranted aggression. But Caesar was always careful to have a tribune or two at Rome in his pay who could veto anything harmful that came up against him.

Finally, the Senate got tired of it all and they ended Caesar's governorship; and they told him "Disband your armies, and you come back to Rome as a private citizen." Caesar knew as soon as he went back to Rome, his enemies would bring lawsuits against him. Caesar now faced a choice: He could obey the senate and maybe face the end of his career, or he could place himself above the state. Caesar decided that his *dignitas* was more important than the Roman state, and so with the famous words, "The die is cast," he crossed the Rubicon River—that's the boundary between his province and Italy—and he marched on Rome at the head of his army. The moment when he crossed that river with troops, technically, under Roman law, he became guilty of treason.

This bold action seems to have caught the Senate completely by surprise; they seem to have expected him just to come home docilely. Faced with this crisis, the Senate was unprepared, they didn't have any troops, and so they now turned for help to the only man with the power to maybe oppose Caesar, and that, of course, was Pompey. Pompey agreed to aid the Senate; and so you had a situation where the man, Pompey, who'd arguably done the most to undermine the institutions of the Republic, now somewhat strangely found himself cast in the role of defender of the Republic against what really was a younger, more aggressive version of himself.

What followed next was a colossal civil war fought between Caesar on one side and Pompey and the Senate on the other. It lasted several years; it's fought all across the Mediterranean, from Spain to Greece; but Pompey in the end was overconfident, and he's eventually defeated at the Battle of Pharsalus. Pompey managed to escape from the battle, and he fled to the last remaining independent kingdom left on the shores of the Mediterranean that the Romans didn't yet control: That was Egypt; Egypt was the last Hellenistic kingdom surviving from the breakup of Alexander's empire, and Egypt was still ruled by direct descendants of Alexander's general, Ptolemy. Unfortunately for Pompey, Egypt didn't prove to be a safe refuge since, fearing Caesar's wrath, the Egyptians murdered Pompey the minute he set foot on the beach. When Caesar arrived right after that in hot pursuit, he was presented with Pompey's head by the Egyptians. That was the rather ignoble end of Pompey the Great.

One other noteworthy event occurred while Caesar was in Egypt: He met the young queen of the country, a woman named Cleopatra. She was the last of the Ptolemaic Dynasty of Macedonian rulers and, as I'm sure you know, embarked on a famous love affair with Caesar.

Caesar returned to Rome victorious in 45 B.C., in control of the entire Mediterranean. He was now the sole ruler of Rome. The problems facing him were how to settle affairs, especially how to deal with all of his veterans who were looking to be rewarded; but secondly, maybe more importantly, he had to find a way to rule Rome as one person, but because of that Romans' traditional hatred for kings, he somehow had to avoid appearing like a king.

Caesar embarked on a very energetic program of reforms and activities. He settled 80,000 veterans in colonies; he granted full or half-citizenship to many of them; he built all kinds of public works at Rome; and he even fixed the calendar. During all the civil wars, the calendar had gotten so messed up that it was actually four months out of alignment with the seasons. But Caesar fixed this all up, and he actually produced a new calendar; and that Julian calendar, with just a couple very minor adjustments made later by Pope Gregory XIII, is basically the same one that we use today.

Caesar's biggest problem, though, was how to control things without looking like a king. To begin with, he simply got himself elected consul over and over again; but after a couple years of this, Roman aristocrats started to get resentful because Caesar was monopolizing one of the two available consulships. Then he turned to Roman tradition, where there'd been a special governmental post called Dictator that occasionally the Romans would appoint in a time of extreme emergency. The Dictator had supreme power over the state, but he was strictly limited to a term of no more than six months. In 44 B.C., Caesar arranged to be given the Dictatorship, but with a lifetime appointment. This really was an insult to the Republic, and it's tantamount to being a king.

As such, this act provoked resentment, and it wasn't helped by the fact that Caesar just didn't behave very modestly. He did things like had the Senate decree that everyone had to take an oath of allegiance to him personally. He renamed one of the months after himself, which is why we have the month of July still today. He had statues of himself put in temples, almost as if he were a god. He had priesthoods established in his honor. He was rude to Senate; he didn't even bother to pretend that they're his peers. All of these actions led to a general feeling that Caesar was acting like a king, and in Roman history, when you have trouble with a king, who do you turn to for help? Remember the oath of Brutus, the man who led the rebellion against the last Etruscan king, Tarquin the Proud? As luck would have it, one of Julius Caesar's closest friends was a man named Brutus. That Brutus was a direct descendant, 500 years down the road, of the Brutus who'd expelled Tarquin and sworn opposition to kings. In the middle of the night, people started to write messages to Brutus on his house and in public places that said things like "Remember your ancestor," or "You're not a real Brutus."

Rome was a society in which family, the past, and tradition had enormous power, so Brutus, even though he's Caesar's friend, really had no choice. In 44 B.C., a conspiracy formed around Brutus, and on March 15, 44 B.C., the Ides of March, Brutus and a group of senators stabbed Julius Caesar to death. In what I suppose you could say was a bit of poetic justice, Caesar fell dead directly beneath a statue of his old enemy, Pompey the Great.

The compulsion that Brutus felt to emulate or to live up to the deeds of his ancestor I think shows a real difference between our society and the Romans, and between their concept of the weight of tradition and ours. After telling this story in class, I always ask my students: How many of you would stick a knife into your best friend because of what your great, great, great, great, great, great grandfather did? Not too many of them raise their hands.

The Romans may have gotten rid of Caesar, but the Roman Republic was now trapped in a pattern of civil war between pairs of strong men vying for supreme control. Over the next couple decades, these continuing internal wars would culminate in the death of the Roman Republic and the creation of the first Roman Emperor.

Augustus—Creator of the Roman Empire
Lecture 29

A fter the assassination of Julius Caesar, several factions emerged to wrestle for control of Rome. The leading figures were Caesar's friend Mark Antony and his adopted son Octavian. After banding together to eliminate their rivals, they turned on one another. While Mark Antony was the better and more experienced military strategist, Octavian waged a superior public relations war, using Mark Antony's lover Cleopatra as a tool to rouse Romans' xenophobia. Transforming himself into Caesar Augustus, the Princeps ("First Citizen"), Octavian became emperor in all but name and ruled brilliantly in every way but one—choosing his heirs.

The Would-Be Heirs of Caesar

- Julius Caesar's death created a power vacuum. A number of different men rushed to fill this void. First there were the conspirators—or, as they called themselves, the liberators—who had killed Caesar. Led by Brutus, they claimed their goal was to restore the Roman Republic.

- The most prominent figure to position himself as Caesar's heir was Marcus Antonius, more commonly known as Mark Antony. He had been Caesar's lieutenant and right-hand man. He was also a good soldier and could relate well to Caesar's veterans.

- When Caesar's will was read, it produced a surprise third candidate. He tapped his utterly obscure grand-nephew Octavian as his primary heir and, posthumously, adopted the 18-year-old youth as his son.

- Antony got control of Caesar's money, records, and legions, but Octavian got the legal rights to use Caesar's name—he was now Gaius Julius Caesar Octavianus—and all over the Mediterranean, there were tens of thousands of hardened veteran soldiers who were used to loyally following the orders of someone named Gaius Julius Caesar.

Another Roman Civil War

- At Caesar's funeral, Antony delivered a laudatory oration in the Forum, during which he displayed Caesar's bloody toga as well as a larger-than-life-size wax replica of Caesar's body depicting all the stab wounds. The crowd rioted and burned down the Senate House. The assassins fled Rome and went to the East, where they had loyal troops.

- Octavian amassed a private army of about five legions from Caesar's veterans, and the Senate was so impressed (or frightened) that they allowed him to be elected consul at the age of 19.

- Conflict between Antony and Octavian seemed inevitable, but both wanted time to prepare. Thus they forged an uneasy alliance against Brutus and the assassins. In 42 B.C., the decisive battle was fought. Octavian was defeated in his part of the battlefield, but Antony was victorious and managed to secure an overall victory.

- Still, neither was ready for open war, so they divided the Roman world. Antony chose the richer eastern half; Octavian was left with the western half. To cement their agreement, Octavian married his sister to Antony.

- Now settled in the East, Antony began his famous affair with Queen Cleopatra and sent Octavian's sister back to him. By aligning himself with Cleopatra, Antony gained the use of the large Egyptian army and navy—and more importantly, the vast Egyptian treasury.

- Octavian, outgunned and underfunded, began to wage what, in modern terms, we would call a war of propaganda against Antony. He posed as the champion of the Roman Republic against a dangerous foreign enemy personified by Cleopatra and depicted Antony as a would-be king.

Cleopatra's legendary affair with Mark Antony was driven as much by political calculation as by great passion. Antony needed her treasury and armies.

- Octavian had Cleopatra officially declared a public enemy of the Roman state. This meant Antony had to sever his ties with her and lose his financial backing or remain loyal to her and find himself in collusion with an enemy of Rome. Antony chose to stay with Cleopatra.

- Eventually open warfare broke out. Antony was a far better general than Octavian, but Octavian had a loyal friend named Agrippa who was an excellent military strategist and willing to let Octavian claim the credit for his victories.

- The decisive battle took place off the coast of Greece at a site called Actium in 31 B.C. Octavian spent the battle below decks, stricken with seasickness. Agrippa outmaneuvered Antony and defeated him. Antony and Cleopatra fled back to Egypt, where they both committed suicide.

From Dictator to Emperor

- While Octavian had gained control of the Roman world, he now faced his greatest challenge: how to rule Rome as one man but avoid looking like a king. Drawing on the negative example set by Julius Caesar, he knew he must not act in an arrogant manner and must not monopolize offices. He also had to respect Republican tradition.

- Much of the success of Octavian's settlement of the Roman state rested on his insight that he could get away with introducing new institutions so long as he preserved the illusion that he was not doing so.

- Initially, like Caesar, Octavian held multiple consulships, but he knew he could not do this indefinitely. He arranged it so that he was given the powers of a consul but not the office itself—he was the power behind the consuls. In fact, he had himself awarded the powers of all the other Roman magistracies as well, including the powers of a tribune.

- Octavian faced one additional problem: what to call himself that suggested his status but did not imply anything like "king." Eventually, he adopted a whole series of names, none of which seemed that overwhelming or threatening but that collectively clearly indicated that he was the head of the state:

  o Augustus, from a Latin root implying either devotion to the gods or an object with divine qualities. This became his proper name, replacing Octavian.

  o Princeps, meaning "first citizen" or "first among equals," from which the English term "prince" is derived.

  o Pater patriae, meaning "father of the country," which to the Romans not only conjured up compassionate, protective images but also a demand for absolute respect and obedience.

- o   Imperator, a well-established term that was a spontaneous acclamation bestowed by soldiers on a victorious general. It is from "imperator" that the English words "emperor" and "empire" are derived.

- The final element in Augustus's consolidation of power was that he acted modestly. He lived in a small house, ate simple food, dressed in a humble fashion, and always treated senators courteously and with respect.

The Early Empire

- After decades of civil war, people were eager for peace. Many were willing to accept, and perhaps even believe, the fiction that the Republic had been restored.

- Augustus's actions were enormously influential. He single-handedly created a new state and a new government, establishing a model that would be followed for hundreds of years. With him, the era of the Republic ended, and the Roman Empire began.

- Augustus ruled for a long time. He eliminated his rivals by 31 B.C. and ruled until his death in A.D. 14. By the time Augustus died, there quite literally was no one left alive who could remember the days of the true Roman Republic.

- Throughout his life, Augustus continued his clever use of propaganda and manipulation of his public image, patronizing poets who crafted laudatory accounts of his actions, and funding massive construction projects whose artwork and decoration eulogized his reign and sugar-coated his machinations.

- Augustus also wrote an autobiography, entitled, with typical understatement and modesty, the *Res Gestae*, which literally means, "Some stuff I did." It is a masterpiece of propaganda.

- Augustus all but stopped the rapid expansion of the empire's borders that had characterized the previous centuries. He concentrated more on solidifying what Rome already had than on gaining new lands. Egypt, however, had been turned into another Roman province, and Rome now controlled a continuous ring of territory circling the Mediterranean Sea.

- The one major instance when Augustus tried to expand the empire's borders, a foray across the Rhine River into Germanic territory in A.D. 9, actually resulted in one of Rome's greatest military disasters.

- Augustus' reign was overall a great success. He finally brought Rome peace and stability after a century of discord, and he figured out a way to hold real power in Rome without looking too obviously like he was doing it.

- Historians continue to debate whether Augustus in some sense restored the Republic as he claimed or was the final step in destroying it. Was he a traditionalist who was merely adapting old institutions to fit new realities, or was he an innovator who was creating completely new institutions and disguising them with old labels?

- Despite all his cleverness, one area in which Augustus failed was in finding a way to pass power to the next generation. Part of the problem was the ambiguous nature of the position he had crafted. How do you transfer an office that does not formally exist?

- Perhaps his greatest misjudgment was choosing the next emperor on the basis of heredity. An unexpected drawback to his long lifespan was that Augustus outlived his first four choices for a successor. The living heir at Augustus's death was not an ideal choice—his step-son Tiberius.

- Already 54 years old, Tiberius was grim, serious, and socially awkward. At least initially, Tiberius was not a bad emperor, but later in his life, he withdrew to a palace on the island of Capri, and gave himself up to sexual indulgence and paranoia.

- The next set of emperors features several names notorious for insanity and debauchery, including Caligula and Nero. Augustus's decision to base imperial succession on the principle of heredity and blood relationships would have dire consequences for Roman history.

Suggested Reading

Levick, *Augustus: Image and Substance.*

Zanker, *The Power of Images in the Age of Augustus.*

Questions to Consider

1. Is it more accurate to say that Augustus restored the Roman Republic (as he claimed) or that he destroyed it, and why?

2. Was Augustus more of a traditionalist (as he claimed) or an innovator, and in what ways could each of these statements be considered true?

Augustus—Creator of the Roman Empire
Lecture 29—Transcript

When Julius Caesar fell dead beneath the statue of Pompey in March, 44 B.C., it created a power vacuum. A whole bunch of different men and groups all tried to jump in and fill that void. First of all, there were the conspirators—or, as they would call themselves, the liberators—the group of senators who'd actually killed Caesar. These were led by Caesar's friend, Brutus, and they claimed that their ultimate goal was to restore the Roman Republic. To reinforce this image, they minted coins that had stamped on them little images of daggers and triangular caps. The daggers represented the assassination of Caesar and the caps were the sort of hat traditionally given to slaves when they received their freedom; and so the symbolic meaning of these coins was that they'd freed the entire Roman people and state from enslavement by Julius Caesar.

On the other hand, there were a number of men who tried to position themselves as the heirs to the legacy of Caesar. By far the most prominent of these was Marcus Antonius, or, as we commonly call him today, Marc Antony. He clearly seemed to be the best positioned to just step right into Caesar's palace. He'd been Caesar's lieutenant for many years; he'd been Caesar's right-hand man, the guy that Caesar would delegate authority to when he himself was somewhere else. Antony was also a pretty good soldier in his own right, and so that enabled him to relate well to Caesar's veterans.

Finally, though, when Caesar's will was opened and read, it produced a surprise third candidate. To the shock of almost everyone—and actually to the very great annoyance of Marc Antony—Antony was not named as Caesar's primary heir. Instead, Caesar tapped an utterly obscure grandnephew of his as the primary heir; and, what's more, he then posthumously adopted that young boy as his son. This nephew was at the time a teenager who's 18 years old and he's named Octavian.

Antony got control of almost everything from Caesar—he got Caesar's money, he got his records, and he got his legions—so on the surface, it doesn't look like Octavian benefited very much from this adoption. Under Roman law, though, when you're adopted, you could take the name of the person who adopted you; and so Octavian legally now became Gaius Julius Caesar Octavianus, and the name that he'd use in daily life that people would call him was just Caesar. This might not seem like such a big deal except for the fact that all around the Mediterranean, there were tens of thousands of battle-hardened veteran soldiers who had been indoctrinated to loyally follow the orders of someone named Gaius Julius Caesar. Even though it may not quite seem entirely logical, many of those men now transferred their allegiance to the "new" Caesar, Octavian; and so overnight, this teenage boy had acquired a substantial personal army and he instantly, therefore, became someone to be reckoned with.

The funeral of Julius Caesar was a very memorable event. Marc Antony delivered a laudatory oration in the Roman Forum, during which he displayed Caesar's bloody toga, and he even had constructed this larger-than-life-size wax replica of Caesar's body. This rather gruesome object was mounted upright on a revolving platform, and it depicted realistically every one of the places where Caesar had been stabbed. The crowd got so worked up by this sight, together with the oration of Antony, that they rioted, and they spontaneously cremated Julius Caesar's body right there in the Roman Forum. To provide fuel for this fire, and also clearly as an expression of anger against the assassins, they burnt down the Senate house. The terrified senatorial assassins fled Rome and ran off to the East, and they went that way because that's where their loyal troops were. This effectively left Rome in the hands of the two rivals, Antony and Octavian.

Octavian managed to put together a private army of about five legions, composed of Caesar's veterans; and the Senate was so impressed by this deed—or maybe we should say it's so frightened by this—that they allowed him to run for and be elected Consul. He, at this point, was just 19 years old.

Conflict between Antony and Octavian seemed pretty much inevitable, but neither was quite ready. Both wanted some time to prepare; both were still worried about Caesar's assassins and the senatorial armies that were off in the East. These two rivals then forged an alliance in which they pledged to work together for awhile against Brutus and the other assassins/liberators. In 42 B.C., the decisive battle was fought between these two factions, and Octavian, who really wasn't a good general, was defeated on his part of the battlefield; but Marc Antony, who was a pretty good general, was victorious in his section, and that was enough to secure an overall victory. Brutus and the other senatorial assassins were captured, killed, or committed suicide.

With the Liberators now out of the picture, the situation had clarified and come down again to the two men squaring off to see who would take over Rome. But still, neither was quite ready for open war, so they decided they'd simply divide up the Roman world between them. Marc Antony was clearly the elder partner in this coalition, the stronger one, and so he got first pick. He chose the eastern half, which, remember, was the richer half. That left Octavian with the western half. To cement their agreement, Octavian married his sister to Antony.

Antony, now established off in the East, Antony renewed his acquaintance with Cleopatra, the queen of Egypt, and soon those two were engaged in their famous love affair. It became so heated that eventually Antony sent back Octavian's sister to him and openly took up with Cleopatra, which was quite offensive to Octavian. By aligning himself with her, Antony then gained the use of the large Egyptian army and navy, and, probably more importantly, the vast Egyptian treasury. Octavian couldn't hope to match Antony's financial resources, so he took a different path. He began to wage what I suppose in modern terms we'd call a war of propaganda against Antony.

Octavian posed as the champion of the Roman Republic, and he tried to portray that he's defending the Republic against a dangerous foreign enemy, personified by Cleopatra. Remember, since Cleopatra was a queen, by presenting himself as her consort, Antony had fallen into the trap of looking like a king—which, remember, the Romans hated—and so Octavian was very adeptly able to exploit that traditional Roman fear and hatred of kings. Octavian did all kinds of things: He spread rumors that Cleopatra wanted to conquer Rome and then move the capital of the entire empire to Alexandria in Egypt. Even Romans who really weren't so crazy about Octavian were offended by the thought that the capital might be moved to Egypt; and so Octavian was very, very successful in painting Antony as having fallen under the seductive power of a foreign queen, and that's a stereotype we still have about Cleopatra today. Octavian transformed what in reality was a civil war between two Romans into what looked like a war of a Roman against an Eastern enemy, and that was a very clever strategy.

Having laid this groundwork, Octavian then manipulated the Senate and had them declare that Cleopatra was officially a public enemy of the Roman state. This was an absolutely brilliant move because it put Antony in a difficult position: Either he had to sever his ties with Cleopatra—and if he did that he'd lose all that financial backing—or he could remain loyal to her and then he'd legally find himself in collusion with someone who's an official enemy of Rome. Antony, who really did seem to have fallen genuinely in love with Cleopatra, chose to stay faithful to her and to stay with her.

All this maneuvering back and forth actually took about a decade, but finally the war between the two men broke out. Antony was clearly a better general than Octavian, but, luckily for Octavian, he had a loyal friend, whose name was Agrippa, who not only was an excellent military strategist, but even better was also willing to let Octavian claim the credit for the victories that he won. Antony also seemed to have a big advantage having a larger army and more resources; but Agrippa, who's a very clever general, seized control of the sea, he blockaded Antony's army, and that caused a lot of starvation and disease and weakened it substantially.

The final decisive battle between these two groups took place just off the coast of Greece at a place called Actium, and we're down now to 31 B.C. The Battle of Actium was a naval battle, and Octavian wasn't only a terrible general but also a lousy sailor; and so one source tells us that he spent the entire battle belowdecks in his bunk, stricken with seasickness and vomiting. Good old Agrippa, however, was also a good admiral and he outmaneuvered Antony and defeated him. Antony and Cleopatra both escaped from the battle and they fled to Egypt, and, I'm sure you know, they there committed suicide.

Octavian had now gained control of the Roman world, but he faced his greatest challenge, and it was the same challenge that Julius Caesar had faced: How do you rule Rome as one man but avoid being killed for looking like a king? Caesar had found himself in this situation, too, and despite all of his talents, Caesar had failed when faced with this dilemma. Octavian at least draw could look back at the negative example that had been set by Caesar, and so he could identify some things that he had to avoid doing. First of all, he had to be sure that he didn't act in an arrogant manner, like Caesar had. Second, he couldn't monopolize offices like the consulship, which Caesar had held a whole bunch of times in a row, because this would cause resentment among the aristocrats who themselves wanted to hold those offices. Third, he knew he had to respect tradition and to not appear to be making any dramatic changes either in the state or in creating new institutions.

It was a good thing that Octavian was a mastermind of propaganda, because his solution to these problems was absolutely brilliant. A lot of the success of his settlement of the Roman state rested upon an insight, and the insight was that he could actually get away with introducing new institutions as long as he gave the illusion that he wasn't doing that. Octavian realized that appearances sometimes matter a lot more than reality, and he exploited that strategy to the maximum.

First of all, like Caesar, he wanted to have the various powers of Roman magistrates, such as being Consul; and the way he engineered this was simple but inspired: Octavian arranged it so he was given the powers of the office of Consul, but not the office itself. In other words, each year, the Romans would go ahead and elect two Consuls, just as they always had throughout the whole history of the Republic; and nominally those two men were running the state for that year. Lurking behind them, however, and holding equivalent powers, was Octavian, who also had the power of a consul, but he wasn't exercising that power on a day-to-day basis. The really smart thing was that Octavian didn't just receive the powers of a Consul, but also had himself awarded the powers of every other Roman magistracy as well. For example, he was granted the powers of a Tribune. That meant he could do things like propose new laws, or he could use the Tribunician veto; but, again, he wasn't formally one of the elected tribunes for any one year. Aristocrats could continue to compete, they could run for offices, just as they always had, and it looked like they're the ones running the state. But floating above this entire system was Octavian, and if he needed to, at any moment he could invoke one of his many powers and get his way. Octavian could somehow legitimately claim that he wasn't doing anything new or innovative since all the powers that he held were old, traditional Republican ones.

He faced another big challenge, though, and that was simply what to call himself. After all, he needed some kind of title or name that would suggest the status held; obviously, though, he couldn't use the term "king," There's no chance of that. At first, since he was making the claim that he'd refounded the Republic, he considered taking the name "Romulus," after the original founder of the city. But very soon he realized that he couldn't do that—that would be bad—because Romulus, of course, actually had been a king. Ultimately, he again found a clever solution that again had to do with manipulation of images: He adopted a whole series of different names, none of which individually seemed that overwhelming or threatening, but collectively they clearly indicated he's the head of the state.

The first of those titles, which became part of his official name, was Augustus. This was derived from a Latin root word that implies either a devotion to the gods or maybe that the object called Augustus itself possesses divine qualities. That very ambiguity of meaning was perfect for Octavian because, on the one hand, then he could claim that this title simply meant that he was very pious, he respected the gods; but, on the other hand, it subtly suggested that he's a little bit closer to the gods than ordinary men. By historical convention, Augustus is the name by which we tend to refer to Octavian once he took over the state, so this is just something historians have decided; and so once he becomes the first Roman emperor, we call him Augustus. From this point on, I'll also call him Augustus, but keep in mind that Augustus and Octavian is the same guy.

Another title/name that he acquired was princeps, and this one literally translates as something like "first citizen" or maybe "first among equals"; and, again, that term has a lot of useful ambiguity to it. On the one hand, you can interpret it fairly modestly, and the title simply seems to say that he's a citizen; it emphasized that status, and that's a status he shared with all other Roman citizens. But on the other hand, it also somehow implied that he's superior to other citizens; he's the first among the citizens, and he's their leader. Also, by the way, this is the word from which the English term "prince" is derived.

The next of his titles that he took was Pater Patriae. Unlike Augustus and Princeps, which have all these possible meanings, this one very precisely translates as "Father of the Country." The ambiguity comes in, though, when you consider the connotations of that term. On the one hand, a father conjures up associations of someone who's compassionate, who's caring, who lovingly looks after his children; but on the other hand, in Roman society, a father was a very imposing figure, and he was someone who demanded absolute respect and obedience from those in his family. By law, Roman fathers even had the power of life and death over the people within his family.

Finally, he took another title, and this one was Imperator. This, again, was a well-established, traditional term. This one had its origins in a kind of spontaneous acclamation or a shout that soldiers would give to a victorious general after a battle if they though the general had done a good job, and so this term carried connotations of military skill and success. It's from this term "imperator" that the English words "emperor" and "empire" are derived, and those are then applied to Rome and its rulers.

Every one of these terms was at the same time an official title but it also was really part of his name, and each one of these terms suggested a different aspect of Augustus's power. Every subsequent Roman emperor that came along after him would also adopt all of these names or titles as part of their official name/title.

The final element in Augustus's consolidation of power was that he acted modestly. He'd learned to avoid the arrogance that Julius Caesar had shown. Augustus he lived in a very small house, ordinary house; he ate simple food; he always dressed in a humble fashion, just looking like every other citizen; and he always treated senators with courtesy and respect. Also working in his favor was the fact that after decades now of civil war, people were simply eager for peace. A lot of Romans, I think, were willing to accept and maybe even believe this sort of fiction being sold by Augustus that the Republic had come back and been restored because it meant there'd be an end to all of the destructive wars that had been plaguing Rome for quite a while.

Augustus's actions were incredibly influential. He'd invented or created a new state and a new sort of government, and he established the model that would be followed for hundreds of years after him. It's with him that the Republic ends and that third and final phase of Roman history, the Empire, begins. One more thing that helped to make his settlement of the Roman state long-lasting was that he himself lived a really long time. He gained power as a teenager, he eliminated all of his rivals by 31 B.C., and then he continued to rule all the way down until his death in A.D. 14. By the time Augustus finally died, there quite literally was almost no one else left alive who could remember the days of the true Roman Republic; he'd outlived everyone else.

All his life, he continued his clever use of propaganda and manipulation of his public image. He'd do things like patronize poets who'd craft laudatory accounts of his actions; he'd fund massive construction projects that were adorned with artwork and decoration, all of which eulogized his reign and sugarcoated his machinations. Augustus also wrote an autobiography, and considering that he'd brought the entire Mediterranean world under his sway, he labeled this work, with typical understatement and modesty, the *Res Gestae*, which literally translates as, "Stuff that I did." It's a masterpiece of propaganda that rather blandly just glosses over the actions he doesn't want remembered while emphasizing the things he wants to stress. Let me read you the opening lines of this. The *Res Gestae* begins: "At the age of nineteen, at my own expense and initiative, I raised an army and used it to defend the liberty of the Republic when it was oppressed by a faction." We might more accurately rewrite that line as: "At the age of 19, I raised a private army to fight a civil war against the lawfully elected magistrates of the Roman state." But he goes on to boast, not about the offices he held, but instead he boasts about the honors that he turned down, and he lists in great detail all of the benefactions that he bestowed on the citizens of Rome. For example, when describing his takeover of power in the Roman state, he rather mildly comments that "I held no office which was inconsistent with the customs of our ancestors." This "restoration" could easily be interpreted as destruction; and while that final phrase is true in a strict sense, it certainly doesn't reflect the realities of his power.

In terms of Augustus's foreign policy, the rapid expansion of the empire's borders, which we've seen in the last couple centuries, mostly stopped. In general, Augustus concentrated on solidifying what Rome already had rather than gaining new lands. After Antony and Cleopatra were defeated at Actium, Egypt was turned into a taxpaying Roman province, and Rome now controlled a continuous ring of territory all the way around the Mediterranean Sea. The one time when Augustus tried to expand the empire's borders actually ended up being one of Rome's greatest military disasters. As a result of Caesar's campaigns, all of Gaul was now Roman provinces, and the border of Gaul with the unknown was the Rhine River. On the other side of the Rhine were a bunch of very fierce Germanic tribes, and Augustus's reign the Romans periodically made incursions into that region. Just five years before Augustus's death, in 9 A.D., a Roman general named Varus was sent with three Roman Legions on such an expedition. Varus, though, was really a lawyer; he was an incompetent general. He was tricked by a local German leader named Hermann who pretended to be an ally of Rome but really lured Varus and his men out into an ambush. The Romans always fought best on open, flat ground where their discipline gave them an advantage, but Varus was enticed by Hermann into the swampy and dense Germanic forests, and there the Germans were able to attack the disorganized Roman formations, and Varus and all three legions were massacred. This was an embarrassing defeat, and Augustus seems to have taken the loss of those legions particularly hard. One source tells us that for the rest of his reign, he was prone to occasionally banging his head against the wall while moaning, "Varus, give me back my legions!"

Despite that one disaster, in general Augustus's reign was a great success. He brought peace and stability after almost a hundred years of discord. He was able to become emperor because he figured out a way to hold real power in Rome without looking at least too obviously like he was doing it. Two interesting questions concerning Augustus continue to be debated today, and these are: Did he in some sense really restore the Republic as he claimed, or did he destroy it? Second, was he a traditionalist who was just adapting old institutions to fit new realities, or was he an innovator who's creating completely new institutions and disguising them with old labels?

Despite all of his cleverness that I've been emphasizing, there's one area in which Augustus failed miserably: finding a way to pass on power to the next emperor and to make sure that the emperor was well-qualified. Part of the problem was the ambiguous nature of the position he'd created; how do you transfer something that really doesn't formally exist? Probably his greatest mistake was choosing to select the next emperor on the basis of heredity. By establishing a precedent of passing power to the nearest male relative, Augustus would doom Rome to a string of incompetent, sometimes even mentally unbalanced, emperors over the next hundred years or so.

One unexpected drawback to his long lifespan was that Augustus actually outlived his first four choices for a successor. These included even two of his grandchildren, who died before him. In the end, the heir who managed to still be alive at the time when Augustus died was not a person that he'd have chosen. This was a stepson of his named Tiberius. At the time Tiberius inherited the throne, he was already 55 years old, and had a very grim, serious personality and also had a social awkwardness. At least initially, though, despite all that he wasn't a bad emperor, he worked conscientiously; but later in his life, he withdrew to a palace on the island of Capri and basically gave himself up to all sorts of paranoia and sexual overindulgence. Tiberius died in 37 A.D.

The next set of emperors will have several names among them who were notorious for insanity and debauchery, including Caligula and Nero. Augustus's decision to base imperial succession on the principle of heredity and blood relationships would end up having dire consequences for all of Roman history.

The next lecture will follow the history of the first two centuries of the Roman Empire, and this is a period when it would experience both notable highs and lows. While the empire would have to endure reigns of people like Caligula and Nero, it would also flourish under the management of good emperors such as Trajan and Marcus Aurelius; and during this time, the empire would reach its greatest geographical extent and achieve its economic and cultural apex. But the factors that would eventually cause its collapse would also begin to show themselves.

Roman Emperors—Good, Bad, and Crazy
Lecture 30

D uring its first two centuries, the Roman Empire reached its greatest heights—and, arguably, some of its lowest depths. Augustus's reliance on bloodlines for the succession led to the unstable reigns of the Julio-Claudian emperors, followed by the nearly as disastrous Flavians. Fortunately, the Five Good Emperors—men selected for talent, rather than heredity—rose to the throne and made the 2nd century A.D. Rome's most successful period in terms of peace, prosperity, and culture. This success could not last, however, and the arrival of the soldier-emperors signaled the return to chaos.

The Julio-Claudian Emperors

- The first two centuries of the Roman Empire would see the empire reach the height of its power and wealth and expand to its largest geographic extent. It would witness many of the Romans' greatest cultural and architectural achievements.

- The rulers of this era would feature both Rome's wisest and most conscientious emperors and several of its most notorious and deranged tyrants. The emperor who followed Tiberius to the throne was one of the latter—Caligula. Still quite young when he became emperor, he quickly embarked on a reign of terror and profligate expenditure.

- His favorite saying was "Let everyone hate me, so long as they fear me." After about four years, Caligula was murdered by the commanders of his own bodyguard. Caligula was the first disastrous result of Augustus's decision to base succession on the principle of heredity, but he would not be the last.

- Caligula had no obvious successor, and while the Senate was dithering, the Praetorian Guardsmen (the emperor's bodyguards) were looting the palace. There they discovered Caligula's uncle, Claudius, in hiding.

- Claudius had never been taken seriously because he had physical handicaps, including a speech impediment, and was regarded as dim-witted. In reality, he had a fairly sharp intellect. On the spur of the moment, the guard proclaimed him emperor. This incident reveals the reality of power in the empire. Whoever had the soldiers' support could be emperor.

- Claudius went through several wives and eventually married his niece and adopted her son, Nero. Claudius ruled a fairly long time, constructing a number of important public works. He died in 54 A.D., possibly as a result of poisoning by his wife and stepson.

- For a few years, while Nero was under the influence of his tutors, including the famous Stoic philosopher Seneca, he was a decent emperor. Soon, however, Nero turned against his mentors, forced Seneca to commit suicide, and seems to have gone insane, embarking on a reign of terror and debauchery.

- In the course of his madness, Nero murdered almost every member of his family. In A.D. 68, he was killed in a palace revolt. This created an interesting moment of crisis: His rampages had been so thorough that there was no obvious heir to the imperial throne.

The Flavian Emperors

- As usual, the Romans solved this succession crisis by having a civil war. During the year 69 the Romans quickly ran through no less than four different emperors. Finally, a man named Vespasian from a family known as the Flavians emerged as the victor.

- In many ways, Vespasian was like another Augustus. He ruled wisely, lived modestly, and undertook a number of public works. He was also fairly old at the time he took the throne and had a long career as administrator and general.

- Vespasian had a popular son named Titus, as well as a younger son named Domitian. Titus had already successfully commanded the Roman armies, so when Vespasian died, there was a smooth transition to Titus. Titus was a good and popular ruler, but unfortunately died after only a few years.

- The next emperor was Vespasian's younger son, Domitian. Domitian unfortunately turned out to be more in the mold of Caligula and Nero. He put many senators to death and enjoyed terrorizing them. He was assassinated in 96, and his death marked the end of the Flavian dynasty.

The Five Good Emperors

- In a rare Roman example of breaking with tradition, the next set of emperors came up with the original idea of selecting the person who seemed best qualified for the job, rather than a blood descendant. This would prove to be a wise policy which led to Rome enjoying its most powerful and stable period.

- This series of leaders, who ruled roughly during the 2nd century A.D., became known as the Five Good Emperors, also known as the Antonines. This century is viewed as the highpoint of the Roman Empire. Rome had grown to encompass about 50 provinces and 50 million inhabitants. The empire stretched from Portugal to Mesopotamia, from Britain to the Sahara desert.

- The first of the Five Good Emperors, Nerva, ruled only a short time. The second was Trajan, and he was notable for being the first emperor from the provinces—namely, Spain. This reflects a similar change in the composition of the senate at this time.

- Trajan had had a substantial, distinguished career before being selected as emperor. His personal life was sober and he was always very respectful to the senate. Interested in expanding Rome's borders, he launched an invasion of Dacia, a region enclosed by a large bend of the Danube River. Conquering Dacia shortened and straightened Rome's frontier.

- Dacia also contained rich gold mines, which were used to construct large and elaborate public works. Next to the original Roman Forum, Trajan built a huge new complex known as the Forum of Trajan, which included Trajan's Column, a Latin library, and a Greek library.

- Trajan acquired a reputation as an ideal emperor and earned the title Optimus Princeps. In later years, the senate would praise emperors by using Trajan as a yardstick.

- Trajan selected as his heir a man named Hadrian, who was another well-qualified choice. Unlike Trajan, Hadrian did not embark on any new military conquests. He was more a patron of the arts. In particular, he loved Greek culture.

- Hadrian's solution to the fact that the empire was becoming too large to be effectively ruled by one man was to travel constantly. Indeed, he spent many years of his reign on a grand tour, visiting every province of the empire. His court was a mobile one that traveled with him.

- The next emperor, Antoninus Pius, proved to be another sound choice, but he was more of a caretaker than an innovator, and simply kept the empire running smoothly.

- Antoninus Pius's successor, Marcus Aurelius, is sometimes known as the philosopher emperor. A Stoic, he wrote a famous book called the *Meditations*, in which he speculates about virtue and the need to do your best even under difficult circumstances.

- Marcus Aurelius had to contend with a number of new external threats, particularly from barbarian groups in the north, and an outbreak of plague that began in the east and spread throughout the empire.

The Return to Chaos

- When it came time to select a successor, Marcus Aurelius finally made a foolish mistake and chose his biological son, Commodus. Commodus was a spoiled child with delusions of godhood. He thought he was the reincarnation of Hercules and degraded the office of emperor by fighting in public as a gladiator in rigged contests.

- Commodus was eventually strangled in his bath. The next emperor was almost immediately murdered by the Praetorian Guard, and this led to one of the more shameful moments in Roman history: The guard staged an auction for the office of emperor.

- At the auction, Didius Julianus offered the highest price to the Praetorians— 25,000 sesterces per man, about 25 years' salary for an ordinary Roman legionary. They hailed him as emperor and accepted his money, but he was murdered almost immediately.

- At this point, the legions in Syria, Britain, and along the Danube each proclaimed their own governor as the new emperor. The three governors, with their armies, all raced to Rome and fought another civil war. Eventually, the Danubian governor, Septimius Severus, emerged as the victor.

- Severus was the first of what might be called the soldier-emperors— men who became emperor neither through adoption nor selection by the senate but because they could command the most troops. Severus was from the North African town of Leptis and thus the first African emperor as well.

- Severus stabilized the empire and ruled effectively, if harshly, from 193 to 211. From this point on, emperors would mostly gain power by brute force, and internal and external problems would multiply.

Suggested Reading

Aldrete, *Daily Life in the Roman City*.

Garnsey and Saller, *The Roman Empire: Economy, Society, and Culture*.

Suetonius, *The Twelve Caesars*.

Questions to Consider

1. What factors do you think led historian Edward Gibbon to assess the Roman Empire of the 2nd century A.D. as "the happiest time in all of history?"

2. Of all the various emperors described in this lecture, which, in your opinion, were the best and the worst, and why?

Roman Emperors—Good, Bad, and Crazy
Lecture 30—Transcript

Augustus had initiated the third phase of Roman history, the Empire, and he'd provided a model for how it would be organized. Tiberius, his successor, then kept things running relatively smoothly. This lecture will trace the fortunes of the Roman Empire over the next two centuries. The rulers of this era would feature both Rome's wisest and most conscientious emperors and several of its most notorious and deranged tyrants.

The next emperor to take the throne was one of the latter, a nephew of Tiberius known by the nickname "Caligula," which meant, literally "little boots"; and these were actual boots given to him as a young boy when he accompanied his father on military campaigns and he wore a miniature pair of legionary boots. Caligula was still very, very young when he became emperor, and he rapidly embarked on what we might call a reign of terror and also of profligate expenditure. Just to give you a sense of the sort of person he was, for entertainment, he liked to watch people being tortured to death. Whenever he kissed his wife, he would whisper in her ear, "You know, I could have this beautiful throat cut anytime I please." His favorite saying was, "Let everybody hate me, so long as they fear me." Finally, how do you think the ruler of the known world spent his idle, free time? At least according to one source, he'd spend hours every day in front of a mirror practicing making horrible and disgusting faces.

He did share one thing in common with the average Roman: He was a fan of horse and chariot racing, and he had a favorite horse that he named Incitatus (it translates literally to something like "Speedy"). Caligula had a special marble stable built for Incitatus, and on race days he'd station troops all around the area with orders to kill anyone who made noise just to make sure that Incitatus got a good night's rest. It's rumored that Caligula planned to have Incitatus, his horse, appointed to the consulship. After about four years of these sorts of actions, Caligula was murdered by the commanders of his own bodyguard who finally just got fed up with his behavior. Caligula, though, was the first disastrous result of Augustus's decision to base succession on the principle of heredity, but he wouldn't be the last.

There was no obvious successor after the murder of Caligula, and for a while the senate debated, "What do we do now?" While they were dithering, the Praetorian Guardsmen—these were the emperor's bodyguards—were looting the palace, and in the process of doing so they saw some feet sticking out from under a curtain. When they pulled back the curtain, they discovered Caligula's uncle. He's a man named Claudius, and despite his close kinship to the emperor, Claudius had really never been taken seriously. He had a number of physical handicaps, he had a speech impediment, and people regarded as dimwitted. In reality, it looks like he actually had a fairly sharp intellect, though he had what we might call today social problems. On the spur of the moment, the Praetorian Guard proclaimed this rather unlikely candidate emperor. This little incident revealed what's really the new reality of power in the Roman Empire: Whoever had the support of the army could be the emperor.

Claudius had a lot of problems in his family life. He went through several different wives; he eventually wound up marrying his own niece and adopting her son. Claudius did manage to rule a fairly long time. Among his other achievements was he constructed several important public works, such as a new harbor for Rome and a major aqueduct. Eventually, he died in 54 A.D., perhaps as a result of eating a bowl of poisoned mushrooms that were provided by his wife/niece and his own stepson.

Claudius's stepson was a teenage boy known as Nero, and at least for a few years, while he's still under the influence of his tutors, which including the famous Stoic philosopher Seneca, Nero was a decent emperor. Soon, however, he turned against his mentors, he forced Seneca the philosopher to commit suicide, and he may perhaps even have gone insane—at the very least, we could say he lost touch with reality—and he embarked on yet another reign of terror and debauchery.

In the course of this, Nero murdered almost every member of his family. In addition to his stepfather, he's thought to have murdered his brother, his aunt, his stepson, and finally even his own mother, although that proved to be a real challenge and resulted in an almost Monty Python-esque sequence of blundered assassination attempts. First, he tried on no less than three separate occasions to poison his mother; but knowing her son, she'd foreseen these attempts, and so before every meal she'd drink antidotes. Thwarted in that strategy, Nero then presented her with a new bedroom, which was equipped with a special ceiling that would drop on her as she slept. But she was tipped off by one of the builders and evaded that trap. Next, he invited his mother out to a picnic on an island, and he had a special collapsible boat designed in an attempt to drown her. Just as planned, the boat fell apart in the water, but—what do you know —Nero's mother could swim, and so she reached shore safely. Finally, in frustration, he simply had one of his servants murder her. Nero also, by the way, married his own stepsister, but eventually killed her, too.

Nero's idea of a fun pastime was to wander around the streets of Rome at night in disguise and basically mug random people. Sometimes he'd even kill them and throw their bodies into the sewer. Nero did many other cruel things, but I think you get the picture by now. Ultimately, in 68 A.D., there was a palace revolt against him and he was killed by one of his own slaves.

That first set of emperors from Augustus through Nero is collectively called the Julio-Claudians. The death of Nero created an interesting moment of crisis. Augustus, the first emperor, had established the principle of succession as being that the throne would go to the nearest male relative. Nero's rampages against his own family had been so thorough that there were no male Julio-Claudians left to take over. The Romans had a dilemma: How do you select the next emperor? In I suppose what's a tradition that goes all the way back to the foundation of the city and Romulus and Remus, the Romans solved that problem by having a civil war. The year 69 A.D. was one of constant warfare among various rivals for the throne. In that one year, the Romans ran through no less than four emperors; but finally, a man named Vespasian from a family called the Flavians emerged as the permanent victor. He became emperor; he brought those civil wars to an end.

In a lot of ways, you can think of Vespasian as almost a second Augustus. He ruled wisely, he lived very modestly, and he built a number of public works. Vespasian also had a coarse sense of humor; we know that he liked making obscene jokes. Vespasian was pretty old by the time he took the throne, and he'd already had a long, distinguished career as an administrator and general. Vespasian, though, had a popular son named Titus, as well as a younger son named Domitian. Titus had already successfully commanded some Roman armies himself. In fact, he'd played a central role in suppressing a very famous revolt by the Jews. When Vespasian died, there was a smooth transition to Titus and everybody was happy because Titus showed a lot of promise. It's during the reign of Titus that the Colosseum, the Flavian Amphitheater, was built. It's also during the reign of Titus that Mount Vesuvius erupted and buried the cities of Pompeii and Herculaneum. Titus in general was regarded as a good and popular ruler, but unfortunately he died prematurely after only a couple years. That meant the throne went to Vespasian's younger son, Domitian, and unfortunately Domitian turned out to be more in the mold of Caligula and Nero. He did the usual things crazy emperors do: He put many senators to death; he enjoyed terrorizing them. One nice story about him is once he invited a number of senators to something he called the Feast of Death at the palace. He had the entire dining room draped in black cloth; he had black plates, black glasses, black silverware, and even black food. Each senator's place at the table was marked with a little miniature tombstone with their name carved onto it. Obviously the terrified senators were all sure that at the end of this meal they'd all be murdered; but when the end of the night came, Domitian just sent them home, content to have savored their fear.

How do you think this ruler of the known world liked to spend his idle hours? Supposedly Domitian would spend several hours every day locked alone in a little room in the palace catching flies and impaling them on pins. That led to an actual Roman joke from this time that survives: One Roman asks another, "Who's with the emperor today?" The reply is: "No one, not even a fly." Domitian was assassinated in 96 A.D., and his death marked the end of the Flavian family of emperors. That now takes us pretty much through the 1st century of the empire, the first hundred years, and by then the institution of having an emperor was firmly established.

There was still, though, the problem of succession, and this whole principle of choosing the emperor based on heredity had obviously resulted in a number of disastrous emperors. Even the Romans, who were always hesitant to change, realized that they couldn't afford to keep picking their emperors this way. The next series of emperors recognized that fact, and in what really was a rare example of the Romans breaking with tradition, instead of picking the next emperor as being from the nearest blood relative, those emperors came up with an original idea: They selected the person who seemed best qualified for the job, and then they adopted that person as their son and they became the next emperor. This would prove to be a wise policy, and it led to Rome enjoying what really was its most powerful and stable period.

The next series of leaders, who ruled roughly during the 2nd century A.D., became known as the Five Good Emperors. That century, the 2nd century A.D., is viewed as the high point of the Roman Empire. It's a time when it reached its greatest extent; it's a time when there was relative peace and prosperity among its inhabitants; and it's a time when the emperors themselves were wise and just rulers generally speaking. The famous historian of Rome, Edward Gibbon, considered this time a Golden Age and he once even called this era "the happiest time in all of history." That's probably overstating things a bit, but it was a good period for Rome. By that time, Rome had grown to encompass about 50 different provinces and about 50 million inhabitants. The empire stretched from Portugal in the west all the way to Mesopotamia in the east, and from Britain up in the north down to the Sahara desert in the south.

The Five Good Emperors are also sometimes called the Antonine Emperors, and that, like Julio-Claudian and Flavian, is a family name. The first of them really only ruled a short time, but it's with the second one that the series really got going. His name was Trajan, and Trajan was notable for being the first emperor to come from the provinces. He was from a town in Spain, and so his accession to the throne illustrated a shift in power from Italy to the provinces. It also mirrored a change in the composition of the Senate that was happening at this time, because as the decades went by, a higher and higher percentage of the members of the Senate weren't actually Italians, but were citizens whose origins were in the provinces. One of the keys to Rome's success and to its longevity as an empire was the way it's willing to incorporate and Romanize talented men from its provinces, and that's a theme that we'll come back to later.

Trajan had already had a substantial, distinguished career before he was selected as emperor; and in many ways, he earned the reputation of being the best emperor since Augustus. In his personal life, he was very sober; he was always very respectful to the Senate. He did have an interest in military conquests and in pushing out Rome's borders a bit more, so accordingly he launched an invasion of a region known as Dacia; this was an area enclosed by a large bend of the Danube River. You could almost see this war as a rational one, because by conquering Dacia, the frontier could be shortened and straightened. He also launched a war against the latest Mesopotamian-based empire, which was a group called the Parthians, and he won at least some temporary victories there. At one point, Mesopotamia itself actually became a province of the Roman Empire.

One of the benefits of the Dacian campaign was that he captured some rich gold mines, and Trajan used a lot of the income from those goldmines to build huge, elaborate public works including a brand new harbor to serve the city of Rome. Also, right in the center of Rome next to the old Roman Forum, he built a gigantic new complex that became known as the Forum of Trajan. The main enclosure of this was an area 600 by 1,000 feet in size, and it was entirely built of the finest imported exotic marbles and decorative stones. Right next to this was Trajan's Column, which depicted and commemorated his Dacian campaign. On one side of that column, he put a Latin library, and on the other side he put a Greek library.

Trajan in general acquired the reputation of nearly being an ideal emperor, so one of the titles that he earned was Optimus Princeps, which means "the best princeps." In later years, the Roman Senate would praise emperors that they regarded as good ones by using Trajan as a kind of yardstick to measure them against. For example, one standard acclamation that the Senate would shout at emperors was "Felicior Augusto, melior Traiano!" That translates as "Luckier than Augustus, better than Trajan! That sort of comparative chant could also be used by the Senate to condemn emperors whom they hated emperors. For example, after the death of the emperor Commodus, who was another crazy emperor, the Senate celebrated by chanting this very memorable phrase: "Saevior Domitiano, impurior Nerone!" which translates as "Crueler than Domitian, filthier than Nero!" That's a great insult.

Trajan selected as his heir a man named Hadrian, and Hadrian was another very well-qualified choice. He also had a long, respectable career before being adopted. Unlike Trajan, though, Hadrian didn't embark on any new conquests. He was more a patron of the arts, and in particular, he loved Greek culture. He was an absolutely enthusiastic admirer of all things Greek.

Hadrian's reign also illustrated one possible solution to the fact that the Roman Empire was simply growing too big to be effectively ruled by one man. Issues of control and communication during an era when technology was really quite low was a problem for all early empires, and that's a topic that we're going to examine more closely in an upcoming lecture. But think: How could an emperor at Rome really understand what was happening in a province far, far away? Hadrian's response to this was to travel constantly, and he actually spent many years of his reign on a grand tour, visiting every province of the empire in turn. His court was a mobile court that traveled along with him.

Hadrian had many mistresses as well, but the great, true passionate love of his life was a young, beautiful, curly-haired Greek youth named Antinoos. Antinoos went with Hadrian on all these travels until, tragically, in Egypt there was an accident and Antinoos drowned in the Nile River. Hadrian was devastated by the loss of his favorite, and he had innumerable marble statues of Antinoos made and distributed all over the empire. Because of the sheer number of these statues that were made, when you go to a museum today they're actually one of the most common Roman statues that you might encounter. Hadrian also founded a city in his honor named, as you might expect, Antinoopolis.

Back in Rome, Hadrian built some famous structures, including the Pantheon. Just outside of Rome, he built an enormous villa for himself in the countryside near the town of Tivoli. In this villa, he built various rooms and structures that reminded him of places that he'd visited on his grand tour. You can still go to the ruins of Hadrian's villa at Tivoli today and see the house that the emperor lived in.

The next emperor, Antoninus Pius, was another sound choice, but he really didn't do anything special or remarkable; we can think of him more as a caretaker rather than an innovator, so he kept the empire running smoothly.

His successor, however, was Marcus Aurelius, and would turn out to be the last of the Five Good Emperors. Marcus Aurelius is sometimes called the Philosopher-Emperor, and that's because he's an adherent of the Stoic school of philosophy, like Zeno and Seneca earlier. Marcus Aurelius even wrote a famous book that's called the *Meditations*, in which he speculates about how you lead a virtuous life and he talks about how one must try to do your best always, even under difficult circumstances. This was more than just an abstract topic for Marcus Aurelius, because he himself had to endure various difficulties in his reign. He had to contend with a number of new external threats to the empire, especially some barbarian groups in the north; a new tribe, the Marcomanni, and another group, the Sarmatians, both started to threaten Rome during his reign. Even more destructive, though, was an outbreak of plague that began in the east and spread throughout the empire and killed many, many people.

Marcus Aurelius was the last of the Five Good Emperors because when it came time for him to select a successor, he looked around, tried to find the best qualified person, and, despite all his supposed wisdom as a philosopher, he foolishly decided that   What do you know?   the best qualified person just happened to be his own son, Commodus. You can probably predict how well that's going to turn out. Commodus became emperor in 180 A.D., and so we regard the era of the Five Good Emperors as having stretched from 96–180 A.D. In addition to being wise, the Five Good Emperors also brought stability to the empire, since there were only five emperors over an 84-year stretch.

But now we have to turn to Commodus. Very far from being the best-qualified person, Commodus in reality was a spoiled child with delusions of godhood. In essence, he's another Caligula. Commodus also thought that he's the reincarnation of Hercules, and so he used to wander around the palace dressed in a lion skin like the Greek hero. Commodus also degraded the office of emperor by fighting in public as a gladiator in rigged contests, and Commodus also embarked on the by now standard course of terrorizing the Senate, engaging in debauchery, and spending too much money. Eventually, he was strangled in his bath.

The next emperor was almost immediately murdered by the Praetorian Guard, and this led to one of the most shameful moments in all of Roman history. That murder had effectively left the Praetorian Guard in charge of Rome, and so they decided they'd simply take advantage of this to make a quick buck. The Guard decided to stage an auction at which the item up for sale was nothing less than the office of emperor itself. Again, this incident, I think, clearly revealed the reality of power: It's the troops who could make or break an emperor. In the next century, as more people realized that fact, more and more emperors would gain the throne by military force.

As for the auction, they held it, and a rich man named Didius Julianus offered the highest price to the Praetorian Guard. He promised them 25,000 sesterces per man; that's about the equivalent of about 25 years' salary for an ordinary Roman legionary. The Guard's response to this offer was "Hail Didius, new emperor of Rome!" I hope he got his money's worth, because almost immediately, he got murdered as well.

At this point, the legions in the provinces decided they should get in on the action as well and, separately, the legions posted in Syria, Britain, and the Danube each proclaimed their own governor as the new emperor. These three governors or self-styled emperors with their respective armies all then raced to Rome and fought it out in a big civil war. The one who eventually emerged the victor from all this was the governor from the Danube region, a man named Septimius Severus.

Severus was the first of what we might call the "Soldier-Emperors"— sometimes books will call them the "Barracks Emperors"—and these were men who became emperor not by adoption or selection or any other thing, but because they simply could command the most troops. As in this example, typically they're provincial governors of frontier provinces that faced dangerous barbarians, and so those provinces had been assigned large armies under the control of the governor.

Severus was also from the town of Leptis Magna in North Africa, and so he represents the first African emperor. Again, that shows how power was shifting out to the provinces. He actually wasn't that bad of an emperor; he stabilized the situation and ruled effectively, if a little bit harshly, from 193–

211 A.D. He really was a military man, so he's very practical. His deathbed advice to his sons I think summarizes his entire philosophy. He said to them, "Enrich the soldiers, and despise everybody else."

From this point on, emperors would mostly gain power by brute force, and internal and external problems would multiply in the Roman Empire. The Empire had now begun what would be a long, mostly downhill slide. What's interesting is that even the Romans who lived at the time recognized this. For example, when writing about the death of the last of the Five Good Emperors, a Roman historian, Cassius Dio, wrote: "Our history now descends from a kingdom of gold, to one of iron and rust." That's an assessment that most modern historians pretty much agree with.

Having surveyed the rise of the Roman Empire, I'd now like to pause in the historical narrative to consider some key aspects of ancient empires in general, and particularly how Rome compared to the Chinese Empire. We'll look at that in the next couple lectures.

Han and Roman Empires Compared—Geography
Lecture 31

Many similarities, as well as some crucial differences, existed between the Roman and Han empires. Both were centralized, conservative, hierarchical, and status-oriented states; but Rome was a more heterogeneous culture, while China was a monoculture. Perhaps most curiously, the two contemporary powers had only the vaguest awareness of each other's existence. The enormous extent of both empires and the constraints of technology and distance presented particular challenges, which were met with similar responses: Construction of an extensive and well-engineered road network and heavy reliance on water transport.

Rome and Han China—Similarities

- The Han and Roman empires both flourished from around the beginning of the 2nd century B.C. until the end of the 2nd century A.D., when the last Han emperor abdicated and the death of the Roman emperor Septimius Severus ended the period of stable succession in Rome and the beginning of political chaos.

- In terms of size, the two empires were almost precisely equal. The Chinese census of 2 A.D. recorded a population of 58 million people, while the Roman Empire at the same date had approximately 55 million inhabitants. Han China formed a solid squarish shape measuring about 1,200 miles from east to west, and the same from north to south. The Roman Empire formed a ring of provinces encircling the Mediterranean Sea totaling about 1.5 million square land miles.

- Both empires had strong centralized governments and developed multilayered bureaucracies staffed with officials drawn from an educated class of landowners.

- Both constructed impressive road systems and massive hydrological projects to aid internal communication and transport.

- Both were threatened by recurrent invasions of nomadic barbarian tribes on their borders. In response, both maintained large armies and erected extensive networks of defensive walls.

- Both brought economic stability and prosperity to large areas while practicing intensive taxation and active regulation of vital foodstuffs.

- Both spread an elite culture and used social integration into this culture as a mechanism to assimilate outsiders and harness their energies on behalf of the state.

- Both viewed themselves as universal empires with a divine mandate to rule the entire world. Both asserted an ideology claiming that they brought civilization to the regions that they conquered, and used this as justification for conquest and as a means of co-opting local elites.

- Both had to endure episodes of weak or inept leadership and were constantly threatened with fragmentation due to internal political rivalries and factionalism.

- Both struggled with technological limitations in maintaining such geographically vast empires.

- Both eventually fell due to a combination of external threats, internal dissension, economic collapse, new religious movements, and endemic diseases. When they did collapse, both empires split into two halves, one of which was quickly taken over by barbarians while the other persisted and preserved the traditional regime for a considerable time.

- Both empires continued to exert a powerful influence on subsequent states through the strength and persistence of the image of empire that they created, and each served as the inspiration for and the ideal model of a successful empire for future generations.

Rome and Han China—Differences

- The Roman Empire arose out of the Roman Republic, and aspects of Republican ideology remained highly influential throughout imperial history, such as concepts of participation in government and the idea of citizenship itself, which had important legal and social privileges.

- China had no comparable concepts. In a sense, nearly everyone was a citizen, but this conferred no particular status or ideology of political participation.

- Romans were at least aware of a variety of possible forms of political organization, from Athenian democracy to the Near Eastern god-kings. In China, there was only a single, unquestioned, and universal model of rulership—monarchism.

- What the Han system of government did have that Rome lacked was a clear philosophical underpinning—Confucian and Legalist thought.

- The scale and use of slave labor were much more extensive in the Roman Empire than they were in Han China.

- The Roman world was an ethnically diverse and multicultural one, whereas Han China was a single, uniform monoculture. Individuals who adopted Roman ways usually retained their native language and customs as well, and in fact Greek culture was widely viewed as superior to and more sophisticated than that of the Romans; elite Romans aped and eventually fused Greek culture with their own. In contrast, Chinese culture was not only unquestionably both the dominant and the elite culture, but it was the only one to be found throughout the entire Han Empire.

Whispers along the Silk Road

- Although these two great empires covered large expanses of the globe—and perhaps even more impressively, between them accounted for an estimated one half of the world's population—they were largely unaware of each other. Their knowledge of one another came primarily from the trade goods that traversed the Silk Road.

- By land, they were separated by 4,500 miles of hostile deserts and mountains. The most direct sea route between them, connecting Egypt and Vietnam, was 6,500 miles long.

- There were a few moments when the two great empires came tantalizingly close to establishing contact. In 139 B.C., Emperor Wudi sent an envoy west to form alliances against the Xiongnu. After many misadventures, the envoy returned with many wondrous tales, including vague accounts of a large, impressive empire even further west—the first time that the Chinese heard about the existence of Rome.

- During the later Han period, several military expeditions brushed up against the border regions of the Roman Empire. In 97 A.D., one Chinese general actually reached the Persian Gulf and brought back information on the lands to the west, including a description of a great empire, but China pushed no further.

The Challenge of Geography

- The size of both empires made them both impressive, but size was also a severe challenge to cohesion. Some of the greatest technological advances of the past 100 years have been in the speed and ease of communication. Without such technology, in the Roman and Han empires, news might take weeks or even months to reach the emperor, and his response would take weeks or months to arrive on the scene.

- The Romans and the Han responded to this challenge in similar ways. Both constructed extensive and sophisticated road networks; both undertook colossal public works projects supporting waterborne transportation; and both set up systems of official couriers to carry government messages.

- In Rome, much of this construction was done by the army, so that when soldiers were not fighting, they were digging. Army units were accompanied by engineering detachments, which provided the direction and expertise to create the road system.

- The main Roman roads were marvels of practical engineering. A deep and solid foundation was excavated; then gravel or sand provided a base; and finally the roads were covered with carefully fitted paving stones.

- Major roads were usually 15 feet wide and crowned so that rainwater flowed off the sides into drainage ditches. The Romans also prided themselves on making their roads straight and level no matter what the terrain, so they became master bridge and tunnel builders as well. At least 350 Roman bridges are still standing, many bearing modern traffic.

- In China, starting during the reign of Shi Huangdi, a network of imperial highways radiating from the capital was built by using conscripted labor. The system included roads, way stations, inns, bridges, and raised causeways.

- No matter how fine the road, in the ancient world, transporting bulk goods by water was always much cheaper than moving them by land, so both empires expended vast resources on facilitating waterborne shipping.

- Most of the food for Rome's inhabitants was transported by water, but for a long time, the city lacked a really good harbor. In 42 A.D., Emperor Claudius tackled this problem by excavating a new artificial harbor called Portus and a series of canals. Trajan improved on Claudius's harbor a few decades later.

- Hundreds of Roman freighters busily plied the Mediterranean, bringing an estimated 600,000 tons of vital grain, olive oil, and wine to Rome's harbors every year.

- In China, the main routes of river communication were the Yellow River in the north and the Yangtze in the south. These and their attendant tributaries provided a good natural foundation for an internal Chinese trade and irrigation network.

- The main problems were that certain regions, particularly in the west, were not reached by these rivers, and both rivers flowed west to east, so there was no route for north-south communication. The solution to both problems was to dig canals.

- The Cheng Kuo canal, excavated under the Qin, opened up 450,000 acres of new land to intensive agriculture. Eventually, many of the existing canals were linked, forming the Grand Canal, which stretches 1,100 miles from Beijing to Hangzhou. This astonishing public work is the longest canal in the world and today serves as a main artery for trade in China.

China's Grand Canal is the culmination of imperial water-transport projects that began during the Qin dynasty.

- Despite all these efforts, the basic technological limitations on movement ensured that the central government could only react sluggishly and with considerable delay to problems arising in distant provinces.

- One of the fastest journeys we know of was made by Julius Caesar, who once achieved a speed of 100 miles per day overland. A more normal rate of travel, as suggested by the average distance between inns along Roman roads, was 16–20 miles per day overland. By sea, the vagaries of wind and weather could obviously greatly affect travel; one study suggests that a journey from the city of Rome to Egypt averaged about 30 days. Thus the optimal time for round-trip communication between Rome and its fringes was at least 2 months.

- This represents an ideal, and does not even take into account that Roman and Chinese highways were infested with bandits and sea travel was perhaps even more dangerous due to pirates, storms, and shipwrecks.

- In China, the roundtrip time for a message from the emperor to reach a border region and get a reply was probably a bit less than in the Roman empire, but it would still have been measured in weeks.

Suggested Reading

Chevallier, *Roman Roads.*

Laurence, *The Roads of Roman Italy.*

Mutschler and Mittag, eds., *Conceiving the Empire.*

Scheidel, ed., *Rome and China.*

1. Which of the similarities and differences between the Roman and Han empires do you think are the most important to keep in mind when attempting to compare the two?

2. People like to compare modern states and ancient ones (especially Rome), but given the fundamental technological limitations on communication and travel in the ancient world, how valid do you think such comparisons are?

Han and Roman Empires Compared—Geography
Lecture 31—Transcript

The Han and Roman empires both flourished from around the beginning of the 2nd century B.C. until the end of the 2nd century A.D. As we've just seen over the last series of lectures on Rome, Rome had been founded much earlier than 200 B.C., but you could say that Rome really didn't become a power affecting the broader Mediterranean until after its decisive victory over Carthage in 202 B.C. In a remarkable coincidence, that same year, 202 B.C. was the year that Liu Bang became emperor in China and founded the Han Dynasty. Four centuries later, the last Han emperor abdicated in 220 A.D., while in the West, the death of the Roman emperor Septimius Severus in 211 A.D. marked the end of the stable succession of emperors and the beginning of a period of political chaos. The Roman Empire would continue to exist for several more centuries, but there's no doubt that from this point on, it's a story of decline. While the Roman Empire existed for several centuries before and after the Han Dynasty, its peak is almost exactly contemporaneous with it.

Furthermore, if we look at the size of the two empires, they're almost precisely equal. The Chinese census of 2 A.D. recorded a population of 58 million people, while the Roman Empire at the same date is estimated to have had 55 million inhabitants. In terms of geographic extent, the Roman Empire at first glance seems to much bigger; it stretched 3,000 miles from Britain to Mesopotamia and 2,000 miles north-south. In contrast, the territory of the Han formed a solid square measuring about 1,200 miles east-west and the same from north-south. But the Roman Empire was really just a coastal empire; it consisted of a ring of provinces encircling the Mediterranean Sea. If we add up just the area of the land portions and omit the sea, then we find that the Roman Empire occupied about 1.5 million square miles, which happens to be exactly the square area of the Han Empire.

The Han and the Roman empires, though, form an interesting pair for comparison for reasons that go way beyond just those basic facts that they existed at the same time and were about the same size. Both empires had strong centralized governments, and both developed multilayered bureaucracies that were staffed with officials drawn from an educated class of landowners. Both empires constructed impressive road systems, and also huge hydrological projects, the purpose of which was to aid internal communication and transport. Both empires found themselves threatened by recurrent invasions of nomadic barbarian tribes on their borders, especially their northern borders; and in response, both empires ended up maintaining large, highly-organized armies and they built extensive networks of defensive walls. Both empires brought economic stability and prosperity to large areas while at the same time practicing intensive taxation, and they both took an active in regulating vital foodstuffs.

Both of these empires also spread an elite culture, and they used social integration into that culture as a mechanism to assimilate outsiders and really to harness their energies on behalf of the centralized state. Both empires viewed themselves as universal empires that had a kind of divine mandate to rule over the entire world. Both asserted an ideology that claimed that they were bringing civilization to the regions that they conquered, and they used that as a justification for those conquests, and they also used it as a way to co-opt local elites. Both empires had to endure episodes where they went through weak or sometimes even inept leadership, and both empires were constantly threatened with fragmentation because of internal political rivalries and factionalism. Both empires struggled with basic technological limitations of the time, and a lot of these had to do with how to maintain such a huge empire with the technology that was available.

Both of these empires would eventually fall due to a combination of external threats, internal dissension, economic collapse, new religious movements, and endemic disease. When they did collapse, interestingly, both empires split into two halves; one of those halves in each case was quickly taken over by barbarians, while the other half in both cases preserved the traditional regime for a long time. Finally, even long after both empires had dissolved and disappeared, each continued to exert a powerful influence on subsequent developments; and this was done through the image of empire that they created, and each empire would serve as an inspiration for and really a kind of ideal model of a successful empire for future generations.

In addition to all those many similarities, there were also some key differences between the two. The Roman Empire arose out of the Roman

Republic, and even after the creation of the emperor, aspects of that old Republican ideology of widespread participation in government remained very influential; and that was tied in with the semi-democratic system of the Roman Republic in which you had the concept of citizenship as being a participatory one. For most of Roman history, citizenship was a highly-coveted and special status, and it's held by only a small minority of people living within the Roman Empire. Being a Roman citizen brought with it important legal and social privileges.

China was completely different; they had no comparable concept. I suppose in a sense, in China everybody was a citizen; but that didn't bring you any particular extra status, and there was no ideology of political participation as there was in Rome. The Romans were very much aware that there were a variety of possible forms of political organization, ranging from things like the radical democracy of 5th-century Athens to the totalitarian god-kings of the Near East. But in China, there was really only the single, unquestioned, and universal model of rulership, and that was monarchy. What the Han system of government had that Rome lacked was a clear philosophical underpinning that offered a consistent and clear rationalization for the structure of the government. Of course, this philosophical foundation was that fusion of Confucian and Legalist thought that played such a central role in training Chinese bureaucrats. Another institution that did play a significant role in both the social and economic structure of the Roman Empire was slavery. The scale and use of slave labor was much more extensive in the Roman Empire than it was in Han China.

Another of the really important differences was that the Roman world was an ethnically diverse and what today we might call a multicultural one, whereas Han China was a single, uniform monoculture. Even though various aspects of Roman civilization spread throughout the cities of the empire, there always were many, many distinct local and indigenous traditions and ethnicities that thrived within the Roman world. Even individuals, they might adopt certain Roman ways, but often simultaneously they'd retain their own native language and their local customs. The culture of one of those groups that was conquered by the Romans, the Greeks, was also widely viewed as a superior one and more sophisticated than the Romans; and indeed, it's one that elite Romans themselves would imitate and eventually fuse in with their own.

Again, China forms a dramatic contrast: Chinese culture was unquestionably the dominant and the elite culture, but more than that it's the only one to be found all throughout the Han Empire. For example, in the Roman Empire, Latin was the official language of law and politics, but a person just walking through the streets of Rome would've heard a myriad of different languages being spoken and that same person would see temples not just to the gods of the Greco-Roman pantheon, but they'd have seen dozens of temples and shrines to an amazingly diverse array of exotic foreign gods and cults.

It's a little bit ironic that although these two empires covered huge expanses of the globe and, maybe more impressively, between them accounted for an estimated one half of the world's population at that time, they seem to have been largely unaware of each other. Their knowledge of one another came mainly from the trade goods that traversed the Silk Road, but there seems to have been no direct contact between their governments and really only the most dim awareness that the other even existed. Of course, that's due to geography: By land, Rome and the Han Empire were separated by 4,500 miles of what really were hostile desert and mountains, and even the most direct sea route, which would connect Egypt and Viet Nam, was about 6,500 miles long.

Nevertheless, there were a few moments when these two great empires came tantalizingly close to establishing contact with one another, but none of those chances seem to have quite panned out. For example, in 139 B.C., Wudi sent an envoy west to try and form some alliances against the Xiongnu. This envoy had all kinds of adventures, including for 10 years he's actually held captive by the Xiongnu; but he's an intrepid guy and eventually he managed to escape and get back to China. In addition to accounts of the various tribes of Central Asia, accounts of the wonders in India, he also brought back vague stories of a large, impressive empire even further to the west. This may well have been the very first time that the Chinese heard about the existence of Rome.

During the later Han period, there were several military expeditions sent westward that brushed up against border regions of the Roman Empire. In particular, in 97 A.D., one Chinese general actually reached the Persian Gulf, and then he turned around and came back. When he returned, he brought back information on the lands further to the west, including a description of a great empire, and this was clearly Rome. According to him, he said this empire ruled over many smaller states and contained many large cities. If he'd only pushed just a little bit further, almost certainly he'd have encountered a Roman outpost; but he didn't, and so what's probably the best opportunity for establishing contact between the two empires was lost.

Thus far in this lecture, I've been mostly noting broad similarities and differences between the two empires. But now I want to focus in on some specific aspects of the Han and Roman empires and look at those in greater detail. For the rest of the lecture, I'll start by considering what is one of the most basic similarities between the Han and Roman empires: their size. The enormous geographic extent of these empires is at the same time one of the characteristics that makes them impressive, but it's also something that proved to be a severe challenge to their cohesion. These were massive political entities, and the fact that their respective governments just managed to exercise any kind of control over such enormous distances is truly an incredible achievement in an era without any form of communications technology.

If you think about it, some of the greatest technological advances of the last 100 years have been in the speed and ease of communication. Today, we think absolutely nothing of being able to send texts, images, and even our voices all around the globe nearly instantaneously. But just stop and think for a moment what life was like prior to, say, 200 years ago. In that era, the fastest that a message could move was limited to how rapidly a human, or maybe an animal such as a horse, could travel, or how quickly a ship could be powered by the wind. Under those circumstances, traveling a 100 miles in 24 hours would be regarded as blindingly fast and exceptional, and really the standard distance that anybody could travel in a day prior to about 200 years ago was 20 miles per day. So in the Roman and Han empires, if there was a rebellion, or a natural disaster, or anything else that required the emperor's attention, it might take weeks or even months for news of that to reach him, and then additional weeks or months for his answer or response to arrive on the scene. That basic technological limitation on the speed of communication in the ancient world constituted maybe the most formidable challenge that any ancient empire had to overcome.

The way that the Romans and the Han responded to that challenge was actually very similar: Both empires constructed very extensive and sophisticated road networks; both of them undertook truly colossal public works projects that were centered around improving water-borne transportation; and both empires eventually set up a system of official couriers who'd carry government messages.

The Romans began work on their famous road network quite early in their history—as I talked about, during their wars to conquer the Italian peninsula, they started building these roads—and by the time of the early empire, it was just standard practice to build an elaborate road in any territories that the Romans acquired. A lot of this construction work was done by the Roman army; so when Roman soldiers weren't fighting, they actually spent an awful lot of time digging. Roman army units were always accompanied by an engineering detachment, so that would provide the direction and expertise to create the road system.

The main Roman roads were marvels of practical engineering. First, they'd make a deep and solid foundation. Then they'd put gravel or sand to provide a kind of base. Finally, the roads were often covered with carefully fitted paving stones. Major Roman highways were usually at least 15 feet wide and were built with a crown so that rainwater would quickly flow to the sides and into drainage ditches. The Romans also had a thing about making their roads straight and level no matter what the terrain was; so if there's a mountain in the way, they'd bore a tunnel through it; if there's a river or a valley, they'd simply build a bridge across it. I think it's a measure of the quality of their construction that at least 350 Roman bridges are still standing today, and a lot of those are actually carrying modern traffic. One of the more common artifacts surviving from the Roman world are milepost-markers that were set up along these roads, and they almost always declare not just the distance— usually measured in miles from Rome—but they also proudly list the military unit that constructed them. The total length of this elaborate road network, counting both the major and the small roads, has been estimated to be about 50,000 miles; and you could say that by the height of the Roman Empire, one could travel every step of the way from Spain to Jerusalem on well-crafted Roman paving stones.

In China, beginning during the reign of the emperor Shi Huangdi, a network of imperial highways radiating out from the capital was built; and in China, it wasn't the army, this was conscripted labor of the peasantry. This served to link the various parts of the country together. These were nice roads; they were wide; they had shade trees planted at 30-foot intervals; and the whole system included not just the roadways, but also way stations, inns, bridges, and raised causeways. Like the Romans, the Han were concerned with providing good access over mountainous regions. For example, in 63 A.D., the officials in southwest Shensi rebuilt just a little segment of the imperial highway that went through the mountains, and that one project resulted in the construction of 67 miles of road, five major bridges, 623 trestles, and 64 other buildings such as rest houses and post stations. By the end of the Qin Dynasty, a core network of high-quality roads stretched about 4,000 miles, and then the later Han emperors added on to that. One highway, which was known as "The Straight Road," ran in a line 600 miles, and it connected the capital to Inner Mongolia. Both the Romans and the Han emperors set up a post service that consisted of way stations and horse relays and riders that could carry messages from the capital to those outlying regions along the roads.

No matter how nice the road was, in the ancient world, transporting goods, especially bulk goods, by water was always much, much cheaper than moving them by land; and so both empires spent a lot of resources on trying to facilitate waterborne shipping. It's been estimated by scholars that the cost of shipping one wagonload of grain from one end of the Mediterranean Sea to the other was actually cheaper than moving that same wagonload 75 miles overland; so water transport's much cheaper than land. While it's a little bit more costly to move goods along a river than over the open ocean, river transport was still many, many times more efficient than land transport.

As you might expect, then, most of the food for Rome's inhabitants came in by water; but for a long time, Rome lacked a really first-rate harbor. The available existing harbor of Ostia didn't have a safe anchorage for ships, so in 42 A.D., the emperor Claudius finally tackled this problem by building a new artificial harbor that was 1,000 yards in width, and he just carved this out of the Italian coastline. This huge basin was connected to Ostia, the port, and to the Tiber River by a whole series of canals. This harbor was known as Portus, and it did have big breakwaters, but still it seems to have been a fairly dangerous anchorage. We know, for example, in 62 A.D., a storm came by that sunk over 200 ships within the harbor. Finally, though, Rome got a first-rate harbor when the emperor Trajan rebuilt Portus, and he added on a new inner harbor where ships would be completely safe from storms. This inner harbor was a giant hexagon in shape, 700 yards wide, and completely lined with very nicely-made quays, mooring points, warehouses, and all kinds of things. Today, when you fly into Rome, the modern airport is actually partially built over Portus, the ancient harbor, and if land on the right runway, you can still see that hexagonal basin of Trajan as your plane comes in for a landing. Hundreds of Roman freighters busily plied the Mediterranean, bringing an estimated 600,000 tons of grain, olive oil, and wine into Rome's harbor every single year.

In China, the main routes of riverine communication were those two great parallel river systems: the Yellow River in the north and then the Yangtze River in the south. Those two rivers, with all their attendant tributaries, provided a very nice natural foundation for an internal waterborne trade and irrigation network. The problem was that were certain regions, especially in western China, which weren't reached by those two rivers. The other problem was that both the rivers flowed from the west to the east, and so trade in that direction was easy, but going north-south was much more difficult.

The solution to both those problems was simply to dig canals. The canals could bring water to the drier regions, and you could dig canals that would establish north-south links between the existing rivers. From a very early date in Chinese history, various dynasties began giant canal projects; and, as you might expect, those efforts intensified under centralized governments such as those of the Qin and the Han dynasties. For example, the Cheng Kuo Canal, which was excavated by the Qin, opened up almost half a million acres of new land to intensive agriculture, and it helped to feed those large armies that the Qin were putting in the field. Eventually, a lot of the existing canals would all be linked together, and they'd form one that's now called the Grand Canal, and it stretches over 1,100 miles from Beijing in the north down to Hangzhou in the south. It's really an amazing public work. It's the longest canal in the world, and even today it's still used as a main artery for trade within China. All those various segments that make up the Grand Canal weren't fully connected together until just after the Han era during the Sui Dynasty, but most of the individual parts were already excavated and working at a regional level at least in the earlier period.

Despite all of those efforts, those basic technological limitations on movement made sure that the central governments of Rome and the Han could only react very sluggishly and with an enormous delay to any problem that arose in the distant provinces. Ancient Roman sources include frequent references to the amount of time it took for information to just travel the roads and sea lanes of the Roman world. From these, we can calculate the maximum speeds for communication in the ancient world, as well as what would've been more typical times.

One of the very fastest journeys that we know of was actually made by a famous man, Julius Caesar, who, in an emergency and really calling upon all of his wealth and the resources that were available to someone like him, achieved a speed of nearly 100 miles per day overland; so that's about the fastest you could go. A more normal rate of travel is suggested by the average distance between inns, how they're spaced, along the Roman roads, and they seemed to always be quite consistently 16–20 miles apart; and so that strongly suggests that that's the length of an average day's journey along the Roman road system. If you're traveling by sea, obviously the variables of wind and weather could affect your travel time, but it's still possible to study the amount of the time it took ships carrying announcements of an emperor's death in Rome to reach Egypt, and looking at those it suggests that an average time for news to go from Rome to Egypt by see was about 30 days. Similar to that same rate of travel are comments by the Roman statesman Cicero, who regarded it a very, very quick passage when letters that he wrote to his son, who was a student off in Athens, made it from Italy to Greece in about three weeks.

All of that indicates that a Roman emperor who wanted to send instructions to one of his governors on the far eastern or western edges of the empire really couldn't expect his orders to get there in let's say less than a month. He'd then have to wait another full month for a reply from that governor to come back; so the optimal amount of time for a basic exchange of information in the Roman Empire between central government and the fringes was probably at least two months.

That even still represents an ideal; it doesn't even take into account the probability that these messages would never even reach the people they're intended for. Roman highways were absolutely infested with bandits who'd rob and murder travelers; and sea travel was maybe even more dangerous, because not only were there pirates all over the seas, but there were considerable perils to be faced from storms and shipwrecks. If you look at Roman tombstones, one very common line that you see on a lot of Roman tombstones is the phrase *interfectus a latronibus*, which means "killed by bandits." Another indication of how big a deal banditry was is that in a surviving list of the duties of a Roman governor, the very first thing mentioned is to suppress bandits.

If we look at China, bandits were also rife there. We see them featuring prominently in all sorts of surviving novels, and they're often very colorful figures, at least in the books. In China, the roundtrip time for a message from the emperor to go to a border region and get a reply was probably a little bit less than the Roman Empire, but it still would've been something that you're measuring in weeks.

In the next lecture, we'll continue this comparison of the Roman and Han empires, and we'll focus in on these systems of administration that each set up in an attempt to try and govern these geographically vast areas. First, we'll look at the various levels of official and unofficial bureaucracies that eventually evolved to do things like control behavior and collect taxes, and then we'll look at the guy at the top of the ladder, the emperor himself, and evaluate aspects of his role and influence in the structure of political power in these two great empires.

Han and Roman Empires Compared—Government
Lecture 32

Both the Romans and the Han effectively administered vast empires, but they did so by very different means. Han administration was a model of clarity, structure, and hierarchy built on Confucian and Legalist principles, while Roman administration was a study in improvisation based on a combination of Republican tradition and convenient local systems. The Chinese and Roman emperors wielded their greatest power through appointing their top officials. They played different roles in the eyes of their people; the Chinese emperor was remote and distant; the Roman emperor, in the Republican tradition, regularly appeared among the masses.

Chinese Bureaucracy—The Epitome of Order

- Just what role did a Chinese or Roman emperor play and, more broadly, what did their governments and administrators do for the people who lived within the borders of their empires? Rome and China form an interesting comparison, since both are renowned for successful and long-lasting political hegemony, yet their methods were quite different.

- The most obvious difference is in the size of their imperial bureaucracies. Han China had a formally defined, rigid hierarchy of 120,000 government bureaucrats. Rome had fewer than 200 senior administrators assisted by an informal network of perhaps 30,000 friends, clients, slaves, and local elites. Han China had perhaps one administrator for every 450 people, whereas Rome had one formal administrator per quarter million people.

- Han administration was a paragon of clarity and organization. At the top were the emperor, his family, and his court. Next were three officials known as the Senior Statesmen who served as the intermediaries between the emperor and the rest of the government.

- Below the senior statesmen were the Nine Ministers; each was the head of a different division of government. Beneath them were 20 grades of government officials arranged in a strict hierarchy. Each grade had a specific salary, a specific document seal, and wore a sash of a certain color.

- Chinese officials were career bureaucrats who started at the bottom and hoped to rise through the ranks. Entrance into this hierarchy was gained by passing the civil service examinations. In theory, these were open to all candidates and a route of social mobility. In practice, only sons of the landed gentry could afford the time and leisure to study the Confucian classics that formed the basis of the exams.

- Geographically, Han China was divided into 80 to 100 provinces and subdivided into 1,500 regions. At the lowest level, village officials were responsible for collecting taxes, enforcing edicts, and keeping accurate records.

- Underlying the entire system was an ethical code of conscientious duty derived from Confucian-Legalist doctrine. Its emphasis on selfless service, obedience, and acting as a positive role model served to curb governmental corruption.

- The civil service exams identified individuals with talent and harnessed their abilities and energy in the service of the state. This brought new talent into the government and prevented frustrated individuals from using their skills to undermine the central authority.

Roman Administration—Ad Hoc and Organic

- The Roman bureaucracy developed as Rome expanded and made great use of informal agents. Romans in general were obsessed with tradition and were reluctant to innovate, and for several centuries they labored to run a far-flung empire with a bureaucracy that had been designed to run a single city.

- By the late 1st century A.D., the Roman Empire consisted of about 50 provinces, each run by a governor figure. There two types of provinces. In senatorial ones, the governor was called a proconsul and was appointed by the senate. Provinces with a substantial military presence were imperial provinces and were governed by a legate appointed by the emperor.

- Most senatorial provinces also had a quaestor in charge of financial affairs, and some senatorial and imperial provinces had one or more assistants to the governor known as procurators. Obviously, this was not enough administrators to run an entire region.

- Each formal administrator retained a large group of personal assistants drawn from the ranks of his friends, clients, slaves, and freedmen. They also made extensive use of local elites—tribal leaders, town councilmen, and local aristocrats who had been in control before the Romans took over a region.

- Early on, this minimalist approach to administration was also made possible by farming out many governmental functions to private concerns. Particularly in the Roman Republic, the majority of taxes were not collected by government officials but rather by private corporations.

- Fascinating insight into the workings of Roman administration can be gained from a set of more than 100 letters written between Emperor Trajan and Pliny the Younger, a governor in Asia Minor. Pliny seeks Trajan's advice even on seemingly trivial matters, and one at times gets the sense of mild annoyance from Trajan.

- The Roman reliance on local elites and city councils meant that many Roman cities were effectively self-governing. The Roman approach was exactly the opposite of the Chinese one: In Han China, the officials were brought in from distant regions to govern, because outsiders were thought to provide more objective administration than locals.

- Whereas many low-level governmental positions in China such as clerks and record keepers were filled by salaried officials, the same sorts of jobs in the Roman Empire were handled by public slaves owned by a city or community. Otherwise, however, in both China and Rome, most officials were drawn from the landed elite.

- Whereas China's officials might be termed scholar-bureaucrats, Rome's were amateur gentleman administrators, analogous to the well-educated gentleman who later administered the British Empire.

- The ideology that underlay Chinese bureaucracy was Confucianism-Legalism; upper-class Roman administrators were motivated by the old Roman pursuit of *dignitas*. Over time, the Roman administration became more like the Chinese one—larger and more rigid and more logically organized.

Comparing Emperors

- In both Rome and China, emperors who were energetic, such as Wudi, or even just dedicated, like Vespasian, could exert their authority to dramatic effect. In both empires, perhaps one of the emperor's most influential functions was appointing senior administrators and generals.

- While the theoretical power of the emperors was unlimited, in reality, they were always struggling against the time and distance constraints on communication. The state bureaucracy had to step in and deal with most local issues on its own.

- The inhabitants of the city of Rome often benefited from the emperor's presence through his benefactions: free monthly distributions of grain from the state, colossal public feasts and handouts of money, and extravagant public spectacles.

- On the other hand, proximity to a bad or crazy emperor could be a dangerous situation. The senators were frequent targets for the wrath of such emperors, and even common people in Rome could unexpectedly fall victim to their outbursts.

- Some emperors found their relative lack of control over affairs outside the capital troubling and attempted to do something about it. Emperor Hadrian literally took his court on the road. He spent much of his reign engaged in a series of grand tours.

- Hadrian's travels have an interesting parallel in the grand tours undertaken by Chinese emperors such as Shi Huangdi, who made five of these great journeys during his reign, visiting a different region each time.

Hadrian spent the bulk of his reign touring the empire.

- Shi Huangdi's itinerary was largely dictated by his desire to visit various sacred spots and perform rituals at them. Although he traveled widely, he was a remote figure who was almost never visible to his subjects.

- Hadrian's trips, on the other hand, sprang in part from Republican tradition. The people of Rome no longer had the power to elect their ruler, but they still had the power to symbolically approve his legitimacy through their shouted acclamations.

Alcock et al., eds., *Empires*.

Millar, *The Emperor in the Roman World*.

Mutschler and Mittag, eds. *Conceiving the Empire*.

1. What are the respective advantages and disadvantages of the Roman and Han systems of bureaucracy, and which in the end do you think was more effective?

2. A striking contrast between Rome and Han China was the way the Roman emperor was expected to be visible and accessible versus the Chinese tradition of seclusion. How does this reflect broader conflicts in fundamental attitudes and values of Roman and Chinese cultures?

Lecture 32: Han and Roman Empires Compared—Government

Han and Roman Empires Compared—Government
Lecture 32—Transcript

According to the ancient historian Cassius Dio, one day the Roman emperor Hadrian was hurrying along a road when he was approached by a woman who shouted out that she had a petition that she wanted to present to him. Hadrian replied that he was too busy to stop, at which the woman angrily shouted out, "Then you should stop being emperor!" This little anecdote raises interesting questions about what the expectations were for an emperor, at least in terms of his duties and the obligations that he owed to the citizens who he ruled over. Of course, in this anecdote, Hadrian, who was a good emperor and was very hardworking, immediately stopped, turned back, and listened to the woman's concerns (though one's tempted to be a bit skeptical of such a positive outcome in the majority of cases).

In this lecture, I want to explore this issue of government and administration for both the Roman and the Chinese empires. First, I'll focus on the structure of the administration and the identity and training of the people who functioned as imperial bureaucrats; and second, I want to begin to consider the man at the top, the emperor himself.

In regards to administration, Rome and China form a very interesting comparison, because both emperors are renowned for having maintained successful and long-lasting political hegemony over huge empires. However, the methods by which they did this were very, very different. The most obvious difference between the two is in the size of the imperial bureaucracy. Both administrations had to oversee about 55 million people spread out over about 1.5 million square miles. Han China did that with a formally defined, rigid hierarchy of 120,000 government bureaucrats. Rome, on the other hand, did that same thing with fewer than 200 senior administrators, though they were informally assisted by a network of maybe 30,000 friends, clients, slaves, and local elites. You could argue that in Han China, there was about one administrator for every 450 people, whereas in Rome, there was only one formal administrator for every quarter million people.

Let's begin with the organization of the Han government. Overall, the Han administration was really a paragon of clarity and organization. At the very top were the emperor, his family, and the imperial court, and we'll look at those in more detail a little bit later. Next were three officials who were known as Senior Statesmen, and their real role was to serve as intermediaries between the emperor and his court and the rest of the government, and because of that they played a key role in setting policy in general. Next, there's a level of nine Ministers, and each of those was the head of a different major division of government, such as religion, the economy, foreign affairs, transportation, the law, security, finance, and the palace. Then beneath those were 20 descending grades of government officials arranged in a strict hierarchy from highest down to lowest. Every single one of those grades had a specific salary, which ranged from 10,000 bushels of wheat per year for the top highest level down to just 100 bushels of wheat per year for the most junior level of bureaucrats. Each grade had a specific seal that they'd use to stamp or mark documents and they'd also carry this as a visible symbol of their status. Each level would wear a sash of a certain color, which also would immediately tell you what level bureaucrat they were. These were career bureaucrats. They'd start at the bottom, and each one would hope to rise through the ranks as high as they possibly could get. They got one day out of every six as vacation, and when they retired, they could hope to get one-third of their ordinary salary as a kind of pension.

Entrance into that hierarchy was gained by passing the civil service examinations. Remember, in theory, those were open to all candidates; and so they offered an important route of potential social mobility. In practice, though, the only people who could really afford the huge amounts of time and leisure to study the Confucian classics that formed the basis of those exams were fairly wealthy landowners. They tended to be the local elites, so the bureaucratic class of China was drawn primarily from the ranks of this sort of landed gentry. The Imperial Academy, the university set up by Wudi, functioned as a feeder of well-prepared candidates for the civil service exams.

Chinese literature is absolutely stuffed full of stories that revolve around success or failure at these civil service exams. Often these stories involve pairs of childhood friends, one of whom passes the exams and the other of whom fails them, and as a result subsequently they have very divergent life-paths. Candidates could take the exams over and over again, so these stories will feature an initially unsuccessful candidate who eventually then goes on to a stellar career. A great many of these exam stories have what we might call humorous punch lines. For example, one well-known story concerns two men from the same village who were named Peng and Zhan and, of course, they're married to a pair of sisters. Peng passed the exams the first time he took them and he became a high-status official and became very full of himself, but Zhan failed. Humiliated, he then devoted himself to study, and after many years he, too, eventually passed the exam. As the story goes, Peng one day was riding a donkey through the countryside when news reached him of his old rival's success, and he was so astonished to hear that he'd finally passed the exam that he fell out of the saddle. As a result, the following little couplet became popular in their district, and it goes: "When Zhan the exams did pass / Peng fell off his ass."

In terms of geographic organization, China during the Han period was divided up into between 80 and 100 provinces; sometimes you'll see these called *commanderies*. These in turn were subdivided into 1,500 regions, sometimes called counties. At these lowest levels of administration, the village officials were responsible for doing almost everything: collecting taxes, enforcing imperial edicts, and keeping accurate records, the most important of which was the land register, which showed who owned what. We'll look at the Chinese military in another lecture, but senior generals were directly appointed by the emperor and they held stipends and rank just below the level of the Nine Ministers.

Overall, the Chinese system was one of perfect clarity and organization. Everyone had precisely defined duties and responsibilities, and the status distinctions between all the officials were clear and public. Remember, underlying this entire system was the ethical code of conscientious duty that was derived from Confucian-Legalist doctrine, and with its emphasis on selfless service, on obedience, and always trying to act as a positive role model, this ethos was cultivated as a way to try and curb governmental corruption. The system of civil service exams performed an important function in identifying individuals who had talent and then harnessing their abilities and energy in the service of the state. It's vital to have some sort of mechanism like that to bring new talent into the government and to prevent frustrated individuals from being tempted to use their talent and their skills to instead undermine the central authority.

When we turn to the administration of the Roman Empire in the 1st and 2nd centuries A.D., we see a very, very, very different picture. The Roman bureaucracy was much less preplanned. It's really just a jumbled assemblage of ad hoc positions and offices that had kind of organically developed as Rome expanded, and it made a lot more use of informal agents to flesh out the lack of formal bureaucratic officials. The Romans, as always, were obsessed with tradition, and so they're very reluctant to innovate; and this stubbornness at times could be one of their great strengths, but it could also be a weakness, and we see this clearly in the case of imperial administration. For centuries, the Romans labored to run this enormous, far-flung empire with a bureaucracy that had really been designed just to run a single city, and it's only with the greatest reluctance that they added new magistrates to the existing system.

By the late 1st century A.D., the Roman Empire consisted of about 50 provinces, and each of those was run by an administrator who, in essence, acted as a kind of governor for that province. Technically speaking, there were really two separate types of provinces. There were senatorial provinces, and in these the governor was called a proconsul and he was appointed by the Senate. Provinces, however, which had a large military presence in them, a big army, were called imperial provinces, and these were governed by a man called a legate and he was a direct appointee of the emperor. Most senatorial provinces also had a quaestor, who was a magistrate in charge of financial stuff. Finally, some senatorial and imperial provinces, though not all of them, had one or more assistants to the governor known as procurators. In a senatorial province, the formal state-appointed bureaucrats might just consist of three men: the proconsul, the quaestor, and the procurator.

Obviously, three men weren't enough administrators to run a huge region; and so this gap was filled, first of all, by the fact that each one of those formal administrators would've come out to the province with a huge retinue of personal assistants. Some of these may have been provided by the state, but most of them were drawn from the ranks of his friends, his clients, his slaves, and his freedmen. In the same way that the informal institution of the patronage system played an important role in the Roman social relations, so also these informal bureaucrats played an important role in Roman political administration.

Secondly, the Romans liked to make extensive use of local elites who could then control their own populations. Tribal leaders, local town councilmen, and local aristocrats all were people who'd be cultivated by the Romans and really pressed into service by them as proxies for the Romans. Often, these were the very same sorts of people who'd been in control before the Romans took over a region, and so now effectively they continued to wield local power while, of course, paying deference to the greater power of Rome. In many ways, this was an efficient system. After all, a local leader was going to be the person who had the greatest knowledge of local problems and probably how to solve them as well, and they'd have all the personal connections to facilitate that sort of thing.

At least early on, this minimalist approach to administration was also made possible by in essence farming out many things that we think of as governmental functions to private concerns. For example, especially during the Roman Republic, the majority of taxes weren't collected by government officials but instead they're collected by private corporations that would bid to get the contract to collect taxes in a certain region.

Due to the constraints on communication that I talked about in the last lecture, governors obviously had to exercise a large amount of autonomous power, but, nevertheless, they'd always at least try to consult with the central authority as much as was possible. The form this often took was direct correspondence with the emperor. A really fascinating insight into the workings of Roman administration can be gained from a set of over 100 surviving letters that were written between the emperor Trajan and one of his provincial governors in Asia Minor, a man named Pliny the Younger. One of the surprising aspects of this correspondence is how Pliny the governor seeks Trajan the emperor's advice even on incredibly trivial matters, as when Pliny bothers the ruler of the entire Roman world with a request for permission to cover over a stinky sewer that runs through the forum of some obscure provincial town. In Trajan's replies, you can sometimes get a sense of mild annoyance with this sort of minutiae with which Pliny's letters were pestering him. For example, in reply to a letter concerning requests by some Greek cities to build various public works, we have a reply by Trajan, and he says: "My dear Pliny, you are on the scene and can best determine what should be done about the theater at Nicaea. Just let me know what you decide." Clearly, he would've preferred that many of these issues were handled locally. Pliny also had an unfortunate penchant for asking Trajan to send experts from Rome out to solve problems in his province, and often Trajan politely but very firmly declined these petitions, as when later in the very same letter he said:

> You decide what to advise the people of Claudiopolis about the bath which they have begun on what seems to me a very unfortunate site. There must be local architects. Every province has its share of clever and skillful professionals. Do not always assume that the quickest solution is to get help from Rome. Most architects come from Greece anyway.

The Roman reliance on local elites and on city councils meant that many Roman cities were effectively self-governing. The Roman approach to government here was exactly the opposite of the Chinese one. In Han China, the officials who were sent out by the state to rule over an area were intentionally chosen so as not to be from that region. These detached state agents were thought to provide a more objective administration than if the bureaucrats had been drawn from that region and that would mean they might be enmeshed in local rivalries and have local prejudices. Also, whereas many low-level governmental positions in China—things like clerks and record-keepers—were all filled by professional, salaried officials, but those same sorts of jobs in the Roman Empire tended to be handled by public slaves that were owned collectively by a city or a community.

There was a kind of basic similarity between the two administrations, however, and that's that the class from which the main administrators were drawn was moderately to very wealthy landowning families. Those were the ones who most frequently took the civil service exams in China, and almost all the higher-ranking Roman officials were exclusively drawn from a group of traditional, landowning, aristocratic families. Whereas we might term China's officials scholar-bureaucrats, in a sense Rome's were amateur gentleman administrators. In a lot of ways, these officials of Rome were analogous to the class of well-educated aristocratic gentleman-landowners that Victorian Britain drew upon to administer its colonial empire. If the ideology that underlay Chinese bureaucracy was Confucianism-Legalism, upper-class Roman administrators were motivated by that old Roman pursuit of status in the form of *dignitas*. Over time, the Roman administration slowly became a little bit more like the Chinese one: It grew larger, it grew more rigid, and it became somewhat more logically organized. In particular, there were a whole series of reforms in the late 3rd century A.D. that resulted in a sweeping reorganization of the provinces, and at the end of that there were now 100 standardized provinces that were grouped into four bigger districts, a there's a very substantial increase in the number of formal bureaucrats. That same reform also separated the civilian and the military commands.

Let's turn now to the top administrator himself, the emperor, and look a little bit at his role in all of this. In both Rome and China, emperors who were by nature energetic, such as Wudi, or even just dedicated, like Vespasian, could exert their authority to very dramatic effect. After all, they had total power, and their will could mobilize huge armies and send them off to conquer new lands, as when Trajan invaded Dacia, or they could begin gigantic construction projects, as when Shi Huangdi erected the earliest version of the Great Wall. In both empires, maybe one of their most important functions, though, was the direct or indirect influence that they had in appointing senior administrators and generals.

While the theoretical power of these rulers seems nearly unlimited, in reality, they're always struggling against those time and distance constraints on communication described earlier. After all, how much control could even an absolute monarch wield over a distant province when the most basic information from there took three months to reach him? The answer is obviously very little, so this is where the structure of the state bureaucracy had to step in and really deal with most local issues all on its own. As we saw with Pliny and Trajan, most decisions were best made locally, and emperors really whether they wanted to or not had to rely heavily on the judgment of their subordinates. If, on the one hand though, an emperor's powers were limited by distance, on the other hand they could very actively control their immediate surroundings. Those people who found themselves within the range of the emperor's sight and within the range of his voice were truly under his sway, and this was a condition that could be alternately beneficial or disastrous, depending on the personality of a given ruler.

The inhabitants of the capital city of Rome often benefitted greatly from the emperor's presence in their midst, so he'd grant them all kinds of benefactions. Some of these included the famous grain dole, by which each citizen in Rome received a free monthly distribution of grain supplied by the state. The people who lived Rome were regularly treated to extravagant public spectacles ranging from chariot races to giant mock naval battles fought on artificial lakes with thousands of combatants. On the other hand, proximity to a bad or a crazy emperor could be a very, very dangerous situation. The senators were frequent targets for the wrath of such emperors, but even common people in Rome could unexpectedly fall victim to their outbursts. For instance, at some games in Rome, Caligula once, entirely on a whim, ordered an entire section of the audience thrown into the arena to be eaten by wild animals. If you were one of those unfortunates who suddenly found yourself transformed from a spectator into the entertainment itself, then living in proximity to the emperor had exacted a fatal price.

Some emperors plainly found their relative lack of control over affairs outside the capital troubling and tried do something about it. Hadrian, one of the good emperors of the 2nd century A.D., tried to exercise better personal supervision of the empire, as we've seen, by literally taking to the road; so he spent much of his reign engaged on those grand tours, traveling throughout the provinces, accompanied by the entire imperial court. In that way, he hoped that he could at least bring his personal attention to every corner of the empire at least occasionally as he rotated through all the different provinces.

Hadrian's perambulations around the Roman Empire have an interesting parallel in the grand tours undertaken by various Chinese emperors such as Shi Huangdi. The First Emperor made five of these great journeys throughout his reign, and he visited a different region in China each time. These trips served a lot of the same purposes as Hadrian's tour. They enabled the emperor to personally assess each region, to check in on its problems, and to see if local officials were doing their jobs. In China, though, these imperial trips had an important additional purpose. If you look at Shi

Huangdi's itinerary, it's largely dictated by his desire to visit various sacred spots and to perform rituals personally at them. This was a lot more than just displaying his piety to the gods; it's intimately linked to the Chinese concept of the emperor ruling by virtue of the divine mandate and approval of Heaven, and the actual performance of those rituals was simultaneously a means of ensuring and advertising that mandate.

Similarly, Hadrian's trips had a purpose that's uniquely Roman in its context, and it's another thing that reveals a profound difference between how Rome and China looked at their respective rulers and what their jobs were. In the Roman world, it's vital for the emperor to be seen, to be visible in a literal sense, by his subjects. This need goes all the way back to the Republican origins of Roman society, in which the leaders of the state were elected by the people, by the citizens. In the Empire, the people of Rome were no longer voting, they no longer had the power to elect their ruler, the emperor. But they still had the power to symbolically approve of his legitimacy through their shouted acclamations; so when he appeared in the street, they'd chant approval of him. In order for this to happen, there had to be frequent opportunities for large numbers of ordinary citizens to interact publicly with the emperor. This at least partially explains why the emperors built huge arenas such as the Coliseum or the Circus Maximus and then filled them with free, spectacular entertainments: Because it's in those kinds of places that they could appear before the adoring crowds and receive public acknowledgment of their status as emperor in the form of applause, cheers, and chanted slogans. In a very literal sense, it's the massed shouts of the Roman people hailing a man as emperor that were what made him the legitimate emperor. This sort of public recognition by the citizens was so fundamental to an emperor's legitimacy that often the very first thing that a new emperor would do upon taking the throne would be to appear at some public games.

If we look at the way that Roman cities were built and laid out, they featured large, open public spaces such as the Roman Forum, and those spaces were there to facilitate these sorts of interactions. In Rome, the emperor was supposed to be seen and recognized by his people. If you look at Roman coins, this is why all imperial Roman coins have an image of the emperor's face on them, and it's also why so many portrait busts were carved of Roman emperors—if you go to museums today, they're full of portrait busts of Roman emperors—and the reason for all these was so that even people in remote provinces would maybe have seen one of these portrait busts and would know what their ruler looked like.

In China, it's totally different. There, the emperor was a remote figure who's almost never visible to his subjects. If you look at the way Chinese capital cities were built, they certainly had big, impressive buildings that were associated with the emperor, such as palaces; but they didn't have any big open public spaces or venues where the common people could interact with the emperor, or even see him. In contrast to those ubiquitous portraits of Roman emperors on every coin and all the portrait busts, there were almost no public images whatsoever of the Chinese emperor. And whereas Hadrian planned his journeys to take him to all the largest cities of the empire where he could be viewed by his subjects, Shi Huangdi's itinerary was focused on visiting shrines, most of which were on desolate, uninhabited mountaintops.

In the next lecture, we'll continue this examination of the role and the power of the emperors, as well as looking at how both empires assimilated newcomers and struggled with outsiders.

Han and Roman Empires Compared—Problems
Lecture 33

ncient Rome and Han China each dealt with three major recurrent problems: Weak or insane emperors; incorporating newcomers into the empire; and fending off dangerous tribes on their borders. While incompetent rulers terrorized those in their immediate circles, they had surprisingly little effect on the empires as a whole. Due to the different natures of their cultures, Rome and China had different challenges when it came to integrating conquered peoples, yet they had similar mechanisms for doing so. Both empires built great walls, but these walls did not serve the purposes one might assume at first glance.

Mad, Bad Emperors

- When an emperor was a wise and conscientious man, his sweeping powers could be an asset, but what happened if he was weak, incompetent, or insane? Such a situation actually occurred repeatedly in both ancient Rome and China, and these instances offer an interesting test of both the extent and the limits of the emperor's powers.

- The behavior of egomaniacal or insane emperors tended to fall into certain patterns. One of the most common was criminal rampages. Nero liked to wander around Rome mugging random people. Wen Xuan was prone to drunken fits in which he would tear off his clothes, run about naked, and kill people.

- Another tendency was for mad emperors to grant extravagant honors to their personal favorites, even animals or inanimate objects. Elagabalus made his favorite dancer Prefect of the Praetorian Guard, and Caligula planned to have his favorite racehorse, Speedy, appointed consul. One northern Qin emperor gave official salaried posts to horses, chickens, and dogs.

- Another recurrent imperial delusion was the power to affect the forces of nature. Caligula once declared war on the ocean. Shi Huangdi once became angry at a mountain and had all the trees on it cut down to punish it.

- Why were so many of Rome and China's emperors seemingly insane? Many of the most popular theories—such as incest and lead poisoning—are not true. One definite pattern, however, is that the overwhelming majority of the most erratic emperors assumed the throne at early ages, often in their teens.

- How much did such behavior affect the empire as a whole? For those who lived directly under the emperor's gaze, perhaps a great deal. However, for those living in the outlying provinces, the emperor's behavior might not have much effect at all. The limitations on communication allowed the bureaucratic body of the state to function smoothly even if its head was inattentive or crazy.

The Barbarian Problem

- Both Rome and China faced the question of what to do with outsiders. How do you incorporate the people that you have conquered into your empire, and how do you deal with threats from outside the empire?

- Chinese rulers faced a much simpler situation because most areas incorporated into the Han Empire already shared their same basic culture. Even if people spoke regional dialects of Chinese, the standardization of the written script under the Qin ensured that documents could be understood everywhere.

- Since one of the most visible mechanisms for social and economic advancement—government service—depended on knowledge of Chinese classics, there was a strong incentive for ambitious locals to assimilate yet further into the mainstream culture. Thus the Qin's aggressive policy of standardizing helped to culturally unify all of China.

- In the Roman world, it was a very different story. There was enormous cultural diversity within the empire, a bewildering number of different ethnic groups, religions, cultures, and languages that continued and thrived under Roman rule. This diversity was not only acceptable to the Romans but one of the reasons for their success.

- The one group that they did often quite deliberately try to Romanize was the local elite. Often the sons of local chiefs were coercively invited to Rome, where they were raised with aristocratic families, exposed to Roman culture and values, and thus assimilated.

- When they returned to their native districts as the next generation of leaders, they sympathized with Rome, represented Roman interests, and enforced Roman policies. Frequently granted Roman citizenship, within a generation or two their descendants had taken Roman names and had fully adopted Roman customs. They even became senators and had careers as administrators.

- The Romans often justified the brutality of their imperialism by claiming they were bringing the benefits of civilization to the conquered: peace, law, public works, order, technology, culture, and even entertainment. Many locals, especially the elites, embraced this argument.

- The other great mechanism of Romanization in the provinces was the army. In addition to legions composed of Roman citizens was the *auxilia*, made up of noncitizens recruited from the most warlike peoples of the empire.

- The *auxilia* were trained in Roman fighting methods, and at the end of their decades of service, they were granted Roman citizenship. Provincials who entered the *auxilia* with their own languages, customs, and cultures emerged as Latin speakers who had adopted Roman ways and beliefs. Retired *auxilia* tended to disperse back to their home villages, where they became local magistrates and representatives of Roman authority and culture.

- This strategy of assimilating and Romanizing provincials was one of the great secrets to the success and longevity of the Roman Empire. It not only redirected the efforts of those who might have fought against Rome into fighting for it, but it also provided a constant source of new talent.

- The frontiers and the fringes of China were more culturally diverse than the core regions, and there the situation was more like that in the Roman Empire, in which locals were seduced into adopting Chinese culture and the army as a mechanism for assimilating outsiders as well as fighting them.

- Another way assimilation took place in China, just as in the Roman Empire, was by employment or incorporation of warlike tribes into the Chinese military. Whether directly conscripted or serving as mercenaries, such warriors often acquired Chinese customs, language, and sympathies.

The Wall Builders

- Two of the most famous archaeological monuments in the world represent another way both the Roman and Chinese empires dealt with dangerous barbarians on their borders: the Great Wall of China and Hadrian's Wall.

- Hadrian's Wall runs about 70 miles across the width of northern England and, for most of its length, is composed of solid stone blocks. About 10 feet wide and 20 feet high, it had watchtowers spaced at roughly 500-yard intervals, and these were further supplemented with over a dozen full-scale forts.

- The Romans established networks of walls, roads, ditches, outposts, watchtowers, and forts on other dangerous frontiers, including the Rhine and Danube rivers and along the Saharan and Arabian deserts.

Hadrian's Wall, in the north of England, probably did little to physically stop invaders. However, it provided the Romans with early warning of raids.

- There is considerable debate among Roman historians regarding the purpose and function of these fortifications. Even the most solid and continuous of them would not have been sufficient to stop a large or determined barbarian incursion.

- Some historians suggest they were built to deter small raiding parties and to detect and slow down major invasions. Alternatively, they have been interpreted as a means of regulating trade and collecting customs taxes. Others view them as symbolic statements of the limits of empire or even as busywork for the army. The truth is probably some combination of all of these factors.

- In China, defensive walls had a long history, going back at least to the 7th century B.C. The earliest walls were built of wood and packed earth, so that little remains of them today.

- The famous extant stone portions of the Great Wall are comparatively recent, dating to the Ming dynasty of the 14th–17th centuries. The original version of this wall may have been yet another project of the energetic Qin emperor Shi Huangdi. How reliable this account is and exactly where this wall ran are topics of dispute, but by the time of the Han dynasty, there seems to have been a well-recognized and extensive wall delineating China's northern frontier.

- Many of the same arguments concerning the purpose and function of Hadrian's Wall exist for the Great Wall of China. Walls were never viewed as a solution in and of themselves. China's policy toward the northern barbarian involved using military force, buying them off with money and gifts, hiring them as mercenaries, and assimilation.

- In both China and Rome, instances of heavy reliance on defensive walls can be interpreted as signs of weakness, since, in stronger moments, both states instead relied on mobile armies for defense.

Rome and China—A Final Assessment

- These lectures have focused on a few issues, such as administration, leadership, assimilation, and scale, which made for interesting comparisons, but there are many other characteristics of these empires that are worth such analysis, such as economy, law, systems of coinage, and struggles with new religions.

- One final comparison worth making between Rome and China is one of attitude. Both empires came to view themselves as world civilizations and as cultures destined to rule over all others.

- In the great foundational epic of Rome, the *Aeneid*, Virgil stated that the gods granted to Rome "empire without end." Even Rome's enemies viewed the Romans as universal conquerors. The Chinese believed their state encompassed "all under heaven," and that China itself was "the Middle Kingdom," of which the rest of the world was merely an insignificant fringe.

Suggested Reading

Di Cosmo, *Ancient China and its Enemies*.

Luttwak, *The Grand Strategy of the Roman Empire*.

Hingley, *Globalizing Roman Culture*.

Waldron, *The Great Wall of China*.

Whitaker, *Frontiers of the Roman Empire*.

Questions to Consider

1. What do you think is the best explanation for the disproportionately high number of crazy emperors of China and Rome?

2. Rome and China both had to incorporate outsiders into their cultures. Which empire do you think was more successful in doing this, and what factors contributed to their success?

Han and Roman Empires Compared—Problems
Lecture 33—Transcript

In this lecture, I'll consider a few of the major problems that were faced by the Roman and Han empires and how they responded to them. We ended last lecture with the figure of the emperor as the person in charge who had the capacity to shape state policy. Of course, when the emperor was a wise or conscientious man, his sweeping powers could be an asset; but what happened if he's a weak or even, let's say, an incompetent ruler? Let's push this even a little bit further and consider a worst case scenario: What would happen if the seemingly omnipotent ruler of one of these empires was actually insane? Such a situation actually occurred repeatedly in both Ancient Rome and China, and oddly enough, these instances offer us an interesting test of both the extent and the limits of the emperor's powers. Accounts of these rulers raise the question: How much did it really matter to the empire as a whole if its leader was crazy?

To begin with, the behavior of egomaniacal or insane emperors always tended to fall into certain patterns. One of the most common of these was the sort of murderous rampages that I've already described with Roman emperors such as Caligula or Nero. We see very similar events in China as well. In the same way that Nero liked to wander around Rome at night mugging random people, the Chinese emperor Wen Xuan was prone to drunken fits in which he'd tear off his clothing, run around naked, and kill people; and his guards actually adopted the practice of always keeping ready at hand some condemned criminals so whenever the emperor was struck with one of these killing urges, these could just be offered up to him.

Another tendency was for these sorts of emperors to give extravagant honors to people who were their personal favorites, and in extreme cases this would even be extended to animals or inanimate objects. The Roman emperor Elagabalus made his favorite dancer the Prefect of the Praetorian Guard; he put his barber in charge of the state grain supply; and he assigned a cook who he liked to be in charge of tax collection in the empire. As we've already seen, Caligula planned to have his favorite racehorse, Speedy, appointed to the very highest political office, the consulship. If we look at China, one emperor of the northern Qin Dynasty gave official salaried posts to horses, chickens, and dogs. Once, when a tree protected emperor Shi Huangdi from a sudden rainstorm, in gratitude he bestowed upon the tree the rank and the salary of an official of the fifth grade.

Another recurrent theme is crazy emperors having the delusion that they were so powerful they could even affect forces of nature. Caligula once declared war on the ocean and he had the Roman legions draw up on the beach and throw their spears into the sea. Then, he declared that he'd vanquished the god of the sea, Neptune, and he had his soldiers go around the beach and collect seashells, which he then displayed as evidence that he'd triumphed over the waters. Once when Shi Huangdi became angry at a mountain, he had all the trees on it cut down as a way to punish the mountain. These sorts of actions weren't unique to the absolute rulers of Rome and China, I should mention. For example, when a storm at sea destroyed the great bridge that was built across the Hellespont by Xerxes, the Persian King of Kings, he responded by ordering his soldiers to flagellate the water with whips as punishment.

Lavish expenditure on palaces and banquets that exceeded even the usual ostentatious living standard of such monarchs was another hallmark of these kinds of rulers. One Chinese empress insisted that exotic fruits had to be brought to her from far in the south by a stream of couriers whose route was so arduous that many of them actually died along the way bringing her these fruits. The palace built by the Han emperors was a huge complex of pavilions and halls, and all of them were furnished in the most extravagant way imaginable. But maybe the most outrageous palace of all was the one built by the emperor Nero, and this was after a fire had destroyed a lot of the city of Rome in 64 A.D. He saw this as an opportunity: He took advantage of the space that had been cleared in the center of the city by this disaster to build for himself a giant new palace that was known as Nero's Golden House. It had all kind of features: It had a triple colonnade that extended for an entire mile; it had an artificial lake; it had elaborate pavilions and gardens that were stocked with all kinds of exotic wild animals; and it even had one complex of over 140 rooms that's just used for hosting feasts and dinner parties, and within that complex there's a special octagonal dining room that had a revolving roof and fountains flowing at the sides. Out in front of the Golden House, he placed what's the crowning touch to this entire complex: Nero put a colossal golden 120-foot-high naked statue of himself. At the dedication of this extraordinary set of structures, Nero's comment was, "Finally, I can begin to live like a human being." By the way, today, some of those rooms of the Golden House, including that octagonal dining room, still survive but they're buried deep beneath the Esquiline hill. I've been down in those cave-like passages and you can see still see down there traces of the once-magnificent wall paintings.

Inevitably when discussion of these sorts of emperors comes up, people always ask: Why did so many emperors seem to have been insane? Certainly if we look at the Roman side, they had a terrible track record in that regard. If we consider just the 1st century of the empire, then at least Caligula, Nero, and Domitian, certainly by modern clinical standards, would probably have been classified as mentally unbalanced. You'll hear a lot of popular theories regarding this—so sometimes you'll hear that this was due to incest or lead poisoning, and this is what caused all the nutty emperors—but those theories simply aren't true. One definite pattern, though, which can be detected among them, is that the overwhelming majority of the most erratically-behaved emperors all tended to assume the throne at a young age, often when they're just teenagers. Maybe there really is something to that old cliché that absolute power corrupts absolutely, and if one is given such total power before your adult personality has been fully formed or stabilized, then maybe it's simply too much to handle. In China, even though the pattern isn't quite as clear as at Rome, indeed many of the weaker or more eccentric emperors also ascended the throne in their youth.

Let's return now to our initial question: How much did this sort of behavior affect the empire as a whole? There's no doubt that for those who lived directly under the emperor's gaze and within the range of his voice, it could matter a great deal. As we've seen, the victims of a mad emperor's rampages tended to be those people who were closest to him: his family, his advisers, and really anybody living in the palace or the capital city. Let's say, though, that you're a farmer living in one of the outlying provinces of either the Han or the Roman empires. Did it really affect you in any meaningful way whether your ruler was a person like Augustus or someone like Nero? Given those limitations on communication and the structure of the administration, a realistic answer would probably have to be, "No, not very much, if at all."

While on the one hand the great size of these empires and the difficulties with communication are usually portrayed as weaknesses, these could at times also cover up or at least alleviate other defects; in this case, it could allow the bureaucratic body of the state to continue to function smoothly and at least adequately even if the head of that bureaucratic body, the emperor, was inattentive or even crazy.

Next, I want to consider two other problems that faced Rome and Ancient China, and both of these had to do with outsiders. First, how do you incorporate the people that you've conquered into your empire, and how do you redirect their energies to work for the state rather than against it? Second, how do you deal with threats to security from outside the empire, most commonly in the form of warlike, nomadic barbarians?

In regard to assimilating conquered territories, the Chinese rulers had a much simpler situation because most of the areas that were incorporated into the Han Empire already shared the same basic culture, and so even if there were local variations, these could be relatively easily absorbed. In addition, Chinese culture really had no competition; it's universally viewed by everybody in the area as the oldest, most superior, dominant culture. Even if people might speak a regional dialect of Chinese, the standardization of the written script that had happened back under the Qin ensured that documents could be understood everyplace. Also, since one of the most obvious mechanisms for social and economic advancement, service in the imperial administration, depended on knowledge of Chinese classic texts in order to be successful at those examinations, this means that there's a very strong incentive for ambitious locals to assimilate even further into the mainstream culture. As much as the Qin Dynasty gets castigated later on, its policy of standardizing things such as the script, weights, measures, and coinage, all of this had sunk in deeply and all of it then helped to unify China in cultural terms.

In the Roman world, it's a very different story. While Rome was successful in conquering the whole Mediterranean basin and forcing political unity over that territory, within it there's enormous cultural diversity. This diversity was perfectly acceptable to the Romans, and indeed it's one of the reasons for the success of their empire because, in general, they didn't try to enforce any sort of cultural, ethnic, linguistic, or religious conformity. They'd allow all these little local variants to thrive within the borders of the empire.

While the Romans were pretty content to allow most people within their empire to retain their indigenous traditions, the one group that they did often deliberately try to co-opt or Romanize were local elites. The Romans as a policy tended to favor certain members of the local elite, whether you define that by social or economic status, and they'd then try to use these people to control the behavior of their subordinates. For example, often the sons of local chieftains would be a little bit coercively invited to Rome where they'd be raised together with aristocratic families, and there they'd be exposed to Roman culture and values; and so, having been assimilated, when they returned to their native districts as the next generation of leaders, they'd now sympathize with Rome, and they'd in essence represent Roman interests and enforce Roman policies. Those men were often given Roman citizenship, and so within a generation or two they'd even dropped their original names and taken Latin, Roman names and they'd fully adopted Roman customs. They could then even hope to become senators themselves and to have careers as Roman administrators. This whole process by which the provincials were assimilated is usually called "Romanization."

In an argument that would be echoed centuries later by European colonial powers, the Romans often justified the brutality of their imperialism by claiming that they're simply bringing the benefits of civilization to the people that they conquered. They'd claim that incorporation into the empire gave to their subjects things like peace, law, public works, order, technology, culture, and even entertainment. This was an argument that many of those locals, especially the elites, were perfectly happy to embrace. The Romans were very well aware of the lure that being associated with the power and success of Rome and that the trappings of Roman civilization exerted upon those ambitious local elites, and they'd cleverly exploit that desire. In his work describing the conquest of Britain, the Roman author Tacitus is very honest about the means by which Rome attempted to suborn and Romanize local leaders. Tacitus wrote that the Britons were offered "the temptations of arcades, baths, and sumptuous banquets," and further that "the sons of the chiefs were educated in the liberal arts so that instead of loathing the Latin language, they became eager to speak it effectively" and that "Our national dress came into favor and the toga was everywhere to be seen." Tacitus also rather cynically noted that these men, the local elites, were more than willing to exchange their freedom for these sorts of amenities, and he concluded that "The Britons spoke of such novelties as civilization, when in fact they were the means of their enslavement."

The other great mechanism of Romanization in the provinces was the army—and we'll look at the Roman army in a future lecture in more detail—but in addition to the legions that were made up of Roman citizens, there's another branch of the army called the *auxilia*. This was made up of noncitizens, and typically they're recruited from the most warlike or recently conquered people of the empire. In the *auxilia*, these provincials would be trained in Roman fighting methods, and then they'd serve a 30 year stint of service; and at the end of that time, when they're discharged, they're given Roman citizenship. Provincials who'd enter into the *auxilia* with their own language, customs, and cultures would come out of it at the end of that time as Latin speakers who'd fully adopted Roman ways, beliefs, and customs. These retired *auxilia* would often disperse back to whatever home village they came from, and there they'd often become local officials or magistrates, and they'd be representatives, almost ambassadors, of Roman authority and culture. In this rather clever way, the energies of thousands of potential enemies of Rome were instead channeled into serving Rome. The military also acted as a means of social mobility, because advancement within its ranks was based on merit and ability.

This strategy of assimilating and Romanizing provincials was really one of the great secrets to the success and the longevity of the Roman Empire. It not only redirected the efforts of the very people who might have fought against Rome into fighting for it, but it also provided a constant source of new talent for the Romans. Scholars have done various studies of the composition of the Roman Senate, and what they've found is that during the empire, the men running Rome very quickly began to be drawn from the provinces. The percentage of actual Italians in the Senate rapidly declined after the 1st century A.D. These statistics show Rome's success in assimilating the best and the brightest of the people that they conquered, and then putting them to work for Rome. We can also see this trend reflected in where the emperors came from, their places of origin. In the 1st century of the empire, all the emperors came from old aristocratic Italian families. But by the beginning of the 2nd century A.D., which is regarded as the highpoint of Rome and the time of the Five Good Emperors, they were starting to come from provincial elites. The model good emperor Trajan was Spanish, the emperor Septimius Severus was African, and Rome thrived, at least partially, because of its openness to incorporating such new talent.

As already mentioned, the core geographic region that made up most of China had cultural uniformity, but the frontiers and the fringe areas around that were much more analogous to the Roman provinces. In those culturally diverse regions, we find a situation very much like that in the Roman Empire, in which locals were often seduced into adopting Chinese culture, and so the army functioned not only as a means of fighting outsiders, but as a mechanism for assimilating them. When tribes of nomadic barbarian invaders would come into contact with China, not infrequently they'd end up imitating Chinese customs; and one of the more successful ways that China dealt with invaders was by simply absorbing them into their ancient and enduring culture. While barbarian nomads might have initially made fun of or scoffed at the soft, luxurious life available to the Chinese, who were made rich by intensive agriculture, at the same time they're intrigued and drawn to that sort of lifestyle. Another way that assimilation took place, just as in the Roman Empire, was by employing or incorporating warlike tribes into the Chinese military. Whether these soldiers were directly conscripted or served as mercenaries, they often then acquired Chinese customs, language, and sympathies.

Two of the most famous archaeological monuments in the world represent one more potential approach that was used by both the Roman and Chinese empires for dealing with dangerous barbarians, and these are the Great Wall of China and Hadrian's Wall in Britain. Hadrian's Wall runs about 70 miles across Northern Britain, and for most of that stretch it's made up of solid stone blocks; so it forms a wall about 10 feet wide and 20 feet high. Watchtowers are spaced at about 500 yard intervals, and these were supplemented by about a dozen full-size forts. While Hadrian's Wall in Britain as well as the more northerly Antonine Wall are the best-known Roman border fortifications, they're by no means the only ones. The Romans also built walls, roads, ditches, outposts, watchtowers, and forts on almost all their other dangerous frontiers, including all along the Rhine River, the Danube River off in the east, and then to the south along the border of the Saharan and Arabian deserts.

There's a big debate among Roman historians concerning the intended purpose and function of all of these walls and fortifications. Even the most solid and continuous of them, something like Hadrian's Wall, would really not have been enough to stop a large or determined barbarian invasion. This has led to theories that these walls were really there to just deter small raiding parties or to serve as a kind of early warning system to detect and maybe slow down major invasions. Alternatively, they've been interpreted as actually having mainly an economic function, where the walls served as a way to regulate trade and made collecting customs taxes much easier. Others see them as symbolic statements of the limits of empire, or even just as busywork for the army. The truth probably lies in some combination of all these different factors.

In China, defensive walls had a very, very long history; they go back at least to the 7th century B.C. Like most structures of those early dynasties, those earliest walls were built of wood and packed earth, so that almost nothing is left of them today. The famous stone sections of the Great Wall that you see in pictures today, those are actually very recent, dating to the Ming Dynasty of the 14th–17th century A.D. The original version of that Great Wall, though, may have been another project of the same energetic Qin emperor Shi Huangdi who, at least according to legend, was said to have employed hundreds of thousands of laborers in building a gigantic wood and earthen wall all the way across China's northern border. How reliable that account is and exactly where that wall was are things that people are debating; but by the time of the Han Dynasty, there does seem to have been a well-recognized and extensive wall that delineated the northern frontier. A surviving treaty between the Han and the nomadic horse archers, the Xiongnu, has a clause that states:

> The land north of the Great Wall where men wield the bow and arrow was to receive its commands from the leader of the Xiongnu, while that region within the wall whose inhabitants dwell in houses and wear hats and belts, was to be ruled by [the Chinese emperor].

This reference clearly shows the wall in existence and that it's used to designate the boundary between China and outside regions.

Many of the same arguments concerning the purpose and function of Hadrian's Wall exist for the Great Wall of China. At least in some of those earlier dynasties, China's walls do indeed seem to have been intended as a direct form of deterrence against invasion, but they're never viewed as a solution all alone. China's policy towards those northern barbarian tribes was always a mixture of different methods. Sometimes they'd use naked military force, sometimes they'd buy them off with money and gifts; other times they'd hire them as mercenaries, and other times they'd try to assimilate them. In China and Rome, instances of heavy reliance on defensive walls can really be interpreted as signs of weakness, since, in stronger moments, both of those states would rely instead on mobile armies for their defense.

Over the last three lectures, we've paused in the historical narrative to indulge in some more in-depth discussion of aspects of the Roman and Han empires; and I've focused on a couple issues, such as administration, leadership, assimilation, and scale, and I thought those made for some interesting comparisons. But there really were many other characteristics of those two empires that one might have picked for a similar analysis. You could look at their economies, systems of law, coinage, or struggles with new religions.

One final comparison that I want to make between Rome and China has to do with attitude. Both civilizations came to view themselves as worldwide civilizations, and more than that, as cultures with a special destiny to rule over all others. In the great foundational epic poem of Rome, the *Aeneid*, the author Virgil famously stated that the gods had given to Rome "empire without end." Even Rome's enemies viewed the Romans as universal conquerors, and we see this exemplified in a Greek author Polybius who himself was a victim of Roman imperialism, and he began his history by stating that he'd explain "how the entire world had been brought under the control of the Romans." The Chinese considered their state to encompass "all under heaven," and China itself, of course, was called "The Middle Kingdom," of which the rest of the world was seen as just an insignificant fringe.

In future lectures, we'll return both to the Mediterranean and to China to see what happens when these empires fall, but first, we'll make a rather dramatic shift in geography to an entirely new region of the world that I haven't even mentioned yet. Whereas all the cultures and regions that we've looked at so far have had at least some tenuous links with one another, we're now going to jump to an area that's been developing in complete and total isolation from the rest of the world. For the next three lectures, we'll turn to North and South America and to the great early civilizations of the New World.

Early Americas—Resources and Olmecs
Lecture 34

The earliest North and South American cultures make an interesting contrast with the other great civilizations we have studied so far for several reasons, not least of which is how geography profoundly influenced their development. In particular, the lack of cereal grains and large domesticable animals made certain technologies common to other civilizations far less useful in the Americas. The first major civilization in this region was the Olmecs, a mother civilization to all American cultures. Their legacies included their art, architecture, religion, calendar, and writing system.

Humans Come to the Americas

- The Americas were among the last portions of the world to be settled by humans. The Atlantic and Pacific oceans acted as effective barriers until glaciers froze up enough water in the Bering Strait to create a bridge between Alaska and Siberia, although exactly when this happened is still much debated.

- These earliest peoples, often termed Amerindians or Paleo-Indians, engaged in a nomadic, hunter-gatherer lifestyle. They fished and hunted game both large and small. About 8,000 years ago, they began to plant some of the foods they found growing wild, such as beans and squash.

- Just as in Mesopotamia, India, and China, the practice of agriculture would profoundly change these peoples; as more and more of their diet derived from farmed crops, the hunter-gatherers settled down. With crop surpluses, villages and small cities arose, and soon followed most of the cultural developments we have been tracing in other civilizations.

- These settlements mostly clustered in two regions: One, called Mesoamerica, stretched from the arid highlands of what is today central Mexico through the jungle regions of the Yucatan peninsula and into Guatemala and Central America. The other was a narrow strip along the northwestern coast of what is today Peru that encompassed portions of the Andes Mountains and the coast.

Geography and Culture in the Americas

- Mesoamerica contained two basic environments. Central and western Mexico contain a high, arid plateau whose cool valleys were a popular place to settle. To the east and south were grassy savannas and steamy tropical rain forests with lush vegetation.

- The major Mesoamerican civilizations tended to arise either in the highlands or the lowlands, but usually not both. A number of the items most prized by these civilizations were only found in one or the other area as well, such as obsidian or cacao. In practical terms, the early Mesoamerican societies were therefore dependent on one another for vital goods.

- All the cultures that developed in Mesoamerica featured a number of common elements. The crops and animals they subsisted on were also the same. They all used glyphs to write; built temple-topped pyramids; had similar calendars; played a ball game with religious overtones; practiced human sacrifice; wrote on bark paper; used cocoa beans as currency; and worshiped pantheons that included a goggle-eyed water deity and often a feathered serpent god.

- In Peru, there were also two distinct climatic zones. The western slopes of the Andes formed a dry, desert-like region ill-suited for intensive agriculture but had access to the sea and abundant fishing. The high mountain plateaus and the eastern slopes of the Andes received moisture from the prevailing Amazon winds; there, it was possible to farm corn, beans, and potatoes on terraced fields.

- Just as in the Mesoamerica, a vibrant trade developed early on between the low coastal lands and the inland highlands of Peru. Fish and shells were exchanged for corn, potatoes, and beans. Certain distinctive cultural constants developed that spanned all the civilizations arising in this region, including mummifying the dead and religions with prominent sun gods.

The Slow Rise of American Civilization

- The civilizations of North and South America got going later than those in the Mediterranean, Mesopotamia, India, and China. They domesticated crops and animals at least 5,000 years later than in these other parts of the world, and they never developed some of the key technologies that these other regions enjoyed at all.

- There have been a number of attempts to explain these discrepancies among world civilizations. Certainly the people of North and South America were no less intelligent or creative than their counterparts elsewhere, but due to environmental factors, they may simply have been at a great disadvantage, specifically in terms of the plants available for cultivation and the animals available for domestication.

- Cereals grains today contribute more than 50 percent of all calories consumed by human beings. But potential sources of domesticated cereals were not distributed evenly around the globe at the time civilizations arose, and these plants cannot grow in all climates. The Mediterranean, for example, gave rise to highly useful farm crops, whereas Africa and South America were almost completely lacking in potential high-yield grains.

- Of all the large mammals on earth only 5 have proven to be well suited for domestication: cows, sheep, goats, pigs, and horses. All 5 of these can be found in Europe and Asia; none are indigenous to North and South America.

- South America has one marginally useful domesticable animal—the llama. North America has none. This may be why the wheel was never developed for transportation in the New World. The natives had no large animals suitable for pulling wheeled carts or wagons.

- A subsidiary effect of raising large domesticated animals is disease immunity. Some of humanity's major killers have been seven infectious diseases—small pox, influenza, tuberculosis, malaria, plague, measles, and cholera—that originated among large domesticated animals. When the Spanish conquistadors reached Mexico, they brought along this array of pathogens, to which the local population had no immunity.

Olmec Civilization

- For almost 2,000 years, New World civilizations evolved in near-total isolation from the rest of the world, and they produced some highly memorable and creative cultures. The earliest Mesoamerican urban culture to emerge was the Olmecs, which emerged around 1200 B.C. along the coast of what are now Veracruz and Tabasco.

- While many aspects of their civilization remain mysterious or debated, the Olmecs are often characterized as a kind of mother culture for the region who established the model for pyramid building, the calendar, the pantheon, and artistic pursuits.

- Almost all of what we know about the Olmecs is derived from archaeological evidence rather than textual or historical accounts. The Olmecs are best known for their huge ceremonial centers and for the art and architecture that adorned them. We know practically nothing about Olmec domestic life.

- The most famous of ceremonial centers is La Venta. It was constructed along a north-south axis with careful attention paid to the geometrical relationships between its various structures. It features a massive earthen pyramid over 300 feet high as well as smaller step pyramids.

The colossal head artifacts of Olmec civilization look similar, but each has individual features, suggesting that they represent specific people.

- Buried in the main courtyard are slabs of jade, granite, and serpentine depicting monster and jaguar heads. These were evidently not meant to be seen, as they were buried right after they were created. Precious offerings such as jade axes were placed in many of the burials.

- It is not known what sorts of rituals were performed by the Olmecs, but it is believed that a priestly elite enjoying the highest social status was in charge of Olmec society. The remains of Olmec ceremonial sites suggest that the designers were skillful engineers with huge amounts of labor at their disposal.

- The most typical and impressive Olmec artifacts are also among the most mysterious, a series of colossal baby-faced basalt heads. About 25 of these six- to nine-foot-tall heads survive, and it is speculated that they may be portraits of Olmec kings. They all have a similar distinctive look, but their scars, blemishes, and gaps in their teeth suggest they represent individuals.

- Atypical Olmec art object are statues of jaguar were-babies eating their mothers while nursing. A later Mesoamerican origin myth says a jaguar mated with a woman, who gave birth to a baby that ate her as she nursed it and eventually became the first ruler. Some scholars believe that the massive rulers' heads might refer to this myth.

- The Olmecs developed an extensive trading network, importing goods such as basalt, obsidian, and iron ore from Mexico's west coast and as far south as Costa Rica. An especially important trade item was jade from Guatemala.

- The Olmecs made jewelry, masks, and ritual objects. Jade was considered the most precious material by Mesoamerican cultures, even more so than gold; later on, the conquistador Hernando Cortes found that he could trade green glass beads for gold.

- The trade links established by the Olmecs no doubt contributed to the cultural homogeneity evident in much of ancient Mesoamerica, especially in terms of religion. Olmec gods, half-human/half-animal supernatural creatures, myths, and religious symbols provided prototypes for later Mesoamerican deities and religious beliefs. The Olmecs also played a ceremonial ball game that would become widespread throughout the region.

- By at least 600 B.C., the Olmecs had created the first known form of writing in Mesoamerica. This was a relatively crude hieroglyphic system that many scholars believe was a forerunner to the Mayan glyphs, but it has yet to be deciphered.

- The Olmecs also are credited with the first calendar in Mesoamerica. Its main application seems to have been to record and track religious cycles.

- For reasons that remain uncertain, Olmec civilization appears to have collapsed or faded away sometime in the 4th century B.C. There is evidence of Olmec sites suffering severe depopulation in this period, and some scholars have ascribed this to shifts in climate.

Diamond, *Guns, Germs, and Steel*.

Diehl, *The Olmecs*.

Questions to Consider

1. Would you agree or disagree with Jared Diamond's argument that the availability of domesticable plants and animals gave the civilizations of certain geographic regions a distinct advantage?

2. The Olmec, Minoan, and Indus Valley civilizations are all known mainly through archaeological evidence. What parallels are there in terms what we know (and do not know) about them?

Early Americas—Resources and Olmecs
Lecture 34—Transcript

A massive stone pyramid with nearly the same footprint as the very largest Egyptian ones; finely carved jade figures of creatures that are half-human baby and half-jaguar; colossal stone heads that weigh over 30 tons; and ceramic pots that are painted with beans sporting human arms and legs and dressed in armor, vigorously beating one another with axes and maces. These are just a few of the impressive and rather creative objects produced by the ancient cultures of North and South America. For the next three lectures, we'll examine the civilizations of this region.

The Americas were among the last portions of the world to be settled by human beings. For a long time, the Atlantic and the Pacific oceans acted as effective barriers; that is, until glaciers froze up enough water in the Bering Strait between Alaska and Siberia that a land bridge emerged above sea level. People first migrated to the Americas by crossing the Bering Land Bridge, although exactly when that happened is still something that's much debated. Originally, that moment was dated to around 100,000 years ago, but some studies that are based on genetics point to a date more around 30,000 years ago. Yet other interpretations based on archaeological evidence would push that key event to as recently as 15,000 years ago. One common theory is that bands of hunters from Asia crossed over the Bering Strait in order to follow bison, caribou, and mammoths at the very end of the Ice Age. Genetic analysis of biological traits such as certain blood proteins and shovel-shaped incisor teeth do indicate that there's a common ancestry for ancient inhabitants of Siberian Asia and Native Americans.

These earliest peoples, often termed Amerindians or sometimes Paleo-Indians, engaged in a nomadic, hunter-gatherer lifestyle. They fished and they hunted various game, both large and small; and there's clear evidence that they killed some huge animals like mammoths and bison, but it's now being questioned to what extent this sort of big game formed a significant part of their diet. But gradually, these peoples moved throughout North America, and then ultimately down into South America as well. These nomads eventually began to plant some of the foods that they found growing wild. These were things like beans and squashes, and seeds have been found that hint that their cultivation began at least 8,000 years ago. Around 6500 B.C., we know that squash, chili peppers, avocados, as well as corn were among the earliest domesticated crops being grown in the highlands of Mesoamerica, although corn cobs at that point were only as large as one's little finger. By the way, it would take another 3,000 years before selective breeding had increased the size of corn up to thumb-sized cobs, and those giant foot-long corn that we enjoy today at the market nicely illustrate just how much we really have warped domesticated plants from their original wild ancestors.

Ultimately, just as in Mesopotamia, India, and China, the practice of agriculture would profoundly change these peoples; so as more and more of their diet was derived from farmed crops, the hunter-gatherers would begin to settle down into more sedentary communities. Once they started to develop crop surpluses, you had villages and small cities developing, and soon thereafter you got all the cultural developments that we've been tracing in the other civilizations around the world.

In the Americas, the groups who made that fundamental leap to farming and urbanism clustered mostly in just two regions. One of those, often called Mesoamerica, stretched from the arid highlands of what today is central Mexico down into the jungle regions of the Yucatan Peninsula and into Guatemala and the other Central American countries. The second region was a narrow strip along the northwestern coast of what's today Peru, and this strip encompassed portions of the high Andes Mountains as well as some coastal zones down to the sea. As always, the geography and natural resources of those two regions will play a determining role in the cultures that developed there; so let's first look a little bit at the environments of those two areas.

First, Mesoamerica: Mesoamerica had two basic environments. In central and western Mexico, there's a high, dry plateau where there are nice cool valleys, and these were attractive places to settle. More to the east and the south were grassy open plains and steamy tropical rainforests with lush vegetation, and the major Mesoamerican civilizations tended to arise either up in the highlands or down in the lowlands but, with the exception of the Maya, usually not both. While certain basic crops and resources could be found in both regions, a number of the items that were most prized by these various civilizations only occurred in one or the other area. For example, obsidian, the sharp-edged, black, volcanic stone that's widely used to make knives and weapons, could only be obtained in the highlands; whereas, on the other hand, cacao and cotton were widely cultivated only in the lowlands. What this meant in practical terms was that the early Mesoamerican societies were always dependent on one another for vital goods, so there's always a lively trade going on between the two regions because neither of them could achieve economic self-sufficiency.

All of the cultures that developed in Mesoamerica featured a number of common elements. First of all, not only were their economies interdependent, as we've seen, but the available crops and animals that they basically subsisted on were also the same. All Mesoamerican cultures farmed primarily corn, beans, and squash. Certain cultural practices that were shared by almost every Mesoamerican civilization included that they all used glyphs as writing; that they built pyramids topped with temples; that they had very similar calendars; that they almost all played a specific ball game that had religious overtones; they all tended to practice human sacrifice; they all wrote on paper made from bark; they used cocoa beans as a form of money; and they worshipped polytheistic pantheons of gods that included a goggle-eyed water deity and also a feathered serpent god as well.

Turning now to the section down in South America, if we look at the northwestern edge of Peru, that's the other origin point of New World civilizations. In that region, there were also two distinct climatic zones: First, you had the western slopes of the Andes Mountains that go down to the coast; and that's basically a desert-like region, so it wasn't very well-suited for agriculture. But what that zone did have was lots of sea life in the waters just offshore. On the other hand, the high mountain plateaus and the eastern slopes of the Andes got a lot of moisture; this came from the prevailing winds that had come in from the Amazon basin. Up in those highlands, it's possible to make terraced fields where all the usual New World staple crops—corn and beans, squash—could be grown. In addition, South American farmers could plant another very useful crop, potatoes. Just as in the north in Mesoamerica, a vibrant trade developed very early on between the low coastal lands and the higher inland areas up in the mountains, and they'd exchange fish and shells for corn, potatoes, and beans. Also as in the north, certain distinctive cultural constants developed that would span all the different civilizations that arose in that region. Some of those that were specific to that region including mummifying the dead and religions that had very prominent sun gods.

The civilizations of North and South America got going considerably later than those in the Mediterranean, Mesopotamia, India, and China. They domesticated crops and animals at least 5,000 years later than the other parts of the world that we've examined, and they never developed at all some of the key technologies that those other regions enjoyed. For example, none of the New World civilizations used wheels for transportation, even though they did sometimes have wheels on toys. Most of these civilizations employed stone for tools and weapons, and they never developed metalworking, or else they did develop metalworking but only applied it to decorative things like jewelry. While some New World cultures did invent various forms of writing, none of them got much past the pictograph stage, and so these were not nearly as flexible as the true alphabetic or sign systems that were used elsewhere in the world.

There have been lots of attempts to try and explain these discrepancies among world civilizations—why one seemed to have developed faster than the other—and one of the more interesting of these attempts was popularized about a decade ago by an author named Jared Diamond who wrote a book called *Guns, Germs, and Steel*. Certainly the people who lived in North and South America were no less intelligent or creative than people elsewhere, but due to environmental factors, he argues that they may simply have been at a great disadvantage. Two especially vital areas in which this may have been the case are in the wild plants that were available for cultivation and the animals that were available for domestication.

There are about 200,000 species of wild flowering plants. Of that enormous number, only a couple hundred are routinely eaten by humans; and of those, just 12 account for 80 percent of the world's crops. (If you're curious, those 12 are wheat, corn, rice, barley, sorghum, soybeans, potatoes, manioc, sweet potatoes, sugar cane, sugar beet, and bananas.) The most important category of crops by far are the cereals, and even today cereals contribute more than

50 percent of all calories that are consumed by human beings. When ancient humans set about domesticating wild grasses into modern crops like wheat, there were 56 possible grasses that contained heavy seeds that were suitable for doing this with. These potential sources of domesticated cereals weren't distributed evenly around the globe, and they wouldn't grow in all climates. In fact, those potential cereal plants were heavily concentrated in certain geographic regions; 32 of the 56 were in the zone of the Mediterranean Sea and the Ancient Near East, including Mesopotamia. By contrast, Eastern Asia had only 6; but luckily for them, one of those was rice, which was very well-suited to being a staple crop, so that worked out ok. If we turn to Africa, though, there were only 4 possible candidates, and not very good ones. Finally, in South America, there were just 2. Purely by geography, the Mediterranean region was predisposed to give rise to highly useful farm crops, whereas areas like Africa and South America were almost completely lacking in potential high-yield grains. This, of course, explains why beans, squash, and corn dominated in the diets of New World cultures.

Secondly, almost the same way with wild crops, while there are many large mammals, there are very, very few that are suitable for domestication, and these, too, are unevenly distributed. As it turns out, there are exactly 148 large mammals that might be considered possibilities for domestication, and of those, there are only 14 that are actually well-suited to be domesticated. All the others all fail due to all kinds of things: diet, growth rate, inability to breed in captivity, the inability to live in herds, or some of them were just simply too mean. Of those 14 potential big animals, 9 are considered marginally suitable, so not very good, and that leaves only 5 that have proven to be really well suited for domestication. Can you guess what those 5 vital animals are? They are cows, sheep, goats, pigs, and horses. All 5 of those can be found in Europe and Asia, but none of them were indigenous to North and South America. South America did have one marginally useful domesticatable animal, that's the llama. North America has none. Incidentally, this may be one reason why the wheel wasn't used for transportation in the New World. It wasn't that they couldn't think of a wheel, but that they had no large animals that you could hook up a cart or a wagon to. The largest domestic animals that the Mesoamericans had were little dogs and guinea pigs, and sure enough, both of those were raised for food. But those were no substitute for big animals like cows and sheep.

A subsidiary effect of raising large domesticated animals has to do with infectious disease. Throughout human history, some of the major killers of humanity have been seven deadly, infectious diseases. These are smallpox, influenza, tuberculosis, malaria, plague, measles, and cholera. Do you know where all of these diseases originally evolved from? They all originated among large domesticated animals and then they spread to humans because of their close proximity with those herds. For example, measles and smallpox originally came from cows; influenza originally developed among pigs; and all of those diseases are most destructive when they become introduced into a population of humans among whom they've previously been unknown. That's exactly what happened, for example, when the Spanish conquistadors reached Mexico and they brought with them all of these animal-derived diseases that the local population had never been exposed to because they didn't have those animals.

By the way, in case you were wondering how Africa stacks up in regards to all these issues, it turns out that Africa was particularly shortchanged by geography. The largest domesticatable animal in Africa was a bird called a Guinea Fowl, and sub-Saharan Africa had absolutely no good grains whatsoever. The best crop available for cultivation there was yams, which indeed a lot of cultures cultivated. It's intensive agriculture and animal domestication that really make it possible to feed large cities, and as we've seen, it's in large cities that most technological innovations are produced. You can argue that these disadvantages left Africa far behind in the technology race.

This is only part of Diamond's larger argument; and, indeed, a number of people have challenged various aspects of his thesis of environmental determinism. But the fundamental lack of good domesticatable plants and animals in the Americas and Africa certainly played an important role in how those civilizations developed. As we'll see in the following lectures, all of these areas still gave rise to highly sophisticated, impressive, and original cultures; but Diamond's theories may help to explain why, when they eventually came into contact with European explorers, they were just at a disadvantage in terms of technology as well as other key factors such as resistance to disease.

For almost 2,000 years, we had these New World civilizations evolving in near-total isolation from the rest of the world, and they produced some very memorable, distinctive, and creative cultures. Over the rest of this lecture, and the next two that will follow, I'd like to examine some of those cultures in greater depth, and we'll look at their art, their architecture, and some of their beliefs as well.

The earliest of the Mesoamerican urban cultures to emerge, and maybe the earliest major one in all of the Americas, was a group known as the Olmecs. They developed around 1200 B.C. in the jungle—the low-lying regions— along the coast of the Gulf of Mexico, and this is what is now today the Mexican states of Veracruz and Tabasco. While many aspects of their civilization remain mysterious or things that people are debating about, these cultures are important, because it's clear that they'd exercise a strong influence on all of the Mesoamerican cultures that came after the Olmecs. They're often characterized as a sort of "mother culture" for the entire region. It was they who established the model for pyramid-building; they came up with a calendar that seems to be very similar to the more famous later Mayan calendar; they developed the pantheon of many gods that seems to have spread all throughout Mesoamerica; and certain artistic pursuits, such as portraiture and obsidian mirror-making, also seem to have originated with the Olmecs.

As with the Harappan civilization in India and the Minoan civilization in Greece, almost all of what we know about the Olmecs is derived just from archaeological evidence rather than textual or historical accounts. The Olmecs are probably best known for their big ceremonial centers, which were constructed on a large scale, and these were hacked out of the dense forests, and the art and architecture that adorned them is very distinctive. These are called ceremonial centers, not really cities, because they seem to have been sites mainly intended just for religious rituals. They don't seem to have economic or residential buildings; but, again, to be honest, we know practically nothing about Olmec domestic life.

The most famous of these centers is at a place called La Venta. It's constructed along a north-south axis, and clearly very careful attention was paid to the geometrical relationships between its various structures. La Venta features a huge earthen pyramid that's over 300 feet high, as well as lots of smaller step pyramids. Buried underneath the main courtyard are slabs of various precious stones—jade, granite, and serpentine—that form images of monster and jaguar heads; and clearly these weren't meant to be seen, they were buried right after they were created. Offerings found there consist of precious items such as jade axes, and these were placed in many of the burials. Unfortunately, we just don't know what sorts of rituals were actually performed at this very impressive architectural setting. The apparent focus of Olmec city planning and art has inspired the theory that maybe there was a sort of priestly elite who enjoyed the highest social status and who were in charge of Olmec society. The remains of Olmec sites clearly show that they were skillful engineers who had huge amounts of labor at their disposal. Their earliest ceremonial center, which seems to have been populated by about 2,500 people, is today called San Lorenzo, and it was made on a man-made artificial earth platform over half a mile long that's elevated up above the surrounding terrain so that it wouldn't be affected by the frequent flooding in the area.

The most stereotypical, as well as the most impressive, surviving Olmec artifacts are also among the most mysterious. These are a series of colossal basalt heads that are between 6 and 9 feet in height. In all, there've been about 25 of these heads found, and it's speculated that they might be actual portraits of Olmec kings. They all have a very similar, distinctive look: They're round-faced, chubby-cheeked, broad-nosed, and they all have a kind of odd leather helmet on their head. Some of them feature scars or blemishes on the face, or even gaps in the teeth, and so this has been interpreted that maybe they represent actual individuals. The largest of these heads weighs 30 tons or more, and the blocks of the volcanic stone out of which these colossal heads were carved in some cases had to be transported from quarries that were over 70 miles away from their find site. Probably for most of that distance they would've been floated down a river and then maybe heaved through the jungle to their final resting places.

There's a later origin myth that says that a jaguar mated with a woman who then gave birth to a baby that ate her as she nursed it, and then eventually sort of grew up to become the first ruler. Another typical Olmec art object are statues that depict jaguar "were-babies" that have fangs, jaguar paws, that helmet thing again, and are sometimes shown eating their mothers while nursing. Some scholars believe that the giant baby-faced rulers' heads might refer to that myth, linking them again with jaguars, which were closely associated with the gods in later Mesoamerican belief. Olmec art in general often mixes up features of babies, jaguars, and all sorts of other animals, including toads, snakes, eagles, and caimans, which are relatives of crocodiles. Again, to be honest, we really don't know for sure what these massive heads represent or symbolize.

The Olmecs developed an extensive trade network. They'd import goods such as basalt, obsidian, and iron ore from Mexico's west coast and even from as far south as Costa Rica. The wealth of Olmec society allowed them to bring in luxury items from very far away, and of these, the most important trade item was jade; jade probably had to come from as far away as Guatemala. Out of that jade, the Olmecs loved to make jewelry, masks, and various ritual objects. In general, jade was considered the most precious material by Mesoamerican cultures, even more so than gold, so that later on, the conquistador Hernando Cortes found that he could trade green glass beads for gold.

The trade links that were established by the Olmecs certainly helped to contributed to that cultural homogeneity that's evident in much of ancient Mesoamerica, especially in terms of religion. The Olmec gods, the sort of half-human half-animal supernatural creatures, some of the core myths and various religious symbols, all of these would provide prototypes for later Mesoamerican deities and religious beliefs. The Olmecs also played a ceremonial ballgame that would spread throughout the region. Olmec centers often had ball courts, and little clay ballplayer figurines have been discovered at La Venta as well as other sites.

By at least 600 B.C., the Olmecs had apparently created the first form of writing in Mesoamerica. This was a fairly crude hieroglyphic system that many scholars believe was a forerunner to the later more famous Mayan glyphs. The Olmec hieroglyphs, which are mostly known from a single slab, have yet to be deciphered. The Olmecs also are credited with the first calendar in Mesoamerica, which was something that they needed for religious purposes, and its main application seems to have been to record various religious cycles and to determine the right dates to hold certain rituals.

For reasons that remain uncertain, Olmec civilization seems to have collapsed, or maybe just kind of faded away, sometime around the 4th century B.C. There is some archaeological evidence of Olmec sites suffering severe depopulation in that period, and some scholars have tried to ascribe that to shifts in climate. But the template, the model, which the Olmecs had established would continue, and it would exert a powerful influence over all later Mesoamerican cultures.

In the next lecture, we'll travel to South America and we'll take a look at the earliest cultures that developed there, as well as coming back to Mesoamerica and looking at some of the later civilizations in that place.

Pots and Pyramids—Moche and Teotihuacán
Lecture 35

O f the many civilizations that thrived in South America, two of the most interesting are the Chavín culture, a particularly influential Peruvian civilization, and the Moche, famous for their creative pottery and the spectacular tomb of the Lord of Sipan. The city of Teotihuacán is the most impressive archaeological site in Mesoamerica. It includes a pyramid that rivals those of Egypt and some remarkable iconography, but who built this city and why remains a matter of much mystery and debate.

Chavín de Huántar and Chavín Culture

- Beginning around 2000 B.C., people living in northwestern Peru began to produce ceramic pottery, and over the next millennium ceremonial urban centers with monumental structures began to appear. The common feature of these sites was massive earthen and brick terraced platforms arranged around three sides of a courtyard to form a distinctive U-shape, often with a pyramidal structure at the base of the U.

- The most influential early Peruvian culture, roughly contemporaneous with the Olmecs, is known as Chavín culture. This name derives from the most famous such site, Chavín de Huántar, founded about 900 B.C. in the highlands of the Andes.

- Chavín de Huántar is located at a strategic transportation node, near mountain passes offering good access to the coast, and it reflects the lively trade and interdependence between the highlands and the coastal regions.

- Along the stone walls of the inner enclosure are a series of larger-than-life sculpted humanoid heads with snouts and fangs. In the center is a recessed circular plaza whose sides are lined with relief sculptures of jaguars and creatures with human bodies, fangs, and clawed hands and feet. These sorts of animal-human hybrids are common features in Chavín art, and many believe that the supreme deity was such a creature.

Moche Culture and Civilization

- The best known later civilization of this region is that of the Inca, but they were relative late-comers to the scene, not forming their great empire until around A.D. 1400—well beyond the endpoint of this course. Between the Chavín and Inca were dozens of other cultures, most of whom shared similar architecture, lifestyles, and religious beliefs, including the Moche.

- Archaeologists spend a lot of time looking at clay pots. Ceramic pots last longer than almost any other type of cultural artifact, and almost every culture mastered the techniques making them. Moche pots display a particularly creative and playful streak that makes them especially fun to study.

- Moche culture, based around a series of high Peruvian valleys, flourished between A.D. 100 and 800. They cultivated corn, beans, squash, peppers, and avocados, and fished for fish, crabs, crayfish, and mollusks. Llamas, guinea pigs, and ducks were domesticated and raised as additional food sources.

- This wealth and variety of sustenance enabled the Moche to develop a relatively dense urban culture and be able to devote time and effort to monumental architecture and sophisticated handcrafted objects.

- The Huaca del Sol is a pyramid-like temple composed of an estimated 130 million adobe bricks, making it the largest indigenous clay structure in the Americas.

- Moche potters created an amazing variety of ceramic vessels decorated with fine-line painting that portrays people, animals, plants, supernatural beings, and gods. Moche potters often formed their vessels in the shape of a variety of birds, animals, creatures, and objects. Some pots are cast as portrait busts with nearly as much detail as the famously realistic Roman portrait busts.

- The basic Moche pot is a distinctive design known as a stirrup spout bottle, a roundish vessel from which two hollow tubes form an upward arc. The tubes meet at the top of the arc and fuse into a vertical spout. In more elaborate versions, the vessel itself is cast in the form of a creature or object, or even as multiple figures.

- Even those pots whose main vessels are just standard ovals can have astonishingly complex images painted on them. One scene frequently painted on these pots is a row of realistically portrayed warriors. Sometimes they are shown fighting; other times, they simply parade past in ranks.

- One common category of figure in these illustrations is strange, monstrous beings that mix elements of humans and animals. The designs often seem to have a playful sense of humor in how they anthropomorphize normally inanimate objects. A large body of surviving pots depict beans that have grown limbs, put on armor, and engage in combat.

- In 1987, a spectacular tomb of a high-ranking Moche man was uncovered. Labeled the Lord of Sipán, he was around 40 at the time of death. His high status was indicated by a vast array of expensive grave goods, including fine gold, silver, and copper metalwork inlaid with turquoise and seashells. Six other individuals were buried around him, as well as a dog and several llamas. Nearby were two other tombs, containing a man identified as a priest and another who, as determined by genetic analysis, seems to have been an older relative, perhaps the previous ruler.

By Quapan.

Scholars debate over who built the city of Teotihuacán. It may have been a group effort by many neighboring cultures.

Teotihuacán and the Descendents of the Olmecs

- Cultures that followed the Olmecs included the Zapotec, Nayarit, and Izapa. The Mesoamerican archaeological site of this era stands out for the sheer scale of its monuments is Teotihuacán. Located just 30 miles northeast of Mexico City, it is one of the most visited tourist sites in Mexico.

- Teotihuacán was a truly gigantic city—three and a half miles long and two miles wide, containing more than 5,000 structures. Around A.D. 500, the city had an estimated population of between 125,000 and 200,000, making it one of the biggest cities in the entire world at that time.

- The city is laid out on a grid along north-south and east-west axes and dominated by two massive stone pyramids, today called the Pyramid of the Sun and the Pyramid of the Moon. At more than 200 feet high and 600 feet wide at its base, the Pyramid of the Sun occupies a similar footprint to Egypt's Great Pyramid of Cheops, although it is considerably shorter. Both pyramids were originally surmounted by temples.

- The main street, known as the Avenue of the Dead, connects the three main monuments of the site, beginning in the north at the Pyramid of the Moon and running south for over a mile, past the Pyramid of the Sun, all the way to the so-called Temple of Quetzalcoatl.

- Located within a larger complex, the Temple of Quetzalcoatl features a six-tiered step pyramid decorated with huge protruding stone heads. Half of these depict the head of the god Quetzalcoatl, the feathered serpent. These alternate with heads equipped with fangs and protuberant round eyes—perhaps the water god, Tlaloc. The entire surface of this structure was originally painted in bright shades of blue, red, white, and green.

- The largest stone statue found in Mesoamerica is a 168-ton colossus traditionally believed to represent Tlaloc and associated with Teotihuacán culture. For years this statue lay abandoned in the modern village of Coatlinchan. Today, it stands outside the main entrance of the National Museum of Anthropology in Mexico City.

- Excavations at Teotihuacán have revealed a number of burials, including more than 200 in and under the Temple of Quetzalcoatl complex alone. These are usually interpreted as sacrifices to the gods.

- Evidence of large marketplaces suggests large-scale trade in both local and imported products, including luxury goods such as cacao, shells, rubber, decorative feathers, and foodstuffs. Certain districts of the city seem to have been occupied by craftspeople. A nearby obsidian mine might have been a factor in the choice of the city's location.

- The basic architectural style of Teotihuacán has been labeled *taludtablero*. Each building starts with a layer that has a sloped outward face known as the *talud*. On top of this is placed another layer with a vertical outward face, called the *tablero*. The alternating layers repeat until the desired height is reached.

- Judging from the surviving art, sculptures, murals, and buildings, the religion of Teotihuacán shared common elements with the Mesoamerican civilizations that came both before and after.

- For all the richness and scale of the archaeological remains at Teotihuacán, many fundamental aspects of this civilization remain mysterious, not least of which is the identity of the people who built it. The name Teotihuacán was given to the site by the much later Aztecs.

- The earliest structures have been dated to around 200 B.C., with the city apparently reaching a peak around A.D. 200–500 and then going into decline, with at least parts of the city showing evidence of having been burned down. By 800 A.D., the city seems to have been abandoned.

- Various scholars have attempted to identify the city's builders, linking them to the Olmec, Zapotec, Maya, Toltec, Totonac, or Nahua. Many now believe that the people were influenced by several or all of these, or were composed of a mixture of different ethnic groups.

Colima Pottery

- Mesoamerica had its share of potters who made creative, beautiful, and entertaining ceramic vessels. One culture whose potters might be compared to those of the Moche lived in the region encompassed by the modern Mexican state of Colima.

- From around 300 B.C. to 300 A.D., these potters cast distinctive pieces in the shape of animals and objects. These do not possess the complex stirrup spout arrangement of the Moche vessels but instead have only a simple opening or single spout at the top.

- The most typical Colima-style vessel is in the shape of a plump little dog. These are often sculpted with a great deal of personality and have been identified as a breed of small, hairless dog called the Xoloitzcuintli.

- There is a darker side to these appealing sculptures. Almost certainly their plumpness is due to the fact that many of them were being fattened up to be eaten by humans.

Suggested Reading

Burger, *Chavín and the Origins of Andean Civilization.*

Donnan and McClelland, *Moche Fineline Painting.*

Pasztory, *Teotihuacan.*

Stone-Miller, *Art of the Andes from Chavín to Inca.*

Questions to Consider

1. Using Moche and Colima pottery as examples, what kinds of social values can be learned by examining such images, and is there a danger of projecting our own values onto these images?

2. Sites such as the Lord of Sipan's tomb and Teotihuacán represent enormous expenditure of resources for ritual purposes. Why were these and other civilizations prone to such lavish but impractical displays?

Pots and Pyramids—Moche and Teotihuacán
Lecture 35—Transcript

In the last lecture, we looked at the Olmecs, who were the earliest major culture in Mesoamerica. Now let's consider their counterparts in South America. Beginning around 2000 B.C., people living in northwestern Peru began to produce ceramic pottery, and over the next millennium ceremonial urban centers with monumental structures began to appear. The common feature of all of these sites was massive earthen and brick terraced platforms, and these were always arranged around three sides of a courtyard to form a distinctive U-shape. Often, across the base of the U, there'd be erected a pyramid-like structure. Most scholars have interpreted this that the U-shape reflects core cosmological beliefs regarding the very nature of the universe to these people. The standard interpretation is that the opposing sides of the U represent the opposing yet complementary forces of the universe, and that the crossbar of the U, where that main pyramid is usually located, symbolically represents a fusion or an integration of those cosmically-opposed forces. This kind of dualism combined with a synthesis underlies many of the myths of the better-known later civilizations that will emerge from this same region. Overall, there are about 20 sites with these U-shaped structures that have been so far identified, and some of the more famous ones include Garagay, Huaca la Florida, and Cerro Sechín.

The most influential early Peruvian culture, which was just about contemporaneous with the Olmecs—it also emerged around 1200 B.C. and it would last until around 300 B.C.—is known as Chavín culture. This name comes from the most famous site, Chavín de Huántar, which was founded about 900 B.C. in the highlands of the Andes. Chavín de Huántar is located at a strategic transportation node as so many early cities were. It's near some mountain passes, but it also has good access down to the coast; and so this obviously reflects that lively trade, as well as the interdependence, between the highlands and the coastal regions. Various domesticated animals—including guinea pigs, which were a key food source, and the llama and alpaca—their remains have been found there, and the two large animals were used to carry loads as well as to supply wool for clothing.

At its height, this complex probably housed maybe about 3,000 people, and Chavín de Huántar has one of those stereotypical U-shaped complexes, and its structures rise up to nearly 50 feet in height, and the base of the U there's nearly 150 feet long. Along the stone walls of that inner enclosure are a series of larger-than-life-sized sculpted humanoid heads, and these heads have snouts of animals and fangs. In the center is a recessed circular plaza, and the sides of that are also lined with relief sculptures of jaguars and various mythical creatures. Some of these are shown holding a staff and they might have human bodies but their faces have fangs, and at the ends of their limbs they have clawed hands and feet; so they're odd sorts of animal-human hybrids. These kinds of creatures are very commonly found in Chavín art. Many have speculated that the supreme deity as he's shown on a number of stone slabs was such a creature, with a more or less human body and also wearing human clothing, but with clawed hands and feet and with a more feline or catlike face with those distinctive protuberant fangs.

The term "Chavín" really reflects more of an artistic style and a set of common religious beliefs that are shared among a number of sites rather than being a distinct culture or a single political unit. While some of the subsequent Andean civilizations might be more famous, nearly all of them are thought to have been heavily influenced by this early Chavín culture.

The best known of those later civilizations is, of course, the Inca, but they were relative latecomers to the scene; they didn't form their great empire until around 1400 A.D., so that places them well beyond the endpoint of this course. But between the Chavín and the Inca were dozens of other cultures, most of whom shared a very similar architecture, lifestyle, and religious beliefs. While there's not time to cover all of these, I do want to look at one representative example of these cultures in a little bit more depth, and this is the civilization known as the Moche.

Archaeologists spend a lot of time looking at clay pots. Maybe the main reason for this is that once clay is fired, it lasts forever unless it's repeatedly broken and ground into dust. Ceramic pots last longer than almost any other type of cultural artifact; wood will rot away fairly quickly, and even metal corrodes, but fired clay endures. From very early on, almost every culture mastered the basic techniques of fashioning clay plates and vessels, and some of them included even learning how to throw them on a potters' wheel and to use glazes to make them both waterproof and to simply look attractive. The next logical step was to render these functional objects aesthetically pleasing by casting them into complex shapes and by decorating them with painted designs. In a professional career as an ancient historian and archaeologist, I've spent a great deal of time looking at lots and lots of different clay pots from very many different civilizations. While this is important, of course, to understanding culture, quite honestly it's often not the most exciting aspect of being an archaeologist. But of all those many pots, those from one culture are my absolute favorites, and these are the pots made by the Moche people of Ancient Peru. Many Moche pots have a creative, even sort of playful, streak that makes them especially fun to study.

Moche culture, which was based around a series of valleys high up in Peru, flourished between 100 and 800 A.D. They took advantage of the rivers that were flowing through those valleys to construct elaborate irrigation canals and to cultivate the usual crops such as corn, beans, squash, peppers, and avocados. Because of where they're positioned, they also had access to the sea; and so the sea provided them with an abundant source of other types of food: fish, crabs, crayfish, and mollusks. In addition, they had llamas, guinea pigs, and ducks as animals that they raised as food sources. All of this together made them fairly wealthy, so the Moche were able to develop a dense urban culture and this also meant that they had the spare time to build monumental architecture and to achieve high levels of sophistication in handcrafted objects. The Huaca del Sol is a pyramid-like temple building that's made up of an estimated 130 million adobe bricks, and that makes it the largest indigenous clay structure in all of the Americas. As we'll see when discussing the grave goods in the tomb of the Lord of Sipán, Moche goldsmiths and metalworkers were extremely skilled.

As impressive as those achievements are, it's the Moche pots that are most famous. Moche potters created an amazing variety of ceramic vessels that illustrate and bring to life almost every aspect of their culture. Moche pots are almost always decorated with fine-line paintings that will show people, animals, plants, supernatural beings, and gods. Sometimes the pots will show scenes from everyday life; you'll see scenes of farming, hunting, fishing, and other basic economic activities. The pots will graphically depict people both making war and making love. It's not only the paintings on the pots that offer interesting visual images; sometimes, it's the pot itself. Moche potters would often form their vessels into the shape of birds, animals, monsters, creatures, or inanimate objects. Some pots are cast as portrait busts of the heads and faces of real individuals, and these might have almost as much detail as the famously realistic Roman portrait busts. Some pots will combine painting with low relief molding of the pot's surface.

The standard Moche pot is a very distinctive design, and it's something called a stirrup spout bottle. What it consists of is a roundish vessel from which two hollow tubes form an upward arc that comes together. Where those two tubes meet at the top of the arc, they fuse together and then there's a little vertical spout with an opening at the top. This so-called stirrup spout bottle was very common in South American cultures, and it's shown in ancient art being carried sometimes in a person's hand using that actual little arch as a handle, or sometimes they'll have it slung over their shoulder with a strap passed through that arch. In its basic form, the main vessel of this is just a spherical shape with a kind of flattened bottom on which the pot can rest. But in the more elaborate versions, the vessel itself is modeled or cast into the form of a creature or an object, or sometimes even multiple figures.

Some of the most memorable Moche pots that I've seen include ones that are actually cast in the shape of a winsome little fox sitting back on its haunches, or a merchant mounted atop a llama, or a multi-lobed squash or gourd. There's one I've seen that's very nice that's a kind of smug-looking parrot with its wings folded back. There's a whole set of them that show amorous couples engaged in sex. Another one shows a fat little frog who's inflating his throat sack. Some are just bundles of peppers. One is a very realistic-looking ferocious jaguar rearing up and clawing at the air. One particularly complex pot shows a helmeted warrior bludgeoning his foe with a mace. A finally one is a really bizarre monster that has the head and arms of a human being but the carapace and the six legs of a crab.

Some of these Moche pots really seem to have just been crafted in order to show off the potter's dexterity and creativity. There are some that have spouts within the spout. There are others that have a circular internal chamber within the main vessel, and there are even little windows carved in the outer layer that let you look right through the pot, so it's a kind of optical illusion. One especially clever one that I've seen suspends the chamber that actually holds liquid inside an outer shell. That outer shell has a bunch of little windows in it, and in those windows the sculptor has placed little three-dimensional human faces that are peering inquisitively out of these windows.

Even the pots whose main vessels are just the standard oval can have astonishingly complex images painted upon them. One scene that you see on a whole bunch of these pots is a row of realistically portrayed warriors dressed in this complex segmented body armor with helmets that have high crests on them, and they're carrying all kinds of different weapons, most typically spears, maces, or axes. Sometimes these warriors will be shown fighting one another, and actually crushing their opponents' skulls and then stripping off their armor to take home as a trophy. Other times, the warriors simply march past in ranks. We also see scenes of temple rituals; sometimes you'll see people who are obviously elites, maybe kings or priests or somebody like that, being carried in litters. One especially odd category of figure in all these illustrations is strange, monstrous beings that again mingle together elements of humans and animals. Some examples of these include men who are shown with the heads of hummingbirds; others are unidentifiable things with the bodies and limbs of crayfish but human heads perched on top; you'll see hybrid owl-men, fox-men, lizard-men, centipede-men, snake-men, and even one remarkable creature that seems to be a cross between a person and a sea urchin. On another pot, you see a thing with the torso and legs of a human being, but also eight octopus tentacles sprouting from its back and two giant eyes on its chest, and it's actually steering a fishing boat.

While these sorts of mutant monsters might strike us as frightening, Moche pot designs often seem to have a very playful sense of humor, and one of the areas that you see this is they'll sometimes anthropomorphize normally inanimate objects. One pot shows a little army of plates, jars, and containers who are helpfully marching around on little legs, bringing food to tables and pouring out drink from themselves into a row of cups while a human in the background watches the whole thing with an approving expression. Another shows a chaotic array of different household objects—spindles, clothing, all kinds of things—sprouting limbs and running about the house. Finally, one pot has an enterprising warrior's helmet that has grown arms and legs and, seemingly on its own initiative, has gone out, captured and subdued an enemy warrior, and is now actually sacrificing him to the gods.

Of all of these animated objects, my personal favorite in terms of category of decoration, and this is something that appears on a number of surviving pots, shows little humble beans. But they're not just beans, these beans have grown human arms and legs, they've put on armor, and they're shown engaging in combat. This genre of decoration is known as "bean warrior" pots, and they come in all kinds of forms and they depict a whole range of exploits of these little militant legumes. Maybe the most bizarre scene is one that shows several well-equipped bean warriors fighting a fierce battle against a group of large-eyed creatures that are some sort of cross between a deer and a human being.

In 1987, one of the more spectacular South American archaeological discoveries was made when a tomb was found of a high-ranking Moche man. This tomb was labeled the Lord of Sipán, and the person buried there was estimated to have been about 40 years old at the time of death. He was obviously someone of high status, because he was buried with a huge array of expensive grave goods, including lots of fine gold, silver, and copper metalwork. He was also buried with ornate headdresses and pectorals, these sorts of chest pieces. Also in there were little ear ornaments that were inlaid with turquoise. There were also a number of seashells and, of course, over 1,000 ceramic pottery items. Six other individuals were buried around the main figure, as well as a dog and a couple of llamas. Found nearby to this tomb were two other tombs, one of which had a man who's been identified as a priest and another that genetic analysis revealed seems to have been an older relative of the Lord of Sipán, maybe he's even the previous Lord or Sipán.

Just as there was a proliferation of cultures that followed the Chavín and that were influenced by them, when we turn our attention northward to Mesoamerica, we find lots of different cultures that followed in the footsteps of the Olmecs and who shared a number of fundamental cultural similarities with them. Some of those included cultures such as the Zapotec, the Nayarit, and the Izapa.

The Mesoamerican archaeological site of this era that most stands out, though, for the sheer, huge scale of its monuments is a place called Teotihuacán. This is located just about 30 miles northeast of Mexico City, and the ancient city of Teotihuacán is probably one of the most visited tourist sites in Mexico today. You can go there and you can explore the remains of what was once a truly gigantic city. It stretched three-and-a-half miles in one direction and two miles in the other, and it contained at least 5,000 structures. At its zenith, which is thought to be around 500 A.D., Teotihuacán had an estimated population of maybe between 125,000 and 200,000 people, which would've made it one of the biggest cities in the entire world at that time, and almost certainly the largest city yet seen in the Americas. Teotihuacán has these very, very large main avenues that run through the city, and the whole thing's laid out on a grid plan, so it's positioned along north-south and east-west axes.

Teotihuacán is dominated by two massive stone pyramids; and we don't know what gods these were actually to, but they've been labeled by later archaeologists the Pyramid of the Sun and the Pyramid of the Moon. At over 200 feet high and 600 feet wide at its base, the Pyramid of the Sun occupies just about the same footprint as Egypt's Great Pyramid of Cheops although, because the Pyramid of the Sun has somewhat squatter proportions, it's shorter than the Egyptian pyramid. There are broad staircases that lead up to the summits of both pyramids, and at the top there were clearly temples where various rites and sacrifices to honor the gods were performed. Unlike the pyramids in Egypt, tourists can climb to the top of the pyramids of Teotihuacán, and from up there you can survey the surrounding city from a very nice, lofty perch. It's a view that I can attest from personal experience is a spectacular one.

The main street at Teotihuacán has been labeled the Avenue of the Dead, and it nicely connects the three main monuments of the site. It begins in the north at the Pyramid of the Moon, it runs south for over a mile to a complex called the Temple of Quetzalcoatl, and along the way it passes by the other big pyramid, the Pyramid of the Sun. The Temple of Quetzalcoatl is one part of a larger complex, but its most prominent feature is a six-tiered step pyramid, and the vertical faces on each level of that pyramid are decorated with huge, carved, protruding stone statues of heads. Half of these heads depict the god

Quetzalcoatl, and this is in his manifestation as a feathered serpent; so it's a snake head with a ring of feathers around it. By the way, that's the literal meaning of the word "Quetzalcoatl"; "Quetzal" is the feathers of the Quetzal bird, "coatl" means "snake." These heads alternate with the head of another god who has fangs and big, protuberant, round eyes, and these are thought to be representations of the water god, Tlaloc, although some people have started to question that identification. The whole surface of this structure, including the heads, originally was painted in bright, bright shades of blue, white, and green.

The largest stone statue found in Mesoamerica is a 168-ton colossus that traditionally has been thought to represent the rain god Tlaloc, and to be associated with Teotihuacáno culture. For years, this particular statue lay abandoned on its back in a brush-filled gulley in the modern little village of Coatlinchan; that's about 30 miles outside of Mexico City. My family is from Mexico, and when my father was a young boy, he and his schoolmates would climb on top of this giant Tlaloc statue and they'd play around on top of it and sometimes eat picnics on top of it. Finally in 1964, archaeologists took away this huge, colossal statue using a specially-built flatbed truck, and today, the Coatlinchan Tlaloc stands upright right outside the main entrance of the National Museum of Anthropology in Mexico City.

Excavations at Teotihuacán have also revealed a number of burials, including at least 200 that are in and around the Temple of Quetzalcoatl complex alone. Because of their position, these are usually interpreted as being sacrifices to the gods. There's also evidence of large marketplaces, so that gives us some sense of the scale of trade in both local and imported products; and trace remains tell us that some of the luxury goods that were imported include cacao, shells, rubber, and decorative feathers, as well as all kinds of foodstuffs. Certain areas of the city seem to have been occupied by groups of craftspeople who shared a specialization; so, for example, all the workers who made jade objects could be found in one zone of the city. Archaeologists have also found a nearby obsidian mine that might have played a role in the choice of the city's location. Obsidian, that shiny black stone, wasn't only held precious throughout Mesoamerica as a favored material for things like art objects, tools, and mirrors, but it's also the substance used to make weapons and sacrificial knife blades.

The basic architectural style of Teotihuacán, which you can see both in the monumental ceremonial buildings but also the ordinary humble residential or commercial structures, is something that's been called the talud-tablero style of architecture. In this style, buildings are constructed by beginning with a layer that has a sloped outward face, and this is called the talud. On top of this is placed another layer that has a vertical outward face, and that's the tablero. Then that's followed by another sloped section, another vertical one, and so on; so you get alternating layers of the sloped and the vertical, and that's the talud-tablero style of architecture.

Judging from the surviving art, sculptures, murals, and buildings, the religion that was practiced by the Teotihuacános clearly shared some common elements, at least in terms of the iconography of the gods and the performance of certain rituals, with other Mesoamerican civilizations that came both before and after them.

For all the richness and scale of the archaeological remains at Teotihuacán, there are a lot of fundamental things that we don't know about that civilization, and not least of these is the identity of the people who built this huge city. The name Teotihuacán was given to that site by the much, much later Aztecs, and all it does is it translates to something like "the place of the gods." Again, we don't know what the real name of this place was or what the people who built it called themselves. The earliest structures there have been dated to around 200 B.C., and the city seemed to have reached a peak around 200–500 A.D. and then went into some sort of decline. There's some evidence, in at least parts of Teotihuacán, that seems like some of those buildings were burned down; but, again, whether that's by invaders or some sort of internal tension, nobody really knows. What archaeology can tell us is by about 800 A.D., the city seems to have been completely abandoned.

As for the people, the Teotihuacános themselves, who they were is uncertain. Various scholars have tried to construct arguments identifying them as belonging to or at least being linked to various other cultural groups in Mesoamerica. Arguments have been made trying to tie them to the Olmec, the Zapotec, the Maya, the Toltec, the Totonac, or the Nahua. But many now believe that the inhabitants of Teotihuacán were maybe influenced by several or all of those different groups, so perhaps they were a mixture of different ethnicities. As we've seen over and over again in this course, when all that survives from a site or culture is physical archaeological evidence, it's very hard to reach firm conclusions even about basic issues such as these.

Mesoamerica also had its share of potters who made creative, beautiful, and even entertaining ceramic vessels. Perhaps one area whose potters might be compared to those of the Moche is the region encompassed by the modern Mexican state of Colima. From around 300 B.C.–300 A.D., the ancient potters of the Colima region, which is in central Mexico along the Pacific coast, produced a very distinctive style of ceramic vessel. Like some of their Andean counterparts, Colima pots are famous for being cast in the shapes of animals and objects. These Colima pots don't have that whole complicated stirrup spout arrangement that we saw in Moche vessels, but instead they just have a simple opening or one spout at the top. Some of these shapes that these pots took are realistically rendered parrots, cacti, gourds, ducks, and fish. Sometimes you see humans, including flute-playing musicians and, a little bit oddly, there are a number of pots in the form of hunchbacks and dwarves.

But the most standard Colima-style vessel by far is in the shape of a plump little dog. These are often sculpted with a great deal of personality, with the pups sometimes looking like they're smiling, or sometimes you even have two dogs standing upright, resting their paws on one another's shoulders as if they're in a kind of dancing posture. These particular pots have been identified as depicting this specific breed of small, hairless dog that's found in Mexico, and it's called the Xoloitzcuintli. While the dog pots are certainly cute—and this factor has made replicas of them a very lucrative item to sell to tourists—there's a darker side to these appealing little sculptures. Unfortunately, the plumpness of these dogs is almost certainly due to the fact that they're being fattened up in order to be eaten by humans. As I mentioned, Mesoamerica lacked large domesticated animals, so that the Xoloitzcuintli dogs were an important source of meat. In contrast to the multicolored paintings found on Moche pottery, Colima pots are almost always unpainted, and they just have a simple glaze that's used to bring out the natural colors of the reddish-orange clay that they're sculpted in. In the next lecture, we'll look at our final and maybe the most sophisticated Mesoamerican culture, the Maya.

Blood and Corn—Mayan Civilization
Lecture 36

The Maya were one of the longest-lasting, most influential, and geographically dispersed cultures in Mesoamerica. They were also one of the most advanced, the first culture in the Americas who left a written historical record as well as archeological evidence behind. Technically not a single empire, the Maya were a group of city-states covering a large geographic area that shared a common culture. Many aspects of their culture are similar to those of other Mesoamerican groups, including their religious rituals and their system of timekeeping, but they refined the common writing system and were advanced mathematicians and astronomers.

The Maya—America's First Historical Culture

- On January 16, 378, an ancient Mesoamerican warrior prepared for battle. His name was Smoking Frog, and he commanded the army of the Mayan city of Tikal on behalf of his king, Great Jaguar Paw. On that day, using new weapons and tactics possibly imported from Teotihuacán, he led his army to a great victory over the forces of the rival city of Uaxactún.

- We know Smoking Frog's name, the exact date of his victory, and the details of these events because, unlike most of early North and South American cultures, the Maya had a fully developed system of writing.

- The achievements of the Maya were many because they were among the longest-lasting, the geographically most extensive, and the culturally most sophisticated of all Mesoamerican peoples. We can also call them a historical civilization in the sense not only ample archaeological evidence but their written records survive.

- Mayan civilization arose in the jungle lowlands of what is today southern Mexico, Guatemala, Belize, El Salvador, and eastern Honduras. By the middle of the 1st millennium B.C., this area was occupied by small city-states who were farming the usual corn, squash, beans, and potatoes.

- The area was also a source of cocoa, a highly sought-after trade product. Chocolate was drunk by the upper classes, and cocoa beans were used as currency. Household gardens supplied herbs, chili peppers, and tomatoes. Pineapples, papayas, guavas, and other fruits grew in orchards. Palm trees were exploited for oil and fronds, which thatched roofs. Copal trees provided resin for incense, which was burnt for the gods.

- Mayan civilization reached its peak, or classic period, between about A.D. 250 and 900. It was not a single unified empire; rather, each local area was ruled over by a hereditary king, who was advised by a council of priests and nobles. Local governments imposed taxes, oversaw justice, administered nearby villages, engaged in foreign policy, conducted war, and constructed ceremonial and monumental structures.

- Skilled craftsmen, scribes, and warriors tended to concentrate around the urban centers, but the vast majority of Mayans were farmers who lived in adobe and thatch huts resembling those used by farmers in the region today.

The City of Tikal

- Tikal was one of the largest and most important urban centers of the classic period. Located in the central Yucatan in what is today Guatemala, it occupied more than six square miles and was surrounded by a moat and rampart. It was probably the second largest urban center of Mesoamerica after Teotihuacan.

- Tikal was not located along a river, and it had no good source of fresh water. The Maya solved this by constructing a series of enormous cisterns and reservoirs for rainwater collection sufficient to supply 30,000 people during a complete drought lasting 6 months. These were so well constructed that the excavators of Tikal were able to refurbish one and use it for their own water needs.

- Tikal city features five tall step pyramids surmounted by temples with distinctive roof crests. The tallest of these pyramids is roughly equivalent in height to the Pyramid of the Sun at Teotihuacan, but the Mayan pyramids have extremely steep sides, giving them a smaller footprint on the ground.

- The ceremonial center at Tikal includes palaces, courtyards, altars, and plazas. These are solidly constructed out of limestone blocks and often adorned with relief carvings and painted plaster. Scattered about the site are many stone steles covered with low-relief images and Mayan glyphs, including ones that tell the stories of king Great Jaguar Paw and his general Smoking Frog.

The Mayan Ball Game

- Tikal also features a number of specialized enclosures devoted to the Mayan ball game. Throughout Mesoamerica, sacred ball games were played both for entertainment and as a religious ritual. The rules of the game are not known, but artistic representations suggest that players had to direct a hard rubber ball through rings high up on the court's walls, using their hips and shoulders but not their hands.

- The players wore protective padding around their arms and knees and large U-shaped belts on their waists to cushion their ribs and hips. For decoration, they wore elaborate animal headdresses often topped with quetzal feathers and had implements called *hachas* in their belts. Oversized, ornately carved stone belts that have been discovered throughout Mesoamerica may have been awarded to victorious players. The unlucky losers were quite often sacrificed to the gods.

- Reliefs show prisoners with their limbs tightly bound up so that their bodies formed a ball, and in this form, they may have symbolically or literally been employed as game balls. These unfortunates were ultimately sacrificed by being rolled down the steep staircases of the temples to their deaths.

- A ball game between twin sibling heroes and the gods played a crucial role in an important Mayan creation myth. The twins are forced to play in the ball court of the underworld. One of them has his head severed by killer bats, and his head is to be used as the ball. The decapitated twin plays with a substitute head made from a squash.

- While a helpful rabbit distracts the attention of the gods, the twin retrieves and reattaches his real head. The twins win the game, decapitate the underworld gods, and resurrect their father, the god of corn, who was buried beneath the ball court. By playing the sacred ball game, the Maya reenacted this myth and sacrificed their blood to thank the corn god who had sacrificed himself to feed them.

Mayan Cosmology and Religion

- For the Mayans, there was not a strict division between natural and supernatural spheres but rather constant interaction between them. The universe was made up of three realms—the Upperworld, Middleworld, and Underworld. Gods, spirits, and ancestors dwelt in the Upperworld and the Underworld. They also shared the Middleworld with human beings.

- The four quadrants of the universe were arranged around a central axis and aligned with the four cardinal directions, with a god connected with each one. Symbolically, the four directions and axis each had their own colors, trees, and birds.

  o The primary direction, East, associated with the rising sun, was symbolized by red.

- The West, where the sun sets, was linked with the underworld and the color black.

- The North, connected with the ancestors and death, was white.

- The South, associated with the sun, was yellow.

- The center, through which ran the great axis of creation, was green.

- The Maya were polytheistic, and their pantheon of deities often overlapped with those of other cultures of the region. While more than 250 names of Mayan divinities have been documented, they did not have 250 different gods. Mayan gods were not distinct entities; they had fluid identities and could shift between various aspects, avatars, or manifestations.

- Gods were even complex in how they were depicted. Sometimes they were shown as humanoid, sometimes as human-animal hybrids, and sometimes as beasts—real or mythical.

- One of the most important gods was Chac, the rain god, who was often portrayed as possessing the features of aquatic creatures. He was believed to frequent caves, where storms were thought to originate, and was sometimes shown carrying a lightning bolt. Chac appears to be one of the oldest gods of Mesoamerica. He can be associated with Tlaloc of Teotihuacan, who was important to the much later Aztecs.

- Religion infused all aspects of Mayan life. Priests were high-status individuals in Mayan society, and they played a key role in government, war, and the economy as well as in religion. Education was mainly for priests, who had to read and write as part of their religious observances and use math and astronomy to timing religious ceremonies. The Maya were far more adept at astronomical observations than their European counterparts of the time.

- Bloodletting played a central role in Mayan religious rituals. Human blood was considered a precious substance and thus was the highest sacrifice that could be presented to the gods. Self-inflicted public bloodletting was a standard form of worship.

- Human sacrifice and removal of the heart were also regularly practiced, as suggested by both artistic and archaeological evidence, and decapitation was another common method of sacrifice. Blood spurting from the chest or neck was sometimes portrayed as quetzal feathers, a highly prized trade item, to emphasize the precious nature of human blood.

Mayan Achievements

- While it is easy to focus on the lurid aspects of Mayan civilization, they were responsible for a number of great intellectual achievements. Foremost among these are their calendar and written language.

- The Maya developed a base 20 mathematical system that included the concept of zero. This system is quite flexible and allowed Mayan mathematicians to calculate sums in the hundreds of millions.

- The Maya were the only Mesoamericans to create a complex form of written language. Their sophisticated system consisted of a mixture of ideographs that represent objects and symbols that represent sounds. Each sign is known as a glyph, and the total number of known Mayan glyphs is around 2,000.

- We have about 15,000 Mayan inscriptions surviving on stone and pottery. The Mayans also wrote on a kind of paper made from bark, but unfortunately, these books were destroyed by the Spanish conquistadors. Only four books survived; perhaps fortunately, these were texts on astronomy and the calendar.

- For a long time, scholars were unable to decipher the Mayan language, but when they noticed the frequent occurrence of symbols for dates in the Mayan calendar, they were able to use these as a starting point for interpreting the glyphs.

- The discovery of a royal tomb in the jungle at Palenque provided an important source for Maya hieroglyphs, which were inscribed all over a huge limestone slab found under the aptly-named Temple of Inscriptions.

Mayan Decline

- In the 8th and 9th centuries A.D., classical Mayan civilization went into decline. The reason is unknown, but various theories include overpopulation, overcultivation, drought, erosion, deforestation, endemic warfare, and internal rebellions. Most likely it was the result of a combination of these factors.

- There was a dramatic drop in population accompanied by a cessation of new construction and even the wholesale abandonment of many cities in this period. Studies of skeletons from Copán also show pronounced signs of malnutrition and disease between 650 and 850.

- Power shifted to the northern Yucatan peninsula, where newer cities such as Uxmal and Chichén Itzá fared better and Toltec civilization, which flourished for a few centuries and then faded away. These regions would continue to develop in isolation for another five hundred years or so until the arrival of Europeans following Columbus.

Suggested Reading

Coe, *The Maya.*

Hunter, *A Guide to Ancient Maya Ruins.*

Thompson, *Maya History and Religion.*

1. How do Mayan myths and values compare to others that we have studied, such as those of ancient Greece or Vedic India?

2. Relatively few of the civilizations we have examined practiced large-scale human sacrifice. Why do you think this was such an important part of Mayan culture and not others?

Blood and Corn—Mayan Civilization
Lecture 36—Transcript

On January 16, 378 A.D., an ancient Mesoamerican warrior prepared for battle. He placed on his head a tall headdress that culminated in a life-size parrot with bright feathers. As decoration and a sign of his rank, he wore large, elaborate spools in the stretched-out lobes of his ears and a heavy necklace of squarish beads hung around his neck. A wide belt was wrapped around his waist, and trailing from it behind his back was a bundle of the long, iridescent blue-green feathers of the quetzal bird. In one hand, he clutched a long, wooden club whose edges were studded with razor-sharp chips of obsidian, while in the other, he held a spear thrower that could accurately fling a deadly dart over 100 yards. The name of this warrior was Smoking Frog, and he commanded the army of the Mayan city of Tikal. He did so on behalf of the king of Tikal, Great Jaguar Paw. On this day, using new weapons and tactics possibly imported from Teotihuacán, he'd lead his army to a great victory over the forces of the rival city of Uaxactún. This city fell to Smoking Frog, and he'd go on to rule it for at least 18 years.

The way we know about Smoking Frog's appearance is because he erected a stone monument that bears his image, and more importantly, we know his name and the exact date of that victory, and the details of all these events including the battle and its aftermath; and that's because, unlike the other North and South American cultures we've been studying, the Maya had a fully developed system of writing. The achievements of the Maya are many, and not least because they're among the longest-lasting of all these cultures. They're also among the geographically most extensive, and culturally they raised their civilization to a high level. Even better, though, they're a historical civilization in the sense that we have surviving from them not only ample archaeological evidence, but also these written records.

Mayan civilization arose in the jungly lowlands of what today is the southernmost part of Mexico and also Guatemala, Belize, El Salvador, and eastern Honduras. By the middle of the 1st millennium B.C., that whole area was occupied by little city-states who, of course, were farming the usual corn, squash, beans, and potatoes. The crucial role of corn as their main food source is suggested by both scientific evidence and Mayan mythology.

Isotopic analysis of Mayan skeletons has shown that over 70 percent of their diet was derived from corn, while according to the Mayan creation myth the gods formed human beings out of a dough that's made of corn and blood. As we'll see, blood and corn are recurrent themes in various aspects of Mayan culture. Corn could even be fermented to produce a popular alcoholic beverage called *chicha*, which tasted something like beer supposedly. When Christopher Columbus's son Ferdinand was offered some by a Maya trading canoe, he reported that he found the brew to be "quite tasty." This area was also a source of cocoa, a highly sought after trade product; and chocolate was drunk by the upper classes, and cocoa beans were used as currency throughout the region, as were, of course, various types of beads, salt, and bolts of cotton cloth. Household gardens supplied families with a wide range of herbs, and also chili peppers and tomatoes. Other tropical fruits that people ate at this time included pineapples, papayas, and guavas. Palm trees could be exploited for their oil and their fronds, which were used to make thatched roofs; and copal trees provided resin that was turned into incense that was then burnt for the gods.

Mayan civilization reached its peak during the so-called Classic Maya Period, which began around 250 A.D. and lasted until about 900 A.D. During that time, the population seems to have steadily increased, peaking probably around the 8th century; and also around then we got some very large urban centers. It wasn't a single unified political empire, but rather each little local area was ruled over by its own usually hereditary king, and he's was typically advised by a council made up of priests and noblemen. These local governments would impose taxes, oversee justice, administer the nearby villages, engage in foreign policy, wage warfare, and they also organized the construction of ceremonial and monumental structures in the main city of each little region. At those centers were concentrated people who were skilled craftsmen, scribes, and warriors, but keep in mind that, as usual, the vast majority of Mayans, like in all the civilizations we've studied, were simple farmers. They lived in adobe and thatch huts, often more out in the jungle, and, in fact, their houses resembled the kind of houses still used by some poor farmers in the region today.

One of the very largest and most important urban centers of the Classic Period was the city of Tikal, one of whose generals was the Smoking Frog that I mentioned in the opening anecdote of this lecture. Tikal is located pretty much in the center of the southern half of the Yucatan peninsula, just over the border in what today is Guatemala. It has many of the stereotypical types and styles of buildings that characterized Mayan architecture in general. The city stretched out over about six square miles, and the whole thing was surrounded by a moat and rampart to give it some protection. For the period at least covered by this course, it's probably the second largest urban center of Mesoamerica after Teotihuacán.

Making the size of Tikal all the more impressive was the fact that it wasn't located along a river and therefore there wasn't a good available source of fresh water at Tikal. The solution to this was to construct a series of enormous or reservoirs into which they'd collect rainwater. In a worst case scenario, these are estimated to have been sufficient to supply about 30,000 people during a drought that lasted six months. These reservoirs were so well-constructed that the original excavators of the site of Tikal were easily about to fix one up and use it for their own water needs while on the site.

Tikal is one of the most photogenic Mayan archaeological sites, and a lot of this has to do with the fact that the city had no fewer than five very tall step pyramids, each of which was surmounted by a temple that has a kind of distinctive roof crest. Today, those tall pyramids poke up in an attractive manner above the level of the dense surrounding jungle, and it's a very memorable image to see all these coming up out of the jungle. It's also an image that's maybe most familiar now because it appears in the movie *Star Wars* as the site of a rebel base. The tallest of these pyramids, which were completed in 741 A.D. as we know from an inscription in the temple at its apex, is 230 feet high. This is about the same height as the Pyramid of the Sun at Teotihuacán, but if you put the two pyramids side by side, their proportions are very different. The Pyramid of the Sun has a far greater volume because its sides are much more gradually sloped, whereas the Mayan pyramids have very steep sloped sides, and that gives them a smaller footprint on the ground.

In addition to the five great pyramids, the ceremonial center of Tikal also has a whole series of palaces, courtyards, altars, and nice plazas. Almost all of these are solidly constructed out of limestone blocks, and those blocks are often adorned with relief carvings and painted plaster. Scattered all around the site are stone steles that are covered with low-relief images and Mayan glyphs, and among these is the one that tells that stories of King Great Jaguar Paw and his general, Smoking Frog.

Finally, Tikal also features a number of specialized enclosures that were devoted to staging a very important Mayan ritual, the ball game. As I've said, all throughout Mesoamerica, a form of sacred ball game was played both seemingly for entertainment and as a religious ritual. Cities and ceremonial centers such as Tikal often have stone ball courts. The exact rules of this game that was played on these courts isn't definitely known, but we can look at artistic representations on vases and these seem to suggest that the players had to direct a small, hard rubber ball through rings that were set high up on the court's walls, and the tricky part was they had to do this using only their hips and their shoulders, but not their hands. For protection, they had padding around their arms and knees and they also wore these large U-shaped belts on their waists that could cushion their ribs and hips. For decoration, they had elaborate animal headdresses, again, often topped with quetzal feathers. They also had an odd sort of implement called a *hacha* in their belt. We have, surviving, these sort of oversized, ornately carved stone belts that have been found all throughout Mesoamerica that may have been perhaps awarded to victorious players at this game.

In keeping with the common Mesoamerican belief that the gods required human blood for sustenance, often the unlucky losers of this ballgame were sacrificed. Ball games could also be used to act out battles against the Maya's enemies. Reliefs show prisoners who've had their limbs tightly bound up so that their bodies almost formed a ball, and in this form they may have been symbolically—or maybe even literally—employed as game balls. But in the end, these unfortunates seem to have been sacrificed by being rolled down that steep staircase of the temples to their deaths below.

In addition, a ball game between two sibling heroes and the gods played a crucial role in one of the most important Mayan creation myths. In this myth, the Hero Twins are forced to play a series of ball games, and the games are held in the ball court of the underworld. As if this wasn't enough of a disadvantage, one of them has his head severed by some killer bats and the

Death gods of the underworld decree that the head is to be used as the ball. Undeterred by this, the decapitated twin plays the game with a substitute head made from a squash, and then, at a key moment while a helpful rabbit distracts the attention of the gods, he manages to retrieve and reattach his real head. The twins go on to win the game, after which they both decapitate the underworld gods and resurrect their own father, who's the god of corn, and he'd previously been killed and buried beneath the ball court. The corn god is reborn in the form of a stalk of maize that sprouts up from a crack in the ball court and grows up out of the underworld and on into the realm of humans. By playing the sacred ball game, the Maya thus in a sense reenacted this myth, and they sacrificed their own blood in order to thank the Corn God, who'd sacrificed himself to feed them. Once again, we see these central roles of blood and corn.

For the Mayans, there wasn't a strict division between the natural and the supernatural spheres, but rather, as we see in this myth, there's a constant interaction between them. In their cosmology, vertically, the universe was made up of three realms: the Upperworld, the Middleworld, and the Underworld. And while gods, spirits, and the ancestors dwelt in the Upperworld and the Underworld, they also shared that Middleworld with human beings. Horizontally, also, there were four quadrants arranged around a central axis, and the Maya believed that these were aligned with the four cardinal directions, and there's a specific god connected with each direction. The whole Mayan concept of the universe was a very orderly, harmonious one.

Symbolically, the Middleworld's four directions and the central axis also each had their own colors, trees, and birds. The primary direction, east, which was associated with the rising sun, was symbolized by the color red. The West, the place where the sun sets, was linked with the Underworld, just like in Egypt; and the color for that direction was black. The North, connected with the ancestors and also death, was white; and the South, associated with the sun, was yellow. The center, through which ran the great axis of creation, was green.

As with all Mesoamerican cultures, the Maya were polytheistic, and their pantheon of deities often overlapped with those of other cultures of the region. Over 250 names of Mayan divinities have been documented, but this doesn't really mean that they had 250 different gods. Mayan gods weren't distinct entities strictly defined by just a couple characteristics and attributes. Instead, interestingly, they had much more fluid, amorphous identities, and they could shift between various aspects, avatars, or manifestations, and each of these had its own different name and abilities. Some scholars like to use the terms "deity complex" or "god cluster" in order to try and describe the multiplicity of identities of these gods. At times, this means that a god might conceivably exhibit opposite qualities, such as in one form being a male god but in another female, or sometimes is very friendly to humans and sometimes hostile. Gods were just in general very complex in the way that they're conceived of and depicted. Sometimes gods were shown as humanoid. But, again, sometimes they're human-animal hybrids; and other times they're just as various beasts, both real and mythical, with only a couple or sometimes no human characteristics whatsoever.

Of all the gods, one of the most important and central was Chac, the rain god. He's often portrayed as having the features or qualities of various aquatic creatures; so he might be shown with scales, with catfish-like whiskers, fangs, or a snout. He was thought especially to hang out in caves, where the Maya believed that storms came from; and so appropriately sometimes he's shown carrying a lightning bolt. Chac was usually seen as a kind god, he's someone to whom farmers prayed for assistance; and he appears to be one of the very oldest gods of Mesoamerica who's worshipped in one incarnation or another longer than almost any other. He can be associated with the rain god Tlaloc of Teotihuacán, and Tlaloc himself was also an important god to the much later Aztecs, so we can see this kind of continuity in the gods. The importance of rain gods in Mesoamerica was, of course, linked to the fundamentally agricultural nature of these societies, in which crops such as maize were dependant on getting a good rainfall.

Religion infused all aspects of Mayan life. Priests clearly were high-status individuals in Mayan society, and they seemed to have played a direct role in things like government, war, and the economy, as well as religion. Education was mainly intended for and limited to priests, and this is because they had to be able to read and write as part of their religious observances, and math and astronomy were focused on issues of timing the ceremonies for the gods and when you'd hold certain festivals. The Maya grew quite adept at astronomical observations, and they kept careful records of astrological phenomenon; and in this regard, Mayan astronomers were far ahead of their European counterparts of the same era.

In Mayan religious rituals, bloodletting played a central role. Human blood was considered to be one of the most precious substances, and so it's the highest type of sacrifice that you could present to the gods. Just as human beings were originally created from blood, so the gods depended on blood for sustenance. Offerings could consist of your own blood, someone else's blood, or an animal's blood; and self-inflicted public bloodletting was a standard form of worshipping the gods. The way this would usually work is you'd draw blood from your own body. The most commonly pierced areas were the tongue, the ears, the arms, or the penis and you'd do this with a thorn, a sharp stone, sometimes a stingray spine, or just a sharpened stick. Then the resulting blood was allowed to drip onto paper made out of bark or sometimes collected in dishes, and it would then be presented as an offering to the gods. One very common scene in Mayan art is men piercing holes through their tongues or their penises and then actually stringing cords through them in order to prolong the bleeding so that it wouldn't coagulate and dry up.

Human sacrifice and removal of the heart were also regularly practiced as a way to appease the gods, and we know this from both artistic and archaeological evidence. There are stelae and murals that portray victims who've been stretched out over stones, they have their limbs held down, and they have their hearts cut out; and the actual sacrificial stones on which they'd do this have also been found. Decapitation was another common method of human sacrifice, and skulls were sometimes displayed on platforms or buried as dedicatory offerings. In scenes in art, the blood spurting from the chest or the neck was often portrayed as quetzal feathers, which, remember, were another highly prized trade item, and I think that's done to emphasize the precious and rare nature of human blood. By giving their own blood to nourish the gods, people were in essence repaying the debt that they owed the gods for their creation, because in that creation the gods had to spill their blood to form human beings.

The first modern interpreters of Mayan civilization tended to depict them as being very peaceful, but more recent scholarship has revealed a greater role both of human sacrifice in their culture and just of warfare generally; and particularly from the middle Classic Period onwards, when there seems to have been greater stress on society because the population was growing, there were clearly frequent wars among the different little Mayan states.

While it's easy sometimes to focus on these lurid aspects of Mayan civilization, they were responsible for a number of great intellectual achievements. Foremost among these are their calendar and their written language. The Maya developed a complete mathematical system, and unlike our base 10 system, their system was a base 20 system. The Maya would count from 1–4 and represent this with simple dots; then the number 5 would be represented by a bar; 6–9 were drawn with a bar plus 1–4 dots above it; and then 10 was two [horizontal] bars. This system could be repeated up to 20, and then finally 0 was represented by a seashell. Numbers that were bigger than this were drawn as stacks consisting of multiples of 20 raised to various powers; in other words, such as 20, 400, 8,000, and so on. It sounds kind of complicated, but this system is actually very flexible, very usable, and it allowed Mayan mathematicians to calculate sums that went up to the hundreds of millions. In terms of the calendar, the Mayan year consisted of 18 months of 20 days each for a total of 360 days. The so-called Mayan long count calendar began at our equivalent in our dating system of August 11, 3114 B.C. and it simply counts forward from that point. The Maya expressed dates in terms of multiples of 20 days, or 360 days, or 7,200 days, or 144,000 days.

The Maya were the only Mesoamericans to create really a fully developed complex form of written language, and their writing system consisted of a mix of ideographs, which represent objects, and symbols, which represent sounds. Each of those two types of signs, whether pictorial or phonetic, is called a glyph, and the total number of known number of Mayan glyphs, at least that have been identified, is around 2,000. Archaeologists have found about 15,000 Mayan inscriptions, and that's counting everything from stuff on stone and pottery. The Mayans also, though, wrote on a sort of paper that was made from bark, and they had books on this bark; but unfortunately, almost all of those were destroyed by the Spanish conquistadors. We have some evidence of this in accounts by some of the Spaniards. For example, Bishop Diego de Landa wrote down, talking about the Maya: "We found a large number of books in these characters and, as they contained nothing in which there were not to be seen superstition and lies of the devil, we burned them all."

Only four of those bark books survived that sort of destruction and, maybe fortunately, the ones that survived were texts about astronomy and the calendar. In general, the Maya seemed to have used their written language mostly to keep very precise and detailed dynastic records; so information about the dates of a ruler's birth, his rise to power, his marriage and death, and these accounts also tended to emphasize war victories. In what documents we have surviving, there's no mention of any lower-class Mayans.

For a long time, scholars were unable to decipher the Mayan language, but when they noticed the frequent occurrence of symbols for dates in the Mayan calendar, they were able to use that as a starting point to interpret the rest of the glyphs. The discovery of a royal tomb in the jungle at Palenque provided an important source for Maya hieroglyphs because they're inscribed all over this big limestone slab that was found beneath the rather aptly-named "Temple of Inscriptions." That slab, when finally deciphered, revealed to us the very first identifiable individual in Mayan history, a ruler named Pacal, and his name glyph sort of translates as "the shield."

In the 8th and 9th centuries A.D., Classical Mayan civilization went into decline; and, once again, the reason for that is unknown. Some of the theories that have been proposed and argued for include overpopulation, overcultivation, drought, erosion, deforestation, constant warfare among the cities, and internal rebellions. Probably the collapse of Classic Mayan civilization was a combination of those factors, with certain of them being more significant in one region and others maybe playing more of a role in another region. But what's clear is that there's a dramatic drop in population, and this was accompanied by a complete cessation of new construction and even the abandonment of many of these cities and ceremonial centers. Estimates for the decrease in population range as high as 80 percent or more in some areas; so this was a catastrophic drop off in population. Studies of skeletons from Copán, another site, also show pronounced signs of malnutrition and disease over the period from about 650–850 A.D.

After those events, power then seems to have shifted a little bit to the northern Yucatan Peninsula, where newer cities such as Uxmal and Chichén Itzá seem to have done better. The city of Chichén Itzá, with its many large, spectacular structures, is probably today the most familiar Mayan site, at least to American tourists. The main reason for this is it's very close to the vacation mecca of Cancun. But even though that city began as a Mayan foundation, a lot of the most famous buildings that you see there actually represent the work of a later people who were known as the Toltecs, and the Toltecs themselves flourished for a couple centuries and then also sort of faded away.

North and South America would continue to develop in isolation for another 500 years or so until the arrival of Europeans following Columbus. The best-known New World civilizations, the Inca in Peru and probably the Aztecs in Mexico, before that contact was made would establish huge imperialistic empires. But both empires and cultures would be spectacularly destroyed by contact with Europe. Inca and Aztec civilizations would be built upon the foundations provided by those civilizations that I've just surveyed, and they shared central characteristics with these earlier cultures, including worshiping a lot of the same gods and practicing wide-scale blood sacrifice. Neither of those empires, though, really began their rise until centuries after the chronological parameters of this course.

The spectacular ruins of the early societies of North and South America draw millions of tourists every year, and they continue to exert a strong fascination to people today. Although the later European conquest destroyed much of these indigenous cultures, other aspects of their civilization survive, and some of those continue to influence our daily lives in everything from language to diet.

Hunter-Gatherers and Polynesians
Lecture 37

A number of successful and sophisticated cultures around the globe either resisted urbanization or maintained predominantly hunter-gatherer lifestyles for thousands of years in an astonishing range of ecological niches, from arctic regions to deserts to Pacific islands. These nomadic peoples—whether living in the Arctic, in a desert, or in Oceana—share certain social, economic, and dietary similarities. In this lecture, we look at the living hunter-gatherer descendents of such cultures, such as the Inuit and the Australian Aborigines, as well as the artifacts of their ancient ancestors.

The Basics of Hunter-Gatherer Cultures

- Some ancient societies developed sophisticated cultures but did not build cities. Instead, they continued to pursue a hunter-gatherer lifestyle long after most other peoples had abandoned it.

- *Homo sapiens* have only been farming for about 10,000 years. Today, only a miniscule percentage of humans continue to practice anything approaching the hunter-gatherer lifestyle—some Inuit in the Arctic and some Aborigines of the Australian Outback.

- During the period that this course covers, nearly all humans had already switched over to farming or pastoralism, but there were still a few societies scattered around the globe that pursued the traditional mode of human existence.

- Hunter-gatherer cultures share certain universal characteristics. They derive their caloric intake from nondomesticated plants and nondomesticated animals—mostly nuts, berries, fish, fruits, wild plants, insects, scavenged carcasses, and small wild game.

- Hunter-gatherers are almost always nomadic, following their food resources. This mobility was a double-edged sword; on the one hand, it gave them great flexibility, but on the other hand, it limited their material possessions.

- Hunter-gatherers typically live in smallish bands of 10–40 related individuals. These societies are usually more egalitarian than farming or pastoral communities, without pronounced class or hierarchical structures. There also tends to be more gender equality. These characteristics probably result from the fact that everyone had to contribute to nearly all group activities, including hunting.

- Many hunter-gatherer bands were also matrilineal, meaning that the women were related by blood and individuals trace their ancestry through their mothers. To avoid inbreeding, male members of the group would join the group from other bands to find a mate. Such exchanges were facilitated by the fact that in many hunter-gatherer societies, there is a designated time of year when a number of different bands temporarily form a larger community to hunt or gather a specific foodstuff.

The Nomads of the North

- Once intensive farming and pastoralism had spread around the globe, the hunter-gatherer groups that survived into the historical era tended to be in locations that were either ill-suited for farming, extremely geographically isolated, or both.

- Regions that fit both criteria were the northernmost fringes of North America, Europe and Asia. The Inuit and Eskimos of North America are descended from such peoples, and they evolved an amazing array of strategies and technologies adapted specifically to their extreme environment.

- In Scandinavia, the forerunners of today's Sami were the Fenni, who seem to have inhabited these areas as early as 2000 B.C. They actually appear in the writings of the Roman author Tacitus, who, in his description, highlights the fact that they do not engage in farming. Today, the Sami herd reindeer, but this practice only seems to have begun 500 or 600 years ago.

The Nomads of the Deserts

- Inhabiting an equally harsh but completely different landscape are a number of societies that adapted to living in deserts. Of these, two whose descendants continue to live traditional lifestyles into the modern era are the San, or Bushmen, of the Kalahari Desert in Africa, and the Aborigines of Australia.

- The Aborigines have been in Australian for 40,000–50,000 years, making their culture perhaps the oldest continuous one in the world. When they first arrived, the landscape of much of Australia was more hospitable than it is today.

- Aborigines lived in smallish, kin-related groups typical of hunter-gatherers, and many different clans and tribal units have been identified. They spoke more than 250 different languages and 600 dialects, although almost all of these have fallen out of use and been forever lost.

- The Aborigines mainly used stone, wood, and bone to make essential tools. The most famous Aboriginal hunting weapon was the boomerang. The bow and arrow, found in almost every civilization around the world, was not used except in a small northern region that had contact with other islanders. Aborigines did have barbed spears and darts.

- Groups living in the various parts of Australia conducted a flourishing trade with one another. Items such as shells, quartz, pearls, and animal products have been found many hundreds of miles away from any possible point of origin.

- Religious beliefs emphasized a sense of continuity between the past, present, and future. There was a perception that spirits or beings had existed from the time of creation and continued to be present in the world. This notion is embodied in the concept misleadingly translated as the Dreamtime or the Dreaming.

- Australian Aboriginal art is particularly well known for its unique and inventive aesthetic, such as the technique of forming pictures from colored dots resembling the canvases of late 19th-century pointillist painters.

- Their art often depicts scenes from everyday life, such as hunting, but much of it also serves as a medium for expressing their rich mythology and spirituality, for illustrating ceremonies and rituals, and for relating histories and stories. Some of their rock engravings date to more than 20,000 years ago, suggesting the antiquity of this artistic tradition.

The Nomads of the Seas

- The various peoples collectively called Polynesians are genetically related to the Aborigines of Australia. They also constitute one of the more remarkable cultures that perfectly adapted to a specific environment—in this case, Oceania.

- Oceania consists of innumerable islands forming a great arc that starts with the Philippines and Indonesia, continues past Australia with New Guinea and the New Hebrides, and then stretches far out into the Pacific with the Marshall Islands, Fiji, Samoa, the Society Islands, and the Marquesas. The northernmost edge of this region is marked by the Hawaiian Islands, the southernmost by New Zealand, and the easternmost by Easter Island.

- Between 3000 and 1500 B.C., an enterprising, seagoing people anthropologists have labeled the Austronesians began to spread out from Asia through these networks of islands. Genetic analysis suggests that their point of origin was somewhere near modern Taiwan.

- The earliest distinct culture for which we have archaeological evidence is a group labeled the Lapita that by 1500 B.C. had settled Melanesia. Lapita culture is best known from a distinctive style of pottery. From Melanesia, the Lapita expanded into western Polynesia, reaching Fiji, Tonga, and Samoa by 900 B.C.

- The Lapita did not practice true farming but instead created temporary fields using slash-and burn-agriculture. They introduced some domesticated animals to the islands, including chickens and dogs.

- Their descendants set out yet further across into eastern Polynesia and had settled the Cook Islands and Tahiti by 300 B.C., then reached Easter Island and the Hawaiian Islands by A.D. 500. Finally, the last of these oceanic explorers settled New Zealand in the 13th century, establishing the roots of Maori culture.

- These islands were not promising zones for intensive agriculture. The only edible indigenous plants were nuts, and most of the plants now associated with these regions, including bananas, coconuts, yams, and breadfruit, were all imported. These volcanic islands often had very poor soil, and hurricanes periodically deposited saltwater across the land, effectively poisoning the soil.

- Luckily, many of these islands were atolls surrounded by extensive reefs that were exceptionally rich marine environments. The inhabitants of these islands became expert fishermen.

- Polynesians did not constitute one political or social entity; each island or part of an island evolved its own variant of the core culture. More than 1,200 different languages have been identified in Oceania as well, although most are closely related linguistically and sometimes mutually intelligible. A chief or king typically ruled over each group, and there was a lively trade and interaction among the islands.

- The key to the spread and success of the Polynesians was their ability as sailors, shipbuilders, and navigators. Without any technological aids, Polynesian sailors crossed thousands of miles of open ocean and found their way to tiny islands. If they missed, they headed off into an endless expanse of ocean and certain death.

- Further complicating this challenge was the fact that they were spreading eastward, but all the main winds and currents moved westward. They had to actively struggle against the forces of nature.

- The Lapita developed sea-going canoes equipped with outriggers that stabilized them. The originals were simply hollowed out logs propelled by paddles and triangular lateen sails that allowed them to tack into the wind fairly efficiently.

- These boats were not large enough to carry the supplies needed for the longer voyages among the more widely spaced islands, so the later Polynesians devised a bigger craft built of planks bound with coconut fibers and glues. These had two hulls linked by a platform on which a superstructure was sometimes even erected. The largest of these craft were over 100 feet long and could carry a substantial crew and cargo thousands of miles.

- The next challenge was navigation, and through a combination of trial and error and the oral transmission of accumulated knowledge, Polynesians learned to use the stars, birds, clouds, currents, and waves to guide their vessels. They could identify land even when it was out of sight by various means, including changes in the ocean's swell, variations in wind and current direction, and the presence of land birds. Sometimes they could even see over-the-horizon landmasses reflected in the undersides of clouds.

- Although the Polynesians built no massive cities, they developed a successful, rich, and long-lasting culture, and in areas such as seafaring and navigation, their achievements are among the most impressive of any civilization.

Suggested Reading

Berndt and Berndt, *The World of the First Australians*.

Jennings, ed., *The Prehistory of Polynesia*.

Panter-Brick, Layton, and Rowley-Conwy, eds., *Hunter-Gatherers*.

Schrire, ed., *Past and Present in Hunter Gatherer Studies*.

Questions to Consider

1. Do the hunter-gatherer societies discussed in this lecture disprove the overall argument presented in this course that civilization is an urban phenomenon, or do they merely demonstrate a few exceptions to a generally valid rule?

2. In cultures based on farming, status and power usually depend on the acquisition and storage of objects (food, money, property, etc.). In hunter-gatherer societies, this is impossible. How has this basic difference shaped the cultures and values of both sedentary and nomadic civilizations?

Lecture 37: Hunter-Gatherers and Polynesians

Hunter-Gatherers and Polynesians
Lecture 37—Transcript

We began this course with the statement that civilization was an urban phenomenon, and while this is almost always true, as with any generalization, there are always exceptions to the rule. In this lecture, I want to examine some of those exceptions: societies that developed sophisticated cultures, but didn't build cities. The most notable category of this sort of culture is those that continued to pursue a hunter-gatherer lifestyle long after most other peoples had abandoned it. Homo sapiens as a species evolved about 200,000 years ago, but we've only been farming for about the last 10,000 years. For all the rest of that time, humans subsisted by living a hunter-gatherer lifestyle. Or, maybe another way to think about this is for over 95 percent of the time that humans have existed on earth, we've been hunter-gatherers. It is, by evolution and genetics, the way that we're biologically adapted to live.

Today, though, only a miniscule percentage of humans continue to practice anything that even remotely approaches that style of life, and it's debatable whether there's anybody left who'd truly qualify as a pure old-style hunter-gatherer. Maybe the closest that anybody comes today would be some Inuit in the Arctic, or some Aborigines who live in the most remote sections of the outback of Australia. But during the period that this course covers, nearly all humans had already switched over from hunter-gathering to farming or pastoralism, but there were still a few societies scattered around the globe that pursued this traditional mode of human existence.

Before we look at those specific groups, let me define a little bit better what I mean by hunter-gatherers and what universal characteristics these cultures tended to share. Basically, hunter-gatherers derive their caloric intake by eating non-domesticated plants and non-domesticated animals. A typical diet would consist of a mixture of nuts, berries, fish, fruits, wild plants, insects, maybe scavenged carcasses, and whatever small wild game, like rabbits or birds, which could be caught with snares or killed using fairly primitive weapons. Hunter-gatherers were almost always nomadic, so they moved around after whatever food resource seemed to be the most promising at the time. This sort mobility was a double-edged sword. On the one hand, it gave them great flexibility to shift from one area to another in response to changes in the type, availability, or scarcity sometimes of food supplies. But on the other hand, it limited their physical possessions to what could be easily carried by each individual. After all, when you have to carry everything that you own, you'll very quickly strip down your personal property to an absolute bare minimum. The typical sum of earthly possessions of many hunter-gatherers in many different eras and places has been surprisingly constant: It consists of just some twine or rope, or maybe vines; a single cloak or some sort of piece of clothing; a bowl or gourd; and a dual-purpose stick that can be used for digging in the ground and for killing small animals.

In terms of social organization, hunter-gatherers typically lived in smallish bands of about 10–40 individuals who often are related to one another. Generally speaking, these societies were usually more egalitarian than farming or pastoral communities, so they tended to have less pronounced class or hierarchical structures. Interestingly, there also tended to be more equality between men and women in hunter-gatherer groups; and both of those characteristics maybe resulted from the fact that nearly everybody in such a community had to contribute to nearly all group activities, and that included even traditionally male things such as hunting. Incidentally, contrary to an image that many modern people have of early man as the mighty hunter, early humans did a whole lot more gathering than they did hunting, and what did get hunted was usually pretty small. Early man was prey far longer than he was predator. If you want to get in touch with your true primitive self, rather than going out hunting, it would be much more accurate if you spent some time cowering fearfully in a tree and then maybe picking some grubs out of the bark.

Many hunter-gatherer bands were also matrilineal, and this means that the women in the group were related by blood and that various individuals traced their ancestry through their mothers. To avoid inbreeding, male members of the group often originated from other bands and they'd join just in order to find a mate. That structure also tended to give more social power to women than in typical agricultural or herding communities. These sort of exchanges to find mates were facilitated by the fact that in many hunter-gatherer societies, there's some designated time of year, often when there's a local abundance of a foodstuff, when a whole bunch of different bands would temporarily come together or join together to form a larger community before once again they dispersed. It should be noted that in some groups, that dynamic was reversed, with the males of a band being related and women being imported from the outside.

By the way, wild chimpanzees and bonobos actually live in exactly the same fashion, so they tend to be found foraging about for the same mixture of foods in little mobile groups of 10–40 individuals.

Once intensive farming and pastoralism had spread around the globe, the hunter-gatherer groups that survived into the historical era tended to be in locations that either were just not well-suited for farming, were extremely geographically isolated, or, in many cases, had both of those characteristics. One region that fits both of those criteria was the northernmost fringe of North America, Europe, and Asia. Up in those frigid, often ice covered zones, various groups of hunter-gatherers not only managed to survive, but also to develop rich and distinctive cultures. The Inuit and Eskimos of North America are the direct descendents of such peoples, and they evolved an amazing array of strategies and technologies that were adapted specifically to that extreme environment. Often they had to specialize in certain food-gathering activities, such as whale or seal hunting, and they managed to do this without any metal or wood; but even without those things, they could construct weapons and boats that enabled them to hunt for those selected prey animals. Analogous groups existed in the northern Arctic regions of Europe and Asia as well.

In Scandinavia, for example, the forerunners of today's Sami were a tribe known as the Fenni, and they seem to have inhabited those areas as early as about 2000 B.C. The Fenni actually show up in the writings of the Roman author Tacitus who, in his description of Europe, highlights the fact that this group doesn't engage in farming. Tacitus writes:

> The Fenni live in complete savagery and extreme poverty. They do not possess weapons, horses, or homes. They eat plants, they clothe themselves in skins, they sleep on the ground. Their only tool is arrows, which they tip in bone for lack of iron. Both men and women hunt and share the prey. But they hold that their lifestyle is happier than groaning over a plow or laboring to construct houses.

It should be noted that while today the Sami herd reindeer and are famous for that, this practice only seems to have begun about 500 or 600 years ago, and the Fenni of Tacitus's era seem have been true hunter-gatherers.

Inhabiting an equally harsh but completely different landscape were a number of long-lasting hunter-gatherer societies that adapted to living in deserts. Of those, two whose existence spans the timeframe of this course, and whose descendants continued to live traditional lifestyles well into the modern era, are the San or the Bushmen of the Kalahari Desert in Africa and the Aborigines of Australia. Both of these groups adapted to living in regions with very, very minimal rainfall, and so they developed a wide range of techniques for finding sustenance in such an unpromising environment. The San, who are also known by the names of some of their subunits, such as the !Kung, were a branch of the far-flung Khoisan people, and they seem to have been present in the Kalahari Desert region at least throughout the historical era.

The story of the Aborigines of Australia is even more remarkable because it appears that they've been living there for 40–50,000 years, and that would make their culture perhaps the oldest continuous culture in the entire world. When they first arrived, the landscape of a lot of Australia was more hospitable than it is today, and the first settlers probably lived along the coastline. Later, though, they spread inland and they occupied drier regions, and that movement intensified with the arrival of Europeans.

Aborigines lived in the usual small, kin-related groups typical of hunter-gatherers, and many, many different clans and tribal units have been identified. Emblematic of this are the more than 250 spoken languages and about 600 sub-dialects that were once used by all these groups. Regrettably, today almost all of those languages have fallen out of use and been forever lost. Life for the Aborigines was regulated by a complex series of rituals and initiation ceremonies that individuals would use to mark the transitions from childhood to adulthood, to married life, and then to the point where they'd begin raising children of their own.

The Aborigines mainly used stone to make their essential tools, and that could be augmented by wooden and bone implements. Of course, the most

218

famous Aboriginal device of all is the boomerang, which was employed for hunting, and it could bring down a bird or a game animal. By at least 10,000 years ago, Aborigines were flinging true returning boomerangs as opposed to the one-way throwing sticks that were found in lots of different cultures. Kind of strangely, the bow and arrow, which almost every civilization around the world used at some point, wasn't utilized in Australia, except for a small northern region where obviously it was brought in by contact with some islanders. Aborigines did have barbed spears and darts that were flung from throwers, and they made use of all sorts of clever techniques to get game. For example, in rivers or swampy regions, they'd make these elaborate cone-shaped traps, and these were specially constructed to catch a variety of large and nutritious eel that lived in those regions.

Groups who lived in the various parts of Australia conducted a flourishing trade with one another. When they met, they'd barter items that might be scarce or nonexistent in one zone for rare goods from another area. Because of that mechanism, certain things such as shells, quartz, pearls, and various animal products have been found hundreds of miles away from any possible point of original origin.

The religious beliefs of these people emphasized a sense of continuity from the past into the present, and the ancestors were always very much alive. All Aboriginal groups shared a belief or a faith in a category of behaviors, activities, rituals, and times that had to do with the sacred and with the numinous. There's a perception or a feeling that there were spirits or beings that had existed from the time of creation and that continued to be present in the world. This whole notion is embodied in a concept that's somewhat often misleadingly translated as the "Dreamtime" or "The Dreaming," but it's really about this idea of an ongoing spirituality that infuses the world, and that creates a continuity of the past, the present, and the future. The colorful myths that were told by various groups often describe origin stories of animals or traditions, and so those help to make sense of the world and to connect those living in it with these underlying fundamental forces of nature and the entire universe. An example is the way in which individual clans would be tied to an ancestral animal, which supposedly played some central role in their history and then also played a central role in their contemporary rituals and art. The Aborigines have often been held up as a laudatory example of a group who lived in balance with nature, and there's a fair amount of truth to that stereotype. Certainly the religious beliefs incorporated a great deal of reverence for nature, the land, and the creatures that live upon it.

Australian Aboriginal art is especially well-known for having a very unique and inventive aesthetic; for example, the technique of forming pictures from little colored dots, and this is somewhat reminiscent of the canvases of late 19th century pointillist painters. Aborigine artists painted on a variety of surfaces; they painted on rock, sometimes animal skins, bark, and, of course, on human bodies. Artists would use charcoal as well as primarily red, brown, yellow, and white ochre and clays. Their art depicts scenes from everyday life, such as hunting, but a lot of it also serves as a medium for expressing that rich mythology and spirituality of the Aborigines, and for illustrating some of the key ceremonies and rituals, and sometimes even for relating their own histories or telling stories in a kind of visual form. Rock art was made both by applying pigments to the rock and sometimes by hammering or abrading the surface of the rock to create engravings. Some of these rock engravings have been found that date to more than 20,000 years ago, and that suggests the antiquity of that artistic tradition.

In addition to true hunter-gatherers like the ones I've been talking about, there are also some interesting non-city-building cultures that aren't necessarily hunter-gatherers; and among these, one that's actually genetically related to the Aborigines of Australia are the various peoples of the Pacific islands who fall under the general category of Polynesians. They also constituted one of the more remarkable cultures who've perfectly adapted themselves to a specific environment; in this case, Oceania. The section of the world known as Oceania consisted of thousands of little bitty islands that form a huge arc that begins near southeast Asia with the islands of the Philippines and Indonesia, then continues past Australia with New Guinea and the New Hebrides, and then stretches far out into the Pacific with the Marshall Islands, Fiji, Samoa, the Society Islands, and the Marquesas. The very northernmost edge of this region is marked by the Hawaiian Islands, the southernmost by New Zealand, and the easternmost by Easter Island.

Between 3000 and 1500 B.C., an enterprising, seagoing people that anthropologists have labeled the Austronesians began to spread out from Asia through all of these networks of little islands. Genetic analysis suggests that their point of origin was probably somewhere near modern Taiwan. The earliest distinct culture for which we have clear archaeological evidence is a group that has been labeled the Lapita, and by 1500 B.C. they'd settled Melanesia, the area just north of Australia. Lapita culture is best known from a distinctive style of pottery that they produced, and so by following and dating finds of these distinctive pots or even pot shards, we can trace their slow progress across the Pacific. From Melanesia, they expanded eastward into western Polynesia, reaching Fiji, Tonga, and Samoa by about 900 B.C. The Lapita didn't practice true farming, but instead they'd just create temporary fields using slash and burn agriculture, and then they'd place into those fields imported plants such as yams and breadfruit that they'd brought with them. They were also the ones who introduced some domesticated animals to some of these islands, including chickens and dogs.

Although the islands of Western Polynesia are as far as definite evidence of Lapita culture and pottery reaches, their descendants, who had pretty much a similar culture and languages, then set out further across the Pacific into Eastern Polynesia, and those peoples had reached the Cook Islands and Tahiti by about 300 B.C. The descendants of those explorers then pushed even more daringly off into the open ocean, and eventually reached Easter Island and the Hawaiian Islands by 500 A.D. Some scholars argue about these dates forwards or backwards a couple centuries, but roughly speaking. Finally, the last of these bold oceanic explorers settled New Zealand in the 13th century, and there they established the roots of Maori culture.

The islands that these seafarers settled upon were really not promising zones for intensive agriculture. The only edible indigenous plants were some nuts, and most of the plants that we now stereotypically associate with these regions—things like bananas, coconuts, yams, and breadfruit—all of those were actually imported. These were volcanic islands, and that means often their soil wasn't very deep, and events like hurricanes could periodically deposit saltwater across all of these small islands, which effectively poisoned the dirt. Nevertheless, by combining limited cultivation of some of these imported plants with raising some imported domesticated animals, life was possible. What made it much more than just a marginal existence, though, was the ocean. A lot of these islands were atolls, and so they're surrounded by extensive reefs that were incredibly rich marine environments just teeming with all sorts of sea life. The inhabitants of these islands obviously became expert fishermen, and they'd use nets, hooks, and harpoons, and with those they could pull a huge wealth of seafood from the warm waters.

Collectively, we refer to the people who lived on these islands as Polynesians, but they didn't constitute a single political or social entity. Each island, or sometimes even each part of an island, evolved its own little variant of the core culture, and often these reflected what resources were locally available. They usually developed their own language or dialect as well, and so over 1,200 different languages have been identified in Oceania, although they all tend to be closely related linguistically and often are intelligible by other groups. Body decoration and art such as tattoos were commonly found among all the various Polynesian subcultures. Some sort of chief or king would typically rule over each island or a region of an island, and there was a lot of trade going back and forth between all of them.

The key to the spread and success of the Polynesians was their ability as sailors, as well as shipbuilders and navigators. Completely without any technological aids such as compasses or astrolabes, Polynesian sailors could cross thousands of miles of open ocean and find their way to little tiny islands. If they missed their goal, they could just head off into an endless expanse of ocean and certain death. Further complicating the challenge for at least the original settlers of these islands was the fact that they're coming from Asia and spreading eastward, but all of the main winds and currents in this area moved in a westward direction. You couldn't simply set out in a boat and let the wind and waves take you to new lands; you had to actively struggle against the forces of nature to explore new territory. How were they able to accomplish these really amazing feats of seafaring?

Let's start by looking at the boats. The Lapita developed seagoing canoes that used a large sail, and they were able to make use of this big sail because they were equipped with outriggers that stabilized them. The original form of these canoes was to simply hollow out some logs, and this was good enough to cross those relatively short gaps between islands as far eastward as Samoa. During this initial stage of expansion, the islands weren't spaced too far apart, so that even though the overall distance covered might be a lot, mariners could sort of hop from one island to another and there really weren't long stretches when they're out of sight of land completely. They'd propel their canoes using paddles and with a triangular lateen sale, and this was sort of advanced technology that allowed them to tack into the wind fairly efficiently.

These boats were not large enough, though, to carry the amount of supplies that were needed for the longer voyages among the more widely spaced out islands east of Samoa. The later Polynesians, who settled eastern Polynesia, devised a new type of canoe; and this was a much bigger craft that's built of actual planks attached end to end and then bound with coconut fibers and glue. Instead of a hull with an outrigger, these large oceangoing versions had two hulls that were linked by a platform on which you could actually build some sort of superstructure. The biggest of these craft were over 100 feet long and could carry large crews and enough cargo to go thousands of miles. They were steered not by a rudder, but by paddles. People have made some reconstructed replicas of these sorts of ships, and they've proven to be surprisingly stable and effective.

The next challenge was navigation, and through a combination of trial and error, orally transmitting accumulated knowledge, and really just lifetimes spent in very close proximity to the ocean, Polynesian sailors became master navigators without any sort of advanced technology. The Polynesians learned to use the stars, birds, clouds, currents, even patterns in the waves to guide their vessels; and they could do things like identify land even when it's out of sight by all sorts of means, such as changes in the ocean's swell, variations in the wind and current direction, or, of course, the presence of land birds. Sometimes they could even see over-the-horizon landmasses that were reflected in the undersides of clouds. They really cultivated a detailed familiarity with the complex movements of the stars, and so they learned to estimate direction and distance just based on these astronomical observations. In the Marshall Islands, navigators developed charts, and to us they look like lattices or webs, and these were made by tying together little sticks or sometimes using the ribs of coconut fronds. They really weren't maps in the conventional Western sense, but instead what these charts did was they indicated patterns and directions of currents. They also showed at least four different types of ocean swells that could be used to guide sailors to particular destinations.

Although the Polynesians built no massive cities, they clearly had a successful, rich, and long-lasting culture, and in areas such as seafaring and navigation, their achievements are among the most impressive of any civilization. While I've only focused on a few representative hunter-gatherer societies, there were many others such as the Ainu of Japan. In a world in which every year a higher and higher percentage of people are living in cities, cultures such as these demonstrate that you can have complex societies without urbanism.

The Art and Architecture of Power
Lecture 38

Empires have a near-universal tendency to erect impressive monumental structures and to use art as expressions of power and domination. The Persian King of Kings constructed a tribute relief that demonstrated to visitors his dominion over 23 specific conquered nations. The reliefs of Cerro Sechin, Peru, may have been intended as a mythological reference, a battle memorial, or a threat. The tomb of Shi Huangdi memorialized the emperor's power even into the afterlife. And the city of Rome itself was a living, ever-growing monument to the power of the empire.

The Apadana of Persepolis

- Across almost every ancient society, those in power shared a predilection for using art and architecture to promote their rule and to publicly illustrate their domination over rivals both internal and external. While such grandstanding might seem arrogant or even distasteful to us, it did produce some of the most impressive, and even beautiful, monuments of the ancient world.

- The centerpiece of the palace of the Persian King of Kings at Persepolis was a structure known as the Apadana. This was a combination throne room and royal reception hall. It was a square 300 feet per side whose roof was held up by 72 magnificent stone columns, each nearly 75 feet high.

- Access to the platform was by sweeping staircases. The walls adjacent to these staircases were decorated with finely carved reliefs of approximately 3,000 human figures, a great parade of the king's subjects. The core of the parade consists of representatives from each of the 23 different lands that had been conquered by the Persians, bearing a staggering array of offerings to place before the feet of the king.

- The basic message of this relief was that all the world bows down before the Persian king. Because of the quality and detail of the carvings, this monument is also one of the most helpful guides for modern scholars to use in identifying the distinctive clothing and jewelry worn by different ancient Near Eastern peoples, but we should not forget that the original purpose of these beautiful artworks was to intimidate and awe.

The Apadana frieze offers details about the dress of ancient cultures.

The Cerro Sechín Carvings

- About 170 miles from Lima, Peru, is an archaeological site known as Cerro Sechín, built by one of the early civilizations of the Andes and associated with Chavín culture. It features a carved procession that is even more blatant in its message than the one at Persepolis.

- The centerpiece of Cerro Sechín is a raised platform with retaining walls originally inset with about 400 granite slabs. These were covered with carvings of a parade of high-ranking armed warriors who seem to emerge from the central doorway and march around the sides of the structure. Interspersed among these figures is a jumbled confusion of corpses, dismembered bodies, and body parts.

- Considering the amount of effort that went into creating this public display of violence, it must have been intended as an important statement. Scholars are divided over whether the relief should be read as a record of a historical conquest or as a representation of a mythological battle, but it functions as a rather frighteningly effective assertion of the power and brutality of the dominant group. Graphic carvings such as these are actually rather commonly found in South American and Mesoamerican cultures.

The Tomb of Shi Huangdi

- China's emperor Shi Huangdi is best known for his spectacular burial complex that includes the famous terra-cotta warriors as well as one of the most impressive and mysterious tombs of any ruler throughout all of history.

- Shi Huangdi started building his tomb almost as soon as he took the throne. The scale of the effort was massive. The actual burial chamber itself was concealed beneath a giant earthen mound over 200 feet in height and whose base forms a square 1,000 feet on a side. The tomb lay a further 100 feet below the original ground level.

- Sima Qian records what was placed within it, a fantastic model of the entire world, including the heavens and the earth:

  > Palaces, scenic towers, and the hundred officials, as well as rare utensils and wonderful objects were brought to fill up the tomb. ... Mercury was used to fashion the hundred rivers, the Yellow river, and the Yangtze, and the seas in such a way that they flowed. Above were set the heavenly bodies, below the features of the earth.

- The terra-cotta warriors were discovered in 1974 in a series of pits located roughly a mile east of the burial mound when the Yang brothers were digging a new well for their farm and began to pull life-size clay heads and body parts from the well shaft. In all, 600 pits were discovered in the vicinity of the emperor's tomb, some containing just a handful of objects and others thousands of them.

- The soldiers were arranged as if they were a real army drawn up for review. They stand at attention facing east, organized by type of weapon. They were equipped with fully functional bronze and wooden weapons, including swords, crossbows, spears, halberds, and arrows. These warriors are one of our best guides to understanding the arms and armor used in China during this period.

- The level of detail and craftsmanship lavished on the warriors is amazing. It has been estimated that 1,000 skilled potters had to work for 12 years in teams of 10 or 12 to create the army. So complex are the figures that each team would have been able to complete only about seven per year.

- Scholars are still debating the purpose of the terra-cotta warriors. Whether the army was supposed to serve the emperor in the next life or express his authority is unknown.

- This was not the only grandiose statement of power indulged in by Shi Huangdi. In his capital city, he symbolically asserted his domination over conquered states by constructing copies of his foes' palaces and filled the halls, walkways, and pavilions with piles of precious objects looted from the original owners.

- As a crowning touch, he inhabited this fantastical landscape with harems of beautiful women, presumably drawn from those regions enslaved by his conquests.

Rome—The City as a Monument

- The Romans not only built monuments celebrating their power, but one useful way of interpreting the city of Rome is as an enormous trophy case. No matter where you looked, you were constantly reminded of Rome's total domination over the Mediterranean and its peoples.

- The Romans were especially fond of erecting large public monuments to commemorate military conquests. Some of the best-known examples of this were triumphal arches. These probably had their origins in temporary structures through which generals celebrating triumphs passed and over time became a standard form of war monument.

- Such arches were surmounted by a bronze statue group of a four-horse chariot being driven by the person or persons being honored. They were usually decorated with carved reliefs depicting scenes from the campaign.

- There are archaeological remains or literary references to nearly 50 triumphal or commemorative arches in ancient Rome, although only three survive. The surviving Arch of Titus was built in A.D. 81 to celebrate his military victories in Judea, including his suppression of the rebellion of the Jews and the capture of Jerusalem.

- Another common Roman victory monument was a column topped by a statue of the victorious general. By the late Republic, there was a veritable forest of these in Rome, many of them clustering in and around the Roman Forum.

- By far the most spectacular columns were those put up by the emperors Trajan and Marcus Aurelius, both of which are still standing. The entire shaft of each column was carved with a spiraling frieze that illustrated the campaigns from beginning to end and can be read like a modern cartoon.

- The Column of Trajan commemorates a series of military campaigns waged by the emperor in Dacia. The shaft of the column is about 100 feet tall. The spiral carved frieze contains 155 different scenes featuring over 2,600 figures. If this frieze were unraveled and stretched out, it would be over 600 feet long. Trajan frequently appears in these scenes directing the campaign, and he is carved slightly larger than the others to emphasize his status.

- The frieze is unblinkingly accurate and honest in its portrayal of the harsh realities of conquest. There are scenes showing the Romans burning native villages, rounding up women and children to be sold into slavery, and displaying the heads of slain barbarian leaders on poles.

- As time went on, not only was the city crowded with innumerable triumphal arches, columns, and statues, but its public spaces were also decorated with items stolen from all over the Mediterranean. Many temples were stuffed to overflowing with trophies, while the streets, gardens, baths, and even the houses of wealthy Romans were adorned with seized works of art.

- The stones that made up the great public buildings of Rome were highly visible reminders of Rome's status. Colored marble and decorative stone was plundered from every corner of the Mediterranean: fine white marble from Mount Pentelikon, green cippollino from Carystos, yellow and purple veined stone from Asia Minor, and hard purple and green porphyry from Egypt.

- Even Rome's inhabitants were a living tribute to Rome's dominance. Hundreds of thousands of foreigners found themselves shipped to Rome as slaves, where they were compelled to serve the whims of their Roman masters. Their myriad languages, accents, costumes, and appearances would also have served as constant reminders of Rome's power and authority.

Suggested Reading

Coulston, *All the Emperor's Men.*

Portal, ed., *The First Emperor.*

Root, *The King and Kingship in Achaemenid Art.*

Samaniego, et al. "New Evidence on Cerro Sechin, Casma Valley, Peru."

Wilber, *Persepolis.*

Questions to Consider

1. Do you think displays of domination and power such as the Persepolis reliefs, Cerro Sechín, and Trajan's Column are effective tools of persuasion?

2. How do the specific details of Shi Huangdi's tomb and the associated terra-cotta warriors reflect key aspects of his personality and policies?

The Art and Architecture of Power
Lecture 38—Transcript

Massed ranks of row after row of well-equipped soldiers ready to do your bidding; an endless procession of supplicants bearing tribute and groveling beneath your throne; blood-drenched heaps of the brutally dismembered bodies of your enemies; these are just a few of the images that ancient rulers chose to have memorialized in art, and that served as not-very-subtle statements of propaganda extolling their might. Across almost every ancient society, those in power had a predilection for using art and architecture to promote their rule and to publicly illustrate their domination over rivals both internal and external. While this sort of grandstanding might seem arrogant or even distasteful to us, it did produce some of the most impressive, and sometimes even beautiful, monuments of the ancient world. In this lecture, I want to examine several of these monuments from very different cultures around the globe, but that all share this common theme of being an expression of power and domination through art and architecture.

I'll begin with a rather obvious example that was featured in the palace of the Persian King of Kings at Persepolis. The centerpiece of this complex was a structure known as the Apadana, which seems to have been a kind of combination throne room and royal reception hall. It was a square about 300 feet per side, and the roof was held up by 72 magnificent stone columns, each of which was almost 75 feet high. Access to the platform on which this room rested was by these sweeping staircases at the sides. The walls adjacent to those staircases were decorated with finely carved stone reliefs of nearly 3,000 human figures, most of which are several feet high. Those figures really form a grand parade consisting of groups of the king's subjects, starting with the noblemen, who are resplendent in their finery and are accompanied by all their retainers; it also includes the Royal Guardsmen, and they're perfectly rendered with all of their weapons very accurately shown; but the core of this parade is representatives from all the different lands that have been conquered by the Persians, and these envoys or ambassadors is each shown in the distinctive costume of his nation, and they bear with them an amazing array of offerings that they brought to lay before the feet of the Persian King of Kings. Some of them bring exotic animals, such as the Susian envoy, who leads a lion on a leash along with two little cubs being carried by his attendants. The Ionians from one of the Greek regions hold beehives of sweet honey and finely wrought textiles. The Ethiopians appropriately enough carry ivory elephant tusks. In all, there are 23 separate delegations that are shown bearing tribute and coming to make their obeisance before the King of Kings.

The tribute procession of Persepolis was plainly intended to act as a reminder to foreign envoys who'd come to speak with the ruler of Persia of the size and the wealth of his domain. It also impressed anyone who looked at it with the aptness of his title of King of Kings, since it overtly shows the representatives of so many different nations offering their submission to him. The basic message of that relief was that all the world bows down before the Persian king. Because of the quality and detail of these carvings, this monument also happens to be one of the most helpful guides for modern scholars to use in identifying the distinctive clothing and jewelry that's worn by different Ancient Near Eastern peoples; but we should never forget that the original purpose of these beautiful artworks was to intimidate and to awe.

In South America, about 170 miles from Lima, is an archaeological site known as Cerro Sechin, and it was built by one of the very early civilizations in the Andes; it may be associated with Chavín culture, which I talked about. It also has a carved stone procession, and this one is, if possible, even more blatant in its message than the one at Persepolis. The centerpiece of Cerro Sechin is a raised platform with retaining walls, and those walls have set into them a series of what originally would've been about 400 granite slabs. These are entirely covered with carvings that depict a parade of what seems to be high-ranking individuals, maybe warriors, bearing staffs, some of them have scepters, and all of them have very ornamental headgear. Those figures are carved to look as if they're emerging from the central doorway and then marching around the sides of this structure. The really attention-grabbing aspect of these reliefs, however, is that interspersed among and between these stately figures is a jumbled confusion of corpses, dismembered bodies, and human body parts. These images are extremely gruesome and graphic. They include things like decapitated torsos gushing thick streams of blood, bodies with their intestines spilling out of huge holes in the abdomen, and everywhere there are piles of human heads, hands, feet, legs, bones, guts, ears, and even some little neatly aligned rows of eyeballs that had been wrenched from their sockets. The victims are shown contorted with pain, their faces frozen in expressions of great anguish. Sometimes their lips are pulled back from their teeth and blood is frequently pouring from their mouth, nose, and eyes. Amidst all of this horrible carnage, you have those marching figures striding by with fixed expressions of determination and purpose.

Considering the sheer amount of effort that went into creating this public display of violence, it must've been intended as an important statement that the builders of Cerro Sechin wanted to make. Scholars are somewhat divided over whether these relief should be read as an actual record of a historical conquest or maybe a representation of a mythological battle; but plainly the marching figures are the victors and the corpses the losers. It serves as a kind of frighteningly effective assertion of the power and the brutality of the dominant group. By the way, there have been some attempts to explain away this monument as something more positive by certain scholars who just didn't want to believe that these early Andean cultures could have been so cruel and so savage. One of these suggestions was that the whole thing was built as a sort of three-dimensional illustrated medical textbook where ancient doctors could come to learn about human anatomy. Very few people take that rather wishful interpretation seriously.

Graphic carvings such as those are actually somewhat common in South American and Mesoamerican cultures. The Mayans as well as others frequently carved into stone images of racks composed of hundreds of human skulls. There's another site in Mexico called Monte Alban that's contemporary with Teotihuacáno culture, and it also has a carved wall showing scores of mutilated human corpses. The excavators at Monte Alban originally called those figures "Dancers" because of the way that the bodies were contorted, and only later did they realize that those postures were due to the fact that they're meant to be in agony rather than engaged in pleasant dances.

If we look at China, the actions and accomplishments of Emperor Shi Huangdi that we've looked at so far in this course would already have been more than enough to earn him an important place in history, but we've yet to look at the single thing for which he's most well-known today, and that's the spectacular tomb complex that he had built to hold his body after death, and it includes the famous terracotta warriors as well as one of the most impressive and mysterious tombs of any ruler throughout all of history.

Shi Huangdi started building his tomb almost as soon as he took the throne, and supposedly he employed 700,000 workers on it. That number is almost certainly an exaggeration, but still, the scale of the effort was obviously massive. The actual burial chamber was hidden beneath a giant earthen mound over 200 feet in height and its base forms a square that's almost 1,000 feet on each side. The tomb lay a further 100 feet below the original ground level, and the Chinese historian Sima Qian records what was placed within that tomb. In the tomb could be found:

> Palaces, scenic towers, and the hundred officials, as well as rare utensils and wonderful objects were brought to fill up the tomb. ... Mercury was used to fashion the hundred rivers, the Yellow river, and the Yangtze, and the seas in such a way that they flowed. Above were set the heavenly bodies, below the features of the earth.

The ruler of the world was buried within a tomb that was itself a fantastic little model of the entire world, including the heavens and the earth. Maybe the most incredible aspect of all this is the map of China that's described, which has bodies of water represented by flowing streams of mercury. Shi Huangdi's tomb hasn't actually been excavated, and for a long time people were doubtful about the veracity of that account, especially concerning that map with the mercury streams. But in the 1980s, geophysical surveys of the tomb mound were undertaken that, among lots of other information they revealed, showed the amount of mercury vapor rising from the soil. It was discovered that an approximately 12,000 square foot section right at the center of the tomb had mercury levels that were between 3 and 50 times the natural soil levels for the region; so that evidence very strongly suggests that the description of the mercury map, and presumably all the other tomb features, should be taken quite literally. That same study showed the existence of a tomb chamber that's 240 feet long, 150 feet wide, and 50 feet high. Maube one day that mound will be excavated, and if so it could easily prove to be the most fantastic such find since the discovery of King Tut's tomb. As for the terracotta warriors, those were found in a series of pits about a mile eastward of the emperor's burial mound, and those have been at least partially uncovered.

Farmers had been finding various buried artifacts in that area for centuries, but the modern discovery and awareness of the tomb and the warriors began on March 29, 1974. On that day, the six Yang brothers were digging a new well for their family farm, and they began to pull life-size clay heads and body parts from the well shaft. Eventually, this would lead to the discovery of all the terracotta warriors, and in the end, 600 pits would be discovered in the vicinity of the emperor's tomb. Some of those have just a handful of objects, but others have thousands of them. The terracotta warriors themselves are concentrated in four main pits: Pit number one is the largest, and it measures 700 feet by 180 feet. It has mostly foot soldiers. Pit number two has a mixture of cavalry, chariots, and some foot soldiers. Pit number three has a single chariot as well as 68 high-ranking officers, and the interpretation is that it's the headquarters unit of this clay army. In all the pits, the floors are paved with bricks and the roof is held up by packed earth walls that separate each row of soldiers.

The soldiers themselves are arranged just as if they're a real army drawn up for review by their general. The individual warriors stand usually at attention facing eastward, they're organized in ranks, and they're categorized by the type of weapon that they carry. The clay soldiers were equipped with fully functional bronze and wooden weapons, so they have perfectly usable swords, crossbows, spears, and halberds; and even the arrows are tipped with real bronze arrowheads. This find, this archaeological site, is one of our best guides to understanding the arms and armor used in China during this period. The warriors are roughly life-sized, although maybe a little bit larger. The terracotta warriors symbolically express the status of the person depicted by variations in height. For example, regular soldiers average about 5'10", but officers average about 6'3", and the clay generals average an impressive 6'6". Within each class, there are also little minor variations that give individuality to the clay soldiers. About 1,500 figures have been unearthed so far, but it's estimated that, taken all together, there will maybe be about 7,000 soldiers, 130 chariots with 520 horses, and maybe 150 cavalry horses.

The warriors are built using multiple parts that were molded and cast separately and then they could be combined, and they're built up from the foot up to the head. There seem to be at least eight basic face designs and six main types of body armor, and so you could mix and match these components to produce a lot of diversity. Specific details such as hairstyles and equipment were sometimes done individually, and that added even more variety to the whole thing. The level of detail and the craftsmanship that's lavished on these warriors is amazing. For example, even the patterns on the soles of the shoes of the soldiers are carefully sculpted. It's been estimated that 1,000 skilled potters had to work for 12 years in teams of about 10 or 12 to create this army; and so complex are the individual figures that each team could only have completed maybe seven per year. Like Ancient Greek sculpture, the terracotta warriors were originally brightly painted in hues of red, blue, green, and purple, so even though we're used to visualizing them in their familiar tan hues, we need to mentally restore the paint in order to get a sense of their intended appearance.

Scholars are still debating the purpose of the terracotta army. Whether this was supposed to somehow serve the emperor in the next life or just to express his authority and add to the magnificence of his tomb is unknown. Certainly this wasn't the only grandiose statement of power that Shi Huangdi indulged in. In his capital city, he symbolically asserted his domination over all the states he'd conquered by constructing copies of his foes' palaces all clustered together in one place in his own palace, and he filled these halls, walkways, and pavilions with heaps of precious objects looted from the original owners. Then, as a sort of crowning touch, he inhabited this fantastical landscape with harems of beautiful women, presumably also drawn from those regions he'd enslaved. So the emperor could walk complacently through this bizarre landscape composed of a hodgepodge assemblage of subjugated structures, objects, and people and basically just marvel at the extent of his own power.

Finally, we come to the Romans. Not only did they, too, build monuments celebrating their power, but one useful way of interpreting the entire city of Rome is as an enormous trophy case; that no matter where you look constantly reminded the viewer of Rome's total domination over the Mediterranean and its peoples.

To begin with, the Romans were very fond of erecting large public monuments to commemorate military conquests. Probably the best-known examples of this were the triumphal arches that were put up by victorious generals or emperors. These seem to have had their origins in more temporary arches that were placed over archways in walls through which generals would come when they celebrated a triumph. But the earliest true free-standing triumphal arches were then placed along the path that those old triumphal processions had followed. Over time, the arch became a standard form of monument, and so they started to pop up in other places all throughout the city. All of these arches would've been surmounted by a bronze statue group of a four-horse chariot being driven by whoever was being honored. These arches either had one big opening or else triple passages, but the central one would've been larger than the ones on either side. In addition to portraits of the person being honored, the arches were usually decorated with carved stone reliefs depicting scenes from the campaign, and most typically these would show Roman soldiers slaughtering barbarians and then carrying booty back to Rome.

There are archaeological remains or literary references to nearly 50 triumphal or commemorative arches that were built in the city of Ancient Rome, but today only 3 out of those 50 survive. One of the surviving arches, that of the emperor Titus, was built in 81 A.D. to celebrate his military victories in Judea, including his suppression of the rebellion of the Jews and the capture of the city of Jerusalem. If you visit the Roman Forum today, you can walk under this arch and you can gaze up at several famous panels that show Roman soldiers carrying away the loot that they'd seized in the Great Temple of the Jews in Jerusalem. If you look carefully, you can even see one scene where the soldiers are carrying a huge menorah, the traditional seven-branched Jewish candlestick-holder.

Another common Roman form of victory monument was to put up a column topped by a statue of the general who'd directed the conquest. By the time of the Late Republic, there's a veritable forest of honorific statues and columns scattered throughout Rome, a lot of them, though, clustering in and around the Roman Forum. By far the most spectacular form that this sort of column took, though, were those put up by the emperors Trajan and Marcus Aurelius, and both of those columns are still standing today. These were erected to celebrate military campaigns, and the entire shaft of each column was carved with a spiraling frieze that illustrated the course of those campaigns from beginning to end. These continuous friezes, which tell that story in visual form, can really be read almost like a modern cartoon.

The Column of Trajan was dedicated on May 18, 113 A.D., and it commemorates a series of military campaigns waged by the emperor in Dacia between 101 and 106 A.D. The shaft of this column is about 100 feet tall and 11 feet wide at the base, and it tapers slightly as it goes upwards. The shaft is composed of 17 separate drums of fine Luna marble, and the carved frieze has 155 different scenes with over 2,600 figures. If you were to take that frieze and manage to unravel it and stretch it out, it would be over 600 feet long. It's meant to be read from the bottom upwards, and the figures increase slightly in size as they go up from the bottom. The interpretation here is that this gives the illusion that when you look at it from below, they're all roughly the same scale.

The emperor Trajan often appears in these scenes and he's usually shown in charge directing the campaign, and he's always carved just a little bit larger than everybody else to emphasize his status as emperor. I like to tell my students that you can read this frieze as a graphic novel that tells the story of the campaign and shows every stage of a typical Roman military campaign, beginning with the generals planning their strategy, then it shows the troops marching out, it has them camping in the field, fighting the enemy, and finally, of course, you see the soldiers marching back home laden with all the captured treasure and leading the enslaved barbarians.

It's also a surprisingly honest and accurate portrayal of the harsh realities of conquest. For example, there are scenes that show the Romans burning down native villages, rounding up women and children to be sold into slavery, displaying the heads of slain barbarian leaders on poles mounted outside the Roman camp, and there are lots and lots of scenes of Roman legionaries methodically chopping down wave after wave of barbarians. It also shows more mundane activities—there are an awful lot of scenes of legionaries chopping firewood as well or building bridges—but the overall impression is to emphasize the irresistible and terrifying military might of Rome. The column, by the way, served not just as a victory monument but also as a mausoleum as well, because after Trajan's death his ashes were put into a golden urn that was placed within the base of the column.

As time went on, the city of Rome itself more and more began to symbolize Rome's conquest of the Mediterranean world through its physical structures. Not only was the city crowded with triumphal arches, columns, and statues, each of which was in essence a giant billboard advertising victorious Romans and showing off vanquished enemies, but the public spaces of the city were decorated with items stolen from all over the Mediterranean during these campaigns. Many temples, such as the great temples of Mars the Avenger, the Forum of Augustus, the Temple of Jupiter Optimus Maximus on the Capitoline Hill, were all stuffed to overflowing with enemy flags, standards, armor, and other military trophies, and just the streets, the gardens, the baths, even the houses of individual Romans were decorated with works of art seized during Rome's conquests, especially in the Greek east.

The very stones that made up the great public buildings of Rome themselves could be seen as highly visible reminders of Rome's status as conqueror of the world, because from every corner of the Mediterranean, the provinces were plundered in order to bring colored marbles and decorative stones to Rome to build these fantastic buildings. Some of the main stones sorts of stones that were imported included things like fine white Greek marble from Mount Pentelikon near Athens and also from the island of Paros in the Aegean Sea. Green *cippollino* came from the island Carystos, and a kind of yellow and purple veined stone was brought in from the Docimian quarries in Asia Minor. Egypt could contribute purple and green porphyry, which was hauled across the desert, and also a grey granite that was mined from an area called Mons Claudianus in Egypt. The very buildings that made up the city were themselves literally composed of booty taken from the conquered territories, and anybody walking around the city of Rome would've been confronted at every turn with reminders of Rome's total authority over the Mediterranean.

Finally, of course, even many of the human beings living in the city were themselves a form of tribute attesting to Rome's dominance, because in the wake of Rome's armies were always slave traders, and so hundreds of thousands of foreigners would find themselves shipped off to Rome as slaves, where they had to serve the whims of their Roman masters. In the streets of Rome, all of their different languages, accents, costumes, and appearances would also have served as reminders of Rome's power and its authority.

This impulse to assert one's power through symbolic statements in art and architecture is certainly not limited to the ancient world, but because so many of these monuments were made out of relatively imperishable materials such as stone, they are one of our best guides to how some rulers and peoples of antiquity wished to see themselves, and maybe more importantly to be viewed by others.

Comparative Armies—Rome, China, Maya
Lecture 39

W hile almost every culture and civilization engages in warfare, how they organize their armies and how they fight varies widely. Looking at the military systems of the Romans, the Chinese, and the Mayans offers an idea of the great breadth of styles different cultures employed. These groups varied in how they recruited and managed their soldiers; how they armed and armored their troops; and even when and why they chose to fight.

The Roman Military Machine

- The Roman army was one of the most famous military organizations of all time. From their success record, it is obvious they were doing something right. The Romans often did not enjoy superior technology or numbers compared with their enemies; what they almost always did have was greater organization, discipline, and determination.

- From the time of the Punic Wars on, Rome's army was what we would today call a professional army—that is, made of full-time soldiers. They devoted all of their effort to training and produced much better soldiers.

- Most Roman legionaries were citizen volunteers who enlisted for 25-year terms of service. This is in contrast to many of their contemporary civilizations, which employed mercenaries in their armies.

- The Roman army elevated organization to an art form. All aspects of the soldier's daily schedule were regulated, his equipment was standardized, and he knew exactly his place and role within the army.

- The smallest unit of men was the *contubernia*, which consisted of eight men; *contubernia* literally translated as "those who share a tent." Ten *contubernia* made up a century, which despite the name contained 80 men, not 100. Six centuries were a cohort (480 men), and 10 cohorts formed one legion (4,800 men).

- In battle, a legion could maneuver as a whole or in independent units ranging from 8 to 480 men. This gave the Romans great flexibility.

- Each legion had a golden eagle on a pole as its standard. The soldier who carried the eagle was known as the *aquilifer*. One of the greatest disgraces that could befall a legion was for its eagle to be captured by an enemy. The eagles and other standards were the focus of religious rituals for the legion.

The eagle was the standard of each Roman legion and the center of many rituals.

- Every legion was commanded by a legate, who had to be of senatorial rank. Under him were six senior officers known as military tribunes. Both legates and tribunes were political appointments. This is one of the greatest weaknesses in the Roman military system: The highest-ranking officers were not professional soldiers.

- Legates and tribunes came and went fairly rapidly, and thus continuity and professionalism were provided by the junior officers, called centurions. Each legion had one centurion per century, or 60 per legion.

- Centurions were promoted from the ranks and thus represented the best and most experienced of the soldiers. Among the centurions, there was a strict hierarchy of seniority. The most senior one, was called the *primus pilus* ("first spear"). In the modern U.S. Army, the centurions would be the equivalent of sergeants. They supervised and trained the men.

- Above all else, soldiers were expected to perform their duty, and if they failed, the penalties were predictably harsh. Offences such as insubordination or falling asleep while on watch were punished by death.

- If any whole unit, from *contubernia* to legion, was derelict in its duty, a lottery was held, and the unit would be decimated—that is, one out of every 10 men would be clubbed to death by his remaining comrades.

- The Roman legionary was what we would call a heavy infantryman. By the early imperial period, they wore body armor called a *lorica segmentata* consisting of bands of steel tied together with leather strips; helmets with cheek guards to protect the face, extensions at the back to cover the neck, and a reinforcing bar across the front; and a large, convex, rectangular shield called a scutum.

- The Roman legionary had two main offensive weapons: a double-edged short sword called the gladius made for combat at close quarters and a set of throwing spears. In battle, the legion would advance to close range, throw their spears in unison, then draw their swords, march forward, and chop their foes to pieces.

- Because of the discipline and organization of the Roman military system, they routinely defeated much larger enemies who battled in less coordinated ways. Roman formations, while similar to the earlier Greek phalanx, were not as rigid, and allowed for flexibility and initiative.

- The Romans also maintained a large group of noncitizen soldiers called the *auxilia*. These were typically not infantry but archers, horsemen, lightly armed skirmishers and other specialty fighters, because certain ethnic or geographic groups within the empire were thought to be especially talented at various specialized forms of warfare.

- *Auxilia* units were organized in groups of either 500 or 1,000. The total number of *auxilia* employed by the Romans was roughly equal to the number of legionaries.

China's Army of Bronze

- Like the Roman army, ancient Chinese armies were primarily composed of well-armed infantrymen. They were also characterized by a high degree of organization. Unlike Rome, more of the Chinese army was made up of forced conscripts and soldiers serving short-term stints.

- In keeping with China's large population, the armies of this period could be massive, perhaps the largest of the ancient world, mustering hundreds of thousands of troops.

- The basic soldier was equipped with a bronze sword and a uniquely Chinese weapon sometimes called a dagger-axe. This was something like a halberd consisting of a long pole topped by a bronze head with both a stabbing point and an axe-like blade. It could be used for thrusting or slashing and was well suited to pulling a cavalryman from a horse.

- Other foot soldiers were armed with powerful crossbows, which the Chinese developed centuries before Western Europe. Unlike a longbow, which requires years of practice to attain proficiency, the crossbow could be mastered quickly, although it had a much slower rate of fire.

- The better-equipped Chinese troops wore metal conical helmets and body armor made by lacing together small plates of toughened leather or metal. Most arms and armor were fashioned of bronze, but by the Han period, weak iron was used as well.

- China employed horsemen to a much greater degree than the Romans, usually as mounted archers, and they also had chariots. Chariots served primarily as transportation for high-ranking officers.

- On the battlefield, Chinese generals tried to exercise a great deal of direct control, and they did this by using complex systems of signal flags, drums, gongs, and bells.

- Chinese armies were heavily conscript armies. How these recruits were obtained varied over time, but a typical approach required every group of five households to supply five men to the army. Five men was also the lowest standard organizational unit in the Chinese army, analogous to the Roman *contubernia*.

- Officers in the army were mainly career professionals. Promotion was based on a combination of skills, performance in battle, and mastery of texts on military theory, such as Sun Tzu's *Art of War*.

- Once nomadic barbarian groups such as the Xiongnu became a serious threat, more attention was given to developing cavalry and fortified frontier outposts. This mirrors the later Roman focus on mobile field armies that could intercept incoming barbarian raids. The Chinese also recruited warlike barbarians or non-Chinese peoples as auxiliaries in their armies, again especially in the frontier regions.

- One aspect of warfare that was always important in China but that played little role in Roman warfare was combat along rivers, which were key strategic boundaries and transportation routes. Many wars among rival Chinese states centered around controlling them. This resulted in combined land/water operations involving fleets of ships and barges.

Mayan Combat—The War of the Seasons

- Mayan combat was greatly affected by the basic level of technology in Mesoamerican society in general. Just as there were no metal tools in Mesoamerica, there were no metal weapons or armor.

- The main hand-to-hand weapons were wooden clubs and short thrusting spears. One uniquely Mesoamerican weapon was a wooden shaft with flakes of razor-sharp obsidian embedded along its edges. This was well-suited for slashing attacks against an opponent's arms or legs. Mayan warriors used slings, javelins, and a type of dart-thrower known as an atlatl as projectile weapons.

- Mayan warriors of the classic period seem to have worn little or no armor, although elites are shown with elaborate feather headdresses. Light shields may have offered some protection. Later Mesoamerican warriors had heavy quilted body armor made of cotton, which may sometimes have been used by Mayan fighters.

- The numerous cities of Mayan culture appear to have engaged in frequent low-intensity warfare consisting of raids and occasional larger assaults. Professional armies seem to have been minimal. Most likely, elite Maya served as officers while the mass of troops was composed of their retainers or conscripted militia.

- Warfare appears to have been fairly common among the Maya. Mayan inscriptions record and celebrate many conflicts. Most warfare seems to have been seasonal, taking place during the dry season from December to May, when farmers could be spared from their fields.

- The scale of Mayan warfare would have been much smaller than that conducted by the massive armies of Rome and China; a large force would have comprised several thousand men rather than tens of thousands.

- Some scholars argue that the main purpose of Mayan warfare was to obtain live captives for sacrifice, and was a significant part of Mesoamerican combat, judging by the nonlethal nature of their weapons. Other scholars contend that Mayan warfare was at times also about territorial conquest or resources and could be just as deadly as elsewhere.

Suggested Reading

De Souza, ed., *The Ancient World at War.*

Goldsworthy, *The Complete Roman Army.*

Peers, *Soldiers of the Dragon.*

Raaflaub and Rosentstein, eds., *War and Society in the Ancient and Medieval Worlds.*

Questions to Consider

1. Do you agree with the argument that central aspects of a state's military system (such as the Roman obsession with organization) embody central aspects of that culture itself?

2. How did the goals of warfare and the types of threats they faced affect the sort of equipment and fighting styles favored by the Romans, the Chinese, and the Maya?

Comparative Armies—Rome, China, Maya
Lecture 39—Transcript

A bit depressingly, one of the oldest human activities, and one that shows little signs of ever going away, is organized warfare. The empires that we've looked at in this course were almost all formed by violence. It seems appropriate to spend at least one lecture discussing the military systems used by some of these civilizations. While this course has covered many cultures whose armies would be worth examining in more detail, in this lecture, I'll focus on three, one each drawn from the continents of Europe, Asia, and North America.

We ended the last lecture with the idea of Rome as a trophy case celebrating its conquest of the Mediterranean, and we'll begin this one with a consideration of one of the most famous armies of all time: the Roman. Since the Romans managed to conquer most of the known world, it's obvious that they were doing something right with regards to how they approached warfare. Throughout Roman history, the main characteristics attributed to Rome's military forces, both by the Romans and by their opponents, were determination, organization, and discipline. In combat situations, the Romans often didn't enjoy superior technology or superior numbers—these are usually decisive factors in battle—but what they almost always did have was greater organization, discipline, and determination.

From the time of the Punic Wars on, Rome's army was what we'd today call a professional army, meaning one in which the members are full-time soldiers who have no other jobs. A professional army can devote all of its effort to training and so produce much better soldiers. Most Roman legionaries were volunteers who enlisted for 25-year terms of service. Also, for most of Rome's history, soldiers were recruited from the ranks of Roman citizens, and so they had a personal stake in what they were fighting for, and that's different from a lot of other ancient societies that employed mercenaries.

We've already seen numerous examples of the determination of the Roman army, such as when they just kept raising new troops after suffering terrible defeats at the hands of talented enemies such as Pyrrhus or Hannibal. But the next characteristic of the Roman army is organization, and it's maybe the first in which you could say that organization was raised almost to an art form. Every aspect of the soldier's daily schedule was regulated, his equipment was standardized, and he knew exactly his place and his role within the army.

The easiest way to illustrate this is to consider the way in which Roman military units were structured. The basic army group was, of course, the Legion, but every legion was elaborately subdivided. The smallest unit of men was something called the *contubernia*, and that consisted of just 8 soldiers. The word *contubernia* can be literally translated as "those who share a tent," and that's exactly what it was. Standard Roman army tents held 8 men, so these *contubernia* were then collected together into groups of 10, and each group of 10 *contubernia* was called a century, which, despite what the name sounds like, then had 80 men, not 100. Six centuries were grouped together to create a cohort of 480 men, and finally 10 cohorts formed one legion, or 4,800 soldiers.

This whole elaborate organization was one of the keys to Rome's success, because in battle, a legion could either maneuver as a whole or it could be broken apart into units that ranged from 8 soldiers to 480, and every one of these levels of different units of men was trained to act both independently and together according to the need. This gave the Romans enormous flexibility, because the legion could react quickly to new situations. For example, in one famous battle that the Romans fought against the Macedonians, at a crucial point in this battle, the Battle of Cynoscephalae, one of the Roman commanders recognized that the Macedonian flank was open to attack, and so he could instantly just spin off a couple of cohorts to exploit that weakness, and so take advantage of even a momentary opportunity.

Each legion had as its standard a golden eagle on a pole. Because of the general importance of eagles and thunderbolts as symbols of the supreme god Jupiter, this was a very potent icon for the Romans. The soldier who carried this eagle into battle was called the *aquilifer*, and that's a coveted post of honor. Over time, those eagles became symbols for the legions themselves, and one of the greatest disgraces that could ever befall a legion was to allow its eagle to be captured by the enemy. The eagles, as well as various other standards, were also the focus of religious ritual for the legionaries. Whenever a legion made camp, its standards would be placed on a special raised platform in front of the commander's tent, right at the center of the camp, and any prayers or sacrifices performed by the legion took place beneath them.

Every Roman legion was commanded by a man called the legate, and he usually had to be of senatorial rank. Then, beneath him, were six senior officers called military tribunes. Both legates and tribunes were really political appointments, so these were held not by men for whom the army was a lifetime calling, but rather by politicians as one stage in their political career hopefully on the way towards the consulship. Serving for a year or two as military tribune was informally regarded as the step just before being elected to the lowest magistracy in the Roman government. This was maybe one of the greatest weaknesses in the Roman military system, because in practice what this meant, then, was that high-ranking officers in the legion weren't professional soldiers, and sometimes their inexperience bordered on incompetence, with disastrous results. What's really more surprising is the number of politicians, I suppose, who actually turned out to be pretty good officers and generals.

Legates and tribunes came and went fairly rapidly, so continuity and professionalism in the Roman army were provided not by those senior officers but instead by the junior officers, and these were guys called centurions. As that name implies, each legion had 1 centurion per century; so there'd be 60 centurions per legion. Centurions were promoted from the ranks, and so they represented the best and the most experienced of all the soldiers. Among the centurions, there's a strict hierarchy of seniority from the most junior centurion all the way up to the most senior one, and that most senior guy was called the *primus pilus*, literally "the first spear" of the legion. In the modern U.S. army, the centurions would be the equivalent of sergeants, and they were the ones who really supervised and trained the men and got most things done. As a symbol of their authority, each centurion carried a vine stick, but it was more than just a symbol, because he'd use this to beat the soldiers whenever he was displeased with them. There's one famous centurion whose nickname was "Bring me another" because he had the habit of beating his soldiers so hard with the stick that he was constantly breaking it, causing him always to be shouting, "Bring me another!"

The third characteristic of the Roman army was discipline. Above all else, soldiers were expected to perform their duty, and if they failed, the penalties were predictably harsh. Things such as insubordination or falling asleep while on watch were punishable by death. A particularly Roman institution that I think illustrates something of this attitude was known as decimation. If a whole unit, whether that's a century or even an entire legion, was judged to have failed to perform its duty, then the Romans had this special way of punishing it. A lottery would be held, and 1 out of every 10 men was selected. The chosen 10 percent were then clubbed to death by their own comrades. As amazing as that might seem, there were multiple attested occasions when decimation was actually employed, most commonly when a unit was thought to have shown some sort of cowardice in the face of the enemy.

The Roman legionary was what we'd call a heavy infantryman, meaning one who's very heavily armored and armed. For protecting the chest, Romans by the early imperial period had body armor that's called a *lorica segmentata*, and this consisted of bands of steel that were tied together with leather strips, and this formed very effective protection. Then, to guard his head, the Romans had a distinctive helmet. It featured cheek guards that would protect the face; it had a nice extension at the back that would protect it from chopping blows from behind; and then you also had a reinforcing bar across the front, and that would help to save your skull from any sort of blows that came in from right above. In their left hand, legionaries had a large shield called a scutum. It was three or four feet high, two or three feet wide, rectangular in shape, and from top to bottom the middle of the shield curved slightly outwards so that the legionary could hide his body within that curvature. These shields were painted, and the most common design was a red background with a gold lightning bolt symbol on it.

The Roman legionary had two main offensive weapons. The first of these was the famous Roman short sword, the *gladius*. It's edged on both sides and it can be used to cut, but it's most deadly as a thrusting weapon to inflict deep injuries that are fatal. This is a sword that's made for combat at close quarters; it's simply designed to kill in the most efficient manner possible. It's not one of these flashy or romantic types of swords, you don't do a lot of showy waving around with it; but, like the Romans themselves, it's highly practical. Each Roman legionary also carried two spears; and in battle, the legion would advance to close range, maybe 10 or 20 feet from the opposing army, they'd throw their spears in unison, then draw their swords, march forward, and chop their foes to pieces.

Because of the discipline and organization of the Roman military system, they were routinely able to defeat much larger numbers of enemies who fought in less coordinated ways, and this was because the Romans fought together as a tightly massed group, where each man supported and protected his comrades rather than just running around as individuals. This is similar to the earlier Greek phalanx, but the Roman formations weren't quite as rigid, so they allowed room for the flexibility and initiative that's made possible by their organizational system.

In addition to the legions, which were made up of citizens, the Romans also maintained a large group of non-citizen soldiers, and these were called the *Auxilia*. While the Roman legionaries were all equipped as heavy infantry, armies often needed other types of troops; you need archers, horsemen, and lightly armed skirmishers. But the Romans chose to train their citizens only as heavy infantrymen, and so what they did is they filled those other needed positions with non-Roman units. Certain ethnic or geographic groups within the empire were often thought to be especially talented at various specialized forms of warfare, and so they're often formed into *auxilia* units based around those specialties. For example, certain North African tribes were excellent horsemen, and so the Romans raised light cavalry *auxilia* from them. The inhabitants of the island of Crete were considered to be unusually skillful archers, and so Rome raised cohorts of Cretan archers. The people of the Balearic Islands were experts at the use of slings, so contingents of Balearic slingers were highly valued.

Auxilia units were organized into groups of either 500 or 1,000, and the total number of *auxilia* employed by the Romans was roughly equal to the number of legionaries. As mentioned in another lecture, upon discharge, auxiliaries received full Roman citizenship, so that serving as an auxiliary became one of the principal forces of Romanization in the empire. A weakness of the Roman army is that while they're almost unbeatable on open ground where their heavy infantry could dominate, if you caught them in thick forests, swamps, or in deserts, they could be much more vulnerable.

Like the Roman army, ancient Chinese armies were primarily composed of masses of well-armed infantry. Also like the Roman army, the Chinese armies were characterized by a high degree of organization. But unlike Rome, more of the Chinese army was made up of forced conscripts and various types of soldiers who were serving relatively short-term stints. In this lecture, I'm focusing on Chinese armies from about 200 B.C. to about 589 A.D.; that's from the Qin up to the Sui Dynasty. In keeping with China's large population, the armies of that time could be huge, maybe the largest in all the ancient world, sometimes mustering hundreds of thousands of troops.

The basic soldier in the ancient Chinese army was a heavily armed infantryman, typically equipped with a bronze sword and sometimes a uniquely Chinese weapon called a dagger-axe. This was something like a later Western Medieval halberd that consisted of a long pole, 10 or more feet in length, topped by a bronze head that featuring both a stabbing point and a sort of axe-like blade. This could be used for thrusting or slashing, and it's also well-suited for pulling down cavalrymen from their horses. Other foot soldiers were armed with powerful crossbows, and those missile troops played a crucial role in Chinese armies. The Chinese developed the crossbow centuries before Western Europe. Unlike a longbow, which requires years of practice to attain proficiency, the crossbow could be mastered fairly quickly, although in battle it had a much slower rate of fire than a bow.

For armor, the better-equipped Chinese troops wore conical metal helmets and body armor that's made by lacing together little plates of toughened leather or metal. Most of the arms and armor in the Chinese army were fashioned of bronze, but by the Han Period, iron began to be used as well, although because it wasn't of that good quality, initially it didn't have a lot different performance from bronze. To a much greater degree than the Romans, the Chinese employed horsemen, usually in the role of mounted archers, and they also had chariots. Chariots had been an important component of armies in earlier phases of Chinese history, but as we get up to about the time of the Qin, they sort of transitioned into serving mainly as transportation for high-ranking officers rather than as actual combat elements. On the battlefield, though, Chinese generals tried at least to exercise a great deal of direct control, and so they'd do this by using complex systems of signal flags, drums, gongs, and bells.

Unlike the mostly voluntary enlistment of Roman legionaries, Chinese armies were heavily conscript armies. How these recruits were obtained varied over time, but a typical approach was that put into practice by the Qin, and they'd require that every group of five households had to supply five men to the army. By the way, five men was also the lowest standard organizational unit in the Chinese army; you can think of it as being analogous to the Roman *contubernia*. Each of those little subunits in the Chinese army would often have been made up of a group of people from the same place, and that practice at least ensured a strong sense of group cohesion among those little units.

Officers in the army were mostly career professionals who could rise through 17 successive ranks, beginning with the officer in charge of one of those little units of 5 men, all the way up to a general. Promotion was based on a combination of things: demonstrating your skills as a soldier, performance in battle, but also your mastery of texts on military theory, such as Sun Tzu's famous *Art of War*. This is parallel to the examination system for civil servants that, of course, tested knowledge of Confucian texts. The Chinese system also offered rewards for those who'd personally killed a certain number of enemies in battle, and officers who were in charge of groups that were bigger than 100 could also earn promotion or sometimes rewards for the total number of enemies killed by the men under their command. All of that's very different from the Roman system of officering. The Romans would officer their legions with aristocrats, most of who went on to political careers; and Rome also didn't demand any theoretical text-based knowledge of warfare from its officers. In the Roman army, the average legionary was a long-serving professional while his senior officers were short-term amateurs, whereas in the Chinese army, the typical soldier was a short-term conscript, while his officers were well-read careerists.

Once nomadic barbarian groups such as the Xiong-nu became a serious threat, more attention was given to developing cavalry and fortified frontier outposts. In a lot of ways, this mirrors the later Roman focus on mobile field armies that could intercept incoming barbarian raids. Like the Romans, the Chinese recruited warlike barbarians or non-Chinese people as auxiliaries in their armies, again especially in those frontier regions. One aspect of warfare that's always important in China but that played almost no role in Roman warfare was combat along rivers. Those great waterways of China were key strategic routes, and many wars that were fought among rival Chinese states centered around controlling those waterways; and you'd have combined land/water operations involving fleets of ships and barges.

When we turn to our third army, to Mayan warfare, one huge difference concerns the available equipment. Mayan combat was greatly affected by the basic level of technology that existed in Mesoamerican society in general. Just as there were no metal tools in Mesoamerica, there were no metal weapons or armor; and so Mayan warriors had to make do with equipment fashioned from stone, wood, and textiles. For hand-to-hand combat, the main weapons were often wooden clubs or short thrusting spears. One uniquely Mesoamerican weapon was a device made by taking a wooden shaft and embedding flakes of razor-sharp obsidian along the edges. This created a sword-like weapon that's very well-suited for slashing attacks; so you could attack an opponent's arms or legs. The sorts of injuries that this would inflict were the sort that were most likely to disable an enemy, but what you couldn't really cause with this was any sort of fatal penetrating wound; and so this weapon in some ways is the exact opposite of the Roman *gladius*, which was designed to thrust and therefore to kill enemies rather than disabling them.

In terms of projectile weapons, Mayan warriors could use slings, javelins, and a sort of dart-thrower that's known as an atlatl. The atlatl could be a very effective and deadly weapon, but even though we have some images in Mayan art of warriors holding them, scholars are currently arguing about whether or not they're actually used commonly in combat. Mayan warriors of the Classic Period seem to have worn very in the way of armor. Sometimes elites are shown with elaborate feather headdresses, but that probably wouldn't offer much protection. They did often carry little shields that may have done something, and later Mesoamerican warriors had heavy quilted body armor that's made of cotton, and that armor may have been used by some Mayan fighters as well.

The numerous separate political entities that made up Mayan culture seem to have engaged in frequent low-intensity warfare that consisted of a lot of raids, but occasionally there were larger assaults. In keeping with the limited available weapons, none of which required very extensive training to master, professional armies composed of specialized warriors seem to have been minimal. By Roman or Chinese standards, Mayan armies would probably have looked like an undisciplined mob rather than any sort of professional army. It's most likely that elite Maya would serve as officers and leaders in warfare while the mass of troops was composed of either their personal retainers or conscripted militia.

In contrast to earlier notions among scholars that the Maya were a peaceful people, warfare now appears to have been fairly common among them. Mayan inscriptions record and celebrate many, many wars conflicts. For example, during just one four-month stretch in 799 A.D., the Mayan town of Naranjo is mentioned as having engaged in no fewer than eight separate battles, although hopefully such a rate of conflict was a bit atypical. In keeping with the non-specialist nature of Mayan combat, most warfare seems to have been seasonal, so they'd fight during the dry season, which lasted from December to May; that's when farmers could be spared from their fields. The whole scale of Mayan warfare would have been much smaller than that conducted by the massive armies of Rome and China. A big Mayan force might have been several thousand men compared to tens or hundreds of thousands in Rome or China.

Some have argued that the main purpose of Mayan warfare was to obtain live captives for sacrifice, and that goal certainly was at least a significant part of Mesoamerican combat in general. If you look at the nonlethal nature of the weapons, such as those obsidian-edged swords that were better suited to disable rather than to kill, this seems to support this interpretation. Mayan warfare has sometimes also been viewed as being mostly ritual in nature, and therefore different in some fundamental way from the sorts of wars of conquest and expansion that we find in other cultures. Other scholars contend that Mayan warfare was, at least at times, also very much about territorial conquest or acquiring new resources, and so it could be just as deadly as elsewhere. Certainly, though, the focus on taking captives for sacrifice was a significant and very distinctive aspect of Mayan warfare, but that doesn't mean that it didn't also serve those same functions as in other civilizations.

For all their superficial differences and similarities, the Roman, Chinese, and Mayan armies each played important roles in their respective cultures, and collectively they offer some interesting insights into how those three societies approached what is, after all, one of the most basic of human activities: organized, armed conflict.

Later Roman Empire—Crisis and Christianity
Lecture 40

D uring the Crisis of the 3rd Century, internal problems and external enemies threatened Rome, but the empire made a surprising recovery under Emperor Diocletian. He changed the very nature of what it meant to be emperor by creating the tetrarchy—or "rule of four"—addressing the problems of the empire's size and the wars of succession with a single solution. His monetary reforms also shored up Rome's ailing economy. It was also during this period that Christianity rose from an obscure cult to a recognized and major faith of the empire, thanks to the conversion of Emperor Constantine.

The Crisis of the 3rd Century

- In the 3rd century A.D., Roman history entered a chaotic period of great political instability and an extraordinarily high turnover rate of emperors. Many rivals for the throne came and went in a single year. Between 238 and 278, there were 26 official emperors and dozens of usurpers; the only qualification needed to claim the title was the loyalty of many men with swords.

- Things were so bad during this time that historians have labeled this period the Crisis of the 3rd Century. Three main factors contributed to this crisis:

  o It was an era of near constant civil war. When an emperor died, generals of the three major frontier armies often bribed their legions to proclaim them emperor. All three armies then converged on Rome to fight it out. Sometimes generals did not even wait for the old emperor to die.

  o There were serious barbarian invasions. New, large barbarian confederations had formed, and when civil war broke out and the Roman armies abandoned the borders, the barbarians saw the opportunity to plunder the empire.

○ Due to these two factors, the economy was in a state of collapse. Villages were burnt, people were killed, and crops were destroyed. Merchants were afraid to travel, and bandits and pirates proliferated. Desperate for income, emperors debased the coinage. People were not fooled by this, however, and raised their prices, sparking terrible bouts of inflation.

- Finally, the empire was really too big to be run effectively by one person. It looked like the end was at hand when a series of tough military emperors managed to stabilize the empire and give it another hundred years or so of life.

Diocletian's Reforms

- The last in this line of military reformers had the longest, most successful reign. His name was Diocletian. He reorganized the army and expanded it to around 600,000 troops, many of them drawn from the barbarian tribes menacing Rome, turning a problem into a solution.

- He also reoriented the armies from a border patrol to a defense-in-depth force in which large, centralized military reserves were posted behind the frontier, from where they could move to intercept and eliminate barbarian incursions.

- He completely separated the civilian and military structures. No longer were legion commanders short-term political appointees; they were now career military men. Governors were now exclusively civil administrators.

- To increase the efficiency of the administration, he split up the provinces into smaller units so each governor had less to do and could concentrate on a more manageable area. Diocletian then combined provinces into a number of larger units called dioceses, each under the control of a vicar. The legions were consolidated into several multilegion armies, each under the command of a dux, from which we got the English cognate duke.

- Realizing that the empire was too big for any one man to govern effectively, he made official what had already happened. He split the empire into four parts, appointing a ruler for each. This system of four emperors was called the tetrarchy.

- To rebuild the people's faith in money, Diocletian issued a new solid gold coin whose purity and weight were guaranteed. Its official name was the solidus. To curb inflation, Diocletian issued the Price Edict, a list of maximum prices for goods and services. Although difficult to enforce, in theory, if you charged more than the price listed, you could be punished with exile or even death.

- Finally, Diocletian explicitly linked the emperors to the gods for the first time. Many emperors had been deified after their deaths or had been unofficially worshiped as gods, but now the emperors began to liken themselves to gods while still alive.

Diocletian and the Persecution of Christians

- One consequence of this was that any religious challenge to this practice took on the nature of a political challenge. For the first time, political unity implied religious unity, and Diocletian began to persecute deviant religious cults. Among these was a small group known as Christians.

- From a historical perspective, there were a number of aspects of Christianity that had considerable appeal to the Romans, including the link between good behavior and the reward of immortality and, in particular, that it did not recognize existing Roman legal and social hierarchies but said all humans had value and dignity and were equal in the eyes of God.

- The Romans were normally quite tolerant of other religions but always had trouble with Judaism and Christianity because of their monotheism. They were puzzled by Christianity's secrecy and troubled by its egalitarian views. Nevertheless, Christians' refusal to worship the emperor as a god was the primary cause of conflict and the trigger for widespread persecution.

The Conversion of Constantine—and the Empire

- Events took an abrupt and unexpected turn early in the next century. Civil wars among rivals for the throne continued. One contender was a man named Constantine. He was known to inspire his troops before battles by claiming that he had had a vision from a god, such as Apollo, promising them victory.

- In 312 A.D., he was attempting to capture Rome at a site called the Milvian Bridge. Constantine's troops were at a disadvantage here—tired and outnumbered. Just before the battle, he claimed to have had a vision in which the Christian god promised victory. His men painted a Christian symbol, consisting of Greek letters chi and rho, on their shields and won the battle

- Constantine took the throne and issued a decree that Christianity was now to be tolerated. Constantine himself converted, but he continued to subsidize pagan temples and sacrifices, to worship the sun god, and to issue coins bearing Apollo's image. Constantine seems to have viewed himself as the head of the Christian church as well as the Roman state, summoning meetings of bishops and presiding over them.

- From this point on, all but one Roman emperor was a Christian. One secular appeal that Christianity had for Roman emperors was to extend the idea of there being only one true god to the concept that there was only one legitimate emperor.

- Administratively, Constantine splits the empire into two halves. He founded a new city to serve as the capital of the Eastern Roman Empire, naming it Constantinople after himself. He equipped it with most of the architectural features of Rome.

- Just like Augustus, Constantine claimed that he had saved or restored the Republic. The old propaganda of Roman politics was still in use, 300 years after it had obviously stopped being a republic.

Suggested Reading

Barnes, *Constantine and Eusebius.*

Jones, *The Later Roman Empire, 284–602.*

Lenski, ed., *The Cambridge Companion to the Age of Constantine.*

Questions to Consider

1. Of the three categories of problems (civil wars, barbarian invasions, and economic collapse) that plagued Rome during the Crisis of the 3rd Century, which do you think was the most dangerous and why?

2. In what ways did Christianity's emphasis on the next world rather than this one, on private rather than public worship, and on the individual rather than the community undermine or conflict with core Roman values?

Later Roman Empire—Crisis and Christianity
Lecture 40—Transcript

We left off the story of the Roman Empire in 211 A.D. with the death of the soldier-emperor Septimius Severus, and he'd ruled just after the Golden Age of Rome and the time of the Five Good Emperors. The next century of Roman history will be a particularly dramatic and traumatic stretch during which the empire will suffer severe political, military, and economic crises and it will end up looking certain to collapse; but then it will stage an unexpected, near-miraculous recovery and finally, will undergo an even more surprising transformation into a Christian empire. This tumultuous era marks the beginning of the period known as the Later Roman Empire.

In the 3rd century A.D., Roman history entered a chaotic time when there was great political instability and really an extraordinarily high turnover rate of emperors. Consider that whereas there'd only been about a half-dozen emperors during the entire 2nd century, in the third that many rivals for the throne would often come and go in a single year. From 238–278 A.D., there were at least 26 official emperors and dozens of usurpers. This was now truly the age of the soldier-emperor; a time when the only real qualification you had to have was the loyalty of a lot of guys with swords.

Typical of these men was a man named Maximinus Thrax, which literally translates as "the big guy from Thrace." True to his name, he began as a simple peasant from the region of Thrace who allegedly was seven feet tall. He enlisted in the Roman legions, he gained the favor of his fellow soldiers, and eventually had them proclaim him emperor; and so he may well have been the first peasant emperor. His success, though, was fairly short-lived, as soon his own troops turned against him and murdered him.

Things were so bad during this time that historians have labeled this period "The Crisis of the Third Century." There are three main factors that contributed to this crisis. The first was that it's an era of near-constant civil war. Most of the Roman legions had gotten grouped in just a couple provinces on the frontiers where danger threatened, and especially that's along the Rhine River, along the Danube River, and on the eastern frontier. The commanders of those three armies realized that they each controlled a significant part of the military; and so when a current emperor died, those generals would often bribe their legions to proclaim them as emperor. Since each of the three groups would declare their own general as emperor, you ended up with a vicious three-way civil war, as all converged on Rome with their armies to fight it out.

Second, there were serious barbarian invasions in this period. Outside of Rome's borders, you had new, larger confederations of barbarians that were forming up; and they wanted to invade and plunder the rich provinces of the empire. Normally, the legions would be standing guard against them. However, when one of these civil wars broke out and all the Roman armies abandoned the borders to go to Rome and fight each other, what do you think happened on the frontiers? The barbarians saw opportunity.

The third aspect of the Crisis of the Third Century was economic collapse, and it's very much a direct effect of the previous two. Cities were plundered both by outside invaders and sometimes by Roman armies fighting each other; villages got burnt down; people were killed; crops were destroyed; merchants were afraid to travel any longer between towns; and with no one to control them, bandits and pirates proliferated. All of those things disrupted the economy and reduced the overall economic output. Even worse, as soon as one of these contenders for the throne managed to kill off his enemies and establish himself as emperor, often the first thing he did was to raise taxes in order to get the funds to rebuild the armies that had just been destroyed; but this was happening at the very time when farmers and merchants could least afford to pay more, so it all formed a vicious circle. Absolutely desperate to gain more income, emperors debased the coinage, and this means that they added less valuable metals to coins but they'd keep the face value the same. People weren't fooled by this, and so the inevitable result was that everybody raised their prices. The problem really was that nobody trusted the coinage anymore, so this sparked terrible bouts of inflation. Finally, all of those old technological limitations on communication that we looked at earlier, such as the time it took messages to travel from the emperor to the provinces, meant that now, when it's under stress, the Empire was really too big to be run effectively by just one person.

By the mid-3rd century, it looked like the end was at hand for the Roman Empire. There were constant civil wars and revolutions, self-proclaimed emperors were coming and going with bewildering rapidity, the economy was a complete mess, and barbarians were roaming unopposed through formerly peaceful Roman territories. Just then, a series of tough military emperors arrived on the scene and they managed to stabilize the empire and even to give it at least another hundred years or so of life. While one of the main causes of the Crisis of the Third Century was that legionary commanders were proclaiming themselves emperor, in a way, this problem ultimately resulted in its own solution, since the men who inevitably rose to the top turned out to be the ones who were the most capable of defeating the barbarians and reestablishing order. These pragmatically-minded soldiers also realized that the strategy that Rome had been using simply had to change.

One of these guys was named Aurelian. Something of his character can be inferred from the nickname that his own troops gave him, which was *Manus ad Ferrum*, which you can loosely translate as "Hand on Sword." In his five-year reign, he first of all defeated several major barbarian groups and restored peace, both in the east and the west; and then, another famous action of his that also shows his pragmatism is that he had a wall built around the city of Rome. Rome hadn't been enclosed by a wall since way back in the time of the Roman Republic, and so sometimes the Aurelian Wall is viewed as an admission of Rome's weakness; but on the other hand, the construction of that wall was a very realistic response to the new sorts of threats that Rome was facing.

The last in this little group of military reformers who turned things around is probably the best-known of them, and he had the longest, most successful reign. His name was Diocletian. Diocletian defeated a number of barbarian groups to secure the borders, but he also instituted a number of other essential reforms. First of all, he reorganized the Roman army and made it larger. Under Diocletian, the total size of the armed forces rose to around 550,000 or 600,000 troops. Many of these new recruits were drawn directly from the most warlike of the barbarian tribes that were threatening Rome; so once again, in a way, Diocletian turned the problem into the solution. He also reoriented the armies from ineffectively being spread thinly all around the borders to what's called a defense-in-depth strategy, and there you have large centralized military reserves posted back behind the frontier, but from there they're able to move to intercept and eliminate barbarian invasions.

Diocletian also finally separated the civilian and military structures. No longer were legion commanders these short-term political appointees, but now they're career military men, professionals. Likewise, governors were now exclusively civil administrators rather than trying to be both military and civilian leaders. To try to increase the overall efficiency of the administration, he split up the provinces into smaller units. Before Diocletian there'd been about 50 provinces, but now there were over 100. In practical terms, what this meant was that each governor now had less to do and so he could concentrate all of his efforts on a smaller, more manageable area. With each governor focusing on local issues, there was a need for an administrator who could still look at the big picture in a whole region. To fill this gap, Diocletian clumped together provinces into a number of larger units called dioceses. Each diocese was under the control of an overall administrator whose title was vicar. Probably you recognize that both of those are titles that the Catholic Church would later adapt to its hierarchy. Although these government posts wouldn't last for long, the terms were later copied for various church officials. Similarly, the legions were consolidated into several large multi-legion armies, and each one of those was placed under the command of an overall general whose title was Dux, a term from which we later get the English cognate "duke."

Finally, Diocletian realized that the empire really was too big for any one man to effectively govern, so he in essence made official what had already happened: He split the empire into four parts, and he appointed a ruler for each part. Now there were four co-emperors who'd rule together, but each was responsible for one section of the empire. This system of four emperors was called the Tetrarchy. There's a very famous porphyry statue that's now embedded in a corner of Saint Mark's cathedral in Venice that shows Diocletian and his three fellow tetrarchs firmly clasping each other's shoulders in a symbolic display of unity and determination. Once again, we see Diocletian cleverly turning the problem into the solution, since for years the empire had been already fragmenting into these different pieces; and so, in a way, he's just making official what had been going on. While not all aspects of this reorganization would last for long, collectively these reforms and attempts at reforms created more attention to detail at the local level as well as more organization and strategy at the broad level.

Eliminating civil wars and barbarian invasions obviously went a long way towards restoring the economy, but there were still the problems of rampant inflation and general distrust of the currency. In order to try and rebuild people's faith in money, a new solid gold coin was issued, and this was a coin whose purity and weight of metal were guaranteed. In a gesture of optimistic propaganda, the official term for this new denomination of coin was the solidus, a name that translates as "a solid bit"; in other words, something you can trust.

Then, in 301 A.D., in an effort to curb inflation, Diocletian issued a document known as the Price Edict. This was a long, long list of goods and services that gave a maximum price that could be charged for each one. This wasn't really that successful since there were obvious difficulties in trying to enforce something like this so broadly, but at least it was an attempt, and it probably did have some effect in areas where there were Romans to enforce it. In theory, if you charged more than the price that's listed, you could be punished, sometimes with exile or even death.

Diocletian's Price Edict survives, and it's a very fascinating document, particularly to economic historians, both for the light it sheds on the relative values of goods and services and just for the absolute range of items that get listed in this thing. For example, it distinguishes between multiple gradations of fineness of various textiles such as linen and wool. It identifies several different grades of animal hides, from the highest quality that it says is suitable for making the soles of shoes to a low-grade material that you could only use to patch things up. It lists fees that could be charged to hire the services of various professionals, everything ranging from blacksmiths to barbers. Can you guess what type of service commanded the very highest fee? The answer might be a familiar one: It was for legal advice and services; so some things really never change.

Finally, another reform of Diocletian was to try to give greater stability to the office of emperor and to create more respect and authority for him by explicitly linking for the very first time the emperors and the gods. In the past, many emperors had been deified after their death or they'd been unofficially worshipped as gods; but now the emperors began to liken themselves to gods while still alive. For example, in their portraits on coins, the emperors were now shown with rays of light coming out of their heads like the sun god. Later, when Christians began to depict God in art, they copied that convention, and so we know that today by the term "halo."

Diocletian and the other emperors also surrounded themselves with more formal court ceremony. Diocletian became the first emperor, or maybe I should say the first sane emperor, to wear a golden cloak and jeweled shoes, and who required people to address him as "Lord" or "God."

One unintended consequence of all this was that since the emperors were associating themselves with certain gods, then any religious challenge to those gods took on the nature of a political challenge. This also meant that, for the first time, political unity at least implied nominal religious unity, and so in connection with this, Diocletian began to discourage and even sometimes to persecute deviant religious cults. Among these was a small group known as Christians.

We've come nearly 300 years past the birth of Christ, but I haven't mentioned Christianity yet, and mostly that's because up until this point, it had really not had much influence beyond a miniscule circle of believers. To a Roman, or really almost to anyone living around most of the Mediterranean Sea at this time, Christianity would've just appeared as one of hundreds of tiny, obscure religions and cults that coexisted within the Roman Empire. But within the next hundred years, Christianity would become the official religion of the Roman state.

To understand both its rise and the conflicts that developed between Christian and non-Christians, let's back up a little bit and consider some of the fundamental differences between Christianity and most other religions of the time. Two key components of standard Roman religious beliefs were, of course, its polytheism and its public nature. Like nearly every other Mediterranean culture except for the Jews, the Romans believed that there were an infinite number of legitimate gods and, in general, they were really quite open to accepting new gods and allowing what today we might term religious tolerance. There were definitely certain gods who were worshipped and various rites that were performed on behalf of the state and other collective public entities, but in addition to that, people could typically chose one or even multiple gods that they personally worshipped, and often these were part of more individually-focused cults such as those of Isis or Mithras.

Christianity, in contrast, was rigidly and strictly monotheistic. They asserted an exclusive belief in one and only one god, their own. Christianity was also much more privately focused as a religion. Christians tended to worship indoors, and they concentrated far more on the relationship between individuals and God. In contrast, Roman religious rituals were almost always held outdoors in highly public settings; and so this apparently furtive nature of Christian worship, at least from a Roman perspective, was one of the things that, to Roman eyes, made Christians seem a little bit suspicious. Another big difference is that Christianity had a sacred written text, the Bible, which helped to define what its worshippers believed.

After the crucifixion of Jesus around 27 A.D., Christianity initially spread very, very slowly. A key figure in its establishment was, of course, Paul who, by traveling and preaching all around the Mediterranean and also by addressing his message both to Jews and non-Jews, greatly widened its audience. If you viewed the spread of Christianity from a historical rather than a religious perspective, there were a number of aspects of Christianity that obviously had considerable appeal, including that it emphasized morality and good behavior; that it offered a link between that behavior and the reward of immortality after death; and also, Christianity didn't recognize the existing Roman legal and social hierarchies, but instead it offered a system in which all humans had value and dignity and were equal in the eyes of God.

The Romans generally speaking were normally quite tolerant of other religions, but they always had trouble with Judaism and Christianity because of their monotheism. The Romans simply couldn't understand Christians's stubborn insistence on the exclusivity of their one god. Romans were puzzled by Christianity's apparent secrecy, and they were troubled by the way in which it could make slaves, women, and non-citizens seemingly equals to citizens. Nevertheless, the primary conflict came from a rather odd source: Some emperors had begun to be deified after their deaths and to become objects of cult activity even while still alive; so, on an emperor's birthday, it was expected that all citizens or people in the empire would say a prayer for the health of the emperor, and they'd direct towards the aspect of him that might become divine. Usually they'd also make a little offering of food or wine. The authorities expected everybody to participate in this, and the only reason they could see why you wouldn't do so was if you were treasonous, or maybe you were some sort of revolutionary trying to overthrow the state. To a Christian, as to a Jew, taking part in this sort of ritual was a clear violation of the first commandment, which says, "Do not to worship other gods"; and so, naturally, they refused to do it. So something that to many Romans was predominantly a political act, something analogous today to maybe reciting the Pledge of Allegiance, was to the Christians a matter of core religious belief. Really, all of this to some degree amounted almost in a kind of tragic failure of communication and understanding, but the actual result could be persecution and violent death.

Until Diocletian, most Roman officials and emperors plainly had fairly little inclination or desire to actively hunt down or punish Christians; there were a couple exceptions. Under Diocletian, during the stresses of dealing with all the various crises facing the state, there's a perception that unity became especially vital, and in this sort of emergency situation, they couldn't afford any margin for forms of dissent. In 299 A.D., for the first time, Christians were officially actively persecuted on an empire-wide scale. Having saved the empire in a sense, Diocletian then voluntarily retired; and he's really the only Roman emperor ever to do this. He spent the rest of his life living in a huge palace that he'd built for himself in what today is the town of Split in Croatia. By the way, if you go to Split today, the remains of that palace have been absorbed right into the buildings of the city, so you can see little bits of the palace scattered around; but if you go down underground, you can still wander around the unchanged basement of Diocletian's palace.

Events would take an abrupt and unexpected turn early in the next century. Under Diocletian and his colleagues, immediate disaster had been staved off but there was still a lot of political instability. Civil wars among all these rivals for the throne continued, and in the early 4th century, one contender for the throne was a man named Constantine. He started out as somewhat of a long shot, but he got lucky, he won a couple of battles, and he began to grow powerful. Constantine had a clever way to inspire his troops before key battles: He'd claim that he'd had a vision from a god who promised them victory. For example, before one battle, he stopped in a temple to the sun-god, Apollo, and then he made the claim that Apollo had appeared to him in a vision and promised him victory. After this, Constantine would identify himself with Apollo, for example by issuing a coin that showed a portrait of him and Apollo together.

In 312 A.D., Constantine marched with his army to try to capture Rome. The battle to determine who'd emerge as the emperor of the western half of the Roman Empire took place at a site just outside of Rome called the Milvian Bridge. Constantine was at a disadvantage; his troops were tired, they were outnumbered, and their morale was low. But right before the battle, he claimed to have had another vision; and along with this vision there were some accompanying dreams, and in these the Christian god appeared to him and promised victory. Following up on this vision, his men painted a Christian divine symbol that consisted of Chi and Rho—that's the first two letters of the name "Christ" when written in Greek—on their shields. His men were inspired, and they won the battle; and Constantine then issued a decree that Christianity was now to be tolerated.

At the time, probably less than 10 percent of the empire's inhabitants were Christian, so Constantine converted when 90 percent of Romans weren't Christian yet. To be honest, his understanding of Christianity's doctrines seems to have been a bit shaky. For example, he continued after his conversion to Christianity to subsidize pagan temples and to supply sacrifices to them from the imperial treasury. He continued after his conversion to Christianity to worship the sun god, and he still kept minting coins bearing Apollo's image. He also seems to have had a somewhat inflated view of his role in the church; he seems to have viewed himself as the head of the Christian church, so he'd summon meetings of bishops and preside over them as if he were a pope. He built a church that contained statues of the 12 apostles and in the center he left a niche for himself, apparently either as the 13th apostle or even as an equal to Christ. But nevertheless, from this point on, all but one emperor would follow his example and would be Christian.

One secular appeal that Christianity may have had for Roman emperors was that they could extend the idea of there being only one true god to the concept that there was only one legitimate emperor: themselves. You can see how this would be a very useful ideology during a time when dealing with lots of different rivals for the throne and when issues of legitimacy were one of the greatest problems facing Roman emperors.

From this moment on, the Roman Empire effectively split into two halves, and there would be separate Eastern and Western Roman emperors and Empires. In acknowledgment of this reality, Constantine founded a new city to serve as the capital of the Eastern Roman Empire. Not very modestly, he named this city Constantinople after himself, and he equipped it with most of the features that were found at Rome, including, of course, a palace, a chariot racing arena, a senate, and even a grain dole. Just like Augustus, Constantine then claimed that he'd saved or restored the Roman Republic. Here we see that old propaganda of Roman politics still in use, 300 years after it had obviously stopped being a republic.

In the next lecture, we'll see if Constantine was as successful in the long run as Augustus in revitalizing the Roman state, and despite all the chaos of the 3rd century, it was a time when crucial new elements were emerging and taking shape, and nowhere was that more true than in the area of religion.

The Decline and Fall of the Roman Empire?
Lecture 41

O ne of the most famous historical questions of all time is when and why the Roman Empire fell. There is a surprising variety of possible answers to these questions. Among the most popular culprits in Rome's fall are the various barbarian tribes on its borders, such as the Goths and Huns, but historians have offered a variety of other explanations as well, from ecological crisis to the rise of Christianity. Part of the difficulty in answering these questions lies in just how we might define the term "Rome."

The Barbarian Invasions Begin

- One of the first problems encountered when attempting to analyze the fall of Rome is that no one can seem to agree on exactly when it happened. One frequently suggested date is the death of the philosopher-emperor Marcus Aurelius in A.D. 180 and the accession of his son, the mad Commodus.

- Another popular date is A.D. 312, which marks the conversion of Constantine to Christianity. Proponents of this date stress that the personal, inward-looking ideology of Christianity was fundamentally antithetical to the outward, public focus of Roman civilization.

- The next set of proposed dates all focus around barbarians. The term "barbarian" was a pejorative label used by the Greeks and Romans to denote almost any group they regarded as less civilized than themselves.

- The barbarians we are concerned with had been present for a long time in Northern Europe. These seminomadic peoples had a social structure organized by kinship and loose tribal groupings. These were largely male-dominated societies in which your status was based on your ability as warrior.

- The people of the time often expressed such differences in terms of diet. To a Greek or Roman, one of the marks being a civilized person was that your diet revolved around the three Mediterranean staples of wheat, wine, and olives. Conversely, you were a barbarian if your diet focused on meat, dairy, and beer.

- In the 4th century, small clan groups began to coalesce into much larger units and to migrate out of their traditional homelands. They started to form confederations, and tens or hundreds of thousands of them began to flow across the borders of the Roman Empire.

The Arrival of the Huns

- Of all the barbarian groups, perhaps the most feared were the Huns. They were truly nomadic, riding small, shaggy, horses, and they fought mainly from horseback using powerful bows. They had an extremely tough, brutal society based on raiding and stealing and could travel vast distances.

- The Huns were excellent warriors. When they invaded, people were often so afraid of them that they would run away rather than fight them. For a long time, historians thought the Huns were the Xiongnu. This is now a matter of great contention, and the scarcity of sources means that we will probably never know for sure.

- In the late 300s, the Huns began to shift westward out of central Asia and toward Eastern Europe. This set up a domino effect: The Huns invaded the territory of the Germanic Ostrogoths. They pushed west into the lands of the Visigoths. When the Visigoths moved westward, they entered Roman territory.

- When the Visigoths and the Ostrogoths began to exert pressure on the borders of the empire, the emperors found it expedient to exchange land for promises that the barbarians would fight for Rome rather than against it. These accommodations frequently broke down due to bad faith on both sides.

- In A.D. 378, disgruntled Goths rebelled against the Eastern Roman Empire. Emperor Valens marched out to suppress the rebellion without waiting for reinforcements; he and his entire army were slain at the Battle of Adrianople. Thus this date is often proposed as marking the fall of the Roman Empire as well.

The Sacks of Rome

- Throughout this period, the empire was shrinking as various barbarians carved off bits off the dying empire's carcass. The Vandals took Spain and invaded North Africa. They eventually settled in Carthage, became pirates, and cut Rome off from many of its main sources of food.

- The next date frequently put forward as the moment when Rome fell is A.D. 410, when a band of Visigoths under the able leadership of King Alaric invaded Italy, captured the city of Rome, and sacked it. This was the first time in 800 years that foreign enemy had set foot in the heart of the empire.

- The physical harm to the city was relatively minor; the Visigoths quickly departed, and the administration of what remained of the Western Empire continued unimpeded. The psychological scars were much deeper.

- Finally, the Huns arrived, united under Attila. An unlikely coalition formed to oppose him, consisting of the Western Roman Empire, the Visigoths, the Franks, the Burgundians, and some Celts. In 451, they fought a bitter battle in Gaul which ended in a stalemate.

- In 452, Attila marched on Rome, but in a rather mysterious episode, the pope went out to meet him. They had lunch together on the banks of a river and to everyone's astonishment, Attila announced that the Huns were going back to Gaul.

- Fortunately for Rome, Attila decided to get married. He held a huge drunken feast to celebrate his nuptials and, at some point during the night—whether from too much food, too much alcohol, or too much girl—Attila the Hun died. The Huns splintered into small groups and would never again pose as serious a threat.

- In A.D. 455, the Vandals, led by King Gaiseric, swept through Italy and sacked the city of Rome once again. This time, the damage was much more extensive and destructive, and Rome did not recover. For these reasons, A.D. 455 and the second sack of Rome are often suggested as indicating the end of Roman power.

- The Western Romans continued to create emperors until A.D. 476, when the last of these, the boy Romulus Augustulus, was kicked off his throne by the barbarian king Odoacer and was not replaced. Therefore, this is most commonly cited as the definitive moment when the Roman Empire ceased to exist.

- While the Western Roman Empire had certainly fallen by the end of the 5th century A.D., the Eastern Roman Empire showed surprising resilience. An unbroken succession of emperors ruled from Constantinople for almost 1,000 years—up until 1453, when the city fell to the Ottoman Turks.

Not When But Why?

- Quite reasonable arguments can be made for A.D. 180, 312, 378, 410, 455, 476, and 1453, and these by no means exhaust the range of possible dates that can be (and have been) proposed as the end of the empire. But why did the empire fall?

- We have already encountered several possible answers: that poor leadership fatally weakened the empire, that Christianity undermined its values, and that Rome was simply overrun by hordes of barbarians.

- Another set of explanations concentrates on economic factors. Some scholars hypothesize that there was a decline in arable land or in available workers. Others have suggested that the soil became exhausted or that climatic changes diminished crop yields. Still other scholars see evidence of a growing inequality between rich and poor or economic stagnation due to overreliance on slave labor, while others assert that there was a shortage of new slaves to provide adequate labor.

- One popular explanation pointed the finger at a supposed descent into moral degeneracy. This argument has both methodological and chronological flaws since it is usually based on atypical anecdotes.

- In the end, the question of why Rome fell may not have a single answer but can legitimately yield various different answers depending on which aspect of civilization or history one is most interested in.

Not the Dark Ages but Late Antiquity

- All these interpretations center around a core assumption: that a powerful civilization fell and that this era was a melancholy period of decline ending in a 1,000-year-long abyss of barbarism and squalor. In recent decades, this basic assumption has been challenged.

- The alternate perspective frames the period between A.D. 200 and 600 as a time of invigorating changes, bold new ideas, and stimulating interactions that transformed the stagnant classical world. It was an era of cultural and intellectual experimentation and innovation that included many of the greatest thinkers in the Eastern and Western traditions; gave birth to new religions, states, and social forms; and laid the foundations for the modern world.

- The traditional view, given influential expression in Edward Gibbon's *The Decline and Fall of the Roman Empire,* has become the dominant basic interpretation. The second view is more recent, dating to the 1970s, and has quickly gathered momentum. It offers a way to look at this period that is positive as well as negative and that sees areas of growth as well as decay.

- Some of the key aspects in the reconceptualization of the Dark Ages as late antiquity were to obsess less over the parts of Roman culture that were destroyed and to center more on the new cultures that were created. The focus shifted from decline to change and from fall to transformation. One topic of special emphasis was the study of religious developments.

- In the last few years, this positive interpretation of late antiquity has provoked a reaction among some scholars who argue that the pendulum has now swung too far. They assert that many of the so-called barbarian "migrations" were real invasions accompanied by killing and devastation. They claim that, at least in the west, a sophisticated civilization really was destroyed that there was substantial drop in the overall quality of life.

- Perhaps it is possible to see late antiquity as a distinct and important period while at the same time acknowledging the real destruction and violence of the period.

Suggested Reading

Brown, *The World of Late Antiquity.*

James, *Europe's Barbarians AD 200–600.*

Maenchen-Helfen, *The World of the Huns.*

Ward-Perkins, *The Fall of Rome and the End of Civilization.*

1. Which date do you think best marks the end of the Roman Empire, and why do you favor that one over the others?

2. Do you think that the period of late antiquity is better characterized as a time of violence and collapse or of change and renewal and why?

The Decline and Fall of the Roman Empire?
Lecture 41—Transcript

Arguably, the single most famous ongoing historical debate, at least in the Western tradition, is summed up by the following two questions: When did the Roman Empire fall? And, why did the Roman Empire fall? Over the centuries, dozens of thinkers have proposed hundreds of different answers to those two questions, and they continue to be the subject of heated debates among both professional historians and the general public as well. Recently, in what's really a triumph of orderliness, one German scholar carefully compiled an alphabetical list of possible causes for the decline and fall of the Roman Empire. He began with Aberglaube (meaning superstition) and methodically proceeded through the alphabet to Zölibat (celibacy); and, in the end, the list contained no fewer than 210 items. In this lecture, we'll examine those questions and the debates that surround them.

One of the first problems encountered when attempting to analyze the fall of Rome is that nobody can seem to agree on exactly when it happened. Depending upon which history book you consult, you'll encounter a bewildering array of dates being listed as the moment when Rome fell. One frequently suggested date is the death of the philosopher-emperor Marcus Aurelius in A.D. 180 and the accompanying accession to the throne of his mentally unstable son, Commodus. The appeal of that date is that it draws a clear line between a period that's usually regarded as the "golden age" of Rome and a time when the empire was challenged by a variety of disasters, both internal and external. Although the empire clearly continued for some time, A.D. 180 is often cited as the moment from which affairs assumed an irreversible downward momentum. Kind of interestingly, this seems to be the date favored by Hollywood, since it's the focal point of several high-profile films, including the bluntly named 1964 classic *The Fall of the Roman Empire* and also the 1999 Oscar-winning epic *Gladiator*.

Another popular date is A.D. 312, and that marks the conversion of the emperor Constantine to Christianity. Proponents of that date stress that the personal, inward-looking ideology of Christianity was in some sense fundamentally antithetical to the outward, public focus of Roman civilization. The values of Christianity could be seen supplanting those of classical paganism, and so that conversion of Constantine could be viewed as perhaps demarcating a fundamental fault line in the history of Rome.

The next set of dates all focus around barbarians, but since I haven't really discussed them yet, it's first worth examining them in a little bit more detail. The term "barbarian," I should mention, was originally a Greek one, and it simply meant "those who couldn't speak Greek"; but over time it became more of a pejorative label used by the Greeks and the Romans to denote almost any group that they regarded as being less civilized than they were. The barbarians we're concerned with had been present for quite a long time in Northern Europe. They're semi-nomadic, they had a social structure organized by kinship, and they tended to form loose tribal groupings. These societies were mostly male-dominated, and within them your status was based on your ability as warrior. They didn't, most of the time, practice intensive agriculture or build large cities, but their economies were usually centered around herding animals, especially cattle. Just as all the cultures that grew up along the shores of the Mediterranean all shared certain basic similarities because they tended to grow the same crops, in the same way many barbarian groups shared fundamental commonalities because their economies depended on pastoralism.

The people of the ancient world often expressed these kinds of cultural differences in terms of diet, in terms of what you ate. To a Greek or a Roman, one of the marks of being a civilized person was that your diet revolved around the three Mediterranean staples of wheat, wine, and olives. Conversely, it almost defined you as being a barbarian if your diet focused around three other specific foodstuffs. Can you guess what those three barbarian foodstuffs might be? I'll give you hint: I'm from Wisconsin, and the barbarian diet is almost precisely the stereotypical Wisconsin diet. Yes, the defining barbarian diet meant that you ate mostly red meat and dairy products, such as cheese, and then you'd wash them down with beer. All of this is very nicely summed up in a surviving letter from a Greek who's serving in the Roman administration, and this poor guy had the misfortune of being sent to a post on the Danube River; so far, far from the shores of the Mediterranean, up in barbarian land. Absolutely miserable at having to eat the local barbarian diet, he wrote a letter home lamenting that, "the local inhabitants lead the most wretched existence of all mankind, for they cultivate no olives, and they drink no wine."

Particularly in the 4th century, small clan groups of these barbarians began to coalesce into much larger units and to begin to migrate out of their traditional homelands. They started to form what are sometimes called barbarian confederations, and whereas a few hundred or even a couple thousand barbarians moving around might not be a big problem, when you have tens or hundreds of thousands of barbarians beginning to flow across the borders of the Roman Empire, this became a threat to its very existence.

Of all the barbarian groups roaming around at this time, perhaps the most feared of all were the Huns. The Huns were true nomads. They rode these little shaggy horses from the steppe; they fought mainly (almost exclusively) from horseback using powerful bows; and they had a tough, brutal society that was almost entirely centered around raiding and stealing things. They could also travel huge distances on those tough little horses. Let's take a look at a famous Roman eyewitness description of the Huns; and I should say that this is obviously a highly biased account, and some might even consider it a racist one, but it gives a good sense of the fear that the Huns instilled in those who met them. The description goes:

> The people of the Huns … are quite abnormally savage. From the moment of their birth they make deep gashes in their children's cheeks. … They have squat bodies, strong limbs, and thick necks, and are so prodigiously ugly and bent that they might be two-legged animals … their way of life is so rough that they have no use for fire or seasoned food, but live on the roots of wild plants and the half-raw flesh of any sort of animal, which they warm [up] by placing it between their thighs and the backs of their horses. They have no buildings to shelter them … not so much as a hut thatched with reeds [is] to be found among them. … They wear garments of linen or of the skins of field-mice stitched together. … Once they have put their necks in some dingy shirt they never take it off or change it until it rots and falls to pieces from incessant wear.

Despite all that, or maybe because of it, the Huns were excellent warriors. For example, 300 Huns once killed 1,100 Visigoths while suffering only 17 casualties themselves. When the Huns invaded an area, people were often so frightened that they'd run away, rather than fight them. For a long time, it was thought that the Huns who showed up in Europe in the 4th century were the same people as the Xiong-nu who'd threatened China a couple centuries earlier. This is currently a matter of great contention among scholars—there are people who believe both sides of this issue, and the issues really are complex—but ultimately, the scarcity of our sources means that we'll probably never know for sure; but whether or not the Xiong-nu and the Huns were ethnically the same, they're certainly very similar in terms of culture and habits.

In the late 300s, the Huns began to shift westward out of Central Asia and moved toward Eastern Europe. This set up kind of a colossal domino effect that would eventually impact the Roman Empire. First, the Huns invaded the territory of a group of Germanic barbarians called Ostrogoths, and many of those were displaced westward. Then the Huns invaded the lands of a related tribe called the Visigoths, and then when some of the Visigoths moved westward, those Visigoths entered Roman territory.

Barbarian groups such as the Visigoths and the Ostrogoths began to exert pressure on the borders of both the Eastern and Western Roman Empires, and emperors in the weakened state that these empires found themselves often found it expedient to exchange land for promises that the barbarians would then fight for Rome rather than against it. As you might imagine, these accommodations often broke down due to bad faith or misunderstandings on both sides; and that's exactly what happened in A.D. 378 when a group of disgruntled Goths rebelled against the Eastern Empire. The Eastern emperor at the time was a man named Valens, and somewhat rashly he marched out thinking he could just suppress the rebellion without waiting for more reinforcements to arrive. The result was that he and his entire army were slain at the Battle of Adrianople. The date of that disaster is often proposed as marking the fall of the Roman Empire. The Battle of Adrianople certainly was an important moment, because it exposed the weakness of the once-invincible Roman legions, and it also demonstrated the ascending power of the barbarians.

All throughout this period, the geographic extent of the Roman Empire in both East and West was being steadily eroded away. Various barbarians groups would just move in and carve off bits of the dying empire's carcass.

One group called the Vandals took Spain, and then they just went over the Straits of Gibraltar and invaded North Africa. They kept going from there and eventually settled in what used to be Carthage. The Vandals then specialized in becoming pirates, and eventually they cut off Rome from many of its main food sources, which had been the southern areas of the Mediterranean.

The core of the empire remained, but even this would soon suffer as well. The next date that's frequently put forward as the moment when Rome fell is A.D. 410. In that year, a band of Visigoths who were being led by a particularly able king named Alaric invaded Italy, captured the city of Rome, and sacked the ancient capital. This was the first time in 800 years that a victorious foreign enemy had set foot in the heart of the empire, and so the seizure and ransacking of Rome was an enormous psychological blow to the Romans. The city of Rome was invested with profound symbolic importance for the Romans, and their inability to protect it exposed for everyone the reduced state of Roman power as almost nothing else could have. While the psychological and symbolic trauma from that event was enormous, the actual physical harm was relatively minor. The Visigoths were only there a day or two and then quickly left, and really caused only minimal damage; and the administration of what remained of the Western Empire just continued unimpeded from there.

But finally, the dreaded Huns themselves arrived on the scene. Even worse, when they appeared they were strongly united under one leader, and that's the famous Attila the Hun. Out of what really amounted to mutual fear, an unlikely coalition of different groups formed to try and oppose Attila, and some of the people who joined together were the Western Roman Empire, the Visigoths, the Franks, the Burgundians, and some Celts. In 451, they fought a bitter battle in France, and it ended in a stalemate. But still, that was seen as a success; it was enough to at least temporarily stop the advance of Attila and the Huns. The next year, he just picked up where he left off and he marched down into Italy heading for Rome, intending to destroy and plunder it. But in a rather mysterious episode, the Pope—and there was a Pope by now—went out to meet him. The Pope and Attila had lunch together on the banks of a river in northern Italy, and at the end of this lunch, to everyone's astonishment, Attila announced that the Huns were going to turn around and go back north up to Gaul. No one's really quite sure what it was that the

Pope said to Attila. If you look at Christian sources, they say that Saints Peter and Paul appeared in the sky with flaming swords and turned him back. If you read other sources, they say that the Pope offered Attila a huge bribe. You can believe whichever version you choose to.

Attila was still a danger, but fortunately for Rome, at this point he decided to get married. His chosen bride was a young German girl, so he held a big drunken feast to celebrate his nuptials, and you can imagine what sort of a party Huns would have; at the end of the evening, though, absolutely stuffed with food, glutted with alcohol, he staggered off to celebrate his marriage night with his young bride. At some point during that night, whether it was too much food, too much alcohol, or too much German girl, Attila the Hun died. Europe was saved. Without his leadership, the Huns simply splintered into little groups, and they'd never again pose as serious a threat.

Rome, though, was still doomed. In A.D. 455, the Vandals, led by their king, swept through Italy and the city of Rome was captured and plundered. This time, the sacking of the city was much more extensive, much more thorough, and much more destructive; so Rome was thoroughly looted. This time Rome wouldn't really recover, and both the city and the empire were left as reduced and pale shadows of their former selves. For these reasons, A.D. 455 and the second sack of Rome are often suggested as indicating the end of Roman power and being the moment when Rome fell.

Although Rome no longer ruled over very much territory, the Western Romans did continue to appoint and name emperors, and that continued up until A.D. 476. In that year, the very last of these, a boy with the rather grandiose name of Romulus Augustulus, was finally kicked off the throne by a barbarian king and wasn't replaced. Romulus Augustulus, who otherwise was just completely undistinguished, a nobody, earned the title of the last Roman emperor in the West, and the date of his removal, 476, is commonly cited as the definitive moment when the Roman Empire ceased to exist.

Was this, then, the end of the Roman Empire? Well, maybe. While the Western Empire had certainly fallen by the end of the 5th century A.D., we still had the Eastern Roman Empire, and that would be surprisingly resilient. They'd appoint an unbroken succession of Roman emperors who'd would rule over that Eastern Empire—which retroactively is called the Byzantine Empire by historians—for another 1,000 years. We will, by the way, look at the Byzantine Empire in much more detail in the next lecture. The Byzantine Empire would last all the way up until 1453, when Constantinople at last fell to the Ottoman Turks. If one accepts the Eastern Roman Empire and its rulers as being Romans, then a perfectly legitimate argument can be made that the Roman Empire didn't fall until 1453; and, indeed, that's a date favored by many historians for the fall of Rome.

When, then, did Rome fall? As we've just seen, you can make quite reasonable arguments for A.D. 180, 312, 378, 410, 455, 476, and 1453, and those by no means exhaust the range of possible dates that can and have been proposed as the end of the empire. What about the second part of the equation, the question: Why did the empire fall? We've already seen several possible answers: that poor leadership fatally weakened the empire; that Christianity undermined its value system; or that Rome was just overrun by hordes of nasty barbarians. That last viewpoint was perhaps given its most vivid and succinct expression by a famous French historian who stated: "Roman Civilization did not die a natural death. It was murdered."

A whole other set of explanations, though, concentrate on economic factors. Some scholars hypothesize that there's a decline in arable land or in available workers, resulting either way in reduced taxes and economic strain. Another group has suggested that the soil became exhausted through overcultivation or that there were climatic changes that diminished crop yields. Others pointed to a growing inequality in the empire between rich and poor. Another theory is there's economic stagnation due to an overreliance on slave labor, while yet others assert that there's a shortage of new slaves to provide adequate labor. One popular explanation pointed the finger at a supposed descent by the Romans into moral degeneracy, and that argument, I think, has both serious methodological and chronological flaws since usually it's based on very atypical anecdotes, and the incidents that are cited are almost always drawn from the period of Roman expansion rather than its decline. In the end, the question of why Rome fell really probably doesn't have a single answer; it's something that can yield legitimately different answers depending upon what aspect of civilization or history you're most interested in.

Whether due to barbarians, economic collapse, Christianity, or some combination of these, all these interpretations center around a core assumption, and the assumption is that a powerful civilization fell, and that the history of this time is really a melancholy one of decline that ended in a thousand-year-long abyss of barbarism and squalor that we call the Dark Ages. But in recent decades, even that basic assumption has begun to be challenged. According to this alternate perspective, the period between A.D. 200 and 600 was instead a time when invigorating new changes, bold new ideas, and stimulating interactions transformed what had become a stagnant Classical world. In this interpretation, they see this time as an era of cultural and intellectual experimentation and innovation, and it included many of the greatest thinkers in the Eastern and Western traditions. This whole vibrant intermingling of cultures gave birth to new religions, states, and social forms, and it really laid the foundations for the modern world in terms of borders, religion, law, and culture. In this narrative, it's a time of exciting change and transformation.

Which of those two perspectives is correct? The first one, that it's a gloomy story of decline, is the traditional view, and that's given very influential expression in Edward Gibbon's book *The Decline and Fall of the Roman Empire*, and, with some variations, that became the dominant basic interpretation for quite awhile. The second one represents a more recent viewpoint that emerged among some historians in the 1970s, and it's very quickly gathered momentum during subsequent decades. It offers us a very different way to look at this period: one that's positive as well as negative; one sees areas of growth as well as decay.

Prior to the 1970s, the span of centuries between 200 and 600 A.D. was often regarded with less interest than the more obviously identifiable Roman Period that preceded it and the Medieval one that followed. Nor was that span of centuries even known by a clear designation or term; so some people would stretch the Medieval Period backwards and call it the Early Middle Ages, while others would lump it in with the Roman Period and call it the Later Roman Empire. In 1971, an eminent historian, Peter Brown, published a book called *The World of Late Antiquity*, and in it he argued that these centuries formed a distinct and vital time all of their own, and one that deserves to be treated on its own and not just as a postscript to the

Classical world or a prelude to the Middle Ages. Since then, the study of Late Antiquity has exploded, and it's now generally recognized as, indeed, a separate and important time that was neither stagnant nor simple.

Some of the key aspects in the reconceptualization of Late Antiquity were to be less obsessed over the parts of Roman culture that were destroyed and to focus more on the new cultures that were created; to concentrate less on battles between barbarians and Romans and more on the sort of interactions and cultural exchanges between them; and to shift the whole focus from decline to change, from fall to transformation. One topic in particular that Brown and various others gave special emphasis to was the study of religious developments in Late Antiquity. Really, the history of religion in Late Antiquity is very rich and includes a number of the intellectual giants of the Christian tradition.

Maybe inevitably, in the last couple years this positive reading of Late Antiquity has provoked a counterreaction among some scholars who say that the whole pendulum has swung too far, and that these rosy portraits of change and accommodation have glossed over a lot of the violence and real economic disruption of the period. They assert that many of these so-called barbarian "migrations" were really invasions that were accompanied by lots of killing and devastation. While acknowledging that the intellectual and religious achievements of the era were important, they still claim that, at least in the West, a sophisticated civilization really was destroyed; that there really was a drop in the quality of life; and that this whole decline was accompanied by bloodshed and brutality.

So the seemingly endless debate about the fall of the Roman Empire goes on. As an undergraduate at Princeton, I myself was a student of Peter Brown, and I have to say that I find his conceptualization of Late Antiquity as a distinct and important period fairly compelling, but I also agree with those who see the real destruction and violence of that period. The debate over when, why, or even if Rome fell is one of those fun and engaging historical discussions that has room for many valid viewpoints. I'd be curious to know how you'd choose to answer these very same questions.

The Byzantine Empire and the Legacy of Rome
Lecture 42

The long-lived Byzantine Empire carried on the legacy of Rome for 1,000 years after the collapse of the empire in Europe, and some of its greatest achievements survive to this day. One of the most important of these was the Roman law code as recorded by Emperor Justinian, which has influenced legal systems around the world. The city of Constantinople was a marvel of architecture and military defense; in its modern incarnation of Istanbul, it is still home to the great Hagia Sophia.

One Empire, Two Names

- By the end of the 5th century A.D., the Western Roman Empire centered on Rome had fallen, or at least transformed into something that was no longer Roman. On the other side of the Mediterranean, the Eastern Roman Empire, with its capital at Constantinople, most certainly did not fall.

- Although they viewed themselves as simply the Romans, later historians have labeled this empire the Byzantine Empire, after the original name of the old Greek colony, Byzantium, where Constantinople was built. Today, this is the city of Istanbul, Turkey.

- Constantinople sits exactly on the geological border between Europe and Asia—a horn-shaped peninsula jutting out from the western shore of the Bosphorus, the narrow strip of water that links the Mediterranean Sea to the Black Sea. Constantinople commanded a vital economic and strategic crossroads.

- This was also a wonderfully defensible site. The city was built on a stretch of high ground and surrounded on three sides by water. It could only be approached by land on its western side, and its inhabitants constructed some of the most massive fortifications of antiquity along this one vulnerable approach.

The city of Constantinople was a marvel of architecture and military defense.

- When Constantine established Constantinople as the capital of the Eastern Roman Empire, he equipped it with all the same structures, institutions, and amenities that were found in Rome. It had a senate and a senate house, an imperial palace, a grain dole, and huge entertainment complexes.

- The entertainment complexes provided a venue not only for games but for the public interactions and massed applause and acclamations that were so vital to the legitimacy of a Roman emperor. They were also decorated with great artworks stolen from all over the empire.

- The fortifications, by the 6th century, were 36 feet high and 17 feet thick, with 96 great towers spaced along them. A massive ditch in front of the walls added another formidable obstacle. A second, taller set of walls was nested inside the first.

- One architectural aspect of Constantinople was different from Rome, but equally impressive. Rome was supplied water by its famous system of aqueducts; Constantinople, built with more concern for attack, required an internal supply of fresh water. The solution was enormous underground cisterns, eventually holding some 86 million cubic gallons of water.

The Reign of Justinian

- Of the approximately 95 emperors who ruled over Constantinople, the most significant of the earlier ones was Justinian. He embarked on an energetic program of building, organization, and conquest.

- Justinian came from a military family and was something of an outsider among the aristocrats of Constantinople. Thus he appointed a number of people to important positions based more on energy and ability than on aristocratic connections. This gave him a core of talented subordinates, but it also earned the enmity of the old aristocracy.

- Justinian also married a woman several decades his junior named Theodora, who apparently came from the lower classes. There were rumors that her father was a bear wrangler and that she had been a prostitute. It is difficult to assess the accuracy of any of these accusations. She seems to have been an intelligent and strong-willed woman who took an active role in government, which was likely to stir resentment in itself.

- Early in his reign, Justinian faced a crisis that almost deposed him from office. In the hippodrome the traditional racing factions, the Greens and Blues, had always engaged in a fierce rivalry that not infrequently resulted in riots and violence. Around this time these factions had become associated with certain rival sects of Christianity.

- When Justinian refused to pardon two criminals, one from each faction, the Blues and Greens joined forces and rioted. The subsequent urban violence spilled out of the hippodrome and into the streets. These riots were known as the Nika riots, after one of the traditional shouts at chariot races. ("Nika" means victory.)

- Much of the city was burnt to the ground, and the rioting continued for a week. Justinian suppressed the rioters and reasserting his authority by calling in the army. Allegedly 30,000 people were killed by the troops.

- Despite this unpromising start, Justinian and Theodora had some impressive achievements. They nearly succeeded in reuniting the eastern and western empires. Justinian had a particularly skilled general named Belisarius who led several successful military expeditions and recaptured most of Italy, including Rome itself.

- As glorious as Justinian's reunification appeared at the time, it would be both short lived and relatively inconsequential. Soon after Justinian's death, almost all of the western Mediterranean territories were once again lost to various barbarian kingdoms.

- Justinian embarked on a great building program, particularly after the destruction of the Nika riots. Among the buildings erected at this time was one of the most impressive of all of history: the Hagia Sophia.

- The architects were two mathematicians, Isidore of Miletus and Anthemius of Tralles. Not only was this a massive structure; it was also an architectural and artistic marvel that remains one the world's great buildings. When Constantinople was captured by the Ottoman Turks, it was converted into a mosque. Today it is officially a museum.

- At Justinian's command, another great project was accomplished that would have long-term effects on the entire world: the compilation of the Code of Roman Law. This was a definitive edition of the accumulated centuries of Roman legal precedent. It has survived to become, either directly or indirectly, the source for many of the world's current legal systems.

Christianity in the Late Empire

- With Christianity now Rome's dominant religion, the Mediterranean world was racked by disagreements over theological doctrine. The Byzantine Empire developed its own version of Christianity and split off from the West, forming the Greek Orthodox Church.

- Many other disputes arose around questions such as the exact nature of Christ and the relationship between him and God. These disputes were often very intense and bitter, even leading to violence.

- One particularly bitter fight that raged during the 300s was called the Arian controversy. The Arians, following a man named Arius, believed that Jesus Christ was created by God the Father—separate, inferior, and subordinate to him. Their opponents maintained that Christ was equal to God the Father.

- After nearly 50 years of debate and 18 church councils, the official view was that "Christ and God contained the same divine essence" This is the basis for the concept of the holy trinity. This was but one of many such debates during the early centuries of Christianity.

- Justinian ruled until 565. He was succeeded by his nephew, and their line ruled all the way through the Middle Ages and into the Renaissance. While still considering themselves Romans, the Byzantine empire in many ways would revert to the underlying Greek roots of the East.

- The power and reach of the empire declined, but safe behind its great walls, the city of Constantinople itself persisted. Finally, after a series of determined attacks and fatally weakened by the Fourth Crusade, Constantinople was captured by the Ottoman Sultan Mehmet II on May 29, 1453.

- For those who enjoy arguing about the date of the fall of the Rome, an excellent case can be made for 1453. If this seems like a stretch, consider this: Charlemagne, the first great king of Medieval Europe, crowned Charles Augustus, Emperor of the Romans, on Christmas Day 800. One of the most coveted titles throughout the Middle Ages was that of Holy Roman Emperor, and there was a continuous string of such emperors until 1806. The Russian title tsar was a corruption of "Caesar," and the last tsar ruled until 1917. Even the United States has a governmental body called the Senate, and the architecture of Washington DC looks very much like the buildings of ancient Rome.

Suggested Reading

Harris, *Constantinople*.

Herrin, *Byzantium*.

Norwich, *A Short History of Byzantium*.

Questions to Consider

1. Why should (or should not) the Byzantine Empire be considered a legitimate extension of the Roman Empire?

2. How does Justinian compare as a leader to some of the other figures we have encountered?

The Byzantine Empire and The Legacy of Rome
Lecture 42—Transcript

By the end of the 5th century A.D., the Western Roman Empire centered around Rome had fallen, or at the very least it had been transformed into something that's no longer truly fully Roman. On the other side of the Mediterranean, the Eastern Roman Empire, with its capital at Constantinople, most certainly didn't fall, and would continue to flourish for another 1,000 years. Although they viewed themselves as simply the Romans, later historians have labeled this empire the Byzantine Empire, and that's done after the original name of the old Greek colony, Byzantium, which was located on the site where Constantinople later would be built. Of course, today that same city has undergone yet another name change and is toiday Istanbul in Turkey. This lecture will consider the fortunes of that long-lasting Eastern Roman—or, if you like, Byzantine—Empire. It's a story that includes one of the most powerful women of antiquity as well as one of the most globally influential legacies of the ancient world to the modern.

As usual, though, let me start with a word about geography. The city of Constantinople sat exactly at the border between Europe and Asia. It's placed on a horn-shaped peninsula that juts out from the western shore of the Bosphorus; the Bosphorus is that narrow strip of water that both links the Mediterranean Sea to the Black Sea and separates Europe from Asia. By geography, Constantinople was situated at and really can control a vital economic crossroads; and all the main trade routes that linked east to west, as well as north to south, converged at that single point. All the lucrative shipping that carried goods to and from the Black Sea had to pass right under the walls of Constantinople; and most of the ships carrying the trade from the Mediterranean to the Middle East and beyond also sailed right past that site.

Constantinople wasn't only a key transportation node, but it's also a frontier or border zone. It's in the streets and the bazaars of the city that the various ideas of the cultures of East and West met and intermingled, a little bit like a northern version of Alexandria in Egypt. This mixture of civilizations at Constantinople gave it a uniquely cosmopolitan and really worldly character, and it also enriched the intellectual life of the city.

Finally, the city was situated on a wonderfully defensible site. The actual city was placed on a stretch of high ground, which was surrounded on three sides by the waters of the Sea of Marmara, the Bosphorus, and the Golden Horn. Constantinople could only be approached by a hostile force by land on its western side, and its inhabitants then constructed some of the most massive fortifications of antiquity along that one vulnerable approach. Given powerful natural defenses due to its location, the city could survive many, many attacks, and it could really defend itself against waves of attackers that would far outnumber the defenders.

Constantinople's location also made it a very beautiful city. Even today, when you approach Constantinople by sea as I've done a number of times, you're greeted with this spectacular vista of spires and buildings that just seem to rise up above the shimmering water. These strategic as well as aesthetic aspects of its location were something that was very well-appreciated in antiquity as well. For example, in describing the city of Constantinople, the 6th-century historian Procopius wrote:

> The sea is set most beautifully all about it, forming curving bays ... and thus it makes the city exceptionally beautiful, and offers the quiet shelter of harbours to navigators, abundantly providing the city with the necessities of life and making it rich in all useful things ... and on either side of it the two continents are placed.

When the emperor Constantine established Constantinople as the capital city of the Eastern Empire, he took enormous effort to try to equip the city with the same structures, buildings, institutions, and amenities that were found in Rome. Constantinople, just like Rome, was divided up into 14 districts. Constantinople, just like Rome, was given a senate and a senate house; it had an imperial palace constructed; it had a grain dole established for its citizens; and it had huge entertainment complexes, most notably a hippodrome for chariot racing. This hippodrome was especially important, because not only was it the scene of great spectacles, but it provided a venue for that sort of public interaction and massed applause and acclamations that I talked about as being so vital to the legitimacy of a Roman emperor. Just as the Circus Maximus in Rome was decorated with great artworks stolen from all over the empire, the hippodrome in Constantinople was similarly adorned. Among these decorations were several that can still be seen there today. Those include a bronze column of intertwined serpents that was taken from Delphi, and an 800-ton Egyptian obelisk that was looted from Karnak. Another famous monument that stood in the hippodrome were four huge bronze horses, and those were later stolen by the Venetians and stuck up on the façade of the Cathedral of San Marco in Venice, where you can see them today.

Other monuments that originally were there but are now lost recall some famous events in Roman history. We know, for example, there was a statue of the she-wolf nursing Romulus and Remus, the founders of Rome. There was also a famous bronze statue of a donkey and its keeper, and this was something that was originally put up by the emperor Augustus near the site of his great victory over Mark Antony at Actium. The story behind this somewhat unlikely-sounding subject matter for an imperial monument is that on the eve of the Battle of Actium, Augustus had encountered a man driving his donkey; and when he asked him who he was, the man replied that he was named Eutychus, and his donkey was named Nikon. In Greek, those names were derived from words that mean respectively "prosperity" and "victory," so Augustus took this encounter as a good omen from the gods and, after he indeed won the battle, he put up that monument to them.

The walls that protected Constantinople were built and rebuilt a number of times by a whole succession of emperors, but by the 6th century they consisted of a very impressive set of fortifications. The walls were about 36 feet high, 17 feet thick, and there were 96 great towers spaced along them. They also dug a huge ditch in front of the walls, so that added another obstacle to attackers; and there were actually two complete sets of walls nested within one another, with the outer wall being lower than the inner wall, so that even if that outer wall was captured, the defenders could simply retreat back to the higher inner wall and then shoot down on the exposed attackers.

One architectural aspect of the city in which Constantinople was different from Rome, but is equally impressive, was in regards to the water supply. Rome, of course, was supplied by its famous system of aqueducts, which brought fresh water to the city from far away; but Constantinople, which was always built with more concern for attack, required some internal supply of fresh water. The solution there was they constructed a series of enormous underground cisterns. In 421 A.D., one such reservoir was built that could hold 66 million cubic gallons of water, and a century later the emperor Justinian added another one with a capacity of 20 million gallons. That later cistern still exists underneath the city today, and it's a very popular tourist attraction. When you go in there, you can walk over these catwalks that are placed above the water and you find yourself in this giant cavern where the roof is held up by over 300 columns arranged in 28 rows. Many of those columns are mounted atop chunks of marble that's been recycled from earlier buildings, and most famously there are a number of columns sitting on top of these giant Medusa heads. If you find yourself in Istanbul, it's well worth a visit to this cistern.

Of the approximately 95 emperors who ruled over Constantinople, the most significant of the early ones was a man named Justinian. His rise to power began when he was just a young boy. His uncle Justin became emperor, and so he took on his nephew as a kind of an assistant. It turned out, Justinian became more than that; he quickly became his uncle's main confidant and advisor. Eventually, when his uncle became somewhat senile, he took over de facto administration of the empire. As you might expect, upon his uncle's death in 527, Justinian became emperor himself and he immediately embarked on an energetic program of building, reorganizing things, as well as conquest.

Despite his ties to the former emperor, Justinian always remained a little bit of an outsider, at least among the aristocracy of Constantinople. Justinian had the habit of appointing people to important positions based on their energy and their ability rather than their family, and so that gave him core of talented subordinates who were able to carry out many of his ambitious schemes; but it also meant that the old aristocracy was a bit hostile to him.

Making things worse was his choice of wife. Justinian married a woman who was several decades younger than him, and she was named Theodora. She genuinely seems to have come from the lower classes. There were all kinds of rumors about her; one of them was that her father may have been a bear wrangler for the Green faction in the hippodrome, and there were also rumors that she herself may have been a prostitute. Honestly, it's very difficult to assess how accurate any of those accusations were because the sources, the ones who recorded this information, were all very hostile towards Theodora, and it's obvious that they're just going out of their way to try and portray her in as negative a way as they possibly could. Some of this was due to the fact that she simply seems to have been an intelligent and strong-willed woman who took an active role in government. She obviously served as a key advisor and helper to Justinian; she played a public role in policymaking; and she was a forceful advocate for what today we might term women's rights. For example, she had some laws passed that gave women better protection from abuse; she had some other laws passed that gave them more rights when they got divorced; and all of this made her at the time a target for resentment and criticism, and so the hostile sources tended to depict her as an immoral, sexually licentious, and conniving woman who exerted an unfortunate degree of control over her husband.

Early in Justinian's reign in 532 A.D., he faced a crisis that almost deposed him from the office. In the hippodrome, the traditional racing factions were the Greens and the Blues, and they had always had a fierce rivalry and often this rivalry had resulted in violence and riots. Adding to the intensity was the fact that around this time those two factions had become associated with certain rival sects of Christianity. When Justinian refused to pardon two criminals, one from each of those factions, the Blues and the Greens then joined forces and rioted against him. The subsequent violence spilled out of the hippodrome and into the streets of the city, and it grew so that the factions even attempted to replace Justinian as emperor and put another man in as the new emperor. These riots were known as the Nika Riots because one of the traditional shouts of the factions at chariot races was "Nika, nika," which meant victory. Things escalated to the point that much of the city was burnt to the ground and this rioting went on for an entire week. Supposedly Justinian was right about to flee the city and give up, his courage had failed, but then he was rallied by Theodora who supposedly berated him and convinced him to stay and fight it out with the rioters. He ended up sending in the army, suppressing the rioters, and reasserting his authority; but the cost of that was that about 30,000 people were killed by the imperial troops.

Despite that somewhat unpromising start, Justinian and Theodora would go on to accomplish some very impressive achievements. One of these was to nearly succeed in bringing the Eastern and Western Roman empires back together, and they did this by conquering many of the barbarian kingdoms that had taken over control of the Western Mediterranean. Here, Justinian was lucky that he had a particularly skilled general, a guy named Belisarius, who led several successful military expeditions for him to the West. The first of those managed to recapture North Africa from the Vandals; and then using that as a base of operations, Belisarius invaded and captured Sicily; and from there, he moved on to Italy itself. In a whole series of campaigns against various Gothic barbarian groups, Belisarius succeeded in recapturing most of Italy, including Rome itself. Other generals managed to take other parts of Spain, and so for a brief time, the Roman Empire of Justinian actually approached the size of the earlier unified empire.

All of these military campaigns cost a lot of money and so the empire's resources were depleted, and then they were further dissipated by a series of serious conflicts with the latest Middle Eastern-based empire who were called the Sassanians; they were heirs to the Persians and then later the Parthians. The Sassanians were a powerful, warlike empire. As glorious as Justinian's reunification might have appeared at the time, and it was an impressive achievement, like many conquests it would be both short lived; and, in the end, it would be relatively inconsequential, at least in terms of its permanent effects. Soon after Justinian's death, almost all of the Western Mediterranean territories were lost once again to various barbarian kingdoms. From that point on, the Byzantine Empire would be confined exclusively to the Eastern Mediterranean, and even within that region, over time the extent of its power steadily contracted.

At Constantinople itself, Justinian embarked on a huge building program, especially after the destruction caused in the city by the Nika Riots. Among the various buildings erected at that time was one of the most impressive of all of history, and it's one that still impresses visitors today. This is the church known as the Hagia Sophia. It was inaugurated on December 26, 537 A.D., and Justinian had chosen two very famous scientists and mathematicians, Isidore of Miletus and Anthemius of Tralles, to be the architects of this giant church. What those two guys came up with was a spectacular design. Not only was it just a really big structure—it covers nearly 60,000 square feet—but it's an architectural marvel. It's centered around a huge suspended dome that was set atop a great square boxlike structure. The space beneath the dome is 100 feet across and 170 feet high, and it's filled with light from rows of windows all around. The center of the giant dome underneath had a mosaic portrait of Christ the all-powerful, rendered in very bright colors on a shining gold background. The columns and the walls were all made out of the finest decorative marbles; they're in vivid shades of purple, red, black, yellow, and green. One ancient source that described the effect of entering this enormous structure and being confronted with its glories said that "a golden stream of glittering rays strikes the eyes of men so that they can scarcely bear to look at it." Unfortunately, that great dome collapsed just 20 years after its completion, but it was rebuilt to a strengthened design and it's still standing today. In antiquity, it's a truly astonishing structure; and even today, it's one the world's great buildings. When Constantinople was later captured by the Ottoman Turks, the Hagia Sophia was converted into a mosque, and so minarets were added to it. Today, those minarets are still there, but it's been deconsecrated and now it's officially a museum.

At Justinian's command, another great project was accomplished that would have longterm effects on the entire world, and that was the compilation of the Code of Roman Law. This was a sort of definitive edition of the accumulated centuries of Roman legal precedent, and it consisted of both actual legal statutes and analysis by various eminent jurists. This thing runs to over a hundred volumes, and this compilation of Roman law survived so that it became the direct source for much of the world's current legal systems, and even those that aren't directly derived from it are influenced by it. The law code became particularly influential because it was found and used at the great early law school established at Bologna in the Middle Ages.

The code of Roman law was used as the basis for almost all the legal systems that evolved in Europe, and then, during the era of colonialism, this was expanded to much of the rest of the world. Countries that seem as dissimilar as Germany, Argentina, and Japan all use legal systems that were derived directly or indirectly from Roman law. England deviated by developing English Common Law, but much of the terminology and the structure was still influenced and derived from Roman law as well. In the long run, the single most wideranging and influential effect of the Roman world on the modern might well be in the realm of law, where Justinian's Code laid the basis for almost all modern legal systems.

Throughout these early centuries of the Byzantine Empire, with Christianity now the dominant religion, the Mediterranean world was racked by disagreements over points of theological doctrine. The Byzantine Empire and the East developed its own version of Christianity and split off from the West, so it formed the Greek Orthodox Church. In the West, the Pope presided over what would eventually develop into the Roman Catholic Church, while in the East the Patriarch was the spiritual leader of the Greek Orthodox Church. That split, of course, still exists today.

Many other disputes arose around questions such as the exact nature of Christ and the relationship between him and God. At the time, these disputes were often very intense, very bitter, and sometimes they'd even lead to violence; people would beat each other up discussing points of theology. Especially at Constantinople, even average people were infamous for engaging in the streets and the bars and the public spaces of the city in spirited squabbles regarding what really were sometimes obscure theological points. One especially bitter fight that raged throughout a lot of the 300s was called the Arian Controversy, and this centered around a debate concerning a central aspect of Christianity. In somewhat simplified form, this debate involved on the one side the Arians—who were named after a man named Arius—and they believed that Jesus Christ was created by God, and that he was separate, inferior, and subordinate to him. Their opponents maintained that Christ was human, yes, but he was also simultaneously truly divine. After about 50 years of debate, after 18 church councils on this point, the official view that finally came out of it was that "Christ and God contained the same divine essence." It is the basis today for the familiar concept of the holy trinity, and this is just one of many debates that happened during these early centuries of Christianity.

The Byzantine Empire was struck by a particularly bad outbreak of plague in the 540s, and even Justinian himself caught the disease, though he managed to survive it. Theodora, his wife, died young in 548, and Justinian continued to rule after her death until his death in 565 A.D. But having no direct heir, then his sister's son became the next emperor. That ruler and his successor would continue to preside in a line of emperors that stretched all the way through the Middle Ages up to the Renaissance. While still considering themselves Romans, the Byzantine Empire in a lot of ways ended up reverting back to those underlying cultural Greek roots that were so strong in the East, and which had remained there all throughout the Roman occupation. For example, the official language of the Byzantine Empire would switch from Latin back to Greek. While the power and the reach of the empire declined, the city stayed safe behind its great walls. Finally, though, after a series of determined attacks and actually having been fatally weakened by the disaster of the Fourth Crusade, Constantinople was finally captured by the Ottoman Sultan Mehmet II on May 29, 1453.

I'll end this lecture by referring back to the great debate discussed in the last one; and for those who like to argue about the date of the fall of Rome, an excellent case could certainly be made that 1453 and the fall of the Byzantine Empire marked the true end of the Roman Empire. If this seems like an improbably late date, then consider just how easy it would be to stretch that even further. For example, if one looks at continuity of titles or at self-proclaimed heirs to the Roman Empire, you can extend dates for Rome's fall nearly up to the present. The title with which Charlemagne, the first great king of Medieval Europe, was crowned on Christmas day A.D. 800 was "Charles Augustus, Emperor of the Romans." All throughout the Middle Ages, one of the most coveted titles was Holy Roman Emperor, and there was a continuous string of Holy Roman Emperors up until the last one was kicked out by Napoleon in 1806. The Russian Tsars—and the "Tsar" is, after all, a corruption of the imperial Roman title "Caesar"—regarded themselves as heirs to the Roman legacy, and the last tsar ruled until the Russian Revolution in 1917. You could easily propose that Rome didn't really fall until the 20th century.

Finally, the founding fathers of the United States were totally obsessed with the Roman Republic as a model of government, and they self-consciously imitated all kinds of aspects of Ancient Rome when they established the American republic. This is why, for example, the U.S. has a body called "the senate"; it's why the architecture of Washington, D.C. looks just like the buildings of Ancient Rome. If one counts the United States as a kind of revived Roman Republic, I suppose you could even argue that Rome still continues today.

China from Chaos to Order under the Tang
Lecture 43

L ike Europe after the fall of Rome in the West, China went through a period of turbulence after the collapse of the Han Empire. This is known as the Three Kingdoms era. The Sui and Tang dynasties eventually reunified and restored order to China. A number of famous rulers of this period stirred both controversy and admiration. Many parallels can be drawn between the acts of the Sui and Tang and their predecessors, the Qin and Han, respectively.

The Decline and Fall of China

- We left the historical narrative of China around A.D. 200, with the dissolution of the Han Empire. Mirroring the collapse of the Western Roman Empire, China dissolved into a number of warring states, some of them controlled by groups that the Chinese would have regarded as barbarians.

- The three and a half centuries that followed constituted the longest stretch of disunity in all of Chinese history. The period 221 until 589 is known as the Era of Three Kingdoms and Six Dynasties. In fact, there were many more than six dynasties, but they came and went so quickly that many are hardly worth noticing.

- Not only was there internal dissention during this period, but the external threats posed by nomadic barbarian groups such as the Huns continued to intensify. Gangs of bandits proliferated and roamed throughout China attacking travelers and villages.

- Northern and southern coalitions of states formed around the river networks of the Yellow River in the north and the Yangtze in the south. This was a split that might well have become permanent, especially considering the marked geographical and cultural differences between the two regions, just as Rome permanently split along east-west lines.

- This chaotic and dangerous time later became an extremely popular setting for stories. For the people living through it, the dangers and economic disruption were no cause for amusement. Census data suggests that China suffered a significant decline in population over this period due to war and disease.

- As during other periods of chaos and uncertainty, this time also spawned new philosophical and religious yearnings. Confucianism had flourished under the stability of the Han but was not as well suited to the Three Kingdoms era, and many an escape from the harsh realities of existence.

- Buddhism was such a belief system. It had reached China at least as early as A.D. 64, but it was not until the chaotic

In the chaos of the Three Kingdoms periond, Confucius's philosophy fell out of favor.

4th century that it grew popular, especially among the poorer, disempowered classes. Buddhist monasteries provided islands of stability and calm in stormy seas.

- Many artists and intellectuals rejected the ordered society of Confucianism, which seemed to have failed them, and adopted Neo-Daoism, which focused on abstruse metaphysical questions. Along with this sometimes came a freer, more unfettered lifestyle. A group of 3rd century A.D. Neo-Daoists were known as the Seven Sages of the Bamboo Grove.

- More traditional Confucians and the government authorities did not appreciate the Neo-Daoists' eccentric behavior. In an incident reminiscent of the trial of Socrates, in 262, one of the Seven Sages was executed on charges of perversion of public morals.

- Over several centuries, an eventual fusion of the belief systems of Buddhism, Confucianism, and Daoism took place.

The Sui Dynasty

- Towards the end of the 6th century A.D., much as Diocletian did in the Roman West, in China a family of tough, pragmatic emperors with military backgrounds came to power. They drove out the barbarians, stabilized the borders, reunited the empire, and founded the Sui dynasty.

- Although it would only last for three generations, the Sui dynasty laid the foundation for a glorious rebirth of Chinese civilization under the subsequent and longer-lasting Tang dynasty.

- The Sui were analogous to the Qin dynasty—they were not popular rulers, nor ones renowned for their empathy and kindness, but were a harsh, pragmatic regime that used force to reestablish unity.

- They raised taxes and exploited the peasantry, but they were also large-scale builders and supporters of the arts. They established the largest library in the world at the time (containing 400,000 books), constructed many Buddhist temples, expanded the network of roads, and rebuilt the Great Wall.

- Using the forced labor of an alleged 6 million workers, they excavated more canals and completed the first version of the Grand Canal connecting the Yangtze and Yellow Rivers. Solidly-built bridges spanned the canals and some of these have lasted up until modern times.

- The Sui emperors were highly organized and warlike, deploying an effective imperial army to conquer territory as well as a centralized government and civil service to administer it. But the Sui dynasty overextended itself, and it overworked and exhausted the Chinese people, who suffered from food shortages and were driven to rebellion.

The Tang Dynasty

- After a brief civil war, the Sui general Li Yuan emerged as emperor and founded the Tang dynasty. He was not from an aristocratic family but from the frontiers. Some sources say that he was of mixed Chinese and so-called barbarian ancestry.

- Just as the Han followed, reacted against, and built on the Qin dynasty, so the Tang dynasty succeeded and echoed the Sui. They responded to the harshness and oppression of the previous regime by reviving the Confucian ideal of the benevolent ruler. The Tang dynasty is considered by many historians as the greatest Chinese dynasty, which served as a model, both politically and culturally, for all its Asian neighbors.

- Li Yuan's rule did not last long; his son, Taizong, staged a coup in 626, during which he killed his brothers and threw his father in prison. Despite this questionable beginning, he enjoyed a subsequent reputation as a wise and conscientious emperor who stabilized the northern and western borders; ruled for over 20 years; and instigated many of the administrative reforms and policies that subsequent Tang emperors would follow.

- The next Tang emperor, Gaozong, resembled his father. He supported education and cultivated an administrative system staffed according to merit. Taizong had unsuccessfully attacked northern Korea, but Gaozong achieved this conquest. He is also known for having the Tang legal code revised.

- The next Tang ruler was one of the more amazing figures in Chinese history, the only woman to officially rule as emperor: Wu. She had been one of Taizong's minor concubines. When Gaozong succeeded his father, Wu steadily acquired more influence over Gaozong, eventually becoming his number two wife.

- When Gaozong suffered a stroke, Wu became a dominant figure at court. After Gaozong's death, she manipulated affairs as the real power behind the scenes while allegedly acting on behalf of her own young children. Finally, she usurped the throne in 690 and proclaimed herself emperor—assuming the male title.

- Wu is a controversial figure, and it is hard to ascertain the truth of her actions. The only surviving sources for her reign are hostile, including the usual accusations leveled against powerful female rulers. How true any of these stories are is impossible to tell. It seems accurate that she could be ruthless; she also must have been exceptionally intelligent and talented as well to have succeeded in such an atmosphere.

- To counterbalance the power of her enemies in the administration, she set up an inner court composed of scholars who favored her. Perhaps to gain a powerbase independent of the Confucian establishment, she favored Buddhism and practiced it herself, becoming a nun. Her enemies finally caught up with her in 705. She was forced to abdicate the throne and died shortly thereafter.

- The next ruler to come to power adopted the title Xuanzong. During his 44-year reign, China grew to unprecedented wealth and population. Towns and trade flourished, and the arts underwent a renaissance. The south saw particular gains in population and prosperity.

- The long reign of Xuanzong would often be looked back on as a golden age, but toward the end of his life, Xuanzong fell under the spell of one of his son's concubines. She and her family ended up running the empire—poorly—and things deteriorated.

- After the mid-8th century A.D., the Tang dynasty went into decline. At the Battle of Talas (near Samarkand) in 751, Arab warriors defeated the Tang, whose military dominance began to fade. Uighur Turks took over Mongolia. Internal enemies also menaced Tang power.

- Although the Tang dynasty lasted another 150 years, it would never achieve such heights of power and culture again. In 907, the Tang dynasty came to an inglorious end when a general sacked the capitol city and forced the last Tang emperor from the throne. However, the model of imperial stability and unity that had been established by the Han and Tang had taken firm root.

Suggested Reading

Lewis, *China Between Empires.*

Twitchett, ed., *The Cambridge History of China.*

Questions to Consider

1. What similarities and differences were there in the problems facing Rome and China in the 3rd century, and why did Rome ultimately fail to solve them, whereas China did?

2. Given the surviving sources' obvious hostility towards Empress Wu and Theodora, is it possible to accurately assess these women and their actions, and how might this be done?

China from Chaos to Order under the Tang
Lecture 43—Transcript

Here's the opening line of perhaps the most famous book of classical Chinese literature, a work called the *Romance of the Three Kingdoms*: "After a long period of [division], the world under heaven tends to unite; after a long period of unity, it tends to divide." This sprawling novel was written in the 14th century, but it's set in the chaotic period during and following the decline of the Han Dynasty, and its first sentence offers a succinct but accurate summary of much of Chinese history, including that of the period that we'll examine over the course of the next two lectures.

We left the historical narrative of China around 200 A.D. with the dissolution of the Han Empire. Very much mirroring the collapse of the Western Roman Empire, China then dissolved into a number of different warring states, some of them controlled by groups that the Chinese would have regarded as barbarians. The three and a half centuries that followed the end of the Han constituted the longest stretch of disunity in all of Chinese history and it lasted from 221 A.D. until 589 A.D. This turbulent period is known sometimes as the Era of Three Kingdoms and Six Dynasties, and that name itself reflects the frequent changes in and fragmentation of government during this period. In fact, there were many more than six dynasties, but they came and went so quickly that many of them are hardly worth noticing.

Not only was there internal dissention during this period, but the external threats posed by nomadic barbarian groups such as the Huns continued to intensify. Finally, with the collapse of central government and the security ans stability that it had brought to the land, gangs of bandits proliferated and roamed all throughout China, smetimes attacking travelers or even raiding villages.

In the period after the fall of the Han, one natural division was into northern and southern coalitions of states, each based around those two great river networks of the Yellow River in the north and the Yangtze in the south. This was a split that might have become permanent, especially considering the geographical and cultural differences that already existed between those two regions. That would have constituted what would have amounted to a final similarity between the Han and the Roman empires, except that where the Roman Empire split into eastern and western halves, the natural fissure in China would've been along north/south lines. If this split had happened, it would've resulted in the north and south each evolving its own distinct version of Chinese culture and civilization. However, the north and the south in China, unlike in Rome, were eventually reunified, and this would have a tremendous impact on all the rest of Chinese history. But, for awhile, in the period we're looking at, this split seemed a plausible outcome and it really would've profoundly altered China as we know it today, where it has its very strong sense of political unity and cultural cohesiveness.

Interestingly, this chaotic and dangerous time when China wasn't unified later on became an extremely popular setting for stories. As exemplified by the huge success and popularity of novels such as *The Romance of the Three Kingdoms*, maybe its very unsettled nature provided a fertile backdrop for colorful fables of larger-than-life heroes and dastardly villains. One tale, which has achieved popularity even in the West thanks to an animated Disney movie, but that's actually based on a 5th-century Chinese ballad, recounts the heroic behavior of a woman named Mulan, who masquerades as a male warrior so that she can join in the fight against some of tthose invading nomadic barbarians. The movie that currently holds the two distinctions of being both the most expensive film ever made in China and the top grossing film of all time in China is called *Red Cliff*. It was released in 2008 by acclaimed director John Woo, and it's based on a series of famous episodes in the *Romance of the Three Kingdoms* and it culminates in the gigantic namesake battle of Red Cliffs that was fought among some of the various warring states of this era.

As entertaining as time in Chinese history has proven to be as a setting for fictional stories, for the people who were actually living through it, the dangers posed by rival emperors, warlords, bandits, and barbarians and all of the economic disruption that they caused was probably no cause for amusement. Census data suggests that China may have suffered a significant decline in population over this period due to things like war and disease.

Just as we've seen all throughout this course with other periods of chaos and uncertainty, this time also spawned new philosophical and religious yearnings. The dominant philosophy in China of Confucianism, which had flourished under the stability provided by the Han, was just not as well-suited to the needs of the inhabitants of the Three Kingdoms Era, and many people of that time were seeking a spiritual system that might offer some sort of otherworldly salvation as maybe an escape from the harsh realities of their existence. Buddhism was such a belief, and although Buddhism is attested as having reached China at least as early as 64 A.D., it wasn't really until the chaotic 4th century that it began to grow rapidly in popularity, especially among the poor, disempowered classes. Amongst all this political confusion, it functioned as a source of comfort; it could offer salvation and, of course, it advocated compassion. Buddhist monasteries provided little islands of security, stability, and calm in a time that you might see as a stormy, turbulent era. A long succession of Buddhist pilgrims traveled to India searching for sacred texts and relics, and they wrote accounts of their journeys. An example of how Buddhism adapted itself to preexisting Chinese beliefs was in the way that it downplayed of the notion of reincarnation, which didn't mesh well with the traditional Chinese emphasis on ancestor worship. While there was at least initially some resistance against Buddhism posed by Confucian intellectuals and by rulers who were fearful of its power among the commoners, Buddhism eventually became firmly rooted in China during this period.

While the Buddhist focus on spirituality was one possible response to a society in crisis, another approach was adopted by many artists and intellectuals. The highly ordered society of Confucianism had fallen apart, so people began to say: Why live in obedience to Confucian rituals and strictures? Instead, may people embraced Daoist philosophy in a sort of new form that's sometimes called Neo-Daoism. This had more of a focus on abstruse metaphysical questions. Along with this, there's also a desire to live maybe a freer, more unfettered, unstructured lifestyle. Again, among artists, this led to the adoption of a Bohemian style of behavior that included spontaneous indulgence in things like wine, music, and art for its own sake.

A famous example of this sort of attitude was a 3rd century A.D. group known as the "Seven Sages of the Bamboo Grove," and they counted poets, painters, and musicians among their number:

One of these sages was always accompanied by a servant who carried a jug of wine and a shovel—the one for pleasure, the other to dig his grave should he die. ... another took a boat to visit a friend on a snowy night, but upon arriving at his friend's door, he simply turned around and went home. When asked to explain this, he said that it had been his pleasure to go, and when the impulse died, it was his pleasure to return.

These sorts of anecdotes reveal a scorn for convention, together with an admiration for inner spontaneity, however eccentric that might be. However, more traditional, conservative-minded individuals, such as Confucians and the authorities in charge, didn't always appreciate this kind of eccentric behavior of these creative types. In an incident that's a bit reminiscent of the trial of Socrates, this led in 262 A.D. to the execution of one of the Seven Sages on charges of "perversion of public morals."

Over several centuries, an eventual fusion of the belief systems of Buddhism, Confucianism, and Daoism took place. In what's a very nice metaphor for the synthesis of all these philosophies, there's a traditional Chinese story that imagines a debate taking place among Confucius, Lao Tzu, and the Buddha. In the story, as they're strolling along talking about the merits of their respective philosophies, they come to a bridge, and a dense mist enshrouds them. When the mist clears away, on the far side of the bridge, only one larger figure remains.

I began this lecture with the famous quote from the *Romance of the Three Kingdoms*, which states, "After a long period of division, the world under heaven tends to unite" and this is exactly what finally happened towards the end of the 6th century A.D. Much as Diocletian and his associated group of tough soldier-emperors managed to do for the Roman West three centuries earlier, in China of the late 500s a family of tough, pragmatic emperors with military backgrounds came to power, and they managed to drive out the barbarians, stabilize the borders, and reunite the empire. These men founded the Sui Dynasty, which, although it would only last for about three generations—from 589–618 A.D.—it would lay a foundation for what would amount to a glorious rebirth of Chinese civilization under the subsequent and much longer-lasting Tang Dynasty.

In a lot of ways, the Sui were analogous to the Qin Dynasty; so they weren't popular rulers, they weren't exactly known for their empathy and their kindness, but after centuries of political fragmentation and chaos they were the sort of harsh, pragmatic regime that was needed to use force in order to reestablish unity and provide stability. The Sui emperors were tyrants; they raised taxes and they openly exploited the peasantry. Also like the Qin, though, they were largescale builders and supporters of the arts. They established the largest library in the world, at least at the time, which was said to contain 400,000 books. They constructed many Buddhist temples, they expanded the network of roads, and they rebuilt the Great Wall. Using the forced labor of supposedly six million workers, they excavated more canals and they completed the first version of the Grand Canal that connected the Yangtze and the Yellow Rivers. The canal was lined with parks planted with shade trees and was equipped with inns for travelers. Very solidly-built bridges spanned these canals and some of those bridges have lasted up until modern times. For example, there's one bridge in Hebei province built between 605 and 616 A.D. that's 130 feet long and 30 feet wide, and was built using more than 1,000 stones that weighed over a ton each.

The Sui emperors were also highly organized and warlike, so they deployed a very effective imperial army to conquer territory as well as having a centralized government and a civil service to administer it. But we see a familiar pattern reoccurring: The Sui Dynasty overextended itself; they tried to conquer too much—for example, they pushed all the way into Korea and Central Asia—and the Chinese people, who were overworked and exhausted, suffering from food shortages, were eventually driven to rebellion.

After a fairly brief civil war among several Sui generals, one of these guys emerged as emperor and he then founded the next dynasty, the Tang. Just like many of the later Roman emperors, the lineage of this man, Li Yuan, wasn't from an old aristocratic Chinese family, but instead he was from the frontiers. Some sources even cliam that he was of mixed Chinese and so-called "barbarian" ancestry; but whatever the case, he founded a dynasty that would last for three centuries, from 618–907 A.D. In a repetition of previous Chinese history, just as the Han followed and in a sense reacted against and built upon the Qin, so now the Tang Dynasty succeeded and in some ways echoed the Sui. They, too, responded to the harshness and oppression of the previous regime by once again reviving the Confucian ideal of the benevolent ruler in order to try and find a balance between authority and openness. As under the Han, the emperor was seen both as the "Son of Heaven" who had that absolute mandate to rule and, following the Confucian model, as a kind of "father" who's responsible for his "family" of subjects. The three centuries of Tang rule are thought by many historians to be the greatest Chinese dynasty, and it would serve as a model, both politically and culturally, for all of its Asian neighbors. For example, even today, the word for "Chinese" in Cantonese means literally "people of the Tang," and Chinatowns all over the world are known as "Tang-people-streets." Their expansionist state eventually spread into Turkish Central Asia, as far as Tibet, and down into northern Vietnam, so that under the Tang Dynasty, China became the largest country in the world.

While the rule of the Tang would last a long time, that of the founder of the dynasty didn't. His own son, Tai Zong, staged a coup in 626 A.D., during which he killed his brothers and threw his own father in prison. Despite this rather questionable beginning, he then went on to enjoy a reputation as a wise and conscientious emperor who stabilized the borders, fought off barbarians, and did other good things. Tai Zong ruled for over 20 years, and it was really he who instigated many of the administrative reforms and policies that subsequent Tang emperors would continue to follow. What's really remarkable is that we have surviving from this very energetic man a document that records his philosophy of rulership. It's in the form of a letter addressed to his son that's written a year before he died, and in it he gives sound, Confucian-tinged advice on how to be a good ruler. Among some of the things preserved in it are the following bits of advice. He says: "[A ruler] cannot soothe and protect his people without compassion and kindness." Another one says: "A wise emperor knows how to choose the right person, for the right task." Another: "Slanderers and flatterers are as harmful to the country, as grubs are to seedlings." And finally: "A wise emperor accepts bitter criticisms that benefit his conduct; a foolish emperor takes sweet flattery that leads him to destruction. Beware!"

For being a document of fairly pragmatic political advice, Tai Zong's treatise is a very charming read, and in a large part this is because he often uses these long, extended metaphors that are lyrically written but kind of down-to-earth. For example, there's a famous passage in which he compares being the emperor to being a carpenter who has to match up his tools to the job at hand. In this passage, he writes:

> [A wise emperor] is like a skillful carpenter who knows how to use straight timber to make shafts, curved timber to make wheels, long timber to make beams, and short timber to make posts. Wood of all shapes and lengths is thus fully utilized. The emperor should make use of personnel in the same way, using the wise for their resourcefulness, the ignorant for their strength, the brave for their daring, and the timid for their prudence. As a good carpenter does not discard any timber, so a wise emperor does not discard any gentleman.

Unfortunately, once his power had become firmly established, Tai Zong's practice of these Confucian virtues somewhat waned during the later part of his reign and he began to pick quarrels with the officials whom he'd once treated with respect. Historians of the period have, maybe understandably, tended to emphasize the earlier part of his reign, when his actions matched his advice to his son.

The next Tang emperor, Gao Zong, resembled his father in being considered a good ruler who supported education and cultivated an administrative system that's staffed according to merit. For the most part, he seems to have just continued his father's policies. Tai Zong had unsuccessfully attacked northern Korea, but now Gao Zong achieved this conquest. He's also known for having revised the entire Tang legal code.

The next ruler is one of the more amazing figures in all of Chinese history, and it's the only woman to officially rule as emperor. One of Tai Zong's minor concubines was a woman named Wu, and when Gao Zong succeeded his father as emperor, he also sort of inherited Wu as one of his concubines. According to legend, when she was a young girl, she'd refused to spend all her time sewing as was expected of her in preference to reading books; and now as a concubine, Wu steadily acquired more influence over Gao Zong, eventually being elevated to the status of his number two wife. When Gao suffered a stroke, she then was able to assume an even greater role, and soon she was dominating things at court. After Gao's death, she manipulated affairs, serving as the real power behind the scenes while allegedly acting on behalf of a series of her own young children. Finally, in what's really an astonishingly bold move, she usurped the throne herself in 690 A.D., and she proclaimed herself emperor, assuming the male title despite her gender.

Known to later history as Empress Wu, she's a bit of a controversial figure, and it's hard to tell the truth about her actions. This is because the only surviving sources for her reign are all hostile ones who tend to malign her with all the usual accusations brought against powerful female rulers, such as sexual promiscuity; so we see the story here of Theodora repeating itself. The Confucian "establishment" just didn't approve of having a woman as ruler, and to secure her position they then made the claim that she'd had many of her opponents and even some of her own children tortured and killed. How true any of that is, is impossible to tell. Certainly it seems accurate that at times she could be ruthless; but obviously she also must have been an exceptionally intelligent and talented person just in order to have maintained power for decades in what was really such a hostile atmosphere. To counterbalance the power of her many enemies in the administration, she set up an inner court composed of scholars who favored and were loyal to her. Maybe also to try and gain somewhat of a powerbase that's independent of the Confucian establishment, she then favored Buddhism and she practiced it herself, even becoming a nun. Also, maybe not surprisingly, she patronized the writing of biographies of famous women. Her enemies did finally catch up with her in 705 A.D. when she was forced to abdicate the throne, and she died shortly thereafter.

After some fighting among various rivals, another ruler came to power who adopted the title Xuan Zong. During his 44-year reign, China would grow to unprecedented levels of wealth and population. It's a time when towns and trade flourished, and the arts underwent a sort of renaissance. The Yangtze Valley and the south also saw big gains in population and prosperity. Xuan Zong's court became especially famous for its cultured, cosmopolitan atmosphere, and this is a topic we'll return to in the next lecture in more detail. The long reign of Xuan Zong would often be looked back upon by later Chinese as a Golden Age that's characterized by a very high level of cultural sophistication. It's a time when many technological achievements were being made, and Chinese power stretched far and the borders and the influence of China achieved some of its greatest extent. However, towards the end of his life, Xuan Zong fell under the spell of one of his son's concubines. She managed to gain a lot of power, and then she and her family and her favorites basically ended up running the empire; but unfortunately, they didn't do a very good job, and things deteriorated.

After the mid-8th century A.D., the Tang Dynasty went into decline. At the Battle of Talas, which is near Samarkand, in 751 A.D., Arab warriors defeated the Tang army, and their military dominance began to fade. Uighur Turks took over Mongolia, and Islam became the main religion in many of the western border regions such as Turkestan, which is a situation that's lasted up until the current times. Internal enemies also menaced Tang power, as various military governors asserted themselves and took control of outlying provinces.

The Tang Dynasty would manage to limp along for another 150 years, but it would never achieve the heights, either in power or culture, ever again. In 907 A.D., the Tang Dynasty came to a rather inglorious end when a general sacked the capital city, killed all the eunuchs, and forced the last Tang emperor from the throne. For about five decades after that, China split up again into several states vying for power—and these are sometimes labeled the Five Dynasties—but that model for imperial stability and unity that had been established by the Han and Tang had managed to take firm root, and powerful dynasties would again in the future rise to take control of unified China with only a few occasional lapses into disorder, and that would be the story for Chinese history for the next thousand years. There's a proverb that sums up the Chinese distaste for disunity, and it goes: "Just as there cannot be two suns in the sky, there cannot be two rulers in China."

We're now getting beyond the chronological parameters of this course, and so this is the point at which I'll end my account of Chinese history. But before we leave China, I want to examine in a bit more detail that great cultural flourishing that took place under the Tang, and it's that cultural renaissance that will be the focus of the next lecture.

The Golden Age of Tang Culture
Lecture 44

Tang civilization was not only an era of political stability; it was a great flowering of cultural and technological achievement. The two most important aspects of Tang culture that allowed this to occur were urbanization, which encouraged people from as far as the shores of the Mediterranean to bring goods and ideas to China, and a cultural openness that delighted in what was exotic and new. Among the areas in which the Tang excelled were horse breeding, printing, chemistry, and sculpture.

Chang'an—The Heart of Tang Culture

- At its high point in the 7th and 8th centuries A.D., Tang China was a geographically vast empire consisting of 50 or 60 million subjects. This period is also commonly regarded as one of the cultural pinnacles of Chinese civilization.

- One of the characteristics of the Tang empire was that it possessed an unusual number of large cities. The Tang capital of Chang'an (modern Xi'an) was probably the largest city in the world, with a population that may have approached one million people. It was also a highly cosmopolitan, cultured, diverse place that drew artists, merchants, students, and pilgrims from all corners of Asia.

- The city encompassed some 30 square miles, and was surrounded by a strong wall made of packed earth and pierced by 12 gates. Taking up much of the northern quadrant was a great walled complex. This was the Imperial Palace and Imperial City, home of the emperor and his court. If you were an ordinary resident of the capital, you could never set foot within these precincts.

- The remainder of Chang'an was given over to commercial, residential, and religious structures. Just inside the main eastern and western gates were two great marketplaces. The city formed the eastern terminus of the Silk Road, so trade goods from all over the world poured into it. Arabs, Indians, Jews, Turks, Japanese, Tibetans, Cambodians, Vietnamese, and others all mingled in the markets.

- The southern sections of the city were residential neighborhoods laid in grid patterns. Each ward was surrounded by its own miniature earthen wall. At sunrise and sunset, drums were beaten announcing that the gates were being opened or closed, and these rhythms marked the start and end of the business day for many of the city's inhabitants.

- The main streets were also laid out in a grid. The largest of these, labeled the Avenue of the Vermilion Bird, was over 300 feet wide and served as the boundary between the eastern and western halves of the city.

- Near the Eastern Market could be found a number of schools where hopeful students feverishly prepared to take the civil service examinations. Restaurants, inns, taverns, and brothels also clustered in this district. Many of the patrons of these establishments were the young men studying for the exams.

- Religious schools, institutions, temples, and shrines abounded in the city and were scattered throughout it. One Japanese visitor reported that there were 300 Buddhist temples in the capital, and a particularly large Buddhist monastery occupied the entire southwest corner. The city hosted at least three dozen major Daoist sites plus buildings serving the adherents of Zoroastrianism, Manichaeism, Nestorian Christianity, and Islam.

Tang China's Economy

- Cities such as Chang'an served as points of stimulus for the economy. An increase in China's agricultural and industrial production, including iron casting, silk processing, porcelain manufacture, and the newly discovered craft of papermaking, stimulated a brisk trade along the Grand Canal, the Silk Road, and the sea.

- Trade led to the development of Tang civilization's most characteristic trait: an openness to other cultures. The Tang are considered among the most outward-looking of all Chinese dynasties.

- Other nations sent tribute to the Tang court, including animals. Foreign music and musicians were extremely popular. Tea, originally from Southeast Asia and used primarily for medicinal purposes, grew widely available and became China's national drink. Another new item, the chair, likely came from the Middle East.

- Two of the most famous Tang obsessions were exotic horses and flowers. Emperor Xuanzong had over 40,000 horses in the imperial stables, and he even had paintings made of his favorites. In fact, there were artists who specialized in nothing but horse portraits. Perhaps the most extreme manifestation of this horse obsession was the emperor's dancing horses.

- Foreign-bred horses were also employed as part of another hugely popular import from Persia: polo. Tang paintings depicting these polo matches reveal that sometimes women played alongside men. The quality of one's polo horses and trappings functioned as a status symbol.

- Tang pursued a craze for flowers, especially peonies. Every year, at the time of peony blossoming, hordes of carriages bearing China's elites would descend on places renowned for their peony gardens. Individuals competed to cultivate the most luxuriant blossoms and acquire plants that produced unusual colors.

- Such luxury hobbies were supported by a vibrant economy. The Tang economy was highly regulated. The government had monopolies on salt, liquor, and tea. It controlled grain shipments from the Yangtze Valley to the capital, and employed licensing to put a stop to illegal business practices.

- The innovation of long-distance credit was fostered by the increased trade (especially in tea) between northern and southern China. Bills of exchange known as "flying money" could be used to pay for goods throughout China. State-run public granaries stockpiled excess grain to prevent famine in times of bad harvests.

- Among the scientific developments of the period were gunpowder, wood-block printing, water pumps, a forerunner to the magnetic compass, and the use of coal as a heating fuel.

- In the fine arts, painting, poetry, and music thrived. The arts were avidly pursued by educated dilettantes as well as professional artists. The practice of calligraphy made a poem as beautiful to look at as it was to listen to.

- Of the thousands of known Tang era poets, several are especially renowned. Du Fu, a socially conscious Confucian, wrote anti-war poems and worried about man's cruelty to man. Li Bo often struck a less serious note, but his poetic persona could also be antiauthority, idealistic, romantic, and occasionally melancholy.

- While we know the names of famous painters from this time, very few examples of Tang painting managed to survive, except for a few wall paintings in tombs. The most common surviving Tang art objects are the beautiful glazed pottery figurines often found in tombs.

- While some poets gave themselves up to indulgence in physical pleasures and fine living, others believed that artistic creation and physical suffering went hand in hand. The common thread that links all of these disparate artists together is the intensity of their passion for their creative activity, whatever the accompanying lifestyle might be.

Suggested Reading

Benn, *China's Golden Age.*

Lewis, *China's Cosmopolitan Empire.*

Questions to Consider

1. How did the relative openness of Tang China to outside influences contribute to the cultural and intellectual flourishing of the Tang era?

2. How does the description of the physical layout and districts of the Tang capital of Chang'an reflect various core aspects of Tang culture?

The Golden Age of Tang Culture
Lecture 44—Transcript

At its high point in the 7th and 8th centuries A.D., Tang China was a geographically vast empire consisting of maybe 50 or 60 million subjects. This period is also commonly regarded as one of the cultural pinnacles of Chinese civilization. In the opening lecture of this course, I stressed how cities and civilization have tended to go together, so it's not surprising to learn that one of the characteristics of the Tang Empire was that it possessed an unusual number of large cities. Intensive urbanization was a Tang phenomenon; several of its cities had over 100,000 occupants, and in the 8th century A.D., the Tang capital of Chang'an (which is modern Xi'an) was probably the largest city in the world, with a population that may have even approached one million people. Like Rome before it, it's also a highly cosmopolitan, cultured, diverse place that drew artists, merchants, students, and pilgrims from all corners of Asia. In this bustling metropolis could be found the most sophisticated examples of contemporary culture as well as the most advanced technological innovations, and a flourishing of the arts ranging from everything from poetry to ceramics. In this lecture, I'll examine some of the more famous and impressive aspects of Tang urban civilization.

Imagine yourself entering the capital city of Chang'an around 740 A.D.; what might you see? The city encompassed about 30 square miles, and it's surrounded by a strong wall made of packed earth and this wall was pierced by 12 gates. Each of the gates was timber-framed and lined with brick. Taking up a lot of the northernmost quadrant of Chang'an was a huge walled complex, somewhat like a city within the city, and this was the Imperial Palace; or, I should say, a sequence of three imperial palaces and, in addition, another zone that was called the Imperial City. The three palaces were the home of the emperor and his court, and the Imperial City housed the offices of government and of its administrators. Separating the palaces from the Imperial City was an open courtyard, and this served as a setting for certain important religious rituals that were performed personally by the emperor. If you're just an ordinary resident of the capital city, you'd never set foot within those two very heavily guarded precincts; and, in fact, they're separated from the rest of the city by their own 33 foot high wall. If you even climbed to a rooftop from which you could look down over that wall into the imperial regions, that's an offense that could carry a penalty of incarceration for one year.

While the Imperial Palace and the Imperial City were strictly off limits to ordinary people, the remainder of Chang'an was accessible, and it's given over to commercial, residential, and religious structures. Just inside the main eastern and western gates you'd find two great marketplaces where goods ranging from staples to the most exotic luxuries could be bought and sold. Within each market, the stalls were organized or grouped into those selling the same or similar items. For example, all the goldsmiths would be together, as would be all the butchers, the apothecaries, the fishmongers, the blacksmiths, the potters, the weavers, and so on. This city formed the eastern terminus of the Silk Road, and so in it you'd find trade goods from all over the world, and these were brought by never-ending streams of caravans, wagons, and barges. All sorts of people—Arabs, Indians, Jews, Turks, Japanese, Tibetans, Cambodians, Vietnamese, and all sorts of other ethnic groups and nationalities—could all be found mingled together in the markets hawking their goods.

The southern sections of the city were a series of residential neighborhoods or wards that were laid out on grid patterns. Each individual ward was surrounded by its own little earthen wall, maybe just 9 or 10 feet high. The troops who were in charge of patrolling these ward areas could just close the gates to them, and by doing so closely monitor traffic in and out of each district. At sunrise and sunset, big drums were beaten as an announcement that the gates were being opened or closed, and so these booming rhythms would've marked the start and end of the business day for many of the city's inhabitants. The main streets that led to each of the major city gates were also laid out on nice, convenient grid patterns; and the very largest of these streets, which was called the Avenue of the Vermilion Bird, was over 300 feet wide and it also served as the boundary between the eastern and western halves of the city itself. In the wards surrounding the Eastern Market, you could find a number of schools where hopeful students would be feverishly studying to take the civil service examinations, and each of them would be dreaming that it could be their stepping stone to eventual wealth and power in the administration. Also in that district tended to cluster restaurants, inns, taverns, and brothels; and the erotic entertainment could range in price and offerings from very high-status establishments where the women would be accomplished musicians, singers, and hostesses, somewhat similar to Japanese geishas, to more ordinary prostitutes roaming around in the streets. Many of the patrons of those establishments were the very same young men who were studying for the exams, so that juxtaposition was natural.

There were many stories and songs that were set among this district with all its lively social interactions. A typical one tells the story of a promising young scholar who's been sent to the big city by his father, and his father, of course, cherishes hopes that his son will shine in the exams and so bring fortune to the entire family. The boy, however, when he gets there becomes infatuated with a local prostitute, and so he squanders all his money and neglects his studies. Discovering what his son has been up to, the father beats him savagely and leaves him for dead in the very same garden where traditionally successful exam candidates would celebrate their academic triumph. Lying there half dead in that garden, the very same prostitute that he'd fallen in love with found him and she then repents that she'd led him astray. She takes him in, she nurses him back to health, and then helps him study for the exams; and eventually he goes on not only to pass the exams, but to achieve the sort of distinction that his father had dreamt of all along. This is a nice story; it ends happily, with father and son reconciled, and even a marriage between the promising young scholar and the now-former prostitute.

Other prominent structures found in the city had to do with religion. There were religious schools, religious institutions, and, of course, temples and shrines that could be found all throughout the city. One Japanese visitor reported that he'd found no fewer than 300 Buddhist temples in the capital, and an especially large Buddhist monastery occupied almost the entire southwest corner of the city. All of those Buddhist buildings were balanced by at least three dozen major Daoist sites as well. In keeping with the cosmopolitan nature of the city, there were lots of other temples serving the adherents of many other religions, including Zoroastrianism, Manicheism, Nestorian Christianity, and, of course, Islam.

Cities such as Chang'an served as points of stimulus for the entire economy. An increase in China's agricultural and industrial production, including iron casting, silk processing, porcelain manufacture, and the newly invented craft of papermaking, all stimulated a brisk trade that tended to flow along the Grand Canal. It also came overland across the Silk Road and across the ocean by sea throughout Southeast Asia. Various southern port cities flourished because of this sea trade, and the trade by sea was also encouraged by the fact that porcelain didn't transport very well in those bumpy camel caravans going across land.

All of this trade activity probably led to the development of one of Tang civilization's most characteristic traits: a general openness to other cultures. The Tang is often considered among the most outward-looking of all the Chinese dynasties. In the Tang capital cities and at the imperial court, there was a taste for exotic, foreign, or unusual things. Other nations would send tribute to the Tang court, including various animals that weren't found in China. There are painted scrolls that show emissaries, for example, bringing a lion and an ibex on a little leash as gifts. Various Tang ceramic figurines that are very attractively glazed in shades of brown, orange, yellow, and green will show barbarian handlers leading camels, which are heavily burdened with trade goods, and sometimes even carrying an entire troupe of musicians. This isn't very surprising, because foreign music and musicians became very popular in the Tang era. These little clay figurines, which are a common find in people's tombs, suggest just how eagerly the Tang anticipated the arrival of various caravans from Central Asia, each of which might bring some new, exciting, and unfamiliar item.

One especially popular imported product that came from Southeast Asia was tea. Tea was originally used mainly for medicinal purposes, but tea was able to be grown widely enough that it became available everywhere and so it ultimately turned into China's "national drink," and teahouses proliferated. Another interesting new item was the chair, which likely originated in the Middle East; and over a couple of centuries, it gradually took over from seating pads, so that the Chinese became the only ancient East Asian people to sit in chairs. Chinese music and art also absorbed foreign influences, and in the early 7th century A.D. there was a kind of craze for foreign fashions among Chinese women.

These sorts of climates often produce fads for certain specific luxury goods, and two of the most famous Tang obsessions were for exotic horses and flowers. Specially bred imported horses from the north and the western regions were especially prized. Emperor Xuan Zong had over 40,000 horses in his imperial stables, and he even had little paintings made of his favorites. In fact, there were artists who specialized in doing nothing else but horse portraits, which were intended to capture not just the physical appearance of the horse but something of its spirit or character as well. The different types of horses were given very poetic-sounding names; for example, some were called "Flying Yellow," or "Night-Lightning," "Drifting Cloud," and "Five Blossom." One very charming stone relief depicts an imperial horse whose name was "Autumn Dew" being lovingly tended to by his groom.

Maybe the most extreme manifestation of this whole horse obsession was the famous dancing horses of the emperor Xuan Zong. He had a special band of 100 highly trained dance horses, and they'd come out dressed in finely embroidered cloths, their harnesses were made of precious metals (gold and silver), and their manes would have pearls and jade ornaments woven into them. A group of musicians would play a tune that's called "The Upturned Cup" (it's about drinking), and in perfect coordination with the rhythm, the horses would shake their heads, flick their tails, prance in unison, and at one point even climb up a three-level platform. One court official wrote poems commemorating these trained horses' amazing skills. Let me read you a sample of this; the poem goes:

> Heavenly horses have come for the ceremony from
> far west of the sea.
>
> They stride slowly with their feet arched, then kneel
> on both knees.
>
> Though high-spirited, they stay in formation and
> stamp with a thousand hooves.
>
> With bent knees and wine cups in their mouths, and
> maintaining the rhythm,

Devotedly they make offerings for the sovereign's
long life.

These celestial thoroughbreds are amazing.
Nimbly prancing, they keep in step with the music.
High-spirited, they step together, never deviating.

That poem captures a bit of the cosmopolitan, wealthy, maybe even
ostentatious nature of the royal court where you might encounter people,
products, and goods from all over the world, and all of this was used by the
emperor and encouraged by him in order to provoke awe among his subjects,
as well as to delight them.

These foreign-bred horses were also employed in another context as part of
another hugely popular foreign import, and this is one that came from Persia
and is the sport of polo. Tang paintings show polo matches, and in these
sometimes women are shown playing right alongside the men. There are also
ceramic figurines of elegant court ladies playing polo, and all of this captured
the graceful movements both of the woman and the horses. Another reason
for the popularity of polo among Chinese aristocrats is that the quality of
your horse and the elaborateness of the trappings on it could function as a
status symbol and a way that you could flaunt your wealth publicly.

Along with horses, the Tang had a craze for flowers, especially peonies.
Every year at the time of peony blossoming, hordes of carriages carrying
China's elites would descend on certain places that were famous for their
peony gardens. One of these was the Buddhist Temple of Mercy and
Compassion, whose flowers consistently would open two weeks earlier
than others. Various individuals would compete with one another to try to
cultivate the most luxuriant blossoms or to try and find plants that would
produce unusual colors of blooms. There's one story that tells of a monk
who had a peony tree that produced blossoms that apparently were some
shade of red that no other flower was like. A group who was envious of this
tricked the monk away from his beloved plant and then they stole it, but they
did leave behind an offering of gold and tea in its place. In many ways, the
intense passion of the Tang for their peonies calls to mind the later "tulip
mania" that famously struck Holland in the 17th century.

Such luxury hobbies were supported by a very vibrant economy. The Tang economy was one that's highly regulated; the government had monopolies on things like salt, liquor, and tea and, of course, it also controlled grain shipments from the Yangtze Valley to the capital. The government employed a licensing system to try to stop or curb illegal business practices. The innovation of long-distance credit was fostered by all of this trade, especially in tea, between southern and northern China. There were things that were bills of exchange called "flying money" that you could use to pay for various goods and products throughout China. As in previous eras, there were state-run public granaries that would stockpile up excess grain in order to prevent famine in times of bad harvests.

Tang scientists and inventors advanced technological knowledge and they came up with a number of very clever devices. Two developments in particular can perhaps be connected to the intellectual and religious currents of the time. Some Neo-Daoists devoted themselves to trying to find elixirs that would grant immortality. Of course, they never found this; but what it did do was it caused them to practice experiments in alchemy, which in turn led to scientific advances in what today we'd call the field of chemistry. Some of these new chemical advances included the discovery of new medicines, new dyes, and even the invention of gunpowder. There's also a huge growth in the printing industry and in printing technology. In the Han Era, ink rubbings had been made on paper that's stretched across stone carvings; but by the 6th century A.D., real block printing had been developed, and by the 9th century A.D., woodblock printing was common in East Asia. The motivation for this technology was the desire to mass-produce Buddhist texts to give to religious believers and also to produce lots of Confucian texts that the students could then study who wanted to take those exams.

An invention that affected rice cultivation was a contraption called "the Dragon's Backbone," and this consisted of a whole series of paddles along a chain that's driven by two men pushing pedals. This whole thing served as a water pump to transfer water among fields and even to raise water from one level to another. Together with all the new canals being built, the resulting increase in rice production helped to feed many of the immigrants who were displaced from the north by nomadic invaders. It also allowed southern China to grow in population and to prosper economically in general. Other technological innovations of this same period included developments in using a magnetized needle to identify north and south, and this, of course, was really a forerunner to the compass; and also they began to use some coal as a heating fuel.

In the fine arts, the early Tang Period had a true cultural flowering in which painting, poetry, and music all thrived. Famous painters, sculptors, and poets all lived at this time, and the arts were also avidly pursued by people we might call educated dilettantes. Scholars and government officials would spend their spare time painting landscape scenes or composing poetry. Those two arts merged together in the practice of calligraphy, which used an inked brush on a silk or paper scroll to render poems as beautiful to look at they are to listen to. Literature was maybe stimulated by the development of papermaking and that invention of block printing.

The Tang Era is regarded as one of the most fruitful in terms especially of poetry. Poetry was very popular among all classes of society, from the emperor all the way down to the average guy in the street. The value placed upon poetry is reflected in the fact that they'd hold annual literary festivals, which would give prizes to poets. The sheer volume of poetry being written is suggested by one Tang Era anthology that collected 49,000 poems by 2,300 different poets.

Of all the thousands of known Tang Era poets, several are especially famous. Two of these, Du Fu and Li Bo, were actually good friends, but they're very different in both their demeanor and their subject matter. Du Fu was a socially conscious Confucian, and so he tended to write antiwar poems, and in his poems he worries about things such as man's cruelty to man. For example, one of his poems laments: "When will men be satisfied with building a wall against the barbarians? When will the soldiers return to their native land? ... And still the heart of Emperor Wu is beating for war."

Li Bo, on the other hand, often struck a less serious note in his poems, many of which were composed under the influence of alcohol. For instance, one poem called "The Joys of Wine," in which he writes: "Since Heaven and Earth love wine, I can love wine without shaming Heaven. With three cups I penetrate the Great Dao. Take a whole jugful and I and the world are one."

His poetic persona could also be somewhat antiauthoritarian; he had many of the characteristics we might call idealistic or romantic; but sometimes also there's a melancholy tone. Following Daoism, he held that a person should try to keep "the heart and mind of a child" and to always remain "carefree." According to legend, this romantic nature eventually led to his death. Once, when he was drunk on a boat, he became enraptured with the moon's reflection on the water, and he leaned out too far gazing at it so that he fell in and drowned. Maybe this story originated in the fact that many of his best-known poems do feature the moon. Here's one example:

> Beside my bed the bright moonbeams glimmer
> Almost like frost on the floor.
> Rising up, I gaze at the mountains bathed in moonlight;
> Lying back, I think of my old home.

While we know the names of famous painters from this time, very few examples of Tang painting have managed to survive except for there are a few wall paintings in tombs. The man who's considered to be the greatest painter of the era was often praised for the extreme realism of his work. There are stories, for example, of how his wall paintings were so lifelike that after finishing one he could just walk into it and vanish. Unfortunately, we can't judge their quality for ourselves because none of these remain. The most common surviving Tang art objects are the beautiful glazed pottery figurines that I've mentioned, and these are often found in tombs. They sometimes depict fantastic creatures who would act as tomb guardians, as well as more ordinary things such as horses, camels, or various kinds of people, including foreigners; and in the depictions of foreigners in these potteries, they're so detailed that we can identify their ethnicity just from their clothing and features.

It's interesting to note that while Chinese art on the whole emphasized order and tradition, there's also room for deviation and experimentation. One Tang artist is known to have shaken ink-saturated hair at silk, somewhat like a 7th-century Jackson Pollack, and another artist would fling paint while dancing. All across the arts, this sort of desire for spontaneity and naturalness seems to have unleashed a torrent of artistic self-expression. Again, poetry in particular was considered the best way to express yourself and to embody emotion.

One popular poetic convention of this time was to adopt in a poem the persona of a complicated individual who's troubled by strong but contradictory emotions. A typical attitude of the followers of this movement is expressed by one poet, who states, "Since youth I have not fit into the common mold ... It's folly to follow propriety and conventions too earnestly." In a poem called "Drinking Alone in the Rainy Season," he further explains,

> I try a cup and all my concerns become remote.
> Another cup and suddenly I forget even heaven.
> But is heaven really so far from this state?
> Nothing is better than to trust your true self.

While some poets gave themselves up to indulgence in physical pleasures and fine living, others believed that artistic creation and physical suffering had to go hand in hand. One of these poets proclaimed, "The poet suffers making poems," and "Poets are usually pure and rugged. They die from hunger, clinging to desolate mountains." The common thread that links all of these disparate artists together is the intensity of their passion for their creative activity, whatever the accompanying lifestyle might be.

Very much like the flowers of which they were so fond, Tang culture blossomed beautifully for a brief moment and then was no more; but the memory of its glory has persisted, and it continues to be a yardstick against which other eras of Chinese history are measured.

The Rise and Flourishing of Islam
Lecture 45

From its surprising origins among the nomads of the Arabian Desert, Islam spread rapidly through spectacular military conquests during the 6th and 7th centuries. The Umayyad and Abbasid caliphates oversaw a powerful dynasty where culture, trade, and learning flourished. At its greatest extent, Islamic dominance reached the border of modern Spain and France in the west, the Indian states in the east, pressed against the walls of Constantinople in the north, and reached into sub-Saharan Africa to the south. In those southern African regions, it encountered the developing kingdoms of Axum and Ghana.

Out of the Desert, a Kingdom

- Despite all the disruptions of the previous centuries, in the year 600, the Mediterranean world remained a place of great empires. In the former Roman West were a number of barbarian kingdoms; in the Mesopotamia was the Sassanian Empire, heir to the Persians and Parthians; and in between was the Byzantine Empire.

- A set of seminomadic desert tribes had lived in the Arabian Peninsula for centuries. These peoples, sometimes called Arabs or Bedouins, lived a hard life on the edges of civilization. They were proud, clannish, aloof, pagan, and possessed no overarching political organization but instead clumped into small familial groupings.

- Within 100 years of their conversion to the last of the three great monotheistic religions to arise from the Mediterranean basin, however, these nomads would sweep out of the desert, toppling kingdom after kingdom, until they had conquered fully half the Mediterranean world.

- In the process, they would permanently shatter the form\ of that world, spin its constituent parts onto divergent paths, establish religious, linguistic, and cultural boundaries that su. exist today.

The Origins of Islam

- This remarkable conquest begins with an unlikely source: a middle-aged businessman who lived in the town of Mecca at the beginning of the 7th century. This man began roaming the wilderness, often meditating in a cave.

- There, in 610, he experienced a vision in which the angel Gabriel appeared to him and taught him a revelation from God. Over the next 20 years, more than 100 further revelations followed, and these collected lessons became known as the Qur'an.

- The religion established by Mohammed advocated a stark form of monotheism in which the primacy of God as the one and only deity was stressed and nothing was allowed to come between God and the worshiper. Acknowledgment of God's omnipotence and submitting oneself to his will were all-important; this concept is reflected in the word "Islam" itself, which means "submission."

- Mohammed identified God (in Arabic, Allah) as the same God who was worshiped by the Jews and the Christians. Biblical figures such as Abraham, Moses, and Jesus were venerated as human prophets who had received earlier divine revelations. Mohammed was the last in this long line of prophets who had been granted the fullest and most accurate version of God's message.

- Early Islam had little formal church structure, with no equivalent of priests or other intercessors between God and his worshipers. Islam stressed that each person would have to stand alone before God and be judged. The Islamic concept of heaven was a paradise of lush green gardens with lots of water—the very opposite of the harsh desert they lived in.

- Islam is based around a set of moral injunctions similar to those found in Judaism and Christianity as well as the Five Pillars of the faith: (1) that Allah is the only god, and Mohammed is his prophet; (2) to pray five times every day while facing Mecca; (3) to fast during the holy month of Ramadan; (4) to make a pilgrimage to Mecca at least once in your life; and (5) to give alms to the poor and assist the needy.

- Mohammed's teachings were initially not very popular among the urban populace of Mecca. Rising tensions with these people peaked in 622, so he and his followers fled to the nearby city of Yathrib, now called Medina, meaning "city of the Prophet." This event is known as the Hejira, literally "the flight." It marks the beginning of the Islamic calendar.

- Islam took hold among the hardy Arab tribes of the surrounding desert. Under the leadership of Mohammed's four caliphs (or successors), the tribes exploded into the Mediterranean world and conquered vast territories. In a sense, these expeditions were a continuation on a grand scale of the raids that had always been part of the lifestyle of these desert nomads.

Islam Becomes an Empire

- Egypt fell to these raids in 642, and the southern Mediterranean coast, encompassing what is today Libya and Tunisia, soon followed. The entire Middle East was overwhelmed. Syria and Mesopotamia were overrun, and the Sassanian Empire was toppled. Jerusalem, the most sacred city in Christendom, fell in 636.

- Over the next several generations, the Umayyad caliphate pushed even further, capturing North Africa through the modern borders of Morocco, crossing the straits of Gibraltar and seizing the Spanish Peninsula. The frontier extended into central Asia to the borders of India.

- In the eastern Mediterranean, the great wave of conquest slowed and eventually stopped by the stubborn resistance of the Byzantine Empire, culminating in the defeat of a Muslim naval expedition before the walls of Constantinople in 717. In France, the Battle of Tours in 732 fixed the high water mark of invasion in the west.

- In a little more than 150 years, these campaigns had fundamentally changed the map of the world, creating new political, religious, linguistic, and ethnic boundaries.

- One special weapon that gave the Muslim armies an edge, particularly in the desertlike regions of North Africa and the Middle East, was the camel. Able to go almost a week without water and carry heavy loads long distances, it could traverse dry terrain in which horses would falter and die.

- These conquests benefited from their timing. The Byzantines and Sassanians had exhausted one another over centuries of conflict and were thus unable to mount an effective or strong defense, and many of the other states around the Mediterranean were weak and disorganized.

- As conquests go, these invasions were relatively non-destructive. Islamic lords were generally tolerant of other religions and left most existing social and political structures in place; they simply took over the top level of administration and collected taxes.

- The Umayyadic capital of the Islamic world was moved from Mecca to Damascus. The Umayyads would not get to enjoy their empire for long. They were overthrown and replaced by the Abbasids around 750.

Baghdad—The Cultural Capital of Islam

- The Abbasids were Persian converts to Islam, and with their ascendancy, the capital of the Islamic world shifted eastward. The new capital city of Baghdad was founded in 762. The lone survivor of the Umayyads escaped to Spain, where he established a cultural center at Cordoba that would thrive for another three centuries.

- Baghdad's location, in a well-irrigated, fertile farming region where important trade routes intersected, allowed it to grow rich and flourish. Goods and ideas from all over the known world arrived and were then passed on to Europe and other parts of Asia. Islam spread along the trade routes.

- Crops from far-flung places, such as rice, sugar cane, lemons, watermelons, spinach, and cucumbers, were planted in this agriculturally productive area and became part of the Muslim diet. Later, the Crusaders would bring some of these foodstuffs back to Europe, from where they eventually diffused throughout the Americas.

- Surplus food fueled rapid population growth and urban expansion. By 900, Baghdad had developed into one of the world's largest cities. Its cosmopolitan atmosphere was enhanced by the presence of many foreign traders, who were shown tolerance by the Abassid rulers and allowed to practice their own religions.

- A large Jewish community arose there, and Persians, many of whom attained high-ranking government posts, exerted a strong influence. Sophisticated economic tools such as banks, joint-stock companies, and bills of exchange (or checks, another Arabic word) further encouraged investment and trade.

- In the 8th century, papermaking was brought from China, which was a crucial step in the diffusion of ideas and scholarship. The manufacture of paper also meant that copies of the Qur'an could be more readily produced, further helping to spread Islam.

- Libraries and universities were established in most large cities. The University of Al-Azhar in Cairo became so renowned that it served as a model for some of Europe's medieval universities.

- The Abbasid caliphate, which lasted for several hundred years, is often regarded as constituting an Islamic golden age. Knowledge, scholarship, and science were highly prized and encouraged. Islamic scholars preserved the intellectual heritage of prior civilizations, both eastern and western, including Egypt, Persia, and classical Greece and Rome.

- Muslim scholars excelled at the synthesis of their ideas with knowledge derived from ancient Greece, Persia, and India. Medicine was pursued with particular zeal. Hospitals, medical schools, and pharmacies were established, and the state required that doctors pass exams before they could legally practice medicine.

- Persian scholar Ibn Sina (or Avicenna) took the writings of ancient Greek physicians such as Hippocrates and Galen and combined these texts with the medical knowledge of the Islamic world. Translated into Latin, this became the primary medical text used in Europe through the 17th century.

- Observatories allowed Muslim astronomers to make detailed observations of the sky, and which honed the accuracy of their calculations of the solar year's length and their predictions of eclipses. Alchemists established the first chemical laboratories.

The Growing Civilizations of Africa

- Even after the initial wave of conquests was over, Islam continued to spread, often along trade routes. This was particularly true in parts of Africa, where the first large, urbanizing kingdoms began to appear in sections of Africa outside of the narrow corridor stretching along the Nile.

- Central and southern African cultures had been heavily influenced by the Bantu migrations, which began around 500 B.C. Most African cultures shared a seminomadic lifestyle that combined slash-and-burn agriculture with some herding and advanced iron-working skills.

- The most notable early sub-Saharan African kingdom was Axum, which arose near the mouth of the Red Sea around the 3rd century B.C. Geographically positioned to control the Red Sea trade, it was also a point from which Mediterranean and Eastern merchants could access the goods of Africa, such as ivory, frankincense, myrrh, and slaves.

- At exactly the same time when the Constantine was converting to Christianity, the king of Axum also became a Christian—in this case, the Coptic form of the religion practiced in Egypt.

- In the 8th century, the Islamic conquests began to push the declining Axum empire away from the rich coastline. Axum was displaced to the highlands of the interior, where it continued to flourish for several more centuries.

- In western Africa, the most important rising kingdom was Ghana, based in the upper Niger River Valley (not in the same location as the modern Ghana). It seems it began developing as early as the late 4th century A.D. and reached a peak in the 9th century.

- The foundation for its wealth was gold, and it enjoyed control over some of the richest mines in Africa. By 800, it was a large, powerful kingdom with several substantial cities. Gold was exchanged with the Mediterranean via trade routes and caravans that crossed the Sahara.

- Muslim merchants crossed the Sahara, transporting loads of precious gold, ostrich feathers, ivory, and animal hides. Ghana would be followed in the next few centuries by other powerful mercantile West African kingdoms, such as Mali, which ruled the fabled markets of Timbuktu.

Suggested Reading

Brockopp, ed., *The Cambridge Companion to Muhammad.*

Kennedy, *The Prophet and the Age of the Caliphates.*

Questions to Consider

1. How do the basic tenets of Islam compare with other religions we have observed such as Zoroastrianism, Buddhism, and Confucianism?

2. What similarities and differences are there in the achievements and attitudes of the Islamic Golden Age compared with those of the Tang at the same time?

The Rise and Flourishing of Islam
Lecture 45—Transcript

Despite all of the various disruptions of the previous centuries, in A.D. 600 the Mediterranean world remained a place of great empires. Dwelling in the former territories of the Western Roman Empire—so places like Spain, Italy, North Africa, and Europe—were a large number of barbarian kingdoms; in the East, stretching from the coast inland to Mesopotamia, was the vast and very powerful Sassanian Empire, which was heir to the Persians and the Parthians; and situated between the west and the east was, of course, the Byzantine Empire, firmly based around Constantinople. The fringes of this world were inhabited by various minor groups.

Among these was a set of semi-nomadic desert tribes who lived in the Arabian Peninsula; and, just as they had for many centuries, these peoples—sometimes called the Arabs or sometimes the Bedouins—lived a very hard life on the very edges of civilization, trying to scrape out a living in what was an extremely hostile climate. As a people, they tended to be very proud, clannish, somewhat aloof, and they're still pagans, and they had no overarching political organization but instead would just group themselves into little familial tribes. In a lot of ways, they resembled desert-dwelling versions of some of the earlier northern barbarian tribes; but within 100 years of their conversion to the last of the three great monotheistic religions to arise from the Mediterranean basin, these formerly obscure nomads would sweep out of the desert and topple kingdom after kingdom until they'd conquered half of the Mediterranean world. In the process, they'd permanently shatter the unity of that world; they'd spin its constituent parts onto divergent paths; and they'd establish religious, linguistic, and cultural boundaries that still exist today.

That remarkable conquest—which, I think, arguably was the greatest in all of history, at least in terms of its scope and its permanence—began with an unlikely source: a less-than-successful middle-aged businessman who lived in the town of Mecca in the Arabian peninsula at the beginning of the 7th century. Unsatisfied with his life, this man began roaming into the wilderness outside of Mecca, often going to a cave where he'd meditate. It's in this cave, in A.D. 610, that he experienced a vision in which the angel

Gabriel appeared to him and taught him a revelation from God. The angel then commanded that he recite back this revelation; and, over the next 20 years or so, more than 100 further revelations followed. Collected together, these lessons became known as the Qur'an, which means literally, "the Recitations". That man, of course, was Mohammed, and the religion that he founded was Islam.

The religion established by Mohammed advocated a very stark form of monotheism in which the primacy of God as the one and the only deity was stressed very heavily, and so nothing was allowed to come between God and the worshipper. Acknowledging God's omnipotence and submitting yourself to his will were all-important within this religion; and we can see this concept reflected in the word "Islam" itself, which can be translated as "submission." Mohammed identified God—or, in Arabic, Allah—as the same God who's worshipped by the Jews and the Christians, and so in Islam, figures such as Abraham, Moses, and even Jesus are venerated as human beings who were prophets and who'd received earlier divine revelations from God. Mohammed, then, was simply the last in this long line of prophets, but he's the one who'd been given the fullest and most accurate version of God's message. The whole figure of the prophet, the Rasul, was very important in early Islam. He's the one sent by God to warn his people. At least in early Islam, there's very little formal church structure; so there's no equivalent to priests or other figures who'd be intercessors between God and his worshippers. The reason for this was that, again, Islam stressed that ultimately each person would have to stand alone before God and be judged, and the fear of that judgment is what should motivate believers. The Islamic concept of heaven, of course, was very obviously also the vision of a desert-dwelling society. Heaven was envisioned as a paradise of lush green gardens with lots and lots of water, which is the very opposite of the harsh desert that these Bedouins lived in.

The core of Islam is based around a set of moral injunctions that generally are pretty similar to those found in Judaism and Christianity. You might even argue that they're stricter than some branches of Christianity, since things like alcohol and gambling are forbidden. But also Islam is based upon the so-called "Five Pillars" of faith. The first of those is to simply affirm and to state the fundamental creed of Islam, which is "Allah is the only god, and Mohammed is his prophet." The second pillar is to, of course, pray five times every day while facing in the direction of Mecca. The third is to fast during the holy month of Ramadan, and Ramadan is the ninth month in the Islamic calendar, and currently that corresponds to late July and August. The fourth is to try to make a pilgrimage to Mecca at least once in your life, and to perform a whole series of rituals there. There's a provision, however, that exempts you from that requirement if you're too poor or physically unable to make such a trip. Finally, the fifth Pillar of Islam is to give alms to the poor and to generally assist those who are needy.

Mohammed's teachings weren't initially very popular among the urban people of Mecca. Rising tensions with those people peaked in 622 A.D., with the result that Mohammed and his followers had to actually flee from Mecca. They ended up going to a fairly nearby city called Yathrib—now that city is Medina, which means the "city of the Prophet"—and that event, which later became a pivotal moment in Islam, is called the Hejira, literally meaning "the flight," or "the escape." So important is the Hejira that it marks the beginning of the Islamic calendar; so the Islamic year 1 is equivalent to the year 622 in the Christian calendar.

While Mohammed steadily gained converts in cities such as Medina, the people among whom the new religion really took hold were the hardy Arab tribes who lived in the surrounding deserts. They're the ones who embraced it enthusiastically and wholeheartedly; and by the time of Mohammed's death in 632, Islam had spread throughout these clans. It's those people who'd form the core of the armies that soon would burst out of the Arabian Peninsula. Under the leadership of Mohammed's four caliphs, or successors, these tribes exploded into the Mediterranean world, and in an incredibly short amount of time conquered vast territories. In a sense, these expeditions were just a continuation on a huge scale of the old Bedouin raids that had been a key part of the lifestyle of these desert nomads. But, nevertheless, mounted on their swift-moving camels, these raiders just rolled irresistibly over all their opponents.

Egypt fell to them in 642; and the southern Mediterranean coast, encompassing what is today Libya and Tunisia, soon followed. To the east, their triumphs were even more impressive, as the entire Middle East was overwhelmed. Syria and Mesopotamia were overrun and even the powerful Sassanian Empire was toppled. Jerusalem itself, the most sacred city in all of Christendom, fell in 636. All of this happened in just the first 30 years after the death of Mohammed. In the next couple generations, which would be known as the Umayyad Caliphate, these Muslim armies would push even further. All the rest of North Africa up through the modern borders of Morocco was captured, and then the Arabic armies even crossed the Straits of Gibraltar and seized most of the Spanish peninsula. To the east, the frontier just kept getting pushed further and further until they got into Central Asia, nearly to the borders of India. In the eastern Mediterranean, this great wave of conquest was only slowed and eventually stopped by the stubborn resistance of the Byzantine Empire, which fought a long series of bitter wars against the invaders, and this culminated in the defeat of a great Muslim naval expedition right in front of the walls of Constantinople itself in 717 A.D.

To the west, in France, the Battle of Tours in 732, at which a coalition of various European powers got together and managed to fight the Muslim forces to a draw, marked the high water mark of invasion in that direction. Just a couple years later, in 738, the Rajahs of Northern India similarly came together and managed to defeat a Muslim army and so put a stop on further expansion in that direction.

This initial great wave of conquest finally subsided around the mid-8th century. Looking back, in a little bit longer than 150 years, these series of campaigns had fundamentally changed the map of the world. They'd created new political, religious, linguistic, and ethnic boundaries. The Arabs themselves were very much aware of the astonishing speed of their conquests, and just how quickly they'd gone from being completely obscure, marginal desert nomads to what really amounted to rulers of much of the world. For example, one Arab ambassador to the Persian court once said, "At one time the Arabs were a wretched race, whom you could tread underfoot with impunity. We were reduced to eating dogs and lizards. But, for our glory, God raised up a prophet among us."

In these lightning-swift military operations, one special weapon that gave the Muslim armies an edge, especially in desert regions, was the camel. Camels can go for almost a week without water, and they can carry very heavy loads, much more than a horse, long distances. Camels could cross dry terrain in which horses would simply die. So the camel gave its riders a range and a speed that would often bewilder the enemies of the Arabs. In warfare, mobility always counts for a lot; the mobility given to the Muslim armies by the camel was a key factor in their success. Because of this, one famous historian has likened the camel to being the tank of the 7th century A.D. In addition, these conquests benefitted a bit because of their timing. They came along at a point at which the Byzantines and the Sassanians had fought one another to a standstill and had exhausted one another; and so when the Arabs showed up, they were unable to mount a very strong or effective defense. For a lot of the states around the Mediterranean, they were also weak and disorganized at this particular moment in time.

As conquests go, these invasions were relatively nondestructive. The new Islamic overseers generally speaking were tolerant of other religions, they tended to leave the existing social and political structures in place; they just simply came in and took over at the top, and then they'd collect the taxes. As this initial phase of expansion came to a close, the Umayyadic capital of the Islamic world was moved from Mecca to Damascus. The Umayyads wouldn't actually get to enjoy their new empire for very long; they were soon overthrown and replaced by a new dynasty of Muslim rulers known as the Abbasids. This began with a revolt in 750 in Persia. Ethnically speaking, the Abbasids were Persian converts to Islam, and so with their ascendancy, the capital of the Islamic world shifted eastward yet again into the former territory of the Persian Empire. The new capital city that's established was Baghdad; that was founded in 762, only a couple miles away from one of the old Persian royal cities, Ctesiphon. Meanwhile, the lone survivor of the Umayyads escaped all the way to Spain, where he established a cultural center at Cordoba that would thrive for at least another three centuries.

Baghdad's location in a very—what was at the time, at least—well-irrigated, fertile farming region was a good location because it's where a lot of important trade routes came together, and this allowed the city to grow rich and to flourish. Baghdad developed into a crucial center of commerce at which goods and ideas from all over the known world arrived, and from which these were then passed on to Europe and to other parts of Asia. The fact that Mohammed himself had been a merchant and had often expressed respect for people who followed that profession—he called them "the couriers of the horizon and God's trusted servants on earth"—and so that made being a merchant a worthy profession in Islam, and so these trade routes spread all throughout Muslim territory.

Crops from all kinds of places—rice, sugar cane, lemons, watermelons, spinach, and cucumbers—were planted in this very agriculturally productive area and became staples of the Muslim diet. Later, the Crusaders who came over to this region would then be exposed to some of these foodstuffs, and they'd take them back to Europe with them from which they'd eventually diffuse throughout the Americas; so the sugarcane plantations in the Caribbean and the orange groves of Brazil have their origins in the Middle East here. Surplus food fueled rapid population growth and urban expansion so that by 900, Baghdad had developed into one of the world's largest cities. Its cosmopolitan nature was enhanced because there were lots of foreign traders there, and they were shown tolerance by the Abassid rulers; so they were allowed to practice their own religions and customs. A large Jewish community arose in Baghdad. Also Persians, many of whom attained high-ranking government posts, continued to have a strong influence in the government there. They developed all kinds of sophisticated economic tools; banks were developed, joint-stock companies, and bills of exchange— or, as they're called in Arabic, "checks"—and these sorts of things further encouraged investment and trade.

In the 8th century, the skill of papermaking was imported from China, and so paper mills were set up in Baghdad; and that also was an important step in the diffusion of ideas. This sudden availability of a nice writing material of paper gave scholarship new energy and it stimulated the publishing of books. The manufacture of paper also meant that copies of the Koran could be more easily produced, helping to spread Islam even further. All sorts of libraries and universities were established in most large Muslim cities, and the university of Al-Azhar in Cairo became so famous that it would serve as a model for some of Europe's later medieval universities.

The Abbasid caliphate would last for several hundred years, and it's often regarded as constituting an Islamic "Golden Age." During this era, and especially at places like Baghdad, knowledge, scholarship, and science were highly prized and were actively encouraged. Islamic scholars would study texts, and one of the things they did was that they preserved the various texts they had that bore the intellectual heritage of earlier civilizations, both Eastern and Western. This included things from Egypt, Persia, as well as Classical Greece and Rome. In fact, it's only because of the preservation of many of these works, such as those of Aristotle, by Arabic scholars that these works survived at all and later were reintroduced into Europe where they'd been lost.

Muslim scholars were especially good at creating a sort of synthesis of ideas; so they'd combine their ideas with knowledge from Ancient Greece, from Persia, and from India. For example, from India, Islamic mathematicians got zero and what's sometimes now erroneously called "Arabic" numerals, while the Ancient Greeks provided them with much knowledge about geometry. Putting together and building upon this fusion of Greek geometry and Indian knowledge of arithmetic, one 9th century Arabic mathematician whose name was Muhammad ibn-Musa al-Khwar-izmi wrote innovative texts on a field that he called *al-jabr*, or "integration." You might recognize that in the modern form of what we call it: algebra.

Science and medicine were also things that were pursued with great zeal. Hospitals were established, medical schools were set up, and pharmacies were set up; and the state required that doctors had to pass medical exams before they could legally practice medicine. By the year 931, Baghdad already had 860 licensed physicians. You can get a sense of their productivity from the work of two famous men. The first was a guy named al-Razi, sometimes called Razes, who's a Persian doctor in charge of the Baghdad hospital, and he wrote 120 books on various medical topics. Among these was a famous one called *On Smallpox and Measles*, and this constituted the very first clear analysis of both the symptoms and the treatments of those diseases. It's also al-Razi who advocated a system of classifying everything into the categories of animal, vegetable, or mineral. The second was another Persian scholar named Ibn Sina, and we know him in the West by his popular name Avicenna. He took the writings of Ancient Greek physicians such as Hippocrates and Galen and, again, combined those texts with the medical knowledge of the Islamic world. The result was a multivolume encyclopedia that was called the *Canon of Medicine*. This was very widely disseminated and eventually it was translated into Latin and became the main medical text used in Europe through the 17th century.

Other scientific fields also flourished. Observatories were built that allowed Muslim astronomers to make detailed observations of the sky, and that honed the accuracy of their calculations of things like the length of the solar year; they were also able to predict eclipses; and in those areas they even went beyond some of the work of the Ancient Greeks. Alchemists worked in Baghdad, seeking to transform base metals into gold or to find a sort of magic elixir that would grant immortality. Of course, they never did either of those two things, but they did establish chemical laboratories, and their experiments led to all sorts of advances including how to conduct evaporation, sublimation, filtration, and crystallization. Around 800, these early chemists discovered distillation and first created a pure form of what was called *al-kuhul*—literally "the essence" in Arabic—or again, in English, what we term "alcohol."

By 800, the Abassid Caliphate governed a population of about 30 million people, and its greatest ruler was probably a man named Harun al-Rashid, whose palace took up one-third of the city of Baghdad. He lived at the same time as the greatest European ruler of that era, Charlemagne, and there was an amicable diplomatic series of exchanges between them. Among the gifts that Harun al-Rashid sent to his Western counterpart was a very finely-crafted, ornate water clock that when it reached Europe was regarded as a technological marvel. These sorts of gifts do reflect the technological sophistication as well as the wealth and the luxury of the Abassid caliphs and of the Islamic world in general in the 9th century A.D.

Even after that first wave of conquests was over, Islam continued to spread, often along trade routes and through merchants; and this was especially true in parts of Africa. We haven't looked at sub-Saharan Africa very much in this course, because the major city-building empires of that region date to later eras; but it's right around the time of these great Islamic conquests that some of the first large, urbanizing kingdoms began to appear in sections of Africa beyond just that narrow corridor along the Nile.

Let's briefly look at what had been happening in some of these regions. Central and southern African cultures had been heavily influenced by a great dispersion of peoples known as the Bantu migration, which seems to have begun around 500 B.C.; and the result was the spread of a bunch of groups who all shared similar cultural and linguistic characteristics. Among these was that they practiced a semi-nomadic lifestyle based around slash-and-burn agriculture, mingled in with a little herding of animals. One common thread among many early African civilizations was that they had a long history of what was really very advanced ironworking, and it extended from this early period all throughout the Middle Ages.

Probably the most notable of the early sub-Saharan African kingdoms was Axum; this arose near the mouth of the Red Sea around the 3rd century B.C. Axum, just by its geographically position, was well-situated to control the sea trade that came from the Mediterranean down through the Red Sea and then off to India and the rest of the East. Axum was also the point from which Mediterranean and Eastern merchants could access the goods of southern Africa, and so there was a very rich trade through this kingdom in things such as ivory, frankincense, and myrrh, as well as slaves. In the early 300s A.D., in a somewhat fascinating coincidence, at exactly the same time when the Roman emperor Constantine was converting to Christianity, the king of Axum also became a Christian. In his case, it was to the Coptic form of Christianity that was practiced in Egypt; and so from that point on, Axum remained predominantly a Christian kingdom.

One of the most impressive physical remains of this culture is a bunch of tall, thin, stone steles—some of these are more than 60 feet tall—and they mark royal tombs. In the 8th century A.D., the Islamic conquests reached down into this region of Africa and those conquests began to push the now declining Axum Empire away from that coastline and the rich trade that went through it. Axum became displaced to the highlands in the interior, where it did continue for a couple more centuries and gave rise to all sorts of legends in Europe of an African Christian ruler called Prester John.

Meanwhile, in West Africa, other kingdoms were just starting to emerge, and the most important of these was Ghana. Ghana was based in the upper Niger River valley in the Sudan, and seems to have begun developing around the late 4th century A.D., but it reached a peak in the 9th century. This political entity, by the way, isn't in the same location as the modern state of Ghana, which is further south. The foundation for the wealth of the ancient kingdom of Ghana was gold. It controlled some of the richest gold mines in all of Africa, and so by 800 A.D., Ghana was a large, powerful kingdom that had begun to build several substantial cities. Gold would be exchanged with the Mediterranean through trade routes and caravans that would go right across the bleak Sahara Desert, and this trade picked up especially after the Islamic conquests. Again, Muslim merchants would go back and forth across the Sahara, transporting loads of gold, ostrich feathers, ivory, and animal hides and taking those to the Mediterranean. Ghana would be followed over the next couple centuries by other powerful mercantile West African kingdoms such as Mali, which ruled over the fabled markets of Timbuktu.

As exemplified by the trans-Saharan trade routes, the Islamic world of the 8th and 9th centuries connected together many disparate cultures and places. Geographically, the Islamic political world stretched from Spain to India, but in terms of its economic and intellectual reach, its influence and its trade routes bound together very tightly the three continents of Europe, Africa, and Asia into a single network that maybe wouldn't be rivaled until much, much more modern times.

Holy Men and Women—Monasticism and Saints

Lecture 46

Christianity dominated almost every aspect of life in medieval Europe. During late antiquity, one of medieval Christianity's most important institutions was formed in the deserts and forests of the Mediterranean: monasticism. In its earliest form, it was an ascetic, individual movement whose practitioners were not unlike the Upanishadic monks of India. Later, under the guidance and rule of Saint Benedict, communal monasticism took on the form that persisted throughout the Middle Ages and is familiar to Christians today.

Saint Jerome—Between Two Worlds

- Before Islam came onto the scene, the late antique Mediterranean world was one in which many religions, cultures, and ethnicities uneasily coexisted and competed with one another. In such a fluid and liminal time, individuals often found themselves slipping back and forth between various worlds.

- One such individual was Jerome, the son of a wealthy Christian family on the northern Roman frontier in the 4th century. He received a thoroughly traditional Roman classical education and was particularly enamored of Cicero but was troubled by whether or not it was possible to be a good Christian while admiring the intellectual achievements of pagans.

- In his late 20s, he had a dream or vision in which Christ appeared before him, and asked, "Who are you?" He answered that he was a Christian, to which Christ declared "You lie! You are a Ciceronian, not a Christian!" This incident prompted a rededication to his religion.

- Jerome spent much of the rest of his life applying the linguistic skills acquired in his classical education to religious writings. He learned Hebrew and Greek and translated the Old and New Testaments of the Bible into Latin. This version, known as the Vulgate, became the standard text used in Europe during the Middle Ages and thus formed the basis of the modern Bible.

The Desert Monks

- By the end of the Middle Ages, hundreds of thousands of men and women all over Europe would be living in monasteries and convents as monks and nuns. Thus, monasticism constitutes not just a religious movement but also one of the largest and most important social and economic developments of the period.

- Although today we think of monasticism as a form of communal living, this is not how the phenomenon began. The original monks were individuals who sought to separate themselves completely from other human beings.

- The story of monasticism starts in late 3rd-century Egypt with a young man named Anthony, another young Christian from a wealthy family. He focused on the passages of the Bible where Christ gives direct instructions to his followers, specifically Matthew 19.21: "Go, sell all that you have, give to the poor … and follow me."

- Anthony took this directive literally, gave away his wealth, donated it to the poor, and wandered out into the fierce Egyptian desert to give himself over to a life of prayer and extreme asceticism. He would ultimately spend 70 years out in the desert, at one point living in complete isolation for 20 years.

- Anthony's deeds proved to be an example that many others would be inspired by and would emulate. In fact, the very extremeness of his actions, especially the sensational way in which he dwelled alone in poverty in the inhospitable desert, ended up making him famous. People started to seek him out to ask his advice or to get his blessing.

- Three times he moved deeper into the desert seeking isolation, but the more extreme his lifestyle grew, however, the more his fame increased. Later followers would take certain elements of his example and intensify them even more.

- Thus was born the ascetic movement, in which monks practiced severe fasting and enduring conditions of excessive heat and cold. The monk in the desert is quite analogous to the Upanishadic forest hermit or the Jain or Buddhist ascetic.

- For some European monks, it was not much of a leap to reason that if the body was a negative thing that distracted you with its desires, then perhaps it should not merely be ignored, but instead actively punished.

- The eastern Mediterranean and Syria had a reputation as the home of some of the most spectacularly dedicated ascetics. Simeon Stylites was determined to escape the crowds of admirers who kept pestering him. He eventually climbed up a 60 foot pillar to live in a basket set atop it for 37 years. His actions inspired a fad of other pillar sitters.

- The monastic movement spread across the Mediterranean. One source notes that, by the early 400s, there were supposedly nearly 20,000 women in Egypt alone pursuing this lifestyle.

Communal Monks and the Rule of Benedict

- As time went on, the authority that these men and women gained by virtue of their dedication to their faith led them to assume important roles in local communities. Some embraced this leadership role and took over some of the traditional functions of the pagan oracles—curing diseases, averting droughts, putting curses on the wicked, bestowing blessings on the devout, and fighting against the forces of evil.

- Tension developed between the monk's desire to live alone and devote himself or herself to spiritual contemplation and the obligations many of them felt to help their local communities. The solution to these contradictory impulses of isolation and service would be found in Italy in the 6th century.

- There lived a man named Benedict who, like Anthony, came from a wealthy Roman family. He wandered off into the remote highlands along Italy's mountainous spine and attracted followers and advice seekers.

- Instead of attempting to flee further into the wilderness, he decided to create a new type of society that was organized around religious principles. At Monte Cassino, which had been the location of a pagan temple, he established a community of monks living and praying together rather than as individuals.

- There had already been some attempts at communal monasteries in the eastern Mediterranean, but Benedict added a document called the Rule of Benedict that laid out the guidelines for how the community would run and how the monks would spend each minute of their lives.

- This would prove to be an incredibly influential document over subsequent centuries. Hundreds of thousands, if not millions, of people would have their lives ordered by Benedict's Rule or similar monastic rules.

- Benedict's monastery was, in a sense, an early attempt at a utopian society. It was conceived as a classless zone—the monks were supposed to all be equals. The one exception was the leader, known as the Abbot. He had sweeping powers to enforce discipline, but he was also accountable to God for his own sins and those of all the monks under his management.

- On a day-to-day basis, monks devoted themselves to manual labor in the fields of the monastery, to contemplation and prayer in their cells, and to communal worship. They engaged in prayer at seven appointed times of the day and night.

- Initiates who wished to join the community had to take a series of vows, including ones of chastity, humility, poverty, and obedience. All private property was forbidden. For clothing, they wore simple robes fastened with a piece of rope.

- Meals were basic, with no more than two cooked dishes and a pound of bread sufficing for the entire day. Red meat was banned, except for the sick or very weak.

- The centerpiece of the Rule is a series of directions called the 12 Degrees of Humility. These include a number of obvious basic injunctions relating to obedience and simplicity of lifestyle and religious practices like confession of their sins to the Abbot.

- The Degrees of Humility go on to discourage not merely speech, but laughter; enforced low self-esteem; and forbidding the exercise of free will. The emphasis is on conformity and obedience. The group mattered more than the individual, and the monks were meant to be anonymous, obedient, unthinking cogs in a smoothly running machine.

- One could make a good argument that, of all the societies that we have studied in this course, the one that was most similar in structure to the monastery was that of ancient Sparta. As monasticism developed, different orders of monks and nuns evolved, each with its own slight variations in practices.

- While monasteries started out as islands of poverty, over time, they began to amass wealth, as well-meaning people donated items or land to their local monastery. Due to the increased wealth, the lifestyle in some monasteries lost a bit of its harsh, ascetic quality.

The Cult of the Saints

- Although monasticism was perhaps the most widespread religious movement of the Middle Ages, another important phenomenon was the cult of the saints. Many martyrs of early Christianity, as well as holy men such as Anthony and Benedict, became elevated to sainthood. They were seen as accessible figures to whom one could pray for assistance or guidance.

- This in turn gave rise to the idea of patron saints, by which certain professions, places, or problems became associated with specific saints who were seen as specialists in solving particular problems.

- An offshoot of the cult of saints was the cult of relics, in which objects connected either with saints or with the life of Christ became the focus of veneration. The most common relics were bones of saints, and soon every church was competing to acquire a finger of Anthony, a rib of Bernard, or a thigh bone of Catherine.

- All of these religious movements and figures vividly testify to the vibrancy and creativity of Christianity during this early formative period. From this point, at least in Europe, Christianity would continue to hold a dominant place in life for the next 1,000 years.

Suggested Reading

Brown, *The Cult of the Saints*.

Dunn, *The Emergence of Monasticism*.

Questions to Consider

1. Which version of monasticism—the solitary life of the desert hermit such as Anthony or the communal existence of Benedict's monks—best embodies the directive of Christ that inspired them?

2. In what ways do you think life as a monk according to the Rule of Benedict and the Spartan social system of training hoplites are similar, and in what ways are they fundamentally different?

Holy Men and Women—Monasticism and Saints
Lecture 46—Transcript

Even before Islam burst onto the scene, the Late Antique Mediterranean world was one in which many different religions, cultures, and ethnicities uneasily coexisted and sometimes even competed with one another. It's not uncommon, for example, for the people of this rather confused era to feel torn between conflicting faiths, cultures, and nationalities. In such a fluid and liminal time, individuals often found themselves slipping back and forth between various worlds. Let me give you a famous example from the sphere of religion.

In the early 4th century, a son was born to a wealthy Christian family on the northern Roman frontier. Despite his religious affiliation, this boy received a very thorough traditional Roman Classical education, and, as it turned out, he quickly displayed an appreciation and a great talent for analyzing the works of Roman pagan authors. Accordingly, he eventually went to Rome itself in order to study rhetoric and Latin literature, and he became especially enamored of the writings of the great Roman statesman and orator, Cicero. But even as his love of this literature grew, so too did his devotion to Christianity, and he's constantly troubled by the question of whether or not it was possible to be a good Christian while admiring the intellectual achievements of pagans. During Lent in 375 A.D., when he's in his late 20s, he had a dream or a vision in which Christ himself appeared before him and asked, "Who are you?" He dutifully answered that he's a Christian, to which Christ sternly declared "You Lie! You are a Ciceronian, not a Christian!" This dream or incident prompted a rededication to his religion, and so the young man swore henceforth never to read any more of his beloved Cicero, but only to read Christian texts.

He then spent much of the rest of his life applying the formal linguistic skills acquired in that Classical education to religious writings. He went on to learn Hebrew and Greek as well as Latin, and he translated the Old and New Testaments of the Bible into Latin. That version of the Bible became known as the Vulgate and eventually became the standard one used in Europe during the Middle Ages, and so it formed the basis of the modern Bible. In both the Western Catholic Church and the Eastern Orthodox Church, he was eventually granted the status of a saint, and so we know him today as Saint Jerome. Appropriately enough, Jerome is regarded as the patron saint of translators, librarians, and writers of encyclopedias. By the way, though, he's unable to keep his promise, and later in his life he did read Classical authors once again.

Jerome was just one of many important church fathers who lived during these centuries and whose actions, ideas, and writings irrevocably shaped the course of Christianity. In this lecture, I want to examine some of these Late Antique and Early Medieval figures more closely and to explore some of the religious phenomena that emerged at this time.

The first of these religious phenomena is the monastic movement. By the end of the Middle Ages, hundreds of thousands of men and women all over Europe would be living in monasteries and convents as monks and nuns, and they'd entirely devoted their lives to serving God and the church by following the strict guidelines of the monastic lifestyle. So monasticism constituted not just a religious movement, but also one of the largest and most important social and economic developments of this entire period.

Today, we tend to think of monasticism as a form of communal living in which monks live together in monasteries; but this isn't at all how the phenomenon began. The word "monk" is derived from a Greek term "monos," which means "to be alone," and the original monks were individuals who sought to separate themselves completely from other human beings. Let's go back to late 3rd century Egypt where the story of monasticism begins, and it starts with a young guy named Anthony. Anthony was a Christian from a wealthy family who took his religion very seriously. In particular, he focused on the relatively few passages in the Bible where Christ gives direct instructions to his followers about what they should do. One of these passages is Matthew 19.21 in which Christ is asked by a wealthy young man, much like Anthony, what he should do to be a good Christian, and Christ replies, "Go, sell all that you have, give to the poor … and follow me." Anthony took this directive literally, so he gave away all of his wealth, he donated it to the poor, and then, dressed in rags, he wandered out into the fierce Egyptian desert to give himself over to a life of prayer. Reasoning that the spiritual world was far more important than the physical one, he'd often starve himself and he practiced a philosophy of denial of the body. He saw the body as a distraction from spiritual contemplation. Ultimately, he'd spend 70 years in the desert; at one point, he lived in total isolation for 20 years.

Anthony's actions were maybe the ultimate form of focusing your life entirely on the next world, and along with that, in many respects rejecting this one. His whole being was devoted to worshipping God, and his actions proved to be an example that many others would be inspired by and would emulate. He became the first monk; literally, the "one who lived alone." After him, others also began to separate themselves from society to live in isolation and to dedicate themselves to the worship of God.

There was a somewhat unforeseen side effect of Anthony's devotion, however. While he's clearly motivated by a personal desire to venerate God, the very extremeness of his actions, especially the rather sensational way in which lived totally alone in total poverty out in the inhospitable desert, all these things ended up making him famous. He acquired a reputation as a holy man, and the result was people began to seek him out. They'd go up to him, they'd ask his advice, they'd ask for his blessing; they'd just seek him out. Ironically, he's so successful at living alone that he became a celebrity and society wouldn't leave him alone. In response to this, three separate times he moved deeper and deeper into the desert seeking isolation. He eventually ended up living in the ruins of an abandoned Roman fort. But the more extreme his lifestyle grew, the more his fame increased; and in the end, he established the precedent not only for a new monastic lifestyle, but also for the public status that such men enjoyed as holy men.

Later followers would pick up on certain elements of his example, and in some cases intensify them even more. One of these aspects was that focus on the denial of the earthly demands of the body as being a distraction from spiritual concerns. Out of this was born the ascetic movement, in which monks would practice severe fasting, they'd subsist on an absolute bare minimum of food, and they'd endure conditions of excessive heat and excessive cold. The monk out in the desert is really a perfect analogy to the Upanishadic forest hermit that we saw in India, or the Jain or the Buddhist ascetic.

For some European monks, it wasn't much of a leap to expand this reasoning and figure that if the body was a negative thing that was always distracting you with all of its desires, then maybe you shouldn't just ignore your body, but actively punish it as well. This led to stereotypes, sometimes accurate, of isolated monks in caves doing things such as flagellating themselves with whips or wearing hair shirts to mortify their own bodies.

These zealots seem to have been especially common in the eastern Mediterranean, and Syria had a reputation as being the home of some of the most spectacularly dedicated ascetics. One example of extreme asceticism was a man named Simeon Stylites, and he decided that even living alone in the desert offered his body too much of a variety of sensory experience. In addition, he was determined to escape from all these crowds of admirers who kept coming and pestering him. First he tried to live in several remote locations, but people kept finding him; so his final solution was to climb up to the top of a 60-foot pillar and to live in a basket set atop it. He ultimately lived on top of that pillar for an incredible 37 years, and his actions then inspired a little bit of a fad of other pillar-sitters who imitated his model.

The monastic movement spread across the Mediterranean, and the whole idea of leaving behind earthly concerns and entirely devoting yourself to the service of God plainly had great appeal. One source tells us that by the early 400s, there were supposedly nearly 20,000 women in Egypt alone pursuing that lifestyle.

As time went on, the authority that these men and women had gained because of their dedication to their faith led them to assume important roles within local communities. Not all holy men and women were so obsessed with completely separating themselves from society, and some of them, while still usually living in some remote mountain or desert region, embraced this new identity as figures to which the common people could look for comfort, for leadership, and for advice. We find some holy men acting as mediators in secular local conflicts, or as sources of advice. In this respect, what they've done is to really take over some of the traditional functions of the pagan oracles such as that at Delphi. Their main purpose in these communities, however, was to summon or represent the powers of the divine in a much more direct and engaged fashion; and so holy men are often depicted as miraculously curing diseases, averting droughts, putting curses on the wicked, giving blessings to those who are devout, and fighting the forces of evil, especially in the form of demons. We can see a rather amusing but revealing echo of this role in a game that's popular among little girls in 4th century Syria that's called "monks and demons," and in this game the girls would pretend to exorcise demons and cast them out from their playmates.

In this early phase of monasticism, a tension developed between the monk's desire to live alone and to devote himself to spiritual contemplation and the obligation that many of them felt to help out their local communities. The solution to these contradictory impulses of isolation versus service would be found in Italy in the 6th century. There, a man named Benedict lived, and his early career was very much like Anthony's. Like Anthony, Benedict came from a wealthy Roman family; like Anthony, Benedict became a fervent Christian; and like Anthony, Benedict fixed on that key passage in Matthew where Christ instructs his followers as to what they should do. Benedict also gave up all of his wealth, gave it to the poor, and, since Italy has no deserts, the next best thing was he wandered off into the remote highlands along Italy's mountainous spine. There, like many holy men of this period, he demonstrated piety and dedication to his faith, and he ended up attracting admiration and people eventually sought him out.

Instead of attempting to maybe escape even further into the wilderness, Benedict now did something innovative. Apparently he decided that if it wasn't possible for people to separate themselves from the rest of society in order to devote themselves to God, maybe he could create a new type of society that's itself organized around religious principles. At a mountaintop site called Monte Cassino, which had formerly been the location of a pagan temple, he established what's often credited as being the first monastery; in other words, a community of monks living and praying together rather than as individuals.

This account is actually a little bit simplified. There'd already been some earlier attempts at communal monasteries; in the eastern Mediterranean there'd been a holy man named Basil who'd set up something very much like this already; but Benedict is usually given the credit because he did one more thing: He wrote a document called the "Rule of Benedict" that laid out the guidelines for how this community of monks would be run, and it regulated nearly every minute of their lives. This would prove to be an incredibly influential document, and over the next couple hundred years, hundreds, if not thousands, if not millions of people would have their lives ordered by Benedict's Rule or similar ones that imitated it.

The Rule of Benedict sought to create a perfect Christian community that would serve as an inspiration for other people. In that way, it's really an early attempt at creating a utopian society. The monastery was conceived of as a classless zone, so all the monks were supposed to be equals; or, in the words of the rule itself, it says: "Let him make no distinction of persons in the monastery. ... Let not one of noble birth be put before him that was formerly a slave." It's basically like a commune where the monks shared tasks and food.

The one exception to this, though, was the leader of the monastery, which was a monk known as the Abbot. On the one hand, the Abbot had sweeping powers to enforce discipline; in fact, he's specifically urged by the Rule to use beatings as a punishment. But on the other hand, he's regarded as being held accountable by God for both his own sins and for those of all the monks under his management.

On a day-to-day basis, monks were supposed to devote themselves to manual labor in the fields, to contemplation and prayer in their individual cells, and to communal worship. To ensure and facilitate this, they're required formally to gather and engage in prayer at seven different appointed times of the day and night. Initiates who wanted to join this community had to take a series of vows, including ones of chastity, humility, poverty, and obedience.

In keeping with the focus on obedience and poverty, all private property was forbidden in the monastery. The Rule states that:

> The vice of private ownership is above all to be cut off
> from the Monastery by the roots. Let none presume ...
> to keep anything as their own, either a book or a writing
> tablet, or a pen, or anything whatsoever. ... Let all things
> be common to all.

For clothing, a monk was supposed to be content with just a simple robe fashioned with a piece of rope. Meals were also supposed to be very basic, with no more than two cooked dishes and a pound of bread sufficing for the entire day. Red meat was banned, except for the sick or the very weak.

The centerpiece of the Rule of Benedict is a series of directions called the Twelve Degrees of Humility, and these further dictated how monks should behave in their daily lives. They include a number of obvious basic injunctions relating to obedience and simplicity of lifestyle. For example, one says "the monk should do nothing except what is authorized by the common rule of the monastery" and, again, "the monk is to be contented with the meanest and worst of everything" Also to be somewhat expected is the Fifth Degree of Humility, which required that monks make confession of their sins to the Abbot.

The Degrees of Humility go on, however, to discourage not just speech, but even laughter; so the rule states: "the ninth degree of humility is that a monk refrain his tongue from speaking, keeping silence until a question be asked of him" and "the tenth degree of humility is that he be not easily moved and prompt to laughter because it is written 'the fool lifteth up his voice in laughter.'" Sometimes modern audiences find these passages difficult to accept as being essential to living a good Christian lifestyle. On the other hand, though, if you think about it, what do people tend to laugh about? If you think about that, at least a large percentage of humor is often derived from the misfortunes of others, which isn't exactly a very Christian attitude.

Another section that conflicts with modern notions of self-esteem is the Seventh Degree of Humility, which reads: "He should not only call himself with his tongue lower and viler than all, but also believe himself in his inmost heart to be so, humbling himself and saying 'I am a worm.'"

Finally, the Rule also seems to forbid monks to exercise free will. It says, "We are, indeed, forbidden to do our own will by Scripture, which saith to us 'Turn away from thine own will.' ... A man should love not his own will, nor delight in fulfilling his own desires."

Throughout the Rule, the emphasis is clearly on conformity and obedience. Unlike modern society, which tends to favor the individual over the group, the early monastery was plainly a place where the group mattered much more than the individual, and so the monks were just meant to be anonymous, obedient, unthinking cogs in a smoothly running religious machine. If we think about the monastery's heavy emphasis on equality, austerity, and obedience, you could make a good argument that of all the different societies that we've studied in this course, the one that's most similar in structure to the monastery was maybe that of Ancient Sparta. Perhaps whenever somebody creates a group that's so singlemindedly dedicated to one goal, whether it's to create the perfect man of violence or the perfect man of peace, you end up emphasizing a lot of these same qualities of conformity and obedience.

As monasticism developed, different orders of monks and nuns evolved, and each had its own slight variations in practice. One big change was that while monasteries started out representing little islands of poverty, over time they began to amass wealth, and this happened quite naturally: Well-meaning people would donate items or often land to their local monastery, and then due to this increased wealth, the lifestyle in some monasteries began to lose a little bit of that harsh, ascetic quality. Take this a couple hundred years down the road, by the 9th or 10th century, we start to get a new stereotype of the monk in which he's a rotund, jovial figure. You can see these shifts very easily by comparing the daily rations that were given to the monks of one monastery around this time, and to contrast that with the austere diet prescribed in the Rule of Benedict. In place of a pound of bread and two simple vegetable dishes, instead we find these later monks enjoying four pounds of bread, a slab of cheese, a pound of meat, a half-pound of vegetables, and a quart and a half of wine, and someone added all that up and that's a diet of about 6,000 calories a day. This was now a very different sort of monasticism from poor Anthony starving out in the desert. As you might expect, that sort of excess eventually prompted a reform movement in monasteries, but that won't occur until several centuries beyond the end of this course.

Although monasticism was maybe the most widespread religious movement of the Middle Ages, another important phenomenon was what's often referred to as the cult of the saints. In this period, many of the martyrs of early Christianity, as well as holy men such as Anthony and Benea became elevated to the status of saints. As such, they gained great popularity because they were seen as accessible figures to whom one could pray for assistance or guidance. This, in turn, gave rise to the idea of patron saints, and with patron saints the idea is that certain professions, places, or problems became associated with specific saints, and so those who belonged to those professions, lived in those places, or suffered from those problems would pray to the appropriate saint, who's seen as a sort of specialist in helping them. A little bit oddly, the way that saints ended up being associated with certain problems often had to do with the ways in which they'd been martyred. For example, Saint Apollonia, who in life was tortured by having her teeth yanked out, became, of course, the patron saint of toothaches and dentists. Saint Laurence was martyred by being burnt alive, so can you guess what profession he became the patron saint of? The answer's a little bit gruesome, but he became the patron saint of cooks.

An offshoot of the cult of saints was the cult of relics, in which objects that were connected either with the saints or sometimes with the life of Christ became the focus of veneration; and the most common form that these relics took was the actual bones of the saints. Soon, churches were competing to acquire a finger of Anthony, or a rib of Bernard, or maybe a thigh bone of Catherine; and the churches of Constantinople, for example, eventually amassed a collection of no fewer than 3,600 bone fragments, representing 476 different saints.

All of these religious movements and figures I think vividly testify to the creativity of Christianity during this early formative period; and from this point, at least in Europe, Christianity would continue to hold an absolutely dominant place in life for about the next 1,000 years.

Charlemagne—Father of Europe
Lecture 47

The first great European empire to arise after the fall of Rome in the West was the empire of the Frankish king Charlemagne. Charlemagne was truly a larger-than-life personality whose many accomplishments included military conquests, excellent diplomatic relations with the Roman Catholic Church and the caliphs of Baghdad, and sponsoring an intellectual and artistic renaissance. His kingdom, like that of many great rulers we have studied, did not long outlast his reign, but in many ways he truly built the foundations of the Middle Ages.

Building an Empire, Step by Step

- In Europe by about 750 A.D., the wave of Islamic conquest had been stopped. Europe now consisted of dozens of smallish kingdoms ruled over by various barbarian peoples. One of these nations was a group known as the Franks, from whom the modern country of France got its name.

- It would prove to be the Franks who would give rise to the first great empire of the Middle Ages. The Franks had a series of strong kings who aided their rise. Among these, the most important dynasty was the Carolingians. The pivotal figure was a man named Charles the Great—in Latin, Carolus Magnus, known today as Charlemagne.

- Charlemagne was an effective warlord, and he expanded the borders of the Frankish Empire. He did not suddenly annex huge territories through enormous, set-piece battles. Instead, he practiced incremental warfare. He set a limited goal for each campaign, acquired only the targeted area, and consolidated it into his kingdom.

- He took the field nearly every year, year after year, and he tended to keep what he had conquered. It has been estimated that, over the course of his lifetime, Charlemagne personally led no fewer than 54 distinct military campaigns.

- By the time of his death, Charlemagne's kingdom encompassed most of the modern countries of France, Germany, Belgium, and significant portions of Italy, the largest empire seen in Europe for the next 900 years.

- These campaigns typically employed around 8,000 soldiers. Compare this to some of the epic battles of ancient Rome, India, and China, which could number up to 100,000 troops per side. This reflects a general trend, as we move from the classical era to the Middle Ages, of everything being on a reduced scale.

- While perhaps not as flashy as someone like Alexander the Great, Charlemagne was an extremely competent general who won victory after victory. Given his overall record, it is a bit unfair that the most famous battle associated with him was a defeat.

- In 778, he led an army into Spain at the invitation of one Arabic leader to fight against another. The expedition proved unsuccessful, but as his army was retreating across the Pyrenees, the rearguard protecting the baggage train was ambushed by local Basque tribes and massacred.

- In military terms, this was an insignificant if unfortunate incident, but it has attained fame all out of proportion to its importance because it became the subject matter for one of the first great works of medieval literature, *The Song of Roland*.

From Classical to Medieval Europe

- The warfare of the Carolingian era can be regarded as marking the rise to dominance of the heavily armed and armored horseman over infantry. This is a trend that would culminate later in the Middle Ages in the figure of the knight, completely encased in plate armor.

- Charlemagne's administration prefigured elements of feudalism. The basic government system was a hereditary monarchy, with the king, at least in the abstract, wielding total power. In practice, his empire consisted of 300 administrative districts. Each was ruled by a count.

- Each count was like a miniature king responsible for ruling the territory and collecting taxes. The counts were obligated to provide the king with troops. In certain frontier regions, Charlemagne established districts called marches, which served as buffer zones.

- Charlemagne seems to have been successful, on the whole, at keeping his counts loyal. To bolster this loyalty, he had a system of personal envoys who circulated around his empire. They kept an eye on the counts, and the counts could use them to relay their concerns back to Charlemagne. These envoys were known as *missi dominici*, or literally, "messengers of the lord king."

- Charlemagne appears to have been a devout Christian, and he was careful to cultivate a good relationship with the pope and the religious establishment. He both constructed and restored a number of churches and other ecclesiastical buildings, and he encouraged his subjects to tithe a part of their income to the Church.

- When the Pope became entangled in an internal dispute at Rome, Charlemagne actively supported him. The payback for these actions came on Christmas Day, 800, when Pope Leo III personally crowned Charlemagne and bestowed upon him the title "Charles Augustus, Emperor of the Romans."

- In this act, the three strands of Roman history came together to form the early medieval world: A Christian pope crowned a barbarian king and gave him a Roman title. It is also a measure of how powerful a grasp the image of the Roman Empire retained on the European political landscape.

- From this point on, Charlemagne was indisputably the greatest leader in Western Europe, and other kings sent representatives and offerings to acknowledge his status. So eminent had Charlemagne become that even the caliph of Baghdad, who was a much more powerful ruler, sent gifts to Charlemagne.

The Carolingian Renaissance

- Charlemagne was a generous and enthusiastic patron of the arts. This period is sometimes termed "the Carolingian Renaissance." The focal point of his labors was the capital he established for his empire in the city of Aachen, today located in Germany.

- Charlemagne liked to refer to Aachen as the New Rome. The city was an old Roman one that had been laid out on a grid pattern derived from Roman legionary camps.

- Charlemagne's architect, a man named Odo of Metz, retained this basic layout and constructed a number of buildings within it. Of these, the only one that survives today was Charlemagne's chapel, known as the Palatine Chapel.

- At the other end of the palace from the chapel was the great council hall, which was modeled after a Roman basilica. Nearby was another reminder of the Roman past: an old Roman bath complex renovated for Charlemagne's use.

- Fueling the Carolingian Renaissance were the intellectuals whom Charlemagne invited to reside in Aachen from all over Europe. Charlemagne also promoted education, and he established a number of schools, mostly limited to clergy.

- Thousands of manuscripts were meticulously inked by hand by Carolingian monks and scribes. A large portion of extant Greek and Latin classical texts only survive because the perishable originals were copied by Carolingian monks during this era.

- Above all, they produced copies of the Bible and other writings important to Christianity. These manuscripts were not only intellectual treasures, but they soon developed into works of art as well. The monks drew pictures and decorations in the margins. Such adorned texts are called illuminated manuscripts, and over 8,000 of these survive from Carolingian monks.

- The copyists of Charlemagne's time wrote on parchment, made from sheepskin, as they did not know about paper and the Muslim conquest of Egypt had cut off the supply of papyrus. To produce a single copy of the Bible in the largish size that was common at the time took somewhere between 300 and 400 sheep.

Charlemagne the Person

- Later monarchs, especially in France and Germany, would look back to Charlemagne as a model of the ideal king, in the way that the later Roman emperors were always comparing themselves to and emulating Augustus.

- One of the main sources for Charlemagne's life is a biography written about him by a man named Einhard. Einhard was a courtier at Aachen, and he knew Charlemagne personally.

- Einhard's biography is quite hagiographic in tone, and he is obviously giving us an idealized version. Recent scholarship has challenged the veracity of portions of this text, but nevertheless, it provides some intriguing details.

- One thing that may have contributed to Charlemagne's succ[ess as] a leader was his physical appearance. At 6'3", a height that w[as] supposedly confirmed by an examination of his bones, he looked like a king, exuding dignity and eliciting respect.

- In addition to swimming and warfare, he delighted in horseback riding and hunting, both of which the Franks were expert in. Once again, we find this link between hunting and royalty that we first saw among the Assyrians.

- He seemingly took pride in his Frankish heritage, since he was known to wear the native Frankish costume, consisting of a linen shirt and pants, a bordered tunic, leggings, and an otter-skin vest, and carried a sword at all times.

- While he plainly projected a tough, manly image, especially among the Franks, he also embraced learning and intellectual pursuits, not just as a patron but also as a practitioner. He was a skilled public speaker, made an effort to learn foreign languages, and even acquired some understanding of Greek and Latin. He enjoyed befriending foreigners, whom he entertained lavishly at his court. Thus, although he was proud to be a Frank, he also cultivated a cosmopolitan, worldly atmosphere around him.

- Charlemagne's great European empire did not persist for long after his own lifetime. It seems to have been his personal charisma and abilities that held it together.

Suggested Reading

Barbero, *Charlemagne*.

Riché, *Daily Life in the World of Charlemagne*.

Story, ed., *Charlemagne*.

1. How would you assess and compare the methods used by Charlemagne as an empire builder to those of Philip of Macedon and Chandragupta?

2. How did various aspects of Charlemagne's personality contribute to his success as a king?

Charlemagne—Father of Europe
Lecture 47—Transcript

In Europe by about 750 A.D., the wave of Islamic conquest had peaked and then been stopped in the West roughly along the border between modern Spain and France, and in the East at the formidable defenses of the Byzantine Empire. Politically, Europe now consisted of dozens of smallish kingdoms ruled over by various barbarian peoples. One of these nations was a group known as the Franks, from whom the modern country of France got its name. During the 4th century, they had settled in what would eventually become France and, at least at that point, there was very little to differentiate them from dozens of similar northern barbarian groups, other than that perhaps the Franks had a predilection for fighting with axes and they seemed to like to wear striped clothing. In the 5th century, one of their kings, Clovis, had converted to Christianity, and he had managed to unite all the various tribes of the Franks under his leadership. Out of the multitude of barbarian kingdoms and clans milling around Europe, it would eventually prove to be these Franks who would give rise to the first great empire of the Middle Ages.

The Franks had a series of strong kings who aided their rise, and among these, the most important dynasty was named the Carolingians. Of those kings, the pivotal figure was a man named Charles the Great, or, in Latin, Carolus Magnus. He is, of course, most familiarly known today as Charlemagne, which is a corruption of the Latin form of his name. There have been many rulers who have gotten that epithet of "the Great" stuck onto their names, and they haven't always deserved it; but Charlemagne did a number of important things that I think fully justify its use in his case. Let's look at his actions in four key areas: war, politics, religion, and culture.

First of all, Charlemagne was an effective warlord; he expanded the borders of the Frankish Empire. Nearly every single year of his very long reign, he would lead his troops out and push those frontiers a bit further. Unlike many of the great empire-builders that we've studied so far, such as Alexander or Chandragupta, Charlemagne didn't suddenly annex huge territories through enormous, set-piece battles. Instead, he practiced a kind of incremental warfare in which he'd identify a relatively limited goal for each campaign and then he'd focus on acquiring just the targeted area and consolidate it firmly into his kingdom. Rather than an empire built up by a small number of big, dramatic victories, each of which resulted in huge territorial gains, Charlemagne's strategy was one of doggedly nibbling away little bits of his neighbors' lands.

What made this especially effective was that he took the field nearly every year, year after year after year, and he tended to keep what he'd conquered. It's been estimated that over the course of his lifetime, Charlemagne personally led no fewer than 54 distinct military campaigns. Through this methodology of gradual persistence, all those little gains in the end added up to a huge empire. By the time of his death, his kingdom encompassed most of the modern countries of France, Germany, Belgium, and a good piece of Italy as well. It would, in fact, be the largest empire seen in Europe for the next 900 years. No European ruler would control more territory until Napoleon came along in the early 19th century.

One significant difference between the sort of warfare practiced by Charlemagne and many of the other conquerors that we've studied is that these campaigns typically employed very small armies. On his various military expeditions, the standard size of the Carolingian army seems to have only been about 8,000 men; and just think back to some of the epic battles of ancient Rome, India, and China where you had forces of up to 100,000 troops per side. To some extent, this disparity in numbers just reflects a general trend: As we move from the Classical Era to the Middle Ages in Europe, everything has become on a reduced scale. For example, whereas Ancient Rome reached a population of around a million inhabitants, during the Middle Ages, it's doubtful that any European city ever got much larger than about 50,000 people.

While maybe not as overtly flashy as someone like Alexander, Charlemagne was obviously a very competent general who won victory after victory in his never-ending sequence of small but often hard-fought campaigns. Given his overall record of achievements, it's maybe a little bit unfair that the most famous battle that's associated with him was actually a defeat. In 778, he had led an army into Spain at the invitation of one Arabic leader to fight against another, and that expedition ultimately proved unsuccessful;

but as Charlemagne and his army were retreating back across the Pyr. Mountains, the rear guard of his army, protecting the baggage train, w ambushed by some local Basque tribes and they were massacred.

In military terms, this was an insignificant if unfortunate incident; but it's attained fame all out of proportion to its importance because this little incident became the subject matter for one of the first great works of medieval literature, and that's an epic poem called "The Song of Roland." This tale wasn't actually composed until the 11th century, and it gives a very romanticized version of the heroic but doomed defense offered by the commander of this rear guard, Count Roland. In the poem, the Basques are transformed into Muslims. However inaccurate that poem may be as military history, it does nicely encapsulate important medieval values, such as the extreme loyalty displayed by Roland to his king. The warfare of the Carolingian Era can also conveniently be regarded as marking the rise to dominance of the heavily armed and armored horseman over infantry. That's a trend that would culminate later in the Middle Ages in the figure of the medieval knight, completely encased in plate armor.

If we turn to Charlemagne in the realm of politics, just as his cavalry-dominated army was a precursor of later things to come, so, too, the administration that Charlemagne established to run his empire prefigured elements of medieval feudalism. The basic government system, of course, was a hereditary monarchy, with the king, at least in the abstract, having total power.

In practice, what Charlemagne did was to divide up his empire into roughly 300 administrative districts. Each of those was placed under the control of a lord; in Charlemagne's system, he was termed a count. Within their respective territories, each count was like a miniature king responsible for ruling the territory and collecting taxes. When summoned by Charlemagne, the counts were obligated to provide the king with soldiers to make up his army. In certain frontier regions that were unstable or being threatened, he set up districts called marches that served as buffer zones. The counts were bound to the king by ties of personal loyalty. As you can probably guess, a recurrent problem throughout the Middle Ages would be counts and lords either trying to break away from their own king, or sometimes setting themselves up as rivals to him.

Charlemagne, though, seems to have been quite successful on the whole at keeping his counts loyal. One strategy that he developed to aid that process was he set up a system of personal envoys who circulated around his empire. They functioned both to help the king keep an eye on what was happening in the various districts and as a way for the local rulers to relay their concerns back to Charlemagne. These envoys were known as *missi dominici*, or literally, "messengers of the lord king," and they always traveled in pairs consisting of one secular noble and one member of the Church.

A third significant area in which Charlemagne's actions deeds reaped him benefits concerned religion. Charlemagne himself appears to have been a devout Christian, and he was always careful to cultivate a good relationship with the Pope and with the religious establishment. For example, at his own expense, he constructed and restored a large number of churches and other ecclesiastical buildings, and he encouraged his own subjects to tithe a part of their income to the Church. At one point, when the Pope became entangled in this internal dispute at Rome, Charlemagne took a public stance supporting him.

The payback for all of these actions came at a specific moment, and that moment was Christmas Day of the year 800. On that day, in Saint Peter's Basilica in Rome, Pope Leo III personally placed a crown on Charlemagne's head and bestowed upon him the title "Charles Augustus, Emperor of the Romans." In its symbolism, this little moment wonderfully captures the three main strands that had all come together to form the early medieval world, because what we basically have is a Christian pope crowning a barbarian king and giving him a Roman title. It represents how Christianity was the dominant religion in Europe, and that the former barbarians had become the established political powers, but also the most impressive title that they all coveted was still derived from the now long-dead Roman Empire. Beginning in the next century, it became traditional to assign a variant of that title to one of the kings of Europe, and this appellation was "Holy Roman Emperor." It's a measure of how powerful a grasp the image of the Roman Empire retained on the European political landscape that for the next 900 years, kings would scramble to be identified with the ancient Romans via that title. Just as no empire equaled Charlemagne's in size until Napoleon's, so too Napoleon would be the one to finally get rid of that long-standing title.

This very public endorsement of Charlemagne by Pope Leo ensured Charlemagne's legitimacy and it really helped to cement his identity as the preeminent king in all of Europe. From that point on, Charlemagne was indisputably the greatest leader in Western Europe, and other kings sent representatives and offerings to him to acknowledge his status. So eminent had Charlemagne become that even the Caliph of Baghdad, who actually was a much more powerful ruler, sent gifts to Charlemagne. Among those gifts was a pet elephant that was reportedly called Abul Abaz. Incidentally, the name of that elephant has provoked an odd degree of contention among scholars who can't seem to agree on what the actual meaning of his name was. The whole thing is complicated by the fact that the recorded name is obviously some sort of mishmash or a corruption of a number of Arabic words. But the three most commonly proposed translations for his name are: First, the rather unimaginatively literal "the elephant of the Abassids"; second, the intriguing moniker "the father of intelligence"; and finally, my personal favorite, a name that you could translate roughly as "Mr. Wrinkles." Charlemagne apparently was quite pleased with his pet elephant; he seems to have enjoyed keeping it close to him, because we know that the elephant died while accompanying the king on one of his military campaigns.

Finally, the fourth area in which Charlemagne made his mark was culture. Charlemagne was a generous and enthusiastic patron of the arts; and the result of all these efforts was that his time is sometimes termed "the Carolingian Renaissance," meaning that there's a distinct flourishing of the arts, culture, and learning. The focal point of all of this was the capital city that he established for his empire. This capital was the city of Aachen, which today is located in Germany. Charlemagne and the artists and architects of the Carolingian Renaissance were very much influenced by, again, the model of Ancient Rome; indeed, Charlemagne himself liked to refer to Aachen as the "New Rome." This admiration for Classical Rome can be seen in the palace that he built at Aachen. The city of Aachen, by the way, was an old Roman one that had been laid out on a grid pattern that was derived from Roman legionary camps.

Charlemagne's main architect was a guy named Odo of Metz, and he retained that basic grid layout from the old Roman city and he constructed a number of buildings within it matching those avenues. Of these, one of the most impressive—and, in fact, the only one that survives until today—was Charlemagne's chapel, which was called the Palatine Chapel. It was a fairly complicated structure, but at its center was a large, domed, octagonal space that was 50 feet wide and 100 feet high; and it was there that Charlemagne placed his throne. The chapel was richly adorned with decorative marbles; it was equipped with gold and silver lamps and vessels, and other things. At the other end of the palace from the chapel was the great council hall, and that structure was modeled after a Roman basilica. That building was 150 feet long and basically consisted of one big, open hall; and this was where Charlemagne would hold official ceremonies such as receiving ambassadors from other countries. It was also the location where he gave an annual speech or address to his subjects.

Nearby was another reminder of the old Roman past: There was a Roman bath complex in the city, fed by natural hot springs; and it was renovated for Charlemagne's use. A little bit unusually for the early Middle Ages here, Charlemagne was an enthusiastic swimmer; and so we know he took great pleasure in swimming around these baths. One source tells us that Charlemagne had the habit of inviting whoever was present to jump in and join him, and these might include family members, noblemen, but sometimes even his own bodyguards; and sometimes upwards of 100 people would end up cavorting in the waters with the king.

Fueling the Carolingian Renaissance were the intellectuals that Charlemagne encouraged and actively invited to come live at Aachen. These men came from all over Europe, and they included a number of the leading Christian thinkers of the day. Charlemagne was also very concerned with promoting education, and so he established a number of schools. Education at this point in time was mostly limited to clergy, to members of the church, and so the same was true of these educational institutions. One aspect of the Carolingian Renaissance that can be seen today in tangible form is the thousands of manuscripts that were meticulously inked by hand by Carolingian monks and scribes. A large portion of extant Greek and Latin Classical texts only survive because the perishable originals were copied by Carolingian monks during this era. Charlemagne played an important role in preserving the legacy of antiquity for the future.

The copyists of Charlemagne's time, though, faced a problem when it came to a material to write upon; so paper, as we've seen, was known in China and the Middle East, but that technology hadn't made it to Europe. In the ancient Mediterranean world, people had written on papyrus scrolls. Papyrus is a paper-like substance that's made from an Egyptian plant. The problem was, now the Muslims had conquered Egypt, and in so doing they cut off the supply of this very useful material to Europe. The monks, therefore, had to find something else to write on, and what they eventually settled upon were treated sheets of sheepskin known as parchment. Monks would spend hours laboriously making copies of texts of all kinds, but above all, they focused on producing copies of the Bible and other writings important to Christianity. These manuscripts weren't just intellectual treasures, but they soon developed into works of art; and this was because the monks would write in beautiful, ornate letters—which we now call calligraphy—and they would also draw little pictures or decorations in the margins of the text. When you have a text with those sorts of decorations, it's called an illuminated manuscript; and over 8,000 of them survive that were made by the hands of Carolingian monks. As you might imagine, the finer examples of these manuscripts were very valuable objects; not just because of all the hours of skilled labor that went into them, but because the raw materials themselves were quite expensive.

Here's a little bit of trivia: How many sheep do you think is required to produce one copy of the Bible in the large size that's common at the time? The answer is somewhere between 300 and 400, and a flock of sheep that big would've represented quite a bit of wealth in that era.

Charlemagne is an interesting character, and he's somebody who exerted an important influence on all of subsequent European history. Later kings, especially in France and Germany, would look back to him as a model of the ideal king, somewhat in the way that later Roman emperors were always comparing themselves to Augustus, the first emperor.

One of the main sources for Charlemagne's life is a biography that was written about him by a man named Einhard. Einhard was a courtier at Aachen, and he knew Charlemagne personally; so his biography gives the hope of gaining firsthand insight into the personality of this important historical figure. I should note, though, that Einhard's biography is very hagiographic in tone. He refers to Charlemagne as "the noblest king—the greatest of all his age," and he's obviously giving us a little bit of an idealized version of Charlemagne. Some recent scholarship has challenged the veracity of various portions of Einhard's text, but nevertheless it gives us some intriguing details about Charlemagne the man that we can use to flesh out the portrait of Charlemagne the King.

One thing that might have contributed to Charlemagne's success as a leader was simply his physical appearance. At 6'3" high, and that's a height that was confirmed by an examination of what are allegedly his bones, he looked like a king; he was big and imposing, so he exuded dignity and elicited respect. Late in life, his hair turned white and his coins will show him without a beard but with a little curled mustache on his upper lip. In addition to swimming and warfare, we know that he delighted in horseback riding and hunting, both of which are things that the Franks generally were expert in. Once again, we see this same link that we've seen a number of times in this course between hunting and royalty; we first saw that among the Assyrians.

In keeping with the idea that a good king must be a good warrior and that the appropriate way to learn and demonstrate martial skills is by hunting, Einhard notes that Charlemagne spent a lot of his free time riding and hunting. To ensure that the next generation of Carolingian rulers would share these qualities, as soon as his sons were old enough, Charlemagne insisted that they, too, practice horseback riding and hunting.

Charlemagne seems to have taken a lot of pride in his Frankish heritage. We know, for example, that he wore the native Frankish costume that consisted of a linen shirt and pants. He had a bordered tunic, these leggings, and an otter-skin vest, and he carried his sword with him at all times. He evidently disliked both foreign clothing and clothing that was too fancy, and he'd only dress up in his finery to please popes or on formal occasions; but most of the time, he was said to dress just like one of his subjects. Einhard also claims that he ate and drank in moderation; and his doctors urged him for the ˌ of his health to give up roasted meat, which was his favorite food, and hˌ couldn't quite bear to do that, so he ended up ignoring their advice.

While he plainly projected a tough, manly image, especially among the Franks, he also embraced learning and intellectual pursuits, not just as a patron of the arts but also as a practitioner. He was a skilled public speaker, always a useful skill for a leader. He made an effort to learn foreign languages, even though he may not have been always successful at that. He even seems to have acquired some understanding of Greek and Latin. He clearly admired teachers of the liberal arts; he'd go to their lectures, and he liked to listen to history being read aloud as he ate his dinner. And even though he might avoid dressing like foreigners, he enjoyed befriending foreigners, and he'd entertain them lavishly at his court; so although he was proud to be a Frank, he also was careful to cultivate a cosmopolitan, worldly atmosphere around him.

As we've seen many times with previous kingdoms, Charlemagne's great European empire didn't last long after his own lifetime; and, once again, it really seems to have been just his personal charisma and his personal abilities that held that empire together. Upon his death in 814, his son, who was called Louis the Pious, inherited his empire. But he turned out to be a pretty weak ruler, and when he died about 30 years later, the once-mighty kingdom was chopped up among his three sons in a document that was known as the Treaty of Verdun. By the way, that document was written in three different languages, and those were early versions of Italian, French, and German; so we can already see that the modern linguistic divisions of Europe were beginning to take shape or form at this particular point in history.

In more ways than just linguistically, and in more places than just Europe, the 9th century represents a pivotal moment in the formation of the modern world, and that's a topic that we'll consider in the next, and final, lecture of this course.

Endings, Beginnings, What Does It All Mean?
Lecture 48

In the West, we have followed the history of global civilizations through the Islamic conquests and the first true European empire as represented by Charlemagne. In the East, we have traced developments through the Tang dynasty of China. So why does this course end here, and how does the ancient world help us understand the world we live in today? Simply put, the 9th century was the moment of transition, when the world was set on the course to become our modern world. Yet many of the ancient developments we have examined are still with us today.

The Historian's Crystal Ball

- If you were a historian living sometime in the 9th century A.D., which states do you think would seem likely to emerge as dominant powers in the future?

  o In India, you would see numerous squabbling dynasties, none of which could gain a foothold over the other.

  o In North and South America, you would find many culturally complex societies limited by a Stone Age level of technology.

  o In Africa, large kingdoms were only starting to emerge.

  o Looking at Europe, you would probably be impressed by the substantial empire momentarily created by Charlemagne, but Europe was also sliding into the long era of technological and economic stagnation.

  o The Byzantine Empire recalled the past accomplishments of the Roman empire, but it was clearly a civilization on the decline.

- o Tang China would have appeared a geographically enormous yet culturally united empire of seemingly unlimited potential.

- o The intellectual glories of Baghdad would have clearly placed that city at the vanguard of scientific and technological advancements and unstoppable military forces.

- We tend to look at history through the lens of hindsight and to see its course as inevitable, but to someone able to survey the 9th century world without knowing what came next, surely he or she would assumed that only China or the Muslim Near East could become a dominant global power.

Europe's Unlikely Hegemony—The Pirenne Thesis

- As we know, the territory that actually achieved this was Europe. As late as the early 1400s, China continued to hold the inside track. Enterprising Chinese admirals began voyages of exploration well before European navigators.

- All this changed when the ill-advised isolationist policies of the Hongxi emperor in the mid-1400s abruptly put a stop to these expeditions and turned the focus of China inwards, with disastrous effects.

- Similarly, the lead gained during the great era of intellectual and scientific flourishing of classical Islamic civilization in Baghdad was frittered away when the Islamic world lost its unity through infighting among rival political powers.

- One view of how Europe became a distinct region in its own right and how it freed itself from its long subordination to the cultures of the Mediterranean was the theory of a brilliant Belgian historian of the early 20th century named Henri Pirenne.

- Pirenne was a prominent historian who was writing a multivolume history of his country when World War I intervened and he was incarcerated by the Germans. During his incarceration, he devised the Pirenne thesis, later published in a book called *Mohammed and Charlemagne*.

- Before Pirenne, most historians had used the supposed fall of Rome to Germanic barbarians in 476 as the dividing line between antiquity and the Middle Ages. The Pirenne thesis proposed that the real moment of rupture occurred when the Arabic conquests split the Mediterranean into two halves—a northern Christian one and a southern Islamic one.

- Pirenne's thesis was actually based less on religion than on economics. He argued that the Islamic conquests effectively cut off the north-south and east-west trade that up until then had linked together all the shores of the Mediterranean.

- The takeover of the Western Roman Empire by barbarian kingdoms was not as important as had been assumed, according to Pirenne, because the barbarian tribes simply adopted and imitated most aspects of Roman culture and did not disrupt trade across the Mediterranean.

- The really clever part of Pirenne's thesis, however, was the way in which it explained subsequent European history. Throughout antiquity, the most important developments had all happened around the shores of the Mediterranean. The Arabic conquests broke the unity of the Mediterranean and in so doing shattered the coastal regions' domination over the hinterlands.

- Those once-subordinate regions were free to develop themselves. So it was that the Franks, a thoroughly Europe-based and inland empire, could only rise to power once Europe was no longer held in thrall to the Mediterranean-based Roman Empire.

Does Pirenne's Thesis Hold Up?

- Consider the location of the region's great cities before the Arabic conquests: Constantinople, Alexandria, Rome, Carthage, Antioch, and Alexandria—all coastal. The capital cities of the first empires that arose after 700—Baghdad and Aachen—are hundreds of miles from the coast of the Mediterranean, and both empires were oriented inland. The situation is similar for London, Paris, Florence, Madrid, Damascus, and Cairo.

- The Islamic conquests separated what used to be one world into three separate worlds—Europe, Africa, and the Middle East—situated on three different continents. Each of these new worlds now turned their backs on the Mediterranean Sea.

- The six-word formulation of Pirenne's thesis is "Without Mohammed, Charlemagne would have been inconceivable." Pirenne is suggesting that, if Mohammed had never come along and sparked the Arabic conquests, then Europe would have remained merely an adjunct to the Mediterranean.

- Pirenne's thesis was immediately influential and also immediately controversial. The part of his thesis that has fared most poorly is probably his contention that the Islamic conquests killed most of the trade in the Mediterranean in the 9th century. More recent scholarship has shown that while Europe was indeed cut off from some goods, but there was still much that was being bought and sold across this boundary.

- What remains a powerful and compelling argument is his underlying assertion regarding the shattering of the unity of the Mediterranean and the subsequent individual reorientation of Europe, Africa, and the Near East inwards on themselves.

- The cultural, linguistic, and religious boundaries that shape the world we live in were laid down at this key moment. The modern borders between the countries around the Mediterranean that are Christian, versus those that are Muslim, are almost exactly those established in the 8th century

- The same goes for those countries that speak Arabic, as opposed to one of the Romance or Germanic languages. Only one country that was part of the initial Arabic conquests is not an Arabic-speaking, Muslim country today—Spain, which in 1492, after 800 years of occupation, expelled the Moors. But Spain is really the exception that proves the rule.

- Today, Charlemagne is widely hailed as the founder of Europe as a discrete entity. But if Pirenne was right, then perhaps it would be more correct to say that the real father of Europe was not Charlemagne but Mohammed.

- Most courses on the ancient world tend to end with the supposed fall of the Roman Empire. By extending this course into the 9th century and the formation of Charlemagne's empire, we can fully perceive not only the true end of the ancient world, but also the crucial formation and birth of the modern one, with the major national, linguistic, cultural, and religious boundaries that we see around us today already established.

- The focus on the formation of Europe is not meant as an endorsement of a Eurocentric view; it is simply an acknowledgement of the global impact that the era of European colonization in the 16th and 17th centuries would exert on the history of the entire world. Whether you view that influence as positive or negative, there is no denying that it happened.

- Ending the course in the 9th century allows us to see how all the main areas of the world initially developed and, in most cases, evolved the distinctive culture or cultures that still characterize those regions today. We are able to directly connect that world with the modern one, but that world still constitutes a distinctly different one from our own.

- The ancient world is still alive and around us in everything that we do and in everything that we are. The influence of the ancient world is present in our modern customs, religions, laws, art, architecture, games, calendars, superstitions, education, clothing, buildings, foods, jobs, holidays, entertainments, governments, and beliefs.

- If you want to understand who you are, and why you do the things you do, in the way that you do them, you have to know about the ancient origins of the beliefs, institutions, and cultures that shape your life.

Suggested Reading

Havighurst, ed., *The Pirenne Thesis*.

Hodges and Whitehouse, *Mohammed, Charlemagne and the Origins of Europe*.

Marcus and Sabloff, eds., *The Ancient City*.

Questions to Consider

1. Do you agree or disagree with the Pirenne thesis and why?

2. In what ways has this course on ancient history given you a better understanding of the world we live in today?

Endings, Beginnings, What Does It All Mean?
Lecture 48—Transcript

We've now reached the end point of this course. In the West, we've followed the history of global civilization up through the Islamic conquests and the first true European empire as represented by Charlemagne; in the East, we've traced developments up through the Golden Age of the Tang Dynasty of China. In this, the final lecture of the course, I want to address two questions. First of all, why does this course end here? Why end in the 9th century A.D., with Charlemagne and the Tang? Second, how does what we've learned about the ancient world help us to understand the world we live in today? I think the answers to those two questions are actually interrelated, so that in investigating one, we'll make sense of the other.

Let's begin, though, by considering what the world looked like at the point we're leaving it, sometime around the 9th century A.D. If you were a historian surveying the world at this point, which states do you think would seem most likely to emerge as the dominant powers in the future? If you looked at India, you'd see a number of different dynasties ruling over various-sized kingdoms and constantly squabbling with one another. In cultural and intellectual terms, India was often at the forefront, but the region's influence on the world beyond the Himalayas was limited by India's lack of political unity. No one faction could ever establish itself as the dominant one and then fuse the country into one unit, as had happened in China.

If you turned to North and South America around the 9th century, again you'd find many culturally complex societies and even a couple of large empires, such as that of the Maya. But the fatal flaw here was that all of those cultures were locked into what was, in many respects, a Stone Age level of technology.

In Africa, you'd see some large kingdoms, such as Ghana, which were just starting to emerge; and others would follow in the next couple of centuries. But these still would have a long way to go to equal the technology, wealth, and size of their rivals in other parts of the globe.

Looking at Europe, you'd probably be impressed by the substantial empire momentarily created by Charlemagne, but Europe was also beginning its slide into the long era of technological and economic stagnation that we call the Middle Ages. On Europe's easternmost edge, the Byzantine Empire recalled the past accomplishments of the Roman Empire, but it's clearly a civilization on the decline rather than one on the rise.

If you were to look around at all the different civilizations of the world in the 9th century, surely the two that would stand out far above the others as being the largest, most powerful, the most technologically advanced, among the most culturally sophisticated, and the most economically thriving would be those of Tang China and the Abbasid Caliphate. To an observer of the time, Tang China would've appeared a geographically enormous yet culturally united empire of seemingly unlimited potential, while the intellectual glories of Baghdad would clearly have placed that city at the very vanguard of scientific and technological advancements; and the rapid Arab conquests of the preceding centuries would've made the armies of the caliphates seem to be unstoppable military forces.

We tend to look at history through the lens of hindsight, and to see its course as somehow inevitable; but to someone able to survey the 9th century world without knowing what came next, there probably would've been little doubt as to which civilizations of the time seemed most important. If such an observer were told that within the next 700 years one geographic region would emerge to establish military and economic domination over almost the entire globe, surely he or she would certainly have assumed that this region had to be either China or the Muslim Near East. As we know, though, the territory that actually achieved that was neither of our two obvious favorites, but instead it's that dark horse, long-shot candidate, Europe. In the race for global domination, as late as the early 1400s, China continued to hold the inside track. In fact, enterprising Chinese admirals had begun a series of great sea voyages of exploration well before those undertaken by European navigators. But all of that changed when the ill-advised isolationist policies of the Hongxi emperor around the mid-1400s abruptly put a stop to those expeditions and turned the focus of China inwards, with disastrous effects. Its technology stagnated, and China ultimately lost the race to Europe despite their sizable head start.

Similarly, the lead gained during the great era of intellectual and scientific flourishing of the Golden Age of Classical Islamic civilization in Baghdad was frittered away when the Islamic world lost its unity through infighting among rival political powers. The whole atmosphere of encouragement that had been given to the development of new knowledge dissipated, and just like in China, there was a turning inward with too much reflection upon past glories rather than on crafting new achievements, and a resultant technological stagnation.

In order to see how the unlikely candidate of Europe rose to power during the era of colonization, we first have to understand how Europe became a distinct region in its own right, and really how it freed itself from its long subordination to the cultures of the Mediterranean Sea. Creating a thesis to explain the cause and effect links among the set of events that made this all happen was the work of a brilliant historian of the early 20th century. The story of his life and how he devised his interpretation is itself a remarkable tale.

Imagine for a moment if you were to come up with an entirely new interpretation of the early Middle Ages, one that caused historians to completely reconsider and redefine how the main events of that era were connected. Imagine if your interpretation not only explained occurrences in that distant time, but also offered a new way to account for and explain why Europe was able to rise to a position of global domination during the colonial era, and by doing so to really set the stage for all of modern history. Further imagine if you found a way to express such an important and complex thesis of historical interpretation in just six words. And finally, imagine if you had to formulate that thesis, not while working in a comfortable setting of a research university surrounded by libraries and archives, but instead while incarcerated in a German prisoner-of-war camp, and completely denied access to any books whatsoever. That rather unlikely-sounding scenario is exactly what happened in the early 20th century to a historian named Henri Pirenne.

Prior to World War I, Pirenne was a prominent Belgian historian whose main contribution to scholarship up to that point was a multivolume history of Belgium that he was in the process of writing when World War I intervened.

When Belgium was occupied by the Germans, he opposed them; and as a consequence, he was tossed into a prisoner-of-war camp. During his incarceration, he devised what would become known as the Pirenne Thesis, and after the war and his release, he published it, most notably in a book he called *Mohammed and Charlemagne*.

Before Pirenne, most historians had used the supposed fall of Rome to Germanic barbarians, which they commonly dated to 476 A.D., as the dividing line between antiquity and the Middle Ages. In that viewpoint, the fall of Rome marked a clear separation between the Classical world of Ancient Greece and Rome and the civilizations of the Middle Ages. The Pirenne Thesis, on the other hand, proposed that the real moment of rupture occurred not in the 5th century, but about 200 years later, when the Arabic conquests split the Mediterranean into two halves, a northern mostly Christian one and a southern mostly Islamic one. Pirenne's thesis was actually based less on religion than on economics because he argued that the Islamic conquests had effectively cut off the north-south and the east-west trade that up until that point had linked together all the shores of the Mediterranean. In Pirenne's view, for most of ancient history, the Mediterranean world was one unified economic and cultural area; but that fundamental unity was irrevocably shattered by the Arabic conquests. He further posited that the takeover of the Western Roman Empire by barbarian kingdoms was really not so important as everybody had been assuming, because those barbarian tribes just adopted and imitated most aspects of Roman culture, and because all those political changes didn't disrupt that fundamental underlying trade across the Mediterranean.

The really clever part of Pirenne's thesis, though, was the way in which it explained subsequent European history. Throughout antiquity, the most important political, economic, social, intellectual, and cultural developments had all been happening around the shores of the Mediterranean. For centuries, every great empire was a Mediterranean-based one, and their magnificent cities—such as Athens, Alexandria, and Constantinople—were all located on the shores of the Mediterranean Sea. In that perspective, the Mediterranean was the center and the focal point of civilization itself, and the great civilizations were all coastal ones. Adjacent inland areas, such as most of Europe and most of the Middle East, were just relegated to the status of being secondary, subsidiary zones of much less importance.

The Arabic conquests changed this, and they changed it forever. They broke the unity of the Mediterranean, and in doing so they shattered the coastal regions' domination over the hinterlands. Now, all of those once-subordinate regions were no longer condemned to just remain in the shadow of more powerful Mediterranean civilizations, but finally they were free to spin off on their own and to develop themselves. So it was that the Franks, a thoroughly Europe-based and inland empire, could only rise to power once Europe was no longer held in thrall to the Mediterranean-based Eastern and Western Roman empires.

This course keeps coming back to that link between cities and civilization, and as proof of Pirenne's thesis, just think about the location of the great cities of this part of the world in the centuries before, versus after, the Arabic conquests. Before that event, all the great cities were cities of the Mediterranean coastline: Constantinople, Alexandria, Rome, Carthage, Antioch. But then think about the location of the capital cities of the first empires that arose after around 700 A.D.: Baghdad and Aachen. Both of those were hundreds of miles from the coast of the Mediterranean, and both of them were the centers of empires that were fundamentally oriented inland, away from the sea. We see the same situation if we keep going in forward in time from there; so later important cities, London, Paris, Florence, Madrid, Damascus, and Cairo, they're all inland.

What the Islamic conquests did was to separate what used to be one world, the Mediterranean world, into three separate worlds: Europe, Africa, and the Middle East, and situated on three different continents. Furthermore, each of these new worlds now effectively turned their backs on the Mediterranean Sea as the wellspring of all political, economic, and cultural developments, and instead they looked to emerging inland centers, such as Aachen and Baghdad.

This brings us to the famous six-word formulation of Pirenne's thesis. In the introduction to his best-known book, he wrote the following line: "Without Mohammed, Charlemagne would be inconceivable." With that succinct statement, Pirenne is suggesting that if Mohammed had never come along and sparked the Arabic conquests, then Europe would have remained just an adjunct to the Mediterranean; and so the great European empire of Charlemagne, the precursor to all later great European empires, would never have had the opportunity to flourish. Europe itself might never have risen to prominence during the era of colonization, and obviously the entire subsequent course of history would have been profoundly different.

Pirenne's thesis was immediately influential, and also immediately controversial. In fact, historians have been actively arguing about it ever since. The part of his thesis that has really fared most poorly is probably his contention that the Islamic conquests killed most of the trade in the Mediterranean in the 9th century. More recent scholarship has shown that while Europe was indeed cut off from many goods as a result, there was still a lot that was being bought and sold across this boundary. We now have a more complex and nuanced understanding of early Mediterranean commerce than was available to Pirenne, and a good number of his specific contentions have been challenged.

While details of his economic claims may have been undermined, what remains a powerful and compelling argument is that underlying assertion regarding the destruction of the unity of the Mediterranean, and the subsequent individual reorientation of Europe, Africa, and the Near East inwards upon themselves. We have only to open a newspaper or read an online article on current events to see the effects of that historical moment still being played out today. If you look at the cultural, linguistic, and religious boundaries that shape the world we live in today, they were laid down at this key moment. The modern boundaries between the countries around the Mediterranean that are Christian versus those that are Muslim are almost exactly those established in the 8th century during the initial wave of conquests. The same goes for those countries that today speak Arabic, as opposed to one of the Romance or Germanic languages. The Arabic conquests of the 7th century were the moment when the modern map of Europe was drawn.

By the way, there was one, and only one, major country that was part of those initial conquests that today is not still an Arabic-speaking, Muslim country. Can you figure out what country that is? The answer is Spain, which in 1492, after 800 years of Muslim occupation, expelled the Moors in a process known as the Reconquista. But Spain is really the exception that proves the rule, because everywhere else the Arabic conquests were decisive and permanent.

If I had to pick a single historical event from this entire course that most explains the world today, it would probably be the Arabic conquests of the 7th century. These are what created the current boundaries of the modern maps of Europe, Africa, and the Middle East in terms of politics, language, religion, and culture. Somewhat ironically, it was also the Arabic conquests that freed barbarian Europe from its centuries-old domination by the Mediterranean world, and that set it upon the path that would ultimately lead to its conquest and/or colonization of the entire rest of the world, including, even, Asia, Africa, and the Middle East. All of that is beautifully summed up in and implied by Pirenne's simple statement, "Without Mohammed, Charlemagne would be inconceivable."

Today, Charlemagne is widely hailed as the father of Europe, at least as a discrete entity, and let me give you three contemporary examples to illustrate that point: Every year since 1950, a prize has been awarded to the statesman who is judged to have contributed the most to European unity and stability over the course of the previous year. The name of that coveted prize is, of course, the Charlemagne Prize. Recently, to mark the 1,200 anniversary of Charlemagne's coronation by the Pope, a series of exhibits about him were held in various European cities, and the title chosen for these was "Charlemagne, the Making of Europe." Finally, the influential news magazine, *The Economist*, always includes a weekly essay about a topic that affects the European Union as a whole; and that feature is called the "Charlemagne Column.

Today, Charlemagne is widely viewed as the "Father of Europe," and indeed, that's a title by which he's frequently called; but, if Pirenne was right, then perhaps it would be more correct to say that the real father of Europe was not Charlemagne, but was instead Mohammed. The phrase "Mohammed, The Father of Europe" may sound strange to our ears, but it might be actually be more accurate.

Let me to return to the two questions with which I began this lecture: Why end the course here? How does the ancient world affect the modern? Regarding the first, most courses on the ancient world tend to end a couple centuries earlier with the supposed fall of the Roman Empire; but I agree with Pirenne that the real transition point was the Arabic conquests of the 7th and 8th centuries that broke the unity of the Mediterranean and that also created Europe, Africa, and the Near East as separate entities. By extending this course just past that moment into the 9th century and the formation of Charlemagne's empire, we can fully perceive not just the true end of the ancient world, but also the crucial formation, the ad birth of the modern one, with the major national, linguistic, cultural, and religious boundaries that we see around us today already established.

By doing this, the focus that I've placed on the formation of Europe isn't meant, by the way, as an endorsement of a Eurocentric view; it's simply an acknowledgement of the global impact that the era of European colonization in the 16th and 17th centuries would exert on the history of the entire world. Whether or not you view that influence as positive or negative, there's no denying that it happened.

Ending the course in the 9th century lets us see how all the main areas of the world initially developed and, in most cases, evolve the distinctive culture or cultures that still characterize those regions today. As we've seen with the Pirenne thesis, it brings us far enough along the path of history so that we're able to directly connect that world with the modern one, but it ends at a point when the ancient world still really constitutes a distinctly different one from our own.

As for the question, "How does what we've learned about the ancient world help us to understand the world we live in today?" Hopefully, over the course of the last 47 lectures, learning about the origins of so many fundamental aspects of our modern culture has already provided part of the answer. The ancient world is still alive and around us in everything that we do, and in everything that we that we are. The influence of the ancient world is present in our modern customs, religions, laws, art, architecture, games, calendars, superstitions, education, clothing, buildings, foods, jobs, holidays, entertainments, governments, and beliefs.

If you encounter someone who doesn't believe that he or she is directly influenced by the ancient world, ask them to consider the following description of a typical daily routine: "At 8 am, I bought a newspaper and a cup of hot chocolate, and got a dollar bill in change." As you now know from taking this course, another way of describing those same activities might be to say, According to a Mesopotamian-derived timekeeping system, I bought a Chinese-inspired product and an ancient Mesoamerican drink, employing a Greek-invented system of currency and, using an Indo-Arabic counting system, I got back change consisting of a bill that was marked with no fewer than three Latin slogans and bore an image of an Egyptian pyramid.

Of course, the very letters, words, and numbers that I used to convey that simple sentence are themselves a mixture of Sumerian, Phoenician, Greek, Latin, Arabic, and Nahuatl.

Ancient history still affects our lives every day, in ways both large and small. If you want to understand who you are, and why you do the things you do in the way that you do them, you have to know about the ancient origins of the beliefs, institutions, and cultures that shape your life. Maybe even more importantly, if you want to understand why other people act, believe, and think, the way that they do, you need to know the history of their pasts as well. Ultimately, it's that deeper comprehension of ourselves and the world around us, and the more knowledgeable decision-making that comes along with it, that I hope you'll take away from this course.

Thank you very much for letting me be your guide on this journey around the history of the ancient world. I've had fun, and I hope you have, too.

Timeline

c. 2000–1000 .... Construction of Cerro Sechín in Peru.

c. 2000 B.C.–250 A.D. .... Pre-classical period of Mayan
civilization in Mexico and
Central America.

c. 1800 .... Aryans reach India.

2nd millennium .... Hebrews establish the states of Israel
and Judah; Old Testament formulated.

1782–1570 .... Egypt's Second Intermediate period;
Hyksos tribe gains control in Egypt
and Egyptians copy their war chariots.

c. 1700–1500 .... Cities of the Indus Valley
civilization are abandoned.

c. 1600–1100 .... Mycenaean civilization in
mainland Greece.

c. 1600–1150 .... Shang dynasty in China.

1570–1075 .... Egypt's New Kingdom.

c. 1500 .... Volcanic eruption of the
Aegean island of Thera.

c. 1500 .... Lapita culture settles in Melanesia.

c. 1500–1200 .... High point of the Hittite Empire.

c. 1500–600 .... Vedas, Mahabharata, Ramayana, and
Upanishads are composed in India.

c. 1500–500 .... Aryan and Vedic eras in India.

c. 1279–1212 .... Reign of Pharaoh Rameses II.

1274 .... Battle of Kadesh—Pharaoh
Rameses II versus the Hittites.

c. 1200 .... Phoenicians create a coastal empire
on the western Mediterranean; Shang
civilization has domesticated horses
and light, spoke-wheeled chariots.

c. 1200–1100 .... Major Mycenaean sites are destroyed.

1200–800 .... Dark Ages in Greece.

c. 1200–400 .... Olmec civilization in Mexico.

c. 1200–300 .... Chavín culture in Peru.

c. 1150–221 .... Zhou dynasty in China.

1075–332 .... Egypt's Third Intermediate period.

c. 1000 and 600 .... Life of Zoroaster (Zarathustra),
Persian religious leader.

c. 900 .... Lapita culture reaches
western Polynesia.

c. 900–600 .... Assyrian Empire.

8th century .... Greeks rediscover writing; cities
and trade revive; population
increases rapidly.

c. 800–400 .... Upanishads collected.

c. 800 B.C.–391 A.D. .... Delphic Oracle is in continuous
operation in Greece.

776 .... First Olympic Games held.

753 .... Traditional date for the founding
of the city of Rome; starting
point for the Roman calendar.

753–509 .... Era of the Roman monarchy.

c. 750 .... Homer's *Iliad* and *Odyssey* written
down; Carthage founded.

750–650 .... 25th Dynasty—the Kushite
pharaohs rule Egypt.

c. 750–550 .... Era of colonization in Greece.

c. 700–509 .... Etruscan civilization dominates Italy.

c. 700–500 .... Era of questioning and
challenging tradition in India,
China, Persia, and Greece.

c. 650–500 .... Archaic style of Greek sculpture.

c. 626–539 .... Babylonian Renaissance; the New
Babylonian Empire; the Chaldean
Empire; the Hanging Gardens
of Babylon; the Tower of Babel;
the Ishtar Gate; astrology.

c. 600 .... Emergence of Ionian rationalists
and pre-Socratic philosophers;
earliest coins minted in Lydia.

6th century.. Life of Lao Tzu, to whom the origins
of Daoism are traditionally traced.

594... Athens chooses Solon to make reforms.

c. 563–480.................................... Life of Siddhartha Gautama,
the Buddha.

551–479... Life of Confucius.

c. 550... Mahavira founds Jainism in India.

c. 550–330.................................... Persian (Achaemenid) Empire.

c. 525–456.................................... Life of Aeschylus, first
great Greek tragedian.

c. 522–486.................................... Reign of Darius I; construction
of the tribute procession relief
at Persepolis, Persia.

509–31... Roman Republic.

508... Cleisthenes sets up the first
real democracy at Athens.

5th century...................................... High point of ancient Greek civilization;
classical style of Greek sculpture.

c. 500... Bantu migrations begin in Africa.

c. 500–221.................................... Warring States period in China;
era of the Hundred Schools
of Chinese philosophy.

c. 496–406.................................... Life of Sophocles, the second
great Greek tragedian.

490.. Battle of Marathon.

c. 490–430...................................... Life of Zeno of Elea,
                                                              founder of Stoicism.

c. 484–425...................................... Life of Herodotus.

c. 485–406...................................... Life of Euripides, third
                                                              great Greek tragedian.

480.. Persia invades Greece; Battles
                                                              of Thermopylae and Salamis.

c. 469–399...................................... Life of Socrates.

c. 460–395...................................... Life of Thucydides.

mid-5th century .... Golden age of classical
                                                              Athens; the Athenian Empire
                                                              at the height of its power.

431–404... Peloponnesian War.

c. 427–347...................................... Life of Plato.

c. 412–323...................................... Life of Diogenes, the
                                                              most famous Cynic.

4th century...................................... Life of Daoist philosphper Chuang Tzu.

4th century–3rd century .... Emergence of Legalism in China.

399.. Trial and death of Socrates.

384–322... Life of Aristotle.

358–336... Reign of Philip II, king of Macedon.

356–323.. Life of Alexander the Great.

c. 341–270...................................... Life of Epicurus, founder
of Epicureanism.

334... Alexander invades Persia;
Battle of Granicus.

c. 325–265...................................... Life of Euclid.

323–31.. Hellenistic era.

c. 322–300...................................... Reign of Chandragupta Maurya in India.

c. 322–184...................................... India's Mauryan Empire.

305... Chandragupta Maurya and
Seleucus, Alexander's one-time
general, sign a peace treaty.

c. 3rd century................... .... Rise of the sub-Saharan
African kingdom of Axum.

c. 300.. Polynesians reach the Cook
Islands and Tahiti.

c. 300 B.C.–300 A.D. .... Mexico's Colima culture.

c. 287–212...................................... Life of Archimedes.

269–232.. Reign of Asoka in India.

264... Rome captures the last remaining
independent Italian city.

264–241.. First Punic War.

259–210.. Life of China's first Qin
emperor, Shi Huangdi.

219–201.. Second Punic War.

216... Battle of Cannae.

206 B.C.–220 A.D............................ China's Han dynasty.

206 B.C.–9 A.D............................... Early (or Western) Han dynasty.

c. 200 B.C.–800 A.D....................... Mexico's Teotihuacán civilization.

184... Last Mauryan king is murdered and
the Mauryan Empire falls apart.

c. 145–86... Life of historian Sima Qian.

141–87.. Reign of Wudi, China's
"Martial Emperor."

133–31.. Late Roman Republic.

133... Tiberius Gracchus elected
Roman tribune.

123... Gaius Gracchus elected Roman tribune.

106–48.. Life of Roman statesman
Pompey the Great.

100–44.. Life of Julius Caesar.

91–88.. Social War between Rome
and its Italian allies.

31.. Battle of Actium.

31 B.C.–14 A.D.............................. Reign of Augustus as the
first Roman emperor.

A.D.

31 B.C.–476 A.D............................. Roman Empire.

14–37.. Reign of Roman emperor Tiberius.

25–220.. Later (or Eastern) Han dynasty.

c. 33... Crucifixion of Jesus.

c. 33–57.. Ministry of Saint Paul.

37–41.. Reign of Roman emperor Caligula.

41–54.. Reign of Roman emperor Claudius.

54–68.. Reign of Roman emperor Nero.

64.. Great Fire of Rome.

c. 64... Buddhism reaches China.

69–79.. Reign of Roman emperor Vespasian.

81–96.. Reign of Roman emperor Domitian.

2nd century .... Reigns of the Five Good
Emperors (the Antonines); high
point of the Roman Empire.

98–117.. Reign of Roman emperor Trajan.

c. 100–800.. Peru's Moche culture.

113	Dedication of the Column of Trajan.
117–138	Reign of Roman emperor Hadrian.
122	Construction of Hadrian's Wall begins Britain.
161–180	Reign of Roman emperor Marcus Aurelius
180–192	Reign of Roman emperor Commodus.
193–211	Reign of Roman emperor Septimius Severus.
200–600	The period of late antiquity in Europe.
3rd century	Period of China's Seven Sages of the Bamboo Grove.
221–589	Era of the Three Kingdoms and Six Dynasties of China.
224–651	Sassanian empire
c. 250–900	Classic period of Mayan civilization.
c. 251–356	Life of Saint Anthony Abbot
284–305	Reign of Roman emperor Diocletian.
c. 285	Saint Anthony begins the monastic movement.
306–337	Reign of Roman emperor Constantine.

Timeline

312 .... Conversion of Constantine
to Christianity.

324–1453 .... Byzantine Empire.

c. 325 .... King of Axum (northern Ethiopia)
converts to Christianity.

c. 347–420 .... Life of Saint Jerome.

c. 5th century .... The Avesta, the holy book of
Zoroastrianism, is written down.

410 .... Visigoths capture and sack Rome.

434–453 .... Attila rules over the Huns.

455 .... Vandals capture and sack Rome.

476 .... Romulus Augustulus, the last Roman
emperor in the West, is deposed.

480–547 .... Life of Saint Benedict

c. 6th century .... Block printing developed in China.

c. 500 .... Polynesians reach Easter
Island and Hawaii.

527–565 .... Reign of Byzantine emperor Justinian;
code of Roman law is compiled.

c. 529 .... Saint Benedict establishes the first
Christian monastery at Monte Cassino.

c. 570–632 .... Life of Mohammed.

589–618 .... China's Sui dynasty.

609 .... First version of China's Grand
Canal is completed.

618–907 .... China's Tang dynasty.

622 .... The Hejira—Mohammed flees
from Mecca to Medina; year
1 of the Islamic calendar.

626–649 .... Reign of Chinese emperor Taizong.

632–738 .... Arabic (or Islamic) conquests.

661–750 .... Umayyad caliphate.

690 .... Empress Wu usurps China's
imperial throne.

712–756 .... Reign of Chinese emperor Xuanzong;
the golden age of the Tang era.

717 .... Defeat of the Muslim naval expedition
at the walls of Constantinople.

732 .... Battle of Tours stops the Muslim
expansion towards the West.

738 .... Rajahs of northern India stop
Muslim expansion to the East.

750–1517 .... Abbasid caliphate.

751 .... Arabs defeat the Tang at
the Battle of Talas.

762.. Baghdad is founded as the capital
of the Abbasid caliphate.

768–814.. Reign of Charlemagne.

786–809.. Reign of Harun al-Rashid.

800.. Charlemagne crowned Holy
Roman emperor by the pope.

c. 865–925...................................... Life of al-Rāzī (a.k.a. Rhazes).

c. 980–1037.................................... Life of Ibn Sīnā (a.k.a. Avicenna)

8th and 9th centuries........................ Decline of classical Mayan civilization.

1453.. Ottoman Sultan Mehmet II
captures Constantinople.

1492.. The Reconquista: Spain expels the
Moors; Columbus reaches the Americas.

1687.. Parthenon, being used for gunpowder
storage by Ottoman Turks, blows up.

1806.. Lord Elgin takes the Parthenon
sculptures to Britain.

1806.. Last Holy Roman Emperor
is deposed by Napoleon.

1827.. Charles Masson discovers the ruins
of the Indus Valley civilization.

1899.. Sir Arthur Evans discovers the
Palace of Knossos on Crete.

1917.. Last tsar is deposed by the
                                                      Russian Revolution.

1924.. Howard Carter discovers
                                                      Tutankhamen's tomb

1952.. Michael Ventris deciphers Linear B

1974.. The six Yang brothers discover Qin
                                                      Shi Huangdi's terra-cotta warriors.

Bibliography

Alcock, Susan, Terrence N. D'Altroy, Kathleen D. Morrison, and Carla M. Sinopoli, eds. *Empires: Perspectives from Archaeology and History.* New York: Cambridge University Press, 2001. A collection of scholarly essays about various ancient and medieval world empires, including several on ancient Rome and China.

Aldrete, Gregory. *Daily Life in the Roman City: Rome, Pompeii, and Ostia.* Norman, OK: University of Oklahoma Press, 2004. If you enjoyed the style of my lectures, you should enjoy this survey of all aspects of what it was like to live in the ancient Roman world, from religion to architecture.

Barbero, Alessandro. *Charlemagne: Father of a Continent.* Berkeley: University of California Press, 2004. Solid standard biography. A bit heavy on military affairs, but still comprehensive.

Barnes, Timothy. *Constantine and Eusebius.* Cambridge, MA: Harvard University Press, 2006. Clever scholarly study of the emperor and his main biographer, Bishop Eusebius. Also discusses Diocletian and the early Christian church.

Beard, Mary. *The Parthenon.* Cambridge, MA: Harvard University Press, 2010. Highly readable account of the building, its construction, and its history.

Beard, Mary, and Michael Crawford. *Rome in the Late Republic.* Ithaca, NY: Cornell University Press, 1985. Short, insightful description of key late Republican institutions. Not a historical survey.

Benn, Charles. *China's Golden Age: Everyday Life in the Tang Dynasty.* New York: Oxford University Press, 2004. An accessible description of Tang social history and culture.

Benson, Hugh, ed. *A Companion to Plato*. Malden, MA: Blackwell Publishing, 2006. A collection of essays that offers good introductions to various aspects of Plato's life and thought, from metaphysics to his influence.

Berndt, Ronald and Catherine Berndt. *The World of the First Australians: Aboriginal Traditional Life: Past and Present*. Canberra, Australia: Aboriginal Studies Press, 1996. Dry but comprehensive treatment of all aspects of Australian aboriginal culture and history.

Boardman, John. *Greek Art*. New York: Penguin, 1985. Older but still reliable standard survey of the topic, with copious illustrations.

Borrelli, Federica, Maria Cristina Targia, Stefano Peccatori, and Stefano Zuffi. *The Etruscans: Art, Architecture, and History*. Los Angeles, CA: J. Paul Getty Museum, 2004. A short, highly accessible, and nicely illustrated little book on various aspects of Etruscan culture. Not the place to go for in-depth scholarship, but an excellent introduction.

Brockopp, Jonathan, ed. *The Cambridge Companion to Muhammad*. New York: Cambridge University Press, 2010. A collection of scholarly essays focusing on Muhammad's life and his subsequent image.

Brown, Peter. *The Cult of the Saints: Its Rise and Function in Latin Christianity*. Chicago: The University of Chicago Press, 1981. Classic account of early Christian holy men.

———. *The World of Late Antiquity*. New York: W. W. Norton and Company, 1989. Immensely influential work by the brilliant scholar who invented the historical era of late antiquity. An easy and entertaining read.

Bryant, Edwin, and Laurie Patton, eds. *The Indo-Aryan Controversy: Evidence and Inference in Indian History*. New York: Routledge, 2005. Up-to-date, balanced coverage of much-debated issues, with an emphasis on linguistics.

Bugh, Glenn, ed. *The Cambridge Companion to the Hellenistic World*. New York: Cambridge University Press, 2006. Good, up-to-date overview of all aspects of Hellenistic history and culture.

Burger, Richard L. *Chavín and the Origins of Andean Civilization.* New York: Thames and Hudson, 1992. Very good, well-illustrated study specifically devoted to Chavín culture.

Chadwick, J. *The Mycenaean World.* New York: Cambridge University Press, 1976. Account of Mycenaean culture by one of the pioneers in the field.

Chevallier, Raymond. *Roman Roads.* London: Batsford, 1989. A good general survey of Roman roads, their construction, and what travel in the Roman Empire was like.

Coe, Michael D. *The Maya.* 4th ed. New York: Thames and Hudson, 1987. Classic, short, accessible text with many illustrations by a pioneer in Mayan Studies.

Confucius. *The Analects.* Translated by R. Dawson. New York: Oxford University Press, 2008. Good, readable translation of Confucius's text, with commentary.

Cornell, Tim. *The Beginnings of Rome: Italy and Rome from the Bronze Age to the Punic Wars (c. 1000–264 B.C.).* New York: Routledge, 1995. Good survey of the early phases of Roman history.

Coulston, J. *All the Emperor's Men: Roman Soldiers and Barbarians on Trajan's Column.* Oxford, UK: Oxbow Books, 2011. A study specifically on the column and its images, with an emphasis on military aspects.

Crawford, Harriet. *Sumer and the Sumerians.* 2nd ed. New York: Cambridge University Press, 2004. A nice account of the achievements of Sumerian civilization.

Curd, Patricia, and Daniel Graham, eds. *The Oxford Handbook of Presocratic Philosophy.* New York: Oxford University Press, 2008. Authoritative survey of Greek philosophers up through the Sophists.

Curtis, John, and St. John Simpson, eds. *The World of Achaemenid Persia: History, Art, and Society in Iran and the Ancient Near East*. New York: I. B. Tauris, 2010. Recent survey of Persian history, art, and culture.

Dawson, Raymond. *Confucius*. New York: Oxford University Press, 1983. A short guide aimed at nonspecialist readers that provides historical background and also examines the role Confucius has played in Chinese society.

De Souza, Philip, ed. *The Ancient World at War: A Global History*. New York: Thames and Hudson, 2008. A well-illustrated volume on ancient warfare aimed at a popular audience, it includes specific chapters on the Maya, Chinese, and Romans, as well as on other cultures discussed in this course.

Diamond, Jared. *Guns, Germs, and Steel: The Fates of Human Societies*. New York: W. W. Norton and Company, 1997. Controversial but thought-provoking attempt from an environmental perspective to explain why Europe was able to conquer most of the world in the colonial era. A fun read.

Di Cosmo, Nicola. *Ancient China and Its Enemies: The Rise of Nomadic Power in East Asian History*. New York: Cambridge University Press, 2002. An interesting analysis of China's interactions with neighboring barbarians, including the Hsiung-nu.

Diehl, Richard. *The Olmecs: America's First Civilization*. New York: Thames and Hudson, 2005. Good, balanced text covering all aspects of Olmec civilization, from history to art.

Dinsmoor, William Bell. *The Architecture of Ancient Greece*. New York: W. W. Norton and Company, 1975. Getting dated, but still a masterful survey, especially on technical matters.

Donnan, Christopher, and Donna McClelland. *Moche Fineline Painting: Its Evolution and Its Artists*. Los Angeles, CA: UCLA Fowler Museum of Cultural History, 1999. Wonderful, richly illustrated book specifically on Moche pottery.

Dunn, Marilyn. *The Emergence of Monasticism: From the Desert Fathers to the Early Middle Ages.* New York: Wiley-Blackwell, 2003. A decent overview that traces the early monastic movement and covers topics such as the early desert fathers, asceticism, the Rule of Benedict, and women in monasticism.

Easterling, P. E., ed. *The Cambridge Companion to Greek Tragedy.* New York: Cambridge University Press, 1997. A collection of essays on thematic topics rather than a survey of plays and authors. Not the place to start, but a good supplemental read.

Finley, M. I. *Early Greece: The Bronze and Archaic Ages.* New York: W. W. Norton and Company, 1981. Dated but still insightful work by an eminent ancient historian.

Fitton, J. L. *Minoans.* London: British Museum Press, 2002. Modern, balanced survey of Minoan civilization.

Flood, Gavin. *An Introduction to Hinduism.* New York: Cambridge University Press, 1996. Modern scholarly introduction to Hinduism, its origins, and its development.

Fontenrose, Joseph. *The Delphic Oracle.* Berkeley, CA: University of California Press, 1978. Scholarly treatment of the oracle and its function that ncludes a catalogue of known questions and responses.

Fowler, Robert, ed. *The Cambridge Companion to Homer.* New York: Cambridge University Press, 2004. Nice collection of essays on a wide range of topics related to Homer, his works, and their themes.

Fox, Robin Lane. *Alexander the Great.* New York: Penguin, 2004. Solid biography of Alexander and his career.

Garnsey, Peter, and Richard Saller. *The Roman Empire: Economy, Society, and Culture.* Berkeley, CA: University of California Press, 1987. The best brief survey of the formal and informal institutions that made the Roman Empire function.

Goldsworthy, Adrian. *The Complete Roman Army*. New York: Thames and Hudson, 2003. Excellent overall summary of the Roman army. Particularly strong on the perspectives and experiences of a typical legionary, but also includes a chronological survey of the Roman army.

————. *The Fall of Carthage: The Punic Wars 265–146 BC*. London: Cassell Military Paperbacks, 2007. Dependable recent account of these crucial wars in Roman history by a leading military historian of ancient Rome.

Green Peter. *Alexander to Actium: The Historical Evolution of the Hellenistic Age*. Berkeley, CA: University of California Press, 1990. Mammoth survey of Hellenistic history that weaves a considerable amount of cultural information into the narrative as well.

————. *The Greco-Persian Wars*. Berkeley, CA: University of California Press, 1998. Comprehensive account of both the first and second wars between Persia and the Greeks.

Grimal, Nicolas. *A History of Ancient Egypt*. Cambridge, MA: Blackwell Publishers, 1992. Standard older account of Egyptian civilization. A bit weak on art and architecture.

Guthrie, W. K. C. *A History of Greek Philosophy*. 6 vols. New York: Cambridge University Press, 1962–1981. Exhaustive and highly detailed chronological description of Greek philosophers. Volumes 1 and 2 cover the Pre-Socratics.

Hammond, Nicolas. *Philip of Macedon*. London: Duckworth, 1998. Solid biography of Philip and his actions by a famous scholar of Macedonian history.

Hanson, Victor Davis. *The Western Way of War: Infantry Battle in Classical Greece*. New York: Oxford University Press, 1989. Revolutionary work on hoplite warfare. Although aspects are now being challenged, it is still the starting point for any discussion of Greek warfare.

Harris, Jonathan. *Constantinople: Capital of Byzantium*. New York: Continuum, 2007. Not a chronological survey, but rather a more impressionistic portrait of aspects of Byzantine civilization. A pleasant read.

Harris, William V. *War and Imperialism in Republican Rome*. New York: Oxford University Press, 1985. Controversial yet influential work arguing that Roman imperialism was deliberate and aggressive in nature.

Havighurst, Alfred, ed. *The Pirenne Thesis: Analysis, Criticism, and Revision*. 3rd ed. Lexington, MA: D. C. Heath and Company, 1976. A collection of essays outlining some of the debates and challenges that have arisen since Pirenne proposed his thesis.

Heckel, Waldemar, and Lawrence Tritle, eds. *Alexander the Great: A New History*. Malden, MA: Wiley-Blackwell, 2009. Good recent collection of essays by leading scholars on various aspects of Alexander's life, policies, and actions.

Herrin, Judith. *Byzantium: The Surprising Life of a Medieval Empire*. Princeton, NJ: Princeton University Press, 2007. A nice balance between offering a general survey and dwelling on interesting cultural aspects of Byzantine civilization.

Hingley, Richard. *Globalizing Roman Culture: Unity, Diversity, and Empire*. New York: Routledge, 2005. A study of Romanization and local elites in the Roman Empire.

Hodges, Richard, and David Whitehouse. *Mohammed, Charlemagne and the Origins of Europe: Archaeology and the Pirenne Thesis*. Ithaca, NY: Cornell University Press, 1983. Assesses the Pirenne thesis from the perspective of what archaeological evidence can reveal about medieval trade networks.

Homer. *The Iliad*. Translated by Richmond Lattimore. Chicago: University of Chicago Press, 1961. In my opinion, the very best translation of the *Iliad*. Very accurate, and captures the tone of Homer's poem.

Hunter, C. Bruce. *A Guide to Ancient Maya Ruins.* 2nd ed. Norman: University of Oklahoma Press, 1986. A guidebook that also provides a nice overview of Mayan art and architecture, including both famous and obscure sites.

James, Edward. *Europe's Barbarians AD 200–600.* New York: Pearson, 2009. A nice current study of European barbarian groups, it focuses on cultural aspects, but also includes a historical survey. However, it does not really cover eastern nomadic groups such as the Huns.

Jennings, Jesse, ed. *The Prehistory of Polynesia.* Cambridge, MA: Harvard University Press, 1979. Nice scholarly but readable accounts of history, ethnology, and archaeology of various Polynesian peoples. Now getting a bit old and some of information is out-of-date, but still a good introduction to the topic.

Jones, A. H. M. *The Later Roman Empire, 284–602: A Social, Economic, and Administrative Survey.* 2 vols. Baltimore, MD: Johns Hopkins University Press, 1986. Two massive volumes: dense, comprehensive, authoritative, and scholarly. The place to look for in-depth information, but probably not something you want to read cover to cover.

Kagan, Donald. *The Peloponnesian War.* New York: Penguin, 2004. This author of a massive four-volume study on the war offers a (relatively) condensed, but still comprehensive, account of the conflict.

Kennedy, Hugh. *The Prophet and the Age of the Caliphates: The Islamic Near East from the Sixth to the Eleventh Century.* 2nd ed. New York: Pearson Education, 2004. Straightforward chronological survey of the expansion of Islamic power from the life of Muhammad through the early caliphates.

Kenoyer, Jonathan. *Ancient Cities of the Indus Valley Civilization.* New York: Oxford University Press, 1998. Standard work on the Indus Valley civilization covering all aspects. Well illustrated, including color images.

Kitto, H. D. F. *Greek Tragedy.* New York: Routledge, 1986. Reprint of an old book that is a solid survey of major authors and their works.

Kuhrt, Amélie. *The Ancient Near East.* 2 vols. New York: Routledge, 1995. Slightly older but solid standard reference work.

Laurence, Ray. *The Roads of Roman Italy.* New York: Routledge, 1999. A study of issues related to mobility in ancient Italy that combines theoretical sophistication with practical analysis.

Lenski, Noel, ed. *The Cambridge Companion to the Age of Constantine.* New York: Cambridge University Press, 2005. A collection of essays by various scholars covering the life and actions of Constantine as well as key issues of early Christianity.

Levick, Barbara. *Augustus: Image and Substance.* New York: Longman, 2010. Readable recent biography of Augustus that examines his career and image manipulation.

Lewis, Mark Edward. *China between Empires: The Northern and Southern Dynasties.* Cambridge, MA: The Belknap Press of Harvard University Press, 2009. Current, authoritative coverage of the confused period in Chinese history between the end of the Han and the beginning of the Sui dynasties. Good on both history and culture.

———. *China's Cosmopolitan Empire: The Tang Dynasty.* Cambridge, MA: The Belknap Press of Harvard University Press, 2009. Very current, authoritative coverage of all aspects of Tang civilization, from history to culture. The best general introduction.

———. *The Early Chinese Empires: Qin and Han.* Cambridge, MA: The Belknap Press of Harvard University Press, 2007. Good recent survey of all aspects of Qin and Han history and society.

Lockard, Craig. *Societies, Networks, and Transitions: A Global History.* New York: Houghton Mifflin Company, 2008. There are lots of world history textbooks, but this is one of the better ones. The author is a specialist in Asian history, and this survey has an approach that is truly global in outlook.

Loewe, Michael, and Edward Shaughnessy, eds. *The Cambridge History of Ancient China from the Origins of Civilization to 221 B.C.* New York: Cambridge University Press, 1999. Dependable and comprehensive (if rather dry) survey of early Chinese history, including the Shang and Zhou dynasties.

Luttwak, Edward. *The Grand Strategy of the Roman Empire.* Baltimore, MD: Johns Hopkins University Press, 1976. An influential study of Rome's frontiers from a military perspective.

Maenchen-Helfen, Otto. *The World of the Huns.* Berkeley: University of California Press, 1973. Old but classic work on the Huns that is still relevant.

Marcus, Joyce, and Jeremy Sabloff, eds. *The Ancient City: New Perspectives on Urbanism in the Old and New World.* Santa Fe, NM: School for Advanced Research Press, 2008. A series of essays evaluating various roles and aspects of ancient cities, from religion to economics, using case studies from all over the world. A bit academic in style, but it raises interesting questions.

McIntosh, Jane. *The Ancient Indus Valley: New Perspectives.* Santa Barbara, CA: ABC-CLIO, 2008. Recent general survey, particularly strong on economic issues.

Millar, Fergus. *The Emperor in the Roman World.* Ithaca, NY: Cornell University Press, 1977. Standard (and highly comprehensive) work on all aspects of the job of being Roman emperor.

Murray, Oswyn. *Early Greece.* 2nd ed. Cambridge, MA: Harvard University Press, 1993. Covers historical developments from the Dark Ages to the Persian Wars.

Mutschler, Fritz-Heiner, and Achim Mittag, eds. *Conceiving the Empire: China and Rome Compared.* New York: Oxford University Press, 2008. A thought-provoking comparison of aspects of the Chinese and Roman empires, with an emphasis on issues of image, self-perception, and historiography.

Nemet-Nejat, Karen Rhea. *Daily Life in Ancient Mesopotamia.* Westport, CT: Greenwood Press, 1998. Comprehensive coverage of social aspects of life in various Mesopotamian civilizations.

Norwich, John Julius. *A Short History of Byzantium.* New York: Vintage Books, 1997. Condensed version of the author's magisterial three-volume standard treatment of the Byzantine Empire.

Ober, Josiah. *Mass and Elite in Democratic Athens: Rhetoric, Ideology, and the Power of the People.* Princeton, NJ: Princeton University Press, 1989. Perceptive scholarly study of certain aspects of Athenian democracy.

O'Connor, David. *Ancient Nubia: Egypt's Rival in Africa.* Philadelphia, PA: University of Pennsylvania Press, 1993. Sound discussion of Nubian culture and its interactions with ancient Egypt.

O'Flaherty, Wendy, trans. *The Rig-Veda.* New York: Penguin, 1986. Accessible translation of the earliest Indian sacred text.

Panter-Brick, Catherine, Robert Layton, and Peter Rowley-Conwy, eds. *Hunter-Gatherers: An Interdisciplinary Perspective.* New York: Cambridge University Press, 2001. Collection of scholarly essays on hunter-gatherers. Concentrates on aspects of this lifestyle rather than any specific culture.

Parrinder, Geoffrey, ed. *World Religions: From Ancient History to the Present.* New York: Facts on File, 1971. Comprehensive overview of world religions with brief but informative chapters on Buddhism, Hinduism, Jainism, ancient Iran (for Zoroastrianism), and China (for Daoism).

Pasztory, Esther. *Teotihuacan: An Experiment in Living.* Norman: Oklahoma University Press. 1997. Up-to-date account of the city of Teotihuacán, including art, architecture, and an attempted analysis of its people and their lifestyle.

Peers, C. J. *Soldiers of the Dragon: Chinese Armies 1500 BC–AD 1840.* New York: Osprey, 2006. A lavishly illustrated compilation of four of the Osprey Men at Arms series books. Particularly strong on equipment.

Pomeroy, Sarah B., Stanley M. Burstein, Walter Donlan, and Jennifer Tolbert Roberts. *Ancient Greece: A Political, Social, and Cultural History.* New York: Oxford University Press, 2007. College textbook that provides an excellent introduction to all aspects of Greek history and culture.

Portal, Jane, ed. *The First Emperor: China's Terracotta Army.* Cambridge, MA: Harvard University Press, 2007. Best and most reliable general introduction to both Shi Huangdi and his terra-cotta army. Written by an authoritative team of scholars, accessible, and lavishly illustrated.

Possehl, Gregory. *The Indus Civilization: A Contemporary Perspective.* New York: AltaMira, 2002. Another reliable standard work on the Indus Valley civilization.

Pritchard, James B., ed. *The Ancient Near East.* 2 vols. Princeton, NJ: Princeton University Press, 1971 and 1975. Extremely useful compilations of primary sources from all civilizations of the Ancient Near East, as well as Egypt.

Raaflaub, Kurt, and Nathan Rosenstein, eds. *War and Society in the Ancient and Medieval Worlds: Asia, the Mediterranean, Europe, and Mesoamerica.* Washington, DC: Center for Hellenic Studies, Trustees for Harvard University, 1999. Scholarly but informative, this book includes specific chapters on Mayan, Chinese, and Roman warfare, as well as on most other cultures in this course. No illustrations.

Rhodes, P. J., ed. *Athenian Democracy.* New York: Oxford University Press, 2004. Essays by different leading scholars on various aspects of Athenian democracy that, collectively, also provides a good survey of the topic.

Riché, Pierre. *Daily Life in the World of Charlemagne.* Philadelphia, PA: University of Pennsylvania Press, 1978. A nice account of every imaginable aspect of Carolingian daily life that provides good context for the historical events.

Robinson, Richard, et al. *The Buddhist Religion: A Historical Introduction.* 5th ed. Belmont, CA: Thomson/Wadsworth, 2005. A solid introductory survey of Buddhism and its beliefs.

Root, Margaret Cool. *The King and Kingship in Achaemenid Art.* Leiden, The Netherlands: Brill, 1979. A scholarly study of all aspects of Persian art as kingly propaganda.

Samaniego, Lorenzo, Enrique Vergara, and Henning Bischof. "New Evidence on Cerro Sechin, Casma Valley, Peru." In *Early Ceremonial Architecture in the Andes*, edited by Christopher Donnan. Washington, D.C.: Dumbarton Oaks, 1985. One of the more reliable articles on Cerro Sechin.

Samons, Loren, II, ed. *The Cambridge Companion to the Age of Pericles.* New York: Cambridge University Press, 2007. Like the others in this series, an accurate, accessible, up-to-date survey of the era, covering both history and culture.

Scheidel, Walter, ed. *Rome and China: Comparative Perspectives on Ancient World Empires.* New York: Oxford University Press, 2009. Innovative study comparing some specific aspects of the Roman and Han empires, including law, coinage, eunuchs, trade, and warfare.

Schrire, Carmel, ed. *Past and Present in Hunter Gatherer Studies.* New York: Academic Press, Inc., 1984. Collection of scholarly essays on hunter-gatherers. Especially strong on groups from Australia and the Kalahari.

Scullard, H. H. *From the Gracchi to Nero: A History of Rome from 133 BC to AD 68.* 5th ed. New York: Routledge, 1982. Old but influential historical survey covering the fall of the Roman Republic and the establishment of the empire. A good place to go for the basic facts.

Shaw, Ian. *The Oxford History of Ancient Egypt.* New York: Oxford University Press, 2004. Very good up-to-date general survey of all phases of Egyptian history.

Sima Qian. *Records of the Grand Historian.* 3 vols. Translated by Burton Watson. New York: Columbia University Press, 1993–1996. Multivolume complete translation of Sima Qian's work. (Most other English translations are just selections or condensed versions.)

—————. *Records of the Grand Historian: Qin Dynasty.* Translated by Burton Watson. New York: Columbia University Press, 1993. Complete passages from the ancient Chinese historian's account of the Qin dynasty, including Shi Huangdi.

Smith, John D., trans. and abr. *The Mahabharata.* New York: Penguin, 2009. Solid selection and translation of passages from a difficult text, with a useful introduction and supplemental material.

Smith, R. R. R. *Hellenistic Sculpture.* London: Thames and Hudson, 1991. Standard survey of the development and characteristics of Hellenistic sculpture.

Smith, W. Stevenson. *The Art and Architecture of Ancient Egypt.* New Haven, CT: Yale University Press, 1981. Authoritative and well-illustrated overview of Egyptian art and architecture.

Stiebing, William H. *Ancient Near Eastern History and Culture.* New York: Longman, 2003. Dependable survey of early civilizations, with wide geographic coverage.

Stoneman, Richard. *Alexander the Great: A Life in Legend.* New Haven, CT: Yale University Press, 2010. Not a biography but an interesting study of later legends about Alexander in a variety of cultures.

Stone-Miller, Rebecca. *Art of the Andes from Chavín to Inca.* 2nd ed. New York: Thames and Hudson, 2002. Standard textbook offering broad (though not detailed) coverage of Andean art.

Story, Joanna, ed. *Charlemagne: Empire and Society*. New York: Manchester University Press, 2005. A collection of short, focused scholarly essays by different authors covering many aspects of Charlemagne, from his personality to his coinage.

Strassler, Robert, ed. *The Landmark Herodotus: The Histories*. New York: Anchor Press, 2009. Reader-friendly version of Herodotus's text, with lots of helpful supplementary material included.

————. *The Landmark Thucydides: A Comprehensive Guide to the Peloponnesian War*. New York: Free Press, 1998. A terrific version of Thucydides' text with lots of helpful supplementary material included.

Suetonius. *The Twelve Caesars*. New York: Penguin Books, 2007. Highly entertaining biographies of the first century of Roman emperors written by a 2nd-century A.D. clerk in the imperial palace.

Talbert, Richard, ed. *On Sparta*. New York: Penguin, 2005. Nicely edited and useful collection of ancient sources in translation that discuss Sparta, including Plutarch and Xenophon.

Tarrant, Harold, ed. *The Last Days of Socrates: Euthyphro, Apology, Crito, and Phaedo*. New York: Penguin, 2003. Collection of Plato's texts (in translation) describing the trial, imprisonment, and death of Socrates.

Thapar, Romila. *Asoka and the Decline of the Mauryas*. Rev. ed. New York: Oxford University Press, 1998. An updated edition of an old but classic book by an influential Indian historian. Particularly strong on Asoka's edicts.

————. *Early India from the Origins to AD 1300*. Berkeley, CA: University of California Press, 2002. Up-to-date overview of civilizations in India. Goes beyond the ancient period, but contextualizes it well.

Thompson, J. Eric S. *Maya History and Religion*. Norman: University of Oklahoma Press, 1970. Detailed study that is particularly strong on Mayan mythology and religious beliefs.

Thorp, Robert. *China in the Early Bronze Age: Shang Civilization.* Philadelphia, PA: University of Pennsylvania Press, 2005. Solid account of Shang history and culture.

Twitchett, Denis, ed. *The Cambridge History of China. Vol. 3: Sui and T'ang China.* New York: Cambridge University Press, 1979. A somewhat dated but comprehensive account of this period in Chinese history. A good reference work.

Twitchett, Denis, and M. Loewe, eds. *The Cambridge History of China. Vol. 1: The Ch'in and Han Empires.* New York: Cambridge University Press, 1986. Exhaustive (if somewhat dry) account of Han history, with an emphasis on political and religious history. Weaker on social and cultural history.

Upanisads. Translated by Patrick Olivelle. New York: Oxford University Press, 2008. Recent translation of the text, with commentary.

Waldron, Arthur. *The Great Wall of China: From History to Myth.* New York: Cambridge University Press, 1990. Excellent, comprehensive survey about not only the Great Wall but also earlier Chinese defensive walls. Particularly strong on debunking popular myths about the Great Wall.

Ward-Perkins, Bryan. *The Fall of Rome and the End of Civilization.* New York: Oxford University Press, 2006. An engaging book that sparked the most recent round of debates over the fall of the Roman Empire by arguing that there indeed was a destructive decline. A good starting point for the entire debate, since it reviews earlier perspectives.

Warren, Allen M., Fritz M. Heichelheim, and Cedric A. Yeo. *A History of the Roman People.* 5th ed. Upper Saddle River, NJ: Prentice Hall, 2009. College textbook that provides a solid and up-to-date survey of all aspects of Roman history and culture.

Warren, James. *Presocratics.* Berkeley, CA: University of California Press, 2007. Narrative account of the main Pre-Socratic philosophers and their beliefs.

Bibliography

Whitby, M., ed. *Sparta*. New York: Routledge, 2001. A collection of scholarly essays on Sparta. Addresses a good cross-section of topics, from military to social.

Whittaker, C. R. *Frontiers of the Roman Empire: A Social and Economic Study*. Baltimore, MD: Johns Hopkins University Press, 1997. A study of the interactions on the Roman frontiers, especially from a social and economic perspective.

Wilber, Donald. *Persepolis: The Archaeology of Parsa, Seat of the Persian Kings*. Princeton, NJ: Darwin Press, 1989. Nice popular account of the art and architecture of Persepolis, with good detail on the tribute procession.

Wolpert, Stanley. *A New History of India*. 7th ed. New York: Oxford University Press, 2003. Aging but influential standard survey text on Indian civilization.

Worthington, Ian. *Philip II of Macedonia*. New Haven, CT: Yale University Press, 2008. Good, up-to-date biography of Philip.

Wright, Rita. *The Ancient Indus: Urbanism, Economy, and Society*. New York: Cambridge University Press, 2010. Up-to-date treatment with focus on urbanism, environment, and economy.

Zanker, Paul. *The Power of Images in the Age of Augustus*. Ann Arbor: University of Michigan Press, 1990. Ground-breaking exploration of Augustus' use of art and architecture as propaganda.

Notes

Notes

Notes